Readings in
Classroom Learning
and Perception

Readings in Classroom Learning and Perception

NEW YORK · WASHINGTON

EDITED BY

RICHARD J. MUELLER
DONALD ARY
AND CHARLES McCORMICK

PRAEGER PUBLISHERS

Published in the United States of America in 1974
by Praeger Publishers, Inc.
111 Fourth Avenue, New York, N.Y. 10003

© 1974 by Praeger Publishers, Inc.

Library of Congress Cataloging in Publication Data

Mueller, Richard, 1927–   comp.
   Readings in classroom learning and perception.

   Includes bibliographies.
   1. Learning, Psychology of—Addresses, essays, lectures.
I. Ary, Donald, joint comp. II. McCormick, Charles,
joint comp. III. Title.
LB1055.M78   370.15′2′08   73-10656
ISBN 0-275-51190-1
ISBN 0-275-84900-7 (pbk.)

Printed in the United States of America

Contents

vii / *Contents*

Introduction

AROUND THE TURN OF THE CENTURY, a mother took her five-year-old boy to school and presented him to his first teacher. This was a momentous occasion for mother and child alike; teachers in those days were formidable bastions of power and authority. "This is my son, George," the mother said anxiously. The teacher took a long, careful look at young George and said, "Well! *He* looks like a bad boy!"

That was educational psychology seventy years ago. Children were regarded more or less as savages, whom the school had the responsibility of civilizing. We have come a long way since that era, at least in terms of developing a more humane psychology of teaching and learning. The evolution of society's conception of the learner has followed a distinct pattern, which can perhaps best be illustrated by tracing the physical evolution of the classroom itself.

The typical schoolroom at the turn of the century consisted of rather small, cramped spaces. The children's desks were fastened to the floor and faced front, the teacher presided over the room from a raised platform, and the children were expected to sit still at all times. It was a distinctly master-servant relationship; all knowledge and supervision emanated from the dais. There were few work spaces or tables for groups of students. The windows were high and small to minimize distraction from outside. The blackboard was indispensable, of course, because it was an extension of the teacher.

Through the decades, the teacher's platform was lowered and then eliminated. The teacher's desk moved to the side and then to the back of the room. Now, in many schools, it is in an office at the rear of the classroom, out of sight. Similarly, the children's desks were freed from the floor and eventually evolved into tables that could be joined together for group work. Many classrooms now have a mix of chairs, seminar areas, and work carrels for individual study. The classroom as a whole has thus been transformed from a lecture hall to a flexibly organized work area that is ancillary to the core of the school's educational program—the Instructional Materials Center.

This development mirrors the evolution of society's conception of the teaching-learning process, from authoritarian, teacher-centered lecture-and-discussion to child-centered learning in an environment of varied educational resources. The teacher is no longer solely a dispenser of knowledge and an arbiter of behavior but, ideally, a facilitator and resource person. The child who enters an innovative school today is the subject of the educational process, not its object. He or she is encouraged to manipulate the environment in order to grow emotionally and intellectually, not merely to react to it.

Paradoxically, as schools encourage children to become more self-directed, the teacher's role becomes more complex. Knowledge of subject matter and skill in presenting it must be combined with knowledge of the child's learning characteristics, such as his general intelligence, verbal skills, self-concept, and attitudes toward school. The articles in this collection were selected because we believe that they provide an excellent introduction to the major areas of the teaching-learning process and learner characteristics—including behavior modification, psycholinguistics, objectives-based teaching strategies, performance assessment, and humanism in the classroom. An important criterion for the inclusion of an article was its value for beginning and experienced *teachers*, not for the school administrator, guidance counselor, or other school authorities. The choice was also based on style as well as content; thus the articles range from experimentally based research reports to expressions of distinctive points of view.

The initial impetus for this book of readings was the wish to supplement *Principles of Classroom Learning and Perception*, an introductory educational-psychology textbook, by Richard J. Mueller. Most of the articles are cited in the textbook and therefore provide supportive reading. However, we believe that this collection can serve as a valuable adjunct to any recent textbook on the learning process and, in some cases, can stand alone. Obviously, only a few examples from the literature in any field can be presented in a single volume. This one is not intended to be an entire course in educational psychology. But we believe that it does supply reading that is basic to the field, reading that will be informative and inspirational.

PART 1

The Process of Learning

CHAPTER ONE

The Scope of Educational Psychology

THE STUDY OF EDUCATIONAL PSYCHOLOGY has much to offer the beginning teacher who is concerned about how well he will function in the classroom. Designing lesson plans, planning classroom activities, and preparing materials are very important aspects of classroom functioning, but the relationship between teacher and pupil is the cement that holds it all together. Arthur Combs has spent virtually a lifetime promoting the view that the self-concepts of teachers and students and their perceptions of each other ought to be of primary concern in teacher training. In Combs's own words: "If the self-concept is as important a determiner of behavior as research suggests, teacher education must actively supply what is known about it." Combs has done extensive research in perceptual theory and its application to teaching, especially with reference to the subject of self-concept and its effects on behavior. His book *Individual Behavior*, written with Donald Snygg, is still of major importance in the field, although it was first published over two decades ago (1944). One of his more recent statements regarding subjectivity in teacher education is "Some Basic Concepts for Teacher Education."

The perceptualists' view of the role of the teacher, however, is not the only picture of teacher training today. The primacy of subjectivity has been questioned by the theories, research, and recent popularity of modern behavioral psychology. Subjectivity in teaching is viewed by many as associated with "charisma" and "mysticism," terms that apply to the realm of chance rather than the realm of science. All professions aspire to depart from chance and build solid systems of theory and prediction. The teaching profession is no exception.

Probably the most compelling proponent of objectivity rather than subjectivity in teaching and learning today is Harvard psychologist B. F. Skinner. Skinner contends that a science of behavior can be developed by delineating the empirical relationships between environmental events and human behavior. He has demonstrated that human behavior is shaped and maintained as a function of the reinforcers provided by the environment. Knowing the relationship between these reinforcing events and behavior, the teacher can control an individual's actions by manipulating whatever constitutes reinforcement to that individual.

Skinner believes that a science of behavior will allow man to control his behavior, reshape his world, and thus alleviate many contemporary problems. He maintains that a technology of education now exists that can be used to create a system of control that is free of punishment, with positive, socially desirable behavior as the objective. This potential for systematic control of human behavior is a central issue in debates over the impact of behaviorism.

Of course, identifying and controlling important reinforcers are much easier said than done. Many of these reinforcers are elusive, and many are idiosyncratic. Further, although most young children respond predictably to such things as a kind word or a gold star, older children have more complex systems of reinforcers, and these are difficult to identify and control, especially for the classroom teacher with responsibility for 25 or 30 pupils. Even when an individual gets his sought-after reward for a particular response, the maintenance of that behavior across other situations is difficult to accomplish. Extensive changes in a person's behavior pattern may require more resources and commitment than the educator can afford to make.

There is considerable research support for both perceptual psychology and Skinnerian, reinforcement-based approaches to learning. It is a challenge to educational psychologists to determine under what conditions one approach is more effective than the other. The beginning teacher will benefit by keeping an open mind to both ways of viewing the teaching/learning process.

The scope of educational psychology is broader than this one issue. It encompasses research ranging from teaching techniques to the chemistry of the brain; from classroom-based, empirical studies to "pure" research carried out in university psychology laboratories; and from first-hand, observational techniques to highly sophisticated, computerized probability studies of behavior. From his intensive analysis of research in education over the past fifteen years, David Griffiths has compiled a list of what he considers to be the ten most significant studies having impact on educational theory and practice. The list touches on many areas within education, from genetics to administrative leadership styles. Each of these studies is significant in part because it is built on an accumulation of research already amassed in that field. This article should give the beginning teacher an idea of the broad range of topics touched upon by educational psychologists and researchers, all with implications for teachers and teaching.

RECOMMENDED READING

B. Bloom. 1972. "Innocence in Education," *School Review* 80(5), 333–52. A scholarly yet readable description of seven major aspects of the educational process about which our society is no longer "innocent." An excellent way for the beginning teacher to get immediately to the frontier of innovative thinking in education.

A. W. Combs. 1967. *The Professional Education of Teachers* (Boston: Allyn & Bacon). A handbook-sized compendium of research findings and perceptual principles applied to the preparation of teachers at all grade levels; anticipates many aspects of humanistic psychology.

B. F. Skinner. 1953. *Science and Human Behavior* (New York: Macmillan). An early work that applies the logic and methods of the physical sciences to the analysis of behavior, with a technology of education as the ultimate goal.

R. Ulrich, T. Stachnik and J. Mabay (eds). 1966. *Control of Human Behavior: Expanding the Behavioral Laboratory* (Glenview, Ill.: Scott, Foresman & Co.). A collection of articles explaining how behavior-modification techniques can be used to improve aspects of behavior ranging from study habits to autism.

G. Watson. 1963. "What Psychology Can We Feel Sure About?" *NEA Journal* 52(3), 20–22. A frequently cited list of 50 principles of learning and behavior derived from both research and direct classroom experience.

1.

ARTHUR W. COMBS

SOME BASIC CONCEPTS
FOR TEACHER EDUCATION

In 1957, the author instituted a series of research studies on the helping professions designed to discover the differences between effective and ineffective practitioners in such professions as elementary teaching, college teaching, nursing, counseling, and pastoral care.[1] These have since been replicated and expanded by others at the University of Florida, and at

From the *Journal of Teacher Education*, 23:3 (1972), 286–90.

the University of Northern Colorado under the leadership of Richard Usher.[2] One outgrowth of these studies was the development of a position paper on the professional education of teachers.[3] With some modification, the program proposed in that document has since been placed in operation at the University of Florida [4] alongside the already existing program. Out of this research and experience a series of propositions for teacher preparation has emerged, some of which are the subject of this paper.

1. *The production of an effective teacher is a highly personal matter, dependent primarily upon the development of an appropriate system of beliefs.*

A unique quality of the helping professions is that they are all dependent upon instantaneous response: teachers, counselors, pastors, social workers, and others must make immediate responses to their students or clients. In much the same way as the solutions provided by a computer depend upon how it is programmed so also do the immediate responses of teachers. To ensure that these are correct requires that teachers be programmed appropriately. In a human being, this programming is provided by his perceptual or belief system.

What makes a person effective in any of the professions is a question of how well he has learned to use his unique self efficiently to carry out his own purposes and those of society. This use of self as instrument in teaching is a very personal thing, dependent upon the perceptual or belief system the student has acquired. It follows, then, that the student's perceptions must be the major target of teacher education. Since they lie inside persons, they are not open to direct manipulation; they can, however, be modified or induced by programs designed to accomplish this purpose.

2. *The production of an effective teacher must be regarded as a problem in becoming.*

This is a question of helping a person find his own unique ways of operating as an effective individual. There are no "right" methods or "right" knowledge. Other professions do not say that an individual is learning "to law" or "to doctor"; instead, they say that he is becoming a lawyer or becoming a physician. Similarly, teacher education must be seen not as a process of teaching how to teach but as a process of becoming, of personal discovery, of helping a person to become a teacher, beginning from where he is.

3. *The process of becoming must start from security and acceptance.*

Maslow's hierarchy of needs applies to the task of teacher preparation.

The need for personal security is so fundamental that higher order needs are unlikely to be sought while this one remains unfulfilled. Until a young teacher knows he can survive in the classroom, he can attend to little else; and consequently, abstract concepts of democracy, psychological and social foundations, or curriculum theory will fall on ears attuned to more personal requirements. Security for students begins from an acceptance of them where they are and as they are, followed by a maximum diet of success and a minimum diet of failure. This principle is frequently violated by teacher educators, who do not really approve of students as they are or who—perhaps with the best of intentions—want desperately to spur them on to higher things. Either way the message gets through to the student that he is not sufficient as he is. A common fallacy in teacher education is the belief that the methods of the experts can be taught directly to beginners. As a matter of fact, many methods of the experts work only because they are expert; for example, expert teachers handle most disciplinary problems by ignoring them, hardly a method to be recommended to the neophyte. There is a common belief in teacher education that students should always be exposed to only the very best models, but if this is carried so far as to create a feeling of inadequacy in the student, its net effect may be destructive. It may be far more important for him to have a less wonderful teacher with whom he is able to identify.

4. *Effective teacher education must concentrate its efforts upon meanings rather than behavior.*

Behavior, it must be understood, is only symptom; the causes of behavior lie in perceptions and beliefs. Exclusive concern with behavior is not likely to be effective. Teaching teachers how to teach, how to behave, hasn't worked because it places too much emphasis on symptoms. If a student is taught the "right" way to teach and this right way doesn't fit when he goes out to try his skills in the blackboard jungle, all he can do is fall back upon what he perceives or believes from previous experience. He then decides that what he was taught at teachers college is for the birds, and other teachers who have been through the same experience corroborate his conclusion. This syndrome has defeated whole generations of teacher educators preoccupied with trying to teach "right" ways of behaving.

Behavior is a product of meaning. The effect of any behavior is also dependent upon the meaning it invokes in the receiver. This explains why much research on the teaching act has so far been disappointing in providing guidelines for teacher education. Cataloguing teaching acts shows what the teacher did as seen by an observer, not what it means to the children experiencing it. For example, a teacher's saying to a child "Not like that, Jimmy, do it like this" might be scored by an observer as engaging in controlling and directing behavior. To the child, it may be nothing of the sort; the meaning for him may be facilitating and helping, or even loving, behavior. In the light of this understanding of the symptomatic character of behavior, teacher education programs preoccupied with behavioral approaches to teacher preparation may be creating their own roadblocks. The concept also raises interesting questions for the current national emphasis upon behavioral objectives and some applications of behavior-modification techniques. It is conceivable that requiring a teacher education program to define precisely the behaviors it hopes to produce may be the surest way to destroy the effectiveness of its products by concentrating everyone's attention on the wrong dynamics.

When a teacher perceives a child differently, he behaves differently toward him. It makes a great deal of difference, for example, whether a teacher approaches a difficult child with the perception that his behavior has to stop, or that the child believes people don't like him. Each of these ways of perceiving calls for quite different constellations of behaviors to deal with the youngster. If we can be sure the teacher's ways of perceiving are accurate and constructive, it may not be necessary to know precisely how he will put his concern into effect. There are thousands of ways to express either of the above perceptions in action. The crucial question for teacher education is not which behavior but how to bring about appropriate shifts in perception.

The Florida studies in the helping professions found—and later studies have confirmed—clear differences between good and poor professional workers on the basis of (a) their sensitivity to people, (b) what they believe about the people they are working with, (c) what they believe about themselves, (d) what purposes they espouse, and (e) the personal fit of the methods they use.

All but the last of these are functions of belief or perception. Sensitivity or empathy is, in reality, a belief about what are the important data in a human interaction: how it looks to the helper or how it looks to the persons he is working with. Purposes have to do with what one believes is important. If beliefs like these are indeed crucial factors in the make-up of effective professional workers, then programs for teacher education must concentrate their efforts on them, since they may hold important clues to the production of more effective teachers.

5. *If sensitivity and empathy are prime characteristics of effective helpers, and if behavior is the product of perception, teacher preparation programs must shift their main concerns from objectivity to subjectivity.*

This will not be easy. The worship of objectivity, scientific method, and industrial approaches to solving all problems is a way of life deeply rooted in the American culture. Nevertheless, if it is true that human behavior is a function of perception, the problems of behavior change must be recognized as fundamentally subjective, having to do with the inner life of persons—their feelings, attitudes, beliefs, understandings. Even a fact, after all, is only what someone believes. It is interesting to note that in the Florida studies objectivity correlates negatively with effectiveness in the helping professions. In that research, one of the most important factors distinguishing good helpers from poor is the capacity to see non-objectively; that is, subjectively, empathically, or sensitively. Good helpers are characteristically concerned about how things look to the people they are working with.

Much of teacher education as it exists today is teaching students *about* teaching instead of helping them to *become* teachers. This can be observed at every phase of the college experience. Courses in the philosophy of education, for example, teach students about philosophies instead of helping them discover a philosophy of their own. If it were true that a knowledge about philosophies made a good teacher, then our professors of philosophy would be the very best! The problem exists also in social foundations: students are required to look at our social scene objectively and so arrive at magnificent descriptions of the state we are in and how we got there. The goal is to make them dispassionate observers—not movers, shakers, and participators. Courses in human growth and development are no better; most are designed to teach students about children instead of helping teachers to understand a child—a quite different question.

In most colleges, educational psychology is still based almost exclusively on stimulus-response schools of thought, no longer adequate for our purposes. In order to humanize teacher education and our public schools, an alternative or additional subjective, humanistic psychology is needed; more specifically, a perceptual psychology capable of producing sensitivity, empathy, and capacity for effective interaction. No teachers college in these times can afford to base its functions on a single psychology. Humanistic approaches to psychological thought have been expressly designed to deal with the very problems of perceiving and becoming basic to current practice. It is time they were more widely adopted into the curriculum.

6. *The dynamic importance of need in learning must be fully exploited.*

Psychologists don't know much about learning, but one thing they do know: that people learn best when they have a need to know. Donald Snygg once said, "The sickness of American education is a consequence of the fact that we are busily trying to teach people answers to problems they don't have yet!" We have made education irrelevant by ignoring the need of the student.

Applying the principle that learning proceeds best when there is first a need to know calls for rethinking the typical internship at the end of a teacher education program, which was put there with the idea that one learned how to teach and then went out and practiced it. Instead, field experience should be a time for discovering what the problems are, not a place to practice preconceived solutions. What the becoming teacher needs is an awareness of problems and help in finding answers. This calls for continuous practical experience throughout the training period. It probably also means the college will have to surrender to the public schools the job of supervision, for a very practical reason: colleges can't afford it. College supervision is feasible if it is concentrated into a single experience. If field experience is to operate continuously throughout the program, however, few college budgets will stand the strain.

The principle that learning proceeds best when it follows needs has even more striking connotations applied to the substantive aspects of teacher training; it runs head on into the traditional curriculum organization into courses. A course is a package, generally arranged in some orderly sequence determined by the nature of the subject and delivered at some predetermined point in the student's program. But student needs to know are maddeningly haphazard and unpredictable. If students are left free to pursue their needs, they do not learn in orderly sequence; they learn first and later discover an order in which to organize what they have learned. A program honestly seeking to provide information in response to developing needs to know would need to abolish or drastically modify its customary course organization.

7. *A final proposition: if the self-concept is as important a determiner of behavior as research suggests, teacher education must actively apply what is known about it.*

Research on effective helpers clearly demonstrates that such people see themselves in essentially positive ways—as being liked, accepted, able, dignified, and worthy—while poor helpers see themselves as unliked, unwanted, unable, and unworthy. If this is true, teacher education must produce teachers who see themselves in positive ways. This can only be done by giving becoming teachers positive experience, a principle at variance with much current practice in selection, evaluation, and the maintenance of standards.

Some persons seeking to produce changes in the self-concepts of others have assumed that the way to do this is to get them to examine and analyze themselves or engage in deep introspection. Such self-evaluations are part of many teacher education programs. In many places, educators have invented all kinds of gadgets and questionnaires to get teachers to analyze themselves. These are rarely helpful. When people look at themselves, the way they perceive themselves does not change much; for example, if a person wants to be more loveable, the thing for him *not* to do is to think about his loveableness. What he must do, instead, is to think about others and feel better toward them. As he feels better toward them, he will behave better toward them. Soon they will discover that he has become a nicer guy and will treat him accordingly.

A person learns about himself from the feedback he receives from others. Good helpers see themselves as liked, wanted, able, and worthy because they are treated that way. To change education, then, one needs to ask: How can a person feel liked unless someone likes him? How can he feel wanted if no one wants him? How can he feel able unless somewhere he has had success? In our answers to these questions, we shall find what we need to do to improve educational practices and produce teachers with positive views of self.

NOTES

1. A. W. Combs and others. *Florida Studies in the Helping Professions*. Social Science Monograph No. 37. Gainesville: University of Florida Press, 1969; R. Brown. "A Study of the Perceptual Organization of Elementary and Secondary Outstanding Young Educators." Doctor's thesis. Gainesville: University of Florida, 1970. (Unpublished); C. Dedrick. "The Relationship Between Perceptual Characteristics and Effective Teaching at the Junior College Level." Doctor's thesis. Gainesville: University of Florida, 1971. (Unpublished); D. Dellow. "A Study of the Perceptual Organization of Teachers and Conditions of Empathy, Congruence, and Positive Regard." Doctor's thesis. Gainesville: University of Florida, 1970. (Unpublished); G. Vonk. "The Relationship of Teacher Effectiveness to Perception of Self and Teaching Purposes." Doctor's thesis. Gainesville: University of Florida, 1969.
2. Richard Usher and John Hanke. "The 'Third Force' in Psychology and College Teacher Effectiveness Research at the University of Northern Colorado." *Colorado Journal of Educational Research* 10: 2–10; 1971.
3. A. W. Combs. *The Professional Education of Teachers: A Perceptual View of Teacher Preparation*. Boston: Allyn and Bacon, 1965.
4. Robert Blume. "Humanizing Teacher Education." *Phi Delta Kappan* 52: 411–15; March 1971.

2.

B. F. SKINNER

A SCIENCE OF BEHAVIOR

The immediate tangible results of science make it easier to appraise than philosophy, poetry, art, or theology. As George Sarton has pointed out, science is unique in showing a cumulative progress. Newton explained his tremendous achievements by saying that he stood on the shoulders of giants. All scientists, whether giants or not, enable those who follow them to begin a little further along. This is not necessarily true elsewhere. Our contemporary writers, artists, and philosophers are not appreciably more effective than those of the golden age of Greece, yet the average high-school student understands much more of nature than the greatest of Greek scientists. A comparison of the effectiveness of Greek and modern science is scarcely worth making.

It is clear, then, that science "has something." It is a unique intellectual process which yields remarkable results. The danger is that its astonishing accomplishments may conceal its true nature. This is especially important when we extend the methods of science to a new field. The basic characteristics of science are not restricted to any particular subject matter. When we study physics, chemistry, or biology, we study organized accumulations of information. These are not science itself but the products of science. We may not be able to use much of this material when we enter new territory. Nor should we allow ourselves to become enamored of instruments of research. We tend to think of the scientist in his observatory or laboratory, with his telescopes, microscopes, and cyclotrons. Instruments give us a dramatic picture of science in action. But although science could not have gone very far without the devices which improve our contact with the surrounding world, and although any advanced science would be helpless without them, they are not science itself. We should not be disturbed if familiar instruments are lacking in a new field. Nor is science to be identified with precise measurement or mathematical calculation. It is better to be exact than inexact, and much of modern

Reprinted with permission of Macmillan Publishing Co., Inc. from *Science and Human Behavior* by B. F. Skinner. Copyright © 1953 by Macmillan Publishing Co., Inc.

science would be impossible without quantitative observations and without the mathematical tools needed to convert its reports into more general statements; but we may measure or be mathematical without being scientific at all, just as we may be scientific in an elementary way without these aids.

SOME IMPORTANT CHARACTERISTICS OF SCIENCE

Science is first of all a set of attitudes. It is a disposition to deal with the facts rather than with what someone has said about them. Rejection of authority was the theme of the revival of learning, when men dedicated themselves to the study of "nature, not books." Science rejects even its own authorities when they interfere with the observation of nature.

Science is a willingness to accept facts even when they are opposed to wishes. Thoughtful men have perhaps always known that we are likely to see things as we want to see them instead of as they are, but thanks to Sigmund Freud we are today much more clearly aware of "wishful thinking." The opposite of wishful thinking is intellectual honesty—an extremely important possession of the successful scientist. Scientists are by nature no more honest than other men but, as Bridgman has pointed out, the practice of science puts an exceptionally high premium on honesty. It is characteristic of science that any lack of honesty quickly brings disaster. Consider, for example, a scientist who conducts research to test a theory for which he is already well known. The result may confirm his theory, contradict it, or leave it in doubt. In spite of any inclination to the contrary, he must report a contradiction just as readily as a confirmation. If he does not, someone else will—in a matter of weeks or months or at most a few years—and this will be more damaging to his prestige than if he himself had reported it. Where right and wrong are not so easily or so quickly established, there is no similar pressure. In the long run, the issue is not so much one of personal prestige as of effective procedure. Scientists have simply found that being honest —with oneself as much as with others—is essential to progress. Experiments do not always come out as one expects, but the facts must stand and the expectations fall. The subject matter, not the scientist, knows best. The same practical consequences have created the scientific atmosphere in which statements are constantly submitted to check, where nothing is put above a precise description of the facts, and where facts are accepted no matter how distasteful their momentary consequences.

Scientists have also discovered the value of remaining without an answer until a satisfactory one can be found. This is a difficult lesson. It takes considerable training to avoid premature conclusions, to refrain from making statements on insufficient evidence, and to avoid explanations which are pure invention. Yet the history of science has demonstrated again and again the advantage of these practices.

Science is, of course, more than a set of attitudes. It is a search for order, for uniformities, for lawful relations among the events in nature. It begins, as we all begin, by observing single episodes, but it quickly passes on to the general rule, to scientific law. Something very much like the order expressed in a scientific law appears in our behavior at an early age. We learn the rough geometry of the space in which we move. We learn the "laws of motion" as we move about, or push and pull objects, or throw and catch them. If we could not find some uniformity in the world, our conduct would remain haphazard and ineffective. Science sharpens and supplements this experience by demonstrating more and more relations among events and by demonstrating them more and more precisely. As Ernst Mach showed in tracing the history of the science of mechanics, the earliest laws of science were probably the rules used by craftsmen and artisans in training apprentices. The rules saved time because the experienced craftsman could teach an apprentice a variety of details in a single formula. By learning a rule the apprentice could deal with particular cases as they arose.

In a later stage science advances from the collection of rules or laws to larger systematic arrangements. Not only does it make statements about the world, it makes statements about statements. It sets up a "model" of its subject matter, which helps to generate new rules very much as the rules themselves generate new practices in dealing with single cases. A science may not reach this stage for some time.

The scientific "system," like the law, is designed to enable us to handle a subject matter more efficiently. What we call the scientific conception of a thing is not passive knowledge. Science is not concerned with contemplation. When we have discovered the laws which govern a part of the world about us, and when we have organized these laws into a system, we are then ready to deal effectively with that part of the world. By predicting the occurrence of an event we are able to prepare for it. By arranging conditions in ways specified by the laws of a system, we not only predict, we control: we "cause" an event to occur or to assume certain characteristics.

BEHAVIOR AS A SCIENTIFIC SUBJECT MATTER

Behavior is not one of those subject matters which become accessible only with the invention of an instrument such as the telescope or microscope. We all know thousands of facts about behavior. Actually there is no subject matter with which we could be better acquainted, for we are always in the presence of at least one behaving organism. But this familiarity is something of a disadvantage, for it means that we have probably jumped to conclusions which will not be supported by the cautious methods of science. Even though we have observed behavior for many years, we are not necessarily able, without help, to express useful uniformities or lawful relations. We may show considerable skill in making plausible guesses about what our friends and acquaintances will do under various circumstances or what we ourselves will do. We may make plausible generalizations about the conduct of people in general. But very few of these will survive careful analysis. A great deal of unlearning generally takes place in our early contact with a science of behavior.

Behavior is a difficult subject matter, not because it is inaccessible, but because it is extremely complex. Since it is a process, rather than a thing, it cannot easily be held still for observation. It is changing, fluid, and evanescent, and for this reason it makes great technical demands upon the ingenuity and energy of the scientist. But there is nothing essentially insoluble about the problems which arise from this fact.

Several kinds of statements about behavior are commonly made. When we tell an anecdote or pass along a bit of gossip, we report a *single event* —what someone did upon such and such an occasion: "She slammed the door and walked off without a word." Our report is a small bit of history. History itself is often nothing more than similar reporting on a broad scale. The biographer often confines himself to a series of episodes in the life of his subject. The case history, which occupies an important place in several fields of psychology, is a kind of biography which is also concerned mainly with what a particular person did at particular times and places: "When she was eleven, Mary went to live with her maiden aunt in Winchester." Novels and short stories may be thought of as veiled biography or history, since the ingredients of even a highly fanciful work of fiction are somehow or other taken from life. The narrative reporting of the behavior of people at particular times and places is also part of the sciences of archeology, ethnology, sociology, and anthropology.

These accounts have their uses. They broaden the experience of those who have not had firsthand access to similar data. But they are only the beginnings of a science. No matter how accurate or quantitative it may be, the report of the single case is only a preliminary step. The next step is the discovery of some sort of *uniformity*. When we tell an anecdote to support an argument, or report a case history to exemplify a principle, we imply a general rule, no matter how vaguely it may be expressed. The historian is seldom content with mere narration. He reports his facts to support a theory—of cycles, trends, or patterns of history.

In doing so he passes from the single instance to rule. When a biographer traces the influence of an early event upon a man's later life, he transcends simple reporting and asserts, no matter how hesitantly, that one thing has caused another. Fable and allegory are more than storytelling if they imply some kind of uniformity in human behavior, as they generally do. Our preference for "consistency of character" and our rejection of implausible coincidences in literature show that we expect lawfulness. The "manners" and "customs" of the sociologist and anthropologist report the *general* behavior of groups of people.

A vague sense of order emerges from any sustained observation of human behavior. Any plausible guess about what a friend will do or say in a given circumstance is a prediction based upon some such uniformity. If a reasonable order was not discoverable, we could scarcely be effective in dealing with human affairs. The methods of science are designed to clarify these uniformities and make them explicit. The techniques of field study of the anthropologist and social psychologist, the procedures of the psychological clinic, and the controlled experimental methods of the laboratory are all directed toward this end, as are also the mathematical and logical tools of science.

Many people interested in human behavior do not feel the need for the standards of proof characteristic of an exact science; the uniformities in behavior are "obvious" without them. At the same time, they are reluctant to accept the conclusions toward which such proof inescapably points if they do not "sense" the uniformity themselves. But these idiosyncrasies are a costly luxury. We need not defend the methods of science in their application to behavior. The experimental and mathematical techniques used in discovering and expressing uniformities are the common property of science in general. Almost every discipline has contributed to this pool of resources, and all disciplines borrow from it. The advantages are well established.

SOME OBJECTIONS TO A SCIENCE OF BEHAVIOR

The report of a single event raises no theoretical problems and comes into no conflict with philosophies of human behavior. The scientific laws or systems which express uniformities are likely to conflict with theory because they claim the same territory. When a science of behavior reaches the point of dealing with lawful relationships, it meets the resistance of those who give their allegiance to prescientific or extrascientific conceptions. The resistance does not always take the form of an overt rejection of science. It may be transmuted into claims of limitations, often expressed in highly scientific terms.

It has sometimes been pointed out, for example, that physical science has been unable to maintain its philosophy of determinism, particularly at the subatomic level. The Principle of Indeterminacy states that there are circumstances under which the physicist cannot put himself in possession of all relevant information: if he chooses to observe one event, he must relinquish the possibility of observing another. In our present state of knowledge, certain events therefore appear to be unpredictable. It does not follow that these events are free or capricious. Since human behavior is enormously complex and the human organism is of limited dimensions, many acts may involve processes to which the Principle of Indeterminacy applies. It does not follow that human behavior is free, but only that it may be beyond the range of a predictive or controlling science. Most students of behavior, however, would be willing to settle for the degree of prediction and control achieved by the physical sciences in spite of this limitation. A final answer to the problem of lawfulness is to be sought, not in the limits of any hypothetical mechanism within the organism, but in our ability to demonstrate lawfulness in the behavior of the organism as a whole.

A similar objection has a logical flavor. It is contended that reason cannot comprehend itself or—in somewhat more substantial terms—that the behavior required in understanding one's own behavior must be something beyond the behavior which is understood. It is true that knowledge is limited by the limitations of the knowing organism. The number of things in the world which might be known certainly exceeds the number of possible different states in all possible knowers. But the laws and systems of science are designed to make a knowledge of particular events unimportant. It is by no means necessary that one man should understand all the facts in a given field, but only that he should understand all the *kinds* of facts. We have no reason to suppose that the human intellect is incapable of formulating or comprehending the basic principles of human behavior—certainly not until we have a clearer notion of what those principles are.

The assumption that behavior is a lawful scientific datum sometimes meets with another objection. Science is concerned with the general, but the behavior of the individual is necessarily unique. The "case history" has a richness and flavor which are in decided contrast with general principles. It is easy to convince oneself that there are two distinct worlds and that one is beyond the reach of science. This distinction is not peculiar to the study of behavior. It can always be made in the early stages of any science, when it is not clear what we may deduce from a general principle with respect to a particular case. What the science of physics has to say about the world is dull and colorless to the beginning student when compared with his daily experience, but he later discovers that it is actually a more incisive account of even the single instance. When we wish to deal effectively with the single instance, we turn to science for help. The argument will lose cogency as a science of behavior progresses and as the implications of its general laws become clear. A comparable argument against the possibility of a science of medicine has already lost its significance. In *War and Peace*, Tolstoy wrote of the illness of a favorite character as follows:

Doctors came to see Natasha, both separately and in consultation. They said a great deal in French, in German, and in Latin. They criticised one another, and prescribed the most diverse remedies for all the diseases they were familiar with. But it never occurred to one of them to make the simple reflection that they could not understand the disease from which Natasha was suffering, as no single disease can be fully understood in a living person; for every living person has his individual peculiarities and always has his own peculiar, new, complex complaints unknown to medicine—not a disease of the lungs, of the kidneys, of the skin, of the heart, and so on, as described in medical books, but a disease that consists of one out of the innumerable combinations of ailments of those organs.

Tolstoy was justified in calling every sickness a unique event. Every action of the individual is unique, as well as every event in physics and chemistry. But his objection to a science of medicine in terms of uniqueness was unwarranted. The argument was plausible enough at the time; no one could then contradict him by supplying the necessary general principles. But a great deal has happened in medical science since then, and today few people would care to argue that a disease cannot be described in general terms or that a single case cannot be discussed by referring to factors common to many cases. The intuitive wisdom of the old-style diagnostician has been largely replaced by the analytical procedures of the clinic, just as a scientific analysis of behavior will eventually replace the personal interpretation of unique instances.

A similar argument is leveled at the use of statistics in a science of behavior. A prediction of what the *average* individual will do is often of little or no value in dealing with a particular individual. The actuarial tables of life-insurance companies are of no value to a physician in predicting the death or survival of a particular patient. This issue is still alive in the physical sciences, where it is associated with the concepts of causality and probability. It is seldom that the science of physics deals with the behavior of individual molecules, atoms, or subatomic particles. When it is occasionally called upon to do so, all the problems of the particular event arise. In general a science is helpful in dealing with the individual only insofar as its laws refer to individuals. A science of behavior which concerns only the behavior of groups is not likely to be of help in our understanding of the particular case. But a science may also deal with the behavior of the individual, and its success in doing so must be evaluated in terms of its achievements rather than any a priori contentions.

The extraordinary complexity of behavior is sometimes held to be an added source of difficulty. Even though behavior may be lawful, it may be too complex to be dealt with in terms of law. Sir Oliver Lodge once asserted that "though an astronomer can calculate the orbit of a planet or comet or even a meteor, although a physicist can deal with the structure of atoms, and a chemist with their possible combinations, neither a biologist nor any scientific man can calculate the orbit of a common fly." This is a statement about the limitations of scientists or about their aspirations, not about the suitability of a subject matter. Even so, it is wrong. It may be said with some assurance that if no one has calculated the orbit of a fly, it is only because no one has been sufficiently interested in doing so. The tropistic movements of many insects are now fairly well understood, but the instrumentation needed to record the flight of a fly and to give an account of all the conditions affecting it would cost more than the importance of the subject justifies. There is, therefore, no reason to conclude, as the author does, that "an incalculable element of self-determination thus makes its appearance quite low down the animal scale." Self-determination does not follow from complexity. Difficulty in calculating the orbit of the fly does not prove capriciousness, though it may make it impossible to prove anything else. The problems imposed by the complexity of a subject matter must be dealt with as they arise. Apparently hopeless cases often become manageable in time. It is only recently that any sort of lawful account of the weather has been possible. We often succeed in reducing complexity to a reasonable degree by simplifying conditions in the laboratory; but where this is impossible, a statistical analysis may be used to achieve an inferior, but in many ways acceptable, prediction. Certainly no one is prepared to say now what a science of behavior can or cannot accomplish eventually. Advance estimates of the limits of science have generally proved inaccurate. The issue is in the long run pragmatic: we cannot tell until we have tried.

Still another objection to the use of scientific method in the study of human behavior is that behavior is an anomalous subject matter because a prediction made about it may alter it. If we tell a friend that he is going to buy a particular kind of car, he may react to our prediction by buying a different kind. The same effect has been used to explain the failures of public opinion polls. In the presidential election of 1948 it was confidently predicted that a majority of the voters would vote for a candidate who, as it turned out, lost the election. It has been asserted that the electorate reacted to the prediction in a contrary way and that the published prediction therefore had an effect upon the predicted event. But it is by no means necessary that a prediction of behavior be permitted to affect the behaving individual. There may have been practical reasons why the results of the poll in question could not be withheld until after the election, but this would not be the case in a purely scientific endeavor.

There are other ways in which observer and observed interact. Study distorts the thing studied. But there is no special problem here peculiar to human behavior. It is now accepted as a general principle in scientific method that it is necessary to interfere in some degree with any phenomenon in the act of observing it. A scientist may have an effect upon behavior in the act of observing or analyzing it, and he must certainly take this effect into account. But behavior may also be observed with a minimum of interaction between subject and scientist, and this is the case with which one naturally tries to begin.

A final objection deals with the practical application of a scientific analysis. Even if we assume that behavior is lawful and that the methods of science will reveal the rules which govern it, we may be unable to make any technological use of these rules unless certain conditions can be brought under control. In the laboratory many conditions are simplified and irrelevant conditions often eliminated. But of what value are laboratory studies if we must predict and control behavior where a comparable simplification is impossible? It is true that we can gain control over behavior only insofar as we can control the factors responsible for it. What a scientific study does is to enable us to make optimal use of the control we possess. The laboratory simplification reveals the relevance of factors which we might otherwise overlook.

We cannot avoid the problems raised by a science of behavior by simply denying that the necessary conditions can be controlled. In actual fact there is a considerable degree of control over many relevant conditions. In penal institutions and military organizations the control is extensive. We control the environment of the human organism in the nursery and in institutions which care for those to whom the conditions of the nursery remain necessary in later life. Fairly extensive control of conditions relevant to human behavior is maintained in industry in the form of wages and conditions of work, in schools in the form of grades and conditions of work, in commerce by anyone in possession of goods or money, by governmental agencies through the police and military, in the psychological clinic through the consent of the controllee, and so on. A degree of effective control, not so easily identified, rests in the hands of entertainers, writers, advertisers, and propagandists. These controls, which are often all too evident in their practical application, are more than sufficient to permit us to extend the results of a laboratory science to the interpretation of human behavior in daily affairs—for either theoretical or practical purposes. Since a science of behavior will continue to increase the effective use of this control, it is now more important than ever to understand the processes involved and to prepare ourselves for the problems which will certainly arise.

3.

DANIEL E. GRIFFITHS

THE MOST SIGNIFICANT EDUCATIONAL RESEARCH

What research in education has proved to be most significant in the last 15 years? Have the lines of inquiry and findings of special importance remained consistent in the past decade or have new concerns and new studies commanded attention?

In the fall of 1966, I compiled a list of the ten most significant educational research findings (listed below). What has happened in the interim? Has the list stood the test of time or have new research insights changed it?

THE TEN MOST SIGNIFICANT EDUCATIONAL RESEARCH FINDINGS
(Revised as of 1971)
*1. Human characteristics: Benjamin S. Bloom, *Stability and Change in Human Characteristics.*

2. Equal educational opportunity: James S. Coleman and others, *Equality of Educational Opportunity.*

*3. Development of the individual: Richard E. Ripple and Verne N. Rockcastle, eds., *Piaget Rediscovered.* Hans G. Furth, *Piaget and Knowledge.*

*4. Nature of intelligence: J. P. Guilford, "Three Faces of Intellect," *American Psychologist,* 1959. Raymond B. Cattell, "Theory of Fluid and Crystallized Intelligence: A Critical Experiment," *Journal of Educational Psychology,* 1963.

5. Methodology of educational research: "Statistics," *Methodology of Educational Research,* December, 1969.

From *Today's Education,* 61:4 (April, 1972), 48–51.
* Starred items also appeared on the list for the years 1956–66.

*6. Principles of learning: Patrick Suppes, "Modern Learning Theory and the Elementary School Curriculum," *American Educational Research Journal*, March, 1964.

*7. Characteristics and styles of administrators: John Hemphill, Daniel E. Griffiths, Norman Frederiksen, *Administrative Performance and Personality*.

*8. Physiological approaches to learning and memory: John Gaito, "DNA and RNA as Memory Molecules," *Psychological Review*, 1963. Edward L. Bennett and others, "Chemical and Anatomical Plasticity of Brain," *Science*, October 30, 1964.

9. Comparative education: Torsten Husen, ed., *International Study of Achievement in Mathematics: A Comparison of Twelve Countries*. Vols. I and II. A. W. Foshay, ed., *Educational Achievements of Thirteen-year-olds in Twelve Countries*.

10. Nature-nurture: Arthur R. Jensen, "How Much Can We Boost IQ and Scholastic Achievement?" *Harvard Educational Review*, Winter, 1969.

First, what is meant by the term "significant educational research findings," and how can one determine them? I resolved the latter problem simply by asking a sample of professionals—researchers, administrators, and teachers—what they thought the list should include.

The former was a bit more complicated. What, for example, is a "finding"? If one chooses to define that word as "a definitive conclusion of a single study," then it has little meaning. Several of the respondents pointed out that a single finding is rarely important in itself but acquires importance because it fits a system of findings. Another way of saying the same thing is that a single study never produces significant findings, with rare exceptions, and that major contributions are usually a series of interconnected studies conducted by a number of investigators. When a single study does produce significant findings, it is the culmination of a number of related researches.

What, then, is a "significant" finding? Lawrence M. Stolurow of the Harvard Computing Center suggests three questions to ascertain the significance of research in education. (a) To what extent has the behavior of individuals in education been changed? (b) How many articles have been written as a result of the findings? (c) To what extent do educators talk about or use the concepts generated by the research in discussing their own problems?

Dr. Stolurow also believes, as do many others, that a critical mass of research evidence triggers behavior change in educational practitioners. The size of the critical mass probably varies with a number of factors, including the readiness of the field, the power of the findings, and the size of the groups to be affected by the study.

"Research" is used to mean applied research and development as well as fundamental, theory-testing research. I accepted a wide range of research methodologies for inclusion in this paper.

Following is the new list of the ten most significant educational research findings.

1. HUMAN CHARACTERISTICS

The work of Bloom published in *Stability and Change in Human Characteristics* is the best example of the proposition that significant findings for education emerge from long lines of inquiry.

Bloom reviewed almost 1,000 studies of selected human characteristics in an attempt to understand the development and change in these characteristics over a period of time. The studies, taken as a whole, summarize what is known about quantitative development of certain human characteristics from near birth to adulthood.

Bloom's major hypothesis is that "the environment in which the individual develops will have the greatest effect on a specific characteristic in its most rapid period of change and will have least effect on the characteristic in its least rapid period of change." He points out, for instance, that general intelligence appears to develop as much from conception to age four as it does from age five to eighteen.

Bloom's second major hypothesis is that "change measurements are unrelated to initial measurements, but they are highly related to the relevant environmental conditions in which individuals have lived during the change period." From this he argues that the home and the school should act in harmony so that one reinforces the other.

Bloom's work points up the tremendous importance of early education. The significance attached to his work is reflected in Head Start, in the interest in nursery school and kindergarten education, and in a revival of concern for primary education.

2. EQUALITY OF EDUCATIONAL OPPORTUNITY

Virtually all the respondents nominated studies in equality of educational opportunity, and most mentioned the Coleman Report, which was made in response to the Civil Rights Act of 1964.

The Report addressed itself to four major questions:

To what extent are racial and ethnic groups separated from each other in the public schools?

Do schools offer equal educational opportunity?

How much do students learn as measured by their performance on standardized achievement tests?

What relationships exist between student achievement and the kinds of schools they attend?

The study is a monumental one, not only because of the vast amounts of data gathered, but because of the skill and ingenuity with which the data were analyzed. While each of the questions had been researched many times before, the Coleman Report is the capstone of such research efforts.

Many of the Coleman Report findings are well known:

Negro students (as of 1966) were nearly completely segregated in the South and were also segregated in all other sections of the country.

With the exception of Oriental Americans, minority groups score lower on all measures of school achievement.

With the exception of Oriental Americans, the achievement decrement increases as minority children progress through school.

When socioeconomic background of pupils is kept constant, schools across the country are remarkably similar in achievement by pupils.

The achievement of minority pupils is more dependent on the schools they attend than is the case with most white children.

If a minority pupil from a home lacking sufficient educational enrichment is put with schoolmates from educationally advantaged homes, his achievement is likely to increase.

The Coleman Report put the issue of school integration into a factual framework, made it possible to evaluate the results of segregation, and laid the foundation for subsequent policies and practices of the federal government.

3. DEVELOPMENT OF THE INDIVIDUAL

Inquiries into the development of the individual have constituted a line of study for a considerable period of time. The work of Gesell has been most influential in this country, but recently it has been overshadowed by that of Piaget, the Swiss psychologist.

As Eleanor Duckworth states, Piaget's theory is that the "development of intellectual capacity goes through a number of stages whose order is constant, but whose time of appearance may vary both with the individual and with the society. Each new level of development is a new coherence, a new structuring of elements, which until that time have not been systematically related to each other."

Four factors are related to the development of individuals: nervous-system maturation, experience, social transmission, and auto-regulation. The last is viewed as more important than the first three.

The chief implication for education in Piaget's work is

a plea that children be allowed to do their own learning. . . . Good pedagogy must involve presenting the child with situations in which he himself experiments, in the broadest sense of that term—trying things out to see what happens, manipulating things, manipulating symbols, posing questions and seeking his own answers, reconciling what he finds at one time with what he finds at another, comparing his findings with that of other children.

Piaget is extremely popular among elementary school educators, psychologists, and specialists in child development. However, although he is referred to constantly, I believe he has influenced conversation more than educational practice.

4. NATURE OF INTELLIGENCE

The study of human intelligence is one of the most notable lines of inquiry, beginning with Galton's two-factor theory, followed by the development of intelligence tests by Binet and Terman, L. L. Thurstone's exploration of factors in intelligence, and Cattell's theory of fluid and crystallized intelligence (which promises the development of culture-fair intelligence tests). Guilford's unified theory of intellect continues the line.

The Aptitudes Project, which Guilford directs at the University of Southern California, has organized the known unique or primary intellectual abilities into a single system called the "structure of the intellect." One basis for the classification is the basic process or operation performed. This classification produced five major groups of intellectual abilities: factors of cognition, memory, convergent thinking, divergent thinking, and evaluation. A second way in which Guilford classifies intellectual factors is according to the kind of material or content involved—figural, symbolic, semantic, and social. The third way of classifying is according to products involved—units, classes, relations, systems, transformations, and implications.

Guilford believes that the most important educational implication of his work is that it changes the conception of the learner and the learning process. He characterizes the prevailing concept of the learner as a kind of stimulus-response device, much like a vending machine. The learner is taught to give out a certain response when a particular stimulus is administered, just as a vending machine emits a given product for a coin. According to the structure of intellect model, the learner should be conceptualized as an electronic computer. The computer receives information, stores it, uses it to generate new information by either divergent or convergent thinking and evaluates its own results. In addition, the learner has an advantage over a computer in that he can discover new information outside himself.

This conception of the learner leads to the idea that learning is the discovery of information, not merely the formation of associations. The acceptance of this idea and its introduction into the schools over the past seven or eight years is evidence of the significance of Guilford's work.

5. METHODOLOGY OF EDUCATIONAL RESEARCH

The remarkable advances in research methodology must be included, although they are not a research finding in the sense of the others included on this list. Educational researchers are now using powerful methodologies in their efforts to advance knowledge. They may still occasionally use "elephant guns to shoot at fleas," but they no longer use "flyswatters to kill tigers." Once they used only the statistic of simple correlation in efforts to understand complex educational situations, but now almost all use multivariate analysis. Educational outcomes are virtually never measured against a single criterion, so methods of analysis are needed which handle all of the criterion variables simultaneously. These are now available.

The availability of advanced statistical tools changed the way researchers think about educational problems. They are now able to devise more appropriate theories because their methods more precisely mirror the complex reality of the school and the classroom. Advances in methods of analysis have made possible great advances in research design, particularly in model building whereby the researcher constructs an analogy (often mathematical) to the situation he wishes to understand better.

Improvement in methods of research is the major reason for the recent dramatic increase in the production of significant educational research.

6. PRINCIPLES OF LEARNING

The application of computer technology to research in learning theory might well be considered as a research breakthrough. The modern era started with James and Thorndike and moved through Hull, Guthrie, Gates, and others to such present-day workers as Bruner. A second line of inquiry—the work in teaching machines by such men as Pressy and Skinner—has a much shorter history. These two lines have now merged, and the new line is the study of learning in computer-based laboratories.

Neither learning-theory research nor teaching machines constituted powerful lines of inquiry, and the hope held for them has now largely been dissipated. The reason is largely technological. It was virtually impossible to handle the empirical data generated by a study of learning in a classroom, and a noncomputerized teaching machine could deal only with learning processes which are too simple to be of much value. The computer has changed both of these conditions.

The work chosen for this list is that of Suppes, the Stanford philosopher, in which he describes research on five principles of learning in a computer-based laboratory. The laboratory is a simulation of a teaching environment created by a tutor working with an individual child. The computer provides not only visual information on a televisionlike screen but also auditory information through speakers or earphones.

An example of the unique value of the computer in learning research is the attempt to apply response latency—the time between a stimulus and the onset of a response—as a criterion of learning. Presumably, the shorter the time, the better the student is learning. Measurements of response latency are impossible in ordinary classrooms; they are feasible in computer-based classrooms.

The potential of learning research in computer-based laboratories is one of the most promising of the present ventures.

7. CHARACTERISTICS AND STYLES OF ADMINISTRATORS

The publication of *Administrative Performance and Personality* capped a long line of inquiry into the characteristics and styles of administrators. The methodology of this study was the creation of a simulated school in which 232 elementary school principals worked. Their administrative activities were scored and factor-analyzed, and the resulting factors were related to a large number of variables.

Eight styles of administration and of the personalities that tended to accompany each style emerged. Each style was related by a large-scale multivariate analysis process to measures of mental ability, basic personality factors, interests, job performance values, group interaction, superiors' ratings, teachers' ratings, professional and general knowledge, and biographical data. The result was a detailing and explanation of the administrative style through description of the people who perform in accordance with it.

The report of research has not been widely distributed nor, apparently, have many people read it. The materials used in the study, however, have had wide use. The kinescopes, tape recordings, and other printed materials developed in this study have been employed in graduate courses for administrators in over 100 universities, and yet recent doctoral research indicates that only two universities used the written report in their instructional program.

8. PHYSIOLOGICAL APPROACHES TO LEARNING AND MEMORY

A number of studies have attempted to determine physiological bases for learning and memory. This work has largely employed neurological and biochemical approaches. Probably the work best known to educators is that of K. S. Lashley (*Brain Mechanisms and Intelligence*. Chicago: University of Chicago Press, 1929. Reprinted by Hafner).

Biochemical studies now appear to be more popular than neurological ones, and some exciting research which bears on the possible involvement of DNA (deoxyribonucleic acid) and RNA (ribonucleic acid) in memory functions has been done. In reviewing the research on DNA and RNA in relation to memory, Gaito concludes that while there is no conclusive direct evidence to indicate that either of these is the memory molecule, inferential evidence of this does exist.

Bennett and his associates found that rats who receive enriched experiences develop greater weight and thickness of cortical tissue than do their littermates without the experience. Further, acetylcholine esterase activity increases in the rest of the brain even though tissue weight decreases with enriched experiences. This demonstrates that "the brain is responsive to environmental pressure—a fact demanded by physiological theories of learning and memory."

These are but two promising examples that the next decade will see important research results in the physiological approach to learning and memory.

9. COMPARATIVE EDUCATION

The study of the educational systems of different countries has long been a distinguished line of inquiry. These studies have been descriptive in nature, and although some, notably certain UNESCO projects, have employed statistical data, the studies were essentially qualitative.

The International Project for the Evaluation of Educational Achievement was conceived to measure objectively the actual achievements of educational systems and to explore empirically the factors related to such achievement. A pilot study of 13-year-old students in 12 countries in the areas of reading comprehension, mathematics, science, geography, and nonverbal ability was completed to test the feasibility of the idea. Foshay reported the results. A number of interesting conclusions were reached:

the United States fared poorly when compared with other countries; boys varied more from country to country than did girls; Scandinavian children who start school at age seven did as well on the tests as children in other countries with longer schooling.

This project raised and answered many questions concerning differences among countries in achievement by relating the differences to a larger number of factors.

10. NATURE-NURTURE

One of the oldest discussions deals with whether heredity or environment has more influence on the development of intelligence. Within this context, Jensen wrote his highly controversial article in which he reported on an analysis of 151 studies. (The reader of Jensen's article is also referred to an analysis of his work which appeared in the Spring, 1969, issue of the *Harvard Educational Review* and Jensen's reply in the Summer, 1969, issue.)

Jensen opened his paper by stating that recent compensatory education efforts have failed. (This statement is not entirely correct: More precisely, Head Start has not been a complete success.) He then questioned a central notion of compensatory education: IQ differences are almost entirely the result of environmental differences and the cultural bias of IQ tests.

After defining the concept of IQ, he analyzed several lines of inquiry which suggest that genetic factors are much more important than environmental ones in producing IQ differences and that prenatal influences may well contribute the largest environmental influence in IQ. He also discussed evidence showing that social class and racial variations in intelligence must be attributed at least partially to genetic differences.

Jensen then examined other mental abilities, such as free-recall and auditory digit memory, and suggested that educational programs might capitalize on these. He concluded that efforts to boost the IQ have been misdirected and that educational programs should match in variety the wide range of mental abilities found in children, should focus on mental abilities other than the cognitive, and should, therefore, teach more specific skills.

CHAPTER TWO

Behaviorism in the Classroom

BEHAVIORISM ASSUMES THAT THE CAUSES OF HUMAN BEHAVIOR can be identified and measured. It assumes, further, that behavior is developed and maintained largely by conditions and reinforcers in the environment. As Clifford K. Madsen says in his article in this chapter:

Behavioral change occurs for a reason: Students work for things that bring them pleasure; they work for approval from people they admire; students change behaviors to satisfy the desires they have been taught to admire; they generally avoid behaviors they associate with unpleasantness; and, finally, students develop habitual behaviors when those behaviors are often repeated.

There is nothing mysterious about the process: circus animal trainers have been applying it for centuries. Although its application to humans is much more complex the basic principle is the same. In fact, successful teachers have been putting this into practice for years, creating an atmosphere in their classrooms in which students feel competent and happy and are reinforced for positive intellectual and emotional responses. Great teachers are great reinforcers; they know how to "stroke" each child with acceptance, recognition, respect, and awareness whenever it is needed or appropriately earned.

Madsen tells us what behavior modification is and how it can be applied. He then discusses major objections that have been directed toward behavior-modification techniques.

Richard R. Abidin also considers some of the problems and limitations of behavior modification in school settings. He describes the preconditions that, if present, increase the likelihood that the behavior program implemented in a school situation will be a success. Included in these conditions is a system of reinforcing the teacher's efforts to maintain a positive atmosphere in the classroom.

Finally, Abidin describes the necessity for making an extensive and accurate assessment of the behavior problem, gathering baseline data, and identifying effective reinforcers. It is clear that behavior modification is not a simple technique. Its successful application requires a clear understanding, not only of theory, but also of the nature of behavior technology and its implications for society.

The issue of freedom and control is at the core of a basic philosophical conflict regarding the systematic modification of human behavior. There is no question that the idea of systematic control of behavior has threatening overtones. Although Skinner and others have offered forceful arguments that control is unavoidable and that personal enhancement rather than dehumanization will be the ultimate outcome of behavior modification, many critics are not fully convinced. To the humanist, nothing that is done by one individual to another can be entirely without taint. Any form of control is unacceptable, no matter how positive or noble is the goal. To the humanist, the only acceptable method of teaching is to develop a learning atmosphere in which it is possible for individuals to do something for themselves without any system of control or supervision.

Peter C. Madden believes that reinforcement is probably the most viable method of making the classroom less rigid and more enjoyable, a goal shared by both behaviorists and humanists. His views exemplify the prevailing desire of behaviorists to shift from a punitive, aversive classroom atmosphere to a positive, optimistic one. On the basis of his experiences as a school psychologist, Madden is convinced that teachers can use the power of positive reinforcement to motivate children to become independent, self-directed, and creative as well as to learn subject matter.

The reinforcement principle is an aspect of psychology that has effectively bridged the gap between theory and practice. Behavior-modification techniques have already made a great impact on teaching methods, instructional materials, and classroom-management strategies. Although many of the best-known successes of behavior modification have been with atypical individuals—mentally ill adults, mental retardates, and in some cases culturally deprived and emotionally disturbed youth—there is a growing interest in using it with normal classroom problems. Programs based on token economies and contingency management are being developed and tested in group situations. Until recently, few teachers had formal instruction in behavior modification, but it is believed that the technique will become an integral part of the professional preparation of teachers at all levels, from preschool to adult education.

Behaviorism has contributed more to the field of educational psychology than behavior-modification techniques. It attempts to explain other phenomena of learning, such as transfer principles, learning curves, spaced vs. massed training, retention, and problem solving. Above all, behaviorism attempts to explain the process of learning in an objective way through the gradual accumulation of a scientifically verifiable body of facts and principles of behavior. Behaviorism can provide a basis for many teaching practices and also a vocabulary useful for communication among teachers and other professionals involved in education.

RECOMMENDED READING

J. D. Krumboltz and C. E. Thoresen. 1969. *Behavioral Counseling: Cases and Techniques*. Specific examples of behavior-modification programs, useful for teachers and counselors who want to apply the techniques.

D. L. MacMillan. 1973. *Behavior Modification in Education* (New York: Macmillan). One of the best books on the subject, dealing with subjects ranging from complex behavioral theory to clinical and classroom applications.

C. H. Madsen, W. C. Becker and D. R. Thomas. 1968. "Rules, Praise and Ignore: Elements of Elementary Classroom Control," *Journal of Applied Behavior Analysis* 1, 139–50. Techniques for the application of behavior modification to classroom control and management of younger children.

B. F. Skinner. 1968. *The Technology of Teaching* (New York: Appleton-Century-Crofts). The application of behavior modification to a technology of teaching, with emphasis on positive rewards and the elimination of punishment.

———. 1971. *Beyond Freedom and Dignity* (New York: Knopf). An expansion of behavior-modification principles to the level of national planning and control, with a better, more orderly, way of life as the ultimate goal.

J. T. Spence. 1971. "Do Material Rewards Enhance the Performance of Lower-Class Children?" *Child Development* 42, 1461–70. A research report on the problem of whether a token system works with lower-social-class children whose ultimate need is for self-reinforcement and self-direction.

C. E. Thoresen (ed.). 1973. *Behavior Modification in Education. The Seventy-second Yearbook of the National Society for the Study of Education, Part I* (Chicago: University of Chicago Press). A review by major authorities of research in behavior modification, dealing with theory, applications, and philosophical and social issues.

4.

CLIFFORD K. MADSEN

VALUES VERSUS TECHNIQUES:
AN ANALYSIS OF
BEHAVIOR MODIFICATION

A teacher stops by a child working on math and checks correct/incorrect responses. This teacher has observed that most students learn more efficiently when they are given academic feedback. She is using a principle of behavior modification to improve academic performance.

The same teacher sees another child engrossed in his work assignment. She moves quickly to his seat, gives him a smile, and whispers in his ear, "I'm so happy to see you working on your assignment." She has noticed that if she can praise him while he does his work, he works much more than when she recognizes him while he is not working. She is again using a principle of behavior modification.

The teacher goes back to her desk to correct more academic assignments. A little boy comes quickly to her desk and asks a question. She ignores him completely and calmly goes about correcting her papers. He stays about 15 seconds, and then goes back to his work. The teacher smiles to herself as she checks a chart designed for this particular boy. She has almost extinguished his habit of running to her desk (only once this week; initially he did it 28 times a day and that was *after* she started recording it). The teacher sets her handkerchief on her desk as a reminder to go to this child after he has been in his seat for a few minutes. She hopes that his question was not a really important one, that it can wait two or three minutes.

She goes back to correcting assignments. It is important to her that she finish them by the end of the day. She has discovered that, by randomly picking out a different day of the week for children to take corrected papers home, she can dramatically increase their academic performance. Again, behavior modification.

She takes the time to check on the child who came to her desk—he wanted to know if he could get a book from the library—then returns to

From *Phi Delta Kappan*, 54:9 (May, 1973), 598–601.

33

her seat. She hears Suzy starting to talk to her neighbor. The teacher immediately gets up, goes to Suzy, and firmly tells her that she should stop visiting until her work is done. The teacher notices that Suzy appears a little sad. She is a sensitive child, and the teacher has long since discovered that a bit of teacher disapproval will halt her inappropriate behavior. Behavior modification.

The teacher remembers that she used to yell nearly all day long (observers actually counted 146 times during one morning session). In those days she used disapproval about 80 percent of the time in efforts to modify social behavior, generally with little effect. Although she found that this percentage is about average for most teachers, she wanted to be more positive. At first it was difficult, not "natural." She had to learn behavior modification techniques: the reinforcement of certain academic and social behaviors. Now, when she hears a loud adult voice in an adjoining classroom, she thinks about a discussion of honesty she had with a colleague. Should a teacher be honestly disapproving most of the time because it is a "natural" response? She has learned better.

She stands in front of her class. "Children, I would like you to look at me. Suzy's looking at me. Sam is looking at me. Now David's looking at me. Now everyone is looking at me. That's nice." (Again, behavior modification.) "You may all stop your individual work and visit now until it's time for music." (When the youngsters helped make class rules earlier in the year, they expressed a desire for talk time. Establishing rules with student help has *nothing* to do with behavior modification.)

As the students visit, the teacher thinks about the token system the school counselor is trying to establish in some of the rooms. She has read many reports about "token economy" systems and understands that they represent an effective application of behavioral principles, but she does not choose the technique for her class. She has never liked material rewards for learning (except for herself!) and prefers to use social reinforcers instead. Besides, she cannot imagine how her class could be much better than it is. She really likes it. She knows also that the counselor sometimes uses very strong disapproval as well as a special "time-out room" for some children. The effects of his procedures are also well documented and consistent with behavioral approaches, but she prefers not to use them.

WHAT IS BEHAVIOR MODIFICATION?

The above paragraphs describe procedures whose efficacy has been documented in behavioral research. In essence, this research shows that behavior is maintained and shaped by its consequences. (Strange, isn't it, that so obvious a truth should be so badly used in practice?) *Behavior* is a common word which is used quite casually in reference to many things. In the literature of behavior modification it refers to *anything* a person does, says, or thinks that can be observed directly or indirectly. Behavior modification theory deals with techniques of changing behavior as well as specific interaction effects. A "well-behaved student" is of course a person who behaves in ways that society (represented in school by the teacher) thinks are appropriate to a given situation.

Some people try to make a case against a behavioral approach by alluding to "attitudes" which are not a part of the process of behavior modification. Actually, these attitudes represent different value systems. *Principles* for teaching (shaping appropriate behaviors) should not be confused with value issues. Many teachers regard the questions of why, what, and who as considerably more important than how. But, after the teacher has decided what is to be learned, why it should be learned, and who is going to learn it, then an effective approach to how it will be taught is vital, or the teacher's efforts as well as the student's will be wasted.

A very simple rationale explains the efficiency of behavioral approaches. *Behavioral change occurs for a reason:* Students work for things that bring them pleasure: they work for approval from people they admire; students change behaviors to satisfy the desires they have been taught to value; they generally avoid behaviors they associate with unpleasantness; and finally, students develop habitual behaviors when those behaviors are often repeated. The behavior modification approach derives from psychological experiments and represents nothing more than simple cause and effect relationships.

The current emphasis on behavior modification, or reinforcement theory (to use an older term), grew from the works of B. F. Skinner. Programmed instruction is the best-known result of his initial work. Other teaching systems, treatments of mental illness, and techniques in clinical psychology are based on Skinner's experiments. Many critics disagree with certain value choices and extensions proposed by Skinner, but this in no way invalidates the empirical relationships in learning established and stated by Skinnerian investigators. Indeed, the entire rationale of behavior modification is that most behavior is *learned*. Behavior thus defined includes emotional responses, attitudes, reading, listening, talking, looking into the mirror, liking a person, wanting to talk out a problem, hitting, being frustrated, sticking with a task, abandoning a task, responding appropriately to the desires of a teacher, not responding to the desires of a teacher, most "good" behavior, most "bad" behavior, disturbing one's neighbors, being "well-behaved," being excited about school work, hating to learn, and so on—and on—and on.

Exactly the same principles may be used to teach good social behavior as are used to teach appropriate academic skills (e.g., providing feedback about correct/incorrect responses). If a teacher wishes students to have a real desire to learn something, the teacher may find it necessary to structure the external environment so students will seek structured rewards for their work tasks. After initial manipulation, the rewards for proper behavior will often come from the reinforcement of the particular task itself, i.e., getting the right answer is often all the structure that is needed. Incidentally, this is precisely what most teachers do when they initially make a "game" out of learning. Students become enthusiastic concerning the game per se, not realizing that its purpose is to stimulate effective work. It is curious that some teachers who try desperately to make work fun also say they reject any "manipulation techniques." The teacher's job is to structure learning experiences. This structuring process involved manipulating the environment (i.e., setting up the correct situation, physical plant, materials, and so on) conducive to effective learning, whether the goal be simple obedience, complex problem solving, or self-discovery. The teacher must structure as wisely as possible, whether the school organization is open, free, pod, modular, or something else. One should know the subparts of any complex task and structure the situation so that each student can have a "rewarding learning experience." Irrespective of our cherished clichés, we actually do practice behavioral manipulation. It appears paradoxical for the teacher to reject manipulation when manipulation is the essence of her task.

BEHAVIOR RESULTS FROM ITS CONSEQUENCES

Behavioral research demonstrates that if work tasks can be (1) geared to the student's own level, (2) presented in logical sequence with (3) appropriate feedback concerning correct/incorrect responses, and (4) rewarded for successively better efforts to reach defined goals, then the student will certainly learn. Exactly the same principles apply to teaching proper social skills.

Critics say, "Yes, but isn't that a cold approach?" Certainly not. While behavior modification is the only branch of applied psychology based on scientific principles verified in the laboratory, it is the nature of the material to be learned that represents important value choices. Actually, because of its consistency and simplicity, behavioral modification effected through contingent reinforcement (approval/disapproval) usually represents a very kind and understandable system to students. The behavioral scientist who observes a school situation can classify almost everything that goes on behaviorally, regardless of how well the teachers involved understand principles of reinforcement. Cause and effect behaviors are always present. For example, some teachers do not realize when they are being sarcastic. "Why don't you just yell louder, Jimmy?" Problems are created when the student is not really sure of the teacher's meaning. Being taken literally is the price one sometimes pays for using sarcasm or irony.

The behavioral clinician can demonstrate how teachers might be more effective in the application of the child's or teacher's own values. Many teachers are surprised to learn how closely they approximate a strict behavioral approach. After being apprised of behavioral principles, many exclaim, "Why that's what I've been doing all the time!"

When learning is defined as a change or modification of behavior, then reinforcement principles constitute a method to promote or expedite this learning. In short, behavioral analysis asks, "How should we go about teaching in the best possible manner to ensure correct association?" Or, more specifically, "How should we go about teaching the student to concentrate, to read, to share, to clean his desk, to be honest, to develop his own values?" If a youngster responds favorably to our presentation, we assume that it functions as a reward for the students. But what if the student does not respond? Then we must restructure the external environment so that the student *does* receive proper motivation.

IF AT FIRST YOU DON'T SUCCEED?

If behaviors can be learned, they can also be unlearned or relearned. Sometimes, in our zeal to get through to our students, we make mistakes. Sometimes we make mistakes regardless of zeal. The efficacy of behavioral techniques with *severe* problem behaviors within mental hospitals and institutions for the retarded and handicapped perhaps should give us the encouragement to move forward. Behavioral techniques have demonstrated that even severely handicapped children can learn much faster and much more than we previously believed possible. And no, one does not need to be a medical or psychological specialist to provide academic and social approval. Teachers have been doing this for years.

What are the dynamics of changing social behavior? Since it is impossible for a person to maintain two contradictory responses, the skillful teacher will program to elicit responses *incompatible* with deviant behavior and thereby obviate the need for punishment. "Count to 10 before you get angry; think before you begin your work; take three big breaths before you cry." Punishment alone may stop deviant behavior, but it will not necessarily teach correct associations. The child who is hit with his spoon because he cannot use it properly will not necessarily learn proper etiquette. Similarly, the child who is punished for faulty reading will not necessarily learn to read efficiently. The one child might shun the spoon;

the other child may stop reading. Setting up incompatible responses is perhaps the most effective behavioral technique of all, because it constitutes a double-edged approach. Not only is the inappropriate behavior eliminated but a correct response replaces it. Thus the child unlearns and relearns at the same time. The procedure eliminates the need for punishment and at the same time teaches correct associations.

Four principles for the teacher are:

1. *Pinpoint:* It is necessary to pinpoint explicitly the behavior that is to be eliminated or established. This takes place at many different levels relating to many differentiated academic as well as social behaviors. It leads to a hierarchical arrangement of skills and behaviors based upon expected specific behavioral objectives.

2. *Record:* This is a necessity in behavior modification and actually is what differentiates it from other techniques. Specified behaviors must be listed as they occur and thereby provide a precise record from which to proceed. The record must be accurate. If the behavior cannot in some way be measured, then one can never know if it has been established or unlearned. As maladaptive responses are eliminated, more time can then be devoted to more productive behaviors.

3. *Consequate:* This unique word, which you won't find in Webster's, means "setting up the external environmental contingencies (including primarily one's own personal responses) and proceeding with the teaching program." Contingencies include approval, disapproval, withdrawal of approval, threat of disapproval, or ignoring. Reinforcers may be words (spoken and written), expressions (facial and bodily), closeness (nearness and touching), activities (social and individual), and things (materials, food, playthings, and money). *Choice of reinforcers is an extremely important aspect of behavior modification* and constitutes an issue which should receive much discussion, debate, and criticism.

4. *Evaluate:* Evaluation should be continuous, but ultimate effects, which may be different from immediate effectiveness, must be ascertained. Hence a program must be allowed to operate for some time before final data analysis.

VALUES VERSUS TECHNIQUES

It should be apparent from the above that behavior modification represents the use of a series of scientifically verified techniques that may be used to promote more effective learning of both social and academic subject matter. A behavioral approach does not help the teacher decide why, what, and who is going to learn. These issues represent important value choices. However, after questions relating to these values have been answered, behavioral principles may be used to enhance learning of appropriate behavior. Of course, the choice of a particular technique as opposed to other approaches represents a value choice. Also, if a behavioral approach is implemented, then selection of specific behavioral procedures (e.g., approval rather than punishment), as well as choice of potential reinforcers, represents another value issue.

Opponents of behavior modification would do well to address themselves to the more important issues concerning learning rather than condemn a technique by alluding to many ancillary detriments that they feel might ensue from its application. (Generally, they make these pronouncements in the complete absence of data).

Figure 1 illustrates this point. Fill in three or four of the most important values you think should be learned by students (academic, social, or both). For example, reading, writing, consideration for others, self-actualization—whatever *you* consider to be positive. It is obvious that behavioral techniques must be used to teach "negative" as well as "positive" values.

The purpose of this exercise is to indicate that behavioral methods, much like any product of man (atomic energy, jet propulsion, govern-

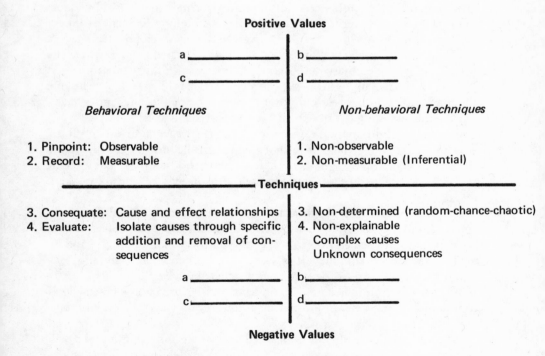

Figure 1. Values / techniques dichotomy chart.

ments), may be used either to the benefit or detriment of other human beings. Behavioral techniques are characterized by definitions of behavior that can be observed (pinpointed) and then measured (recorded and counted). These techniques include the isolation of specific cause and effect relationships and thereby provide a scientific methodology for the evaluation of learning.

TEACHING—ART OR SCIENCE?

Through trial and error, it would seem that every teacher who cares can find effective ways to stimulate students to realize their full learning potential. With or without a full understanding of behavioral principles, this teacher will find better methods of behavioral control and character development.

The ability to recognize individual differences and structure the school environment with contingencies relevant to specific situations represents an outstanding accomplishment. Good sense and good taste are important, of course. I know of one seventh-grade teacher who controlled her class by having the problem children participate in a mock wedding ceremony if they were "very, very bad." When the children evidenced proper behavior, they were allowed to "get divorced." This disciplinary procedure was tremendously effective and used behavioral principles. However, the teacher's choice of activity raises serious questions regarding the acquisition of other behaviors and attitudes. Another teacher told me of a technique she used with 8- and 9-year-old boys: "When one of the boys misbehaves, I make him wear a girl's ribbon in his hair." Does it work? Very well; but again one must question the insensitivity of this teacher to other values. It is ironic that this same person thought it "terrible" to suggest to parents that occasionally they might send their problem children to school without breakfast, in order to promote proper behavior through *rewards* of cookies, cereal, and milk.

It seems apparent that no teaching technique can be effectively divorced from the person who uses it. This point, however, makes a case for more rigorous screening of prospective teachers, not for the abandonment of effective techniques. It is a curious argument that maintains that effective techniques must be kept from teachers because then teachers may actually teach more efficiently. Because of the effectiveness of behavioral techniques, perhaps the profession may now get down to the truly important issues:

—What specifically should be learned? Or, more importantly, who will decide what is to be learned, both socially and academically? What values and accompanying behaviors evidencing selected values should be learned? When, where, and by whom?

—Who should be given the responsibility to interact purposefully in the learning process, i.e., to teach?

—Should society require any objective evidence for this learning, i.e., data from observation or other formal means?

—If continued research demonstrates the efficacy of empirical cause and effect relationships (data based on observation), ought derived principles to be systematically implemented within the schools?

—If so, then what should be the boundaries concerning choice and application of reinforcers, i.e., approval versus disapproval; punishment versus ignoring; the structuring of incompatible responses; the use of academic subject matter only as reward; social as opposed to material reinforcers? These issues represent the most important value issues within the technique of behavior modification.

Let us not waste time with such irrelevant arguments as "it's unfair." (Of course it's unfair, if unfair is defined as any individualization or discriminative assessment, e.g., differential grading.)

Then there is the charge: It's totalitarian. Nonsense! Who decides what values/behaviors should be taught to whom has nothing to do with behavior modification. Some schools are run mostly by teachers; others are controlled mostly by students. Another criticism goes something like this: Behavior mod teaches students to work for rewards. Right! Perhaps after awhile they may even find their subject matter rewarding.

Another criticism: It militates against internal control. Not so; actually, the process of partial reinforcement teaches youngsters to go for longer and longer periods of time without any external rewards. Incidentally, how long do adults maintain appropriate behavior without the occasional reinforcement from a loved one or perhaps a more tangible reward for professional behavior?

Then it is sometimes alleged that behavior modification denies human reasoning. If anything it *teaches* human reasoning—specifying in clear, consistent, and honest ways the cause and effect relationships of life.

Another charge: *It may teach other nonspecified behaviors.* Perhaps. But let's worry about those, if indeed they exist, when there is some evidence for them. And is anyone so naive as to believe that teachers are not already approving or disapproving certain student behaviors with or without a full understanding of behavior modification?

Finally, if we cannot agree on the above, at least we may begin to take data—i.e., make systematic observations concerning what is presently going on in schools, in order to build a sounder basis for the development of teaching techniques.

It is readily apparent that, regardless of how many "behavioral recipes" are available, the insensitive teacher will still be found wanting. The art of being a good teacher seems directly related to the behaviors of that teacher as a person. Modeling effects of an outstanding individual are still among the most powerful and far-reaching of teacher influences. The truly effective teacher will combine the science of behavior with the art of living to create that exceptionally rare atmosphere: an environment where children not only take excitement from discovery but learn to be nice people.

5.
RICHARD R. ABIDIN, JR.

WHAT'S WRONG WITH
BEHAVIOR MODIFICATION

All professional activity, be it educational, legal, medical, or psychological, has its excesses and abuses. It seems that whenever a new and worthwhile tool or technique comes along, many members of a professional group jump on the bandwagon and ride it into the ground. This is especially true when the new technique is not well understood and its users have little experience with it. With the technique excessively and often ineptly applied, disenchantment sets in. One hears: "It doesn't work" and "I have read the articles but when you apply it to real life it doesn't work." Behavior modification appears to be currently undergoing such a fate. I am sure that in the future it will find its appropriate place in the range of techniques available to school and clinical psychologists and, hopefully, to classroom teachers.

To my knowledge no profession has a universally applicable procedure; penicillin, for example, is great for bacterial pneumonia, but it fails in the case of acute appendicitis.

As with all remediation or intervention procedures, in all professions there are certain parameters within which techniques are applicable. This article is addressed to the consideration of some of the parameters, issues, and problems which must be evaluated and dealt with before and during

From *Journal of School Psychology*, 9:1 (1971), 38–42.

the application of behavior-modification techniques. It focuses primarily on issues related to behavior modification in the classroom. The issues raised have developed out of the author's experiences with behavior modification over the past six years and out of his students' experiences as they have attempted to apply the techniques in the classroom. The conclusions, therefore, are not empirical facts; they are experientially developed hypotheses (opinions).

PRELIMINARY CONSIDERATIONS

Often a psychologist encounters a child or a situation which was "made for behavior modification," and so, on the basis of the child's needs and the psychologist's understanding of these needs, he attempts to institute a behavior-modification program. Now, as is generally known, he doesn't institute the behavior-management program; he essentially recommends it and helps set it up. The teacher is supposed to carry it out. Here the problem begins. The school psychologist with his new-found tool may fail to conduct the necessary evaluation and training of the teacher prior to the use of the technique. What neurosurgeon would have a pediatric nurse assist in surgery without some training specific to the job's demands? Further, not every nurse has the personal characteristics, needs, and motivation to be an assistant in surgery.

PRECONDITIONS

Step 1. The psychologist must evaluate the teacher's teaching style and personality in relation to the demands of the behavior-modification program to be instituted. Our experience has indicated that in order for a teacher to work successfully in a behavior-modification program she must have average or above-average organizational ability; in fact, being mildly compulsive is generally helpful. Teachers who tend to be very nondirective, highly intuitive, or very existentially oriented generally do not work out well in the application of a behavior-modification program.

Step 2. The psychologist must train the teacher in basic concepts as well as in the psychomotor skills necessary in the behavior-modification program. Failure to meet this preliminary condition is the single most common cause of failure in behavior-modification programs. Although the basic concepts and the behavioral demands on the teacher appear simple, in practice the simplicity turns out to be quite elusive. In one program, for example, the teacher assumed that if the child was rewarded with tokens for good behavior, she would take tokens away for bad behavior.

The "bad" behavior was unrelated to the target behavior; the program turned out to be a capricious system whereby the teacher threatened to take back tokens whenever she felt it appropriate.

Recognition of the selection and training requirements will hopefully prevent the psychologist from approaching the use of behavior modification offhandedly. Our experience has indicated that it is reasonable to expect a school psychologist to expend 150 hours of professional time in a school year to assist a teacher in setting up a token economy in a classroom. This time includes planning sessions, teaching the teacher, classroom observation, weekly follow-ups, crisis consultation, etc. When the teacher has no prior knowledge, training, or experience in behavior modification, we have found that assisting her in instituting a behavior-modification program for one child will take approximately 30 hours.* It is our belief that if the psychologist recognizes how much time is involved, he will be more discriminating in recommending the institution of a behavior-modification program.

Step 3. The school psychologist must, after discussion with the teacher, decide how she is to be reinforced for her efforts. A teacher experienced in using behavior modification may need little reinforcement. However, since most teachers are not experienced in this area, there is a definite need for frequent and positive reinforcement. We have found that for most teachers weekly or daily verbal encouragement by the psychologist and principal is a powerful reinforcer. Comments recognizing the teacher's effort, work, interest in her children, and the progress of her children are but some of the obvious and natural reinforcers. It has been our experience that the teacher should be assisted in the collection of baseline data and verbally reinforced for plotting and recording countable behavior on a daily basis. We have found that without baseline data teachers will frequently become discouraged, since the first noticeable difference is usually a rather large step, requiring several days. For example, if a child's baseline for out-of-seat behavior is 50 incidences per day, and after the institution of a contingency-management program that behavior is reduced to 40 incidences by the end of the first week, the average teacher will be ready to give up. There is just not sufficient difference between 50 and 40 out-of-seat incidents, in terms of the emotional demands on the teacher. However, we have found that seeing tangible proof of the downward trend in the plotting of a curve frequently becomes a reinforcing event. Further, when these changes are suitably paired with verbal reinforce-

---

* These time demands may be cut to one-quarter with the same teachers in subsequent years.

ments from the psychologist, the changing frequency curve can itself become a reinforcing event.

COMMON PROCESS ERRORS

Error 1. Failure to Define the Problem Behavior Both on an Operational Level and on a Feeling-Tone Level. A teacher's initial statement of a problem might be "Johnny disrupts the class and he is hostile to me. He doesn't like me." Hopefully, after observation the school psychologist might be able to help the teacher see that "disrupts class behavior" may be operationally defined by the number of times Johnny is out of his seat when the teacher is not standing next to him. Further, he might point out that the hostility issue turns out to be an inference that the teacher makes because she feels the child rejects her, and this despite the fact that he gets more individual attention and instruction than any other child. The school psychologist can reassure the teacher that the child seems to like her very much, that her attention is so rewarding to him that he has learned that he can gain her attention by his out-of-seat behavior. The failure to deal with the teacher's feelings about the child or situation prior to the development of a behavior-modification plan frequently results in miscommunication and resistance. Having met or at least recognized the teacher's needs and feelings, the psychologist may then help the teacher select a specific behavior or set of behaviors which are communicable to and understandable by the child. Often the teacher's natural inclination in setting up a contingency program is to tell the child that she doesn't want him to "disrupt the class." The child may find this difficult to understand: Is talking loudly or softly to a friend disrupting the class, is his sitting up and looking mad disrupting, or is his getting his books too rapidly or too slowly disruptive, etc.? The target behavior must be clearly defined.

Error 2. Failure to Collect Baseline Data. Many school psychologists and teachers tend to feel this step is unnecessary, but from a technical standpoint and from our experiences with behavior modification, we have come to feel that it is crucial. We have found that collecting baseline data often leads to a redefinition of the problem. The teacher may believe she recognizes the problem, but in the course of having to attend closely to the child's behavior she will often find that the behavior she is counting may not be the one that is most disturbing to her or that it occurs so seldom as to be less important than some other behavior.

Having a baseline and then noting changes from the baseline, once a response contingency contract has been developed, tend to provide a clear picture of the reinforcers' efficacy. For example: (a) M & M's are not necessarily reinforcers for middle class children who have access to all the candy they want; (b) model airplanes may turn out to be a punishment if the child's father makes him work on the model at home under his direction. The only way that we know that a response-contingent event is reinforcing is the extent to which it modifies the behavior in relation to the baseline.

Error 3. Ineffective or Inappropriate Reinforcement. Often a teacher or a school psychologist assumes he has a reinforcer and makes this "reinforcer" contingent upon some behavior. Nothing happens. It is felt that three steps must be taken in attempting to locate reinforcers for a given child: (a) observe what the child does and what he likes; (b) ask him what would be reinforcing for him; and (c) set up a reinforcing menu, not just one item.

Both the psychologist and the teacher must remember that reinforcers change in their reinforcing strength with time. This expected change must be fully recognized in advance.

Error 4. The Attitude of the School Psychologist. Often the behavior most destructive to any given behavior-modification program is the naively simplistic attitude of the school psychologist. He oversells his idea. The school psychologist must recognize that behavior modification is merely a tool to support good teaching. Many emotional components of teaching which do not lend themselves to a behavior-modification program are essential for good teaching. "Positive regard," "love," "affection," etc., are but some of the complex behaviors which set the tone and determine the learning atmosphere. The school psychologist must recognize that there are many good teachers who do a good job by using less formalized approaches. We must realize that a child's life goes on outside of the behavior-modification program and that the teacher's and psychologist's expectancies must be tempered with reality. No behavior-modification program controls all of the contingencies of a child's life; often it doesn't control the most important contingencies. A child's generalized feelings of inadequacy and inferiority may lead to school failure. Behavior modification may change the school failure and help alleviate the problem, but those circumstances and contingencies which created the generalized feelings of inadequacy and inferiority outside of the school will continue to operate and to have their effect.

Certainly behavior-modification principles and programs have been demonstrated to be highly effective. When properly handled and applied, behavior modification represents one of the best systems for dealing with many behaviors in the classroom. Nevertheless, like all intervention procedures and systems, it has its limits and problems. It also has potentials which have not been adequately explored; it could, for example, be used in systematic analysis of complex human behaviors such as love, affection, and teaching, which most psychologists and educators recognize as learned behaviors. Hopefully, some day we will be able to utilize the tools of the behavioral sciences such as behavior modification to provide the circumstances in which the most creative loving and teaching behaviors can be developed by all teachers.

6.   PETER C. MADDEN

SKINNER AND THE OPEN CLASSROOM

Now that the furor over the publication of B. F. Skinner's new book, *Beyond Freedom and Dignity,* is dying down, it may be possible to examine the implications of this major work from some different perspectives. It appears that the detailed points of the behaviorist position were largely overlooked in the critical shock created by Skinner's sweeping conclusions and proposals. No doubt the tendency of some ardent behaviorists like Skinner to pontificate rather than persuade has contributed to the hostility his observations received.

That is unfortunate, for it is details that behavioral research has always handled most successfully. While I must confess that I became rather mystified as Skinner expanded his theory on an increasingly grand scale, I discovered in the early chapters many ideas of great relevance to the attempt . . . to find ways to make classrooms less rigid and more humane.

From this point of view, *Beyond Freedom and Dignity* offered these suggestions about our cultural system:

1. The study of behavior has demonstrated by now that techniques like positive reinforcement offer a more effective way of changing and controlling behavior than such traditional means as punishment or requests for cooperation.

From *School Review*, 81:1 (1972), 100–107. Copyright © 1972 by The University of Chicago. All rights reserved.

2. There is no real freedom for the individual from the controlling pressures of either the natural or social environment. However, it is possible for the controls to become less visible in a free society since most of its members conform out of a sense of loyalty, peer-group pressure (real or perceived), or simply out of habit and convenience.
3. Advocates of human dignity object to large-scale adoption of behavioral theories by insisting that people continue to get credit for voluntary "good" acts. But in order to deal with those who refuse to be good voluntarily, a society is forced to maintain numerous punitive and disciplinary institutions.
4. While there is general acceptance of a belief that a poor environment can often explain failures of both individuals and groups, there is less willingness to accept the other side of that coin. Individual and group successes may be equally attributable to environmental forces and not actually the personal triumphs often envisioned.
5. Various types of positive reinforcements are available which could largely replace the aversive conditions and punishments which now operate in our society. The most effective reinforcers are those which simultaneously serve the need of the individual for gratification and the need of his society for cultural survival.

It seems to me these are Skinner's major observations in relation to the operation of societies in general and schools in particular. When taken in smaller doses, Skinner's ideas are neither as novel nor as provocative as the early criticism indicated. It has been almost a cliché for years that a greater investment in (positive) education, for example, should eventually lead to a lesser need for (negative) prisons. As to the effects of the environment, there is also consensus that the slums are surroundings which make solutions to educational and social problems difficult if not impossible.

There is also widespread recognition that punishment is a rather ineffective means of changing behavior. Despite centuries of using punitive methods to control classroom behavior, student conduct (as traditionally defined by teachers and parents) remains a major problem in today's schools and consumes an enormous investment in time and effort. Massive expenditures on law enforcement and "rehabilitation" notwithstanding, the recidivism rate of most prisons remains at 80 per cent or more.

As a psychologist who practices in schools, I often find it useful to view a school as a minisociety with a well-defined cultural system. Looking at schools and classrooms from Skinner's point of view, it is obvious that there is *always* control of conduct in the school. In an open classroom the teacher may have made a conscious decision to abandon some of the more traditional procedures, goals, and controls in order to substitute those of his own choosing. Among the ideals often selected by teachers in open classrooms are independent study, self-selection of curricular materials, creative expression by students, and development of a free, humane classroom atmosphere.

Many prominent writers concerned with open classrooms seem to suggest that these independent, creative activities will develop naturally if the child is just released from teacher-directed pressure and left free to choose what he wants to do in the classroom. This point of view is often reinforced by educators and students in colleges which are trying to develop teachers for open classrooms.

My experience tells me that the system just does not work that way, and I think a close examination of Skinner's ideas will reveal why. For one thing, a child is not—in fact—free simply because the teacher chooses not to exert obvious control over his behavior. Children enter a classroom filled with expectations derived from the conditioning of their previous experiences in schools. Graduates of the New School sometimes report strong initial pressure to reproduce the system to which the child has become accustomed. Both parents and students often ask for the workbooks to be brought back and complain that they do not know what to do under the new classroom system. Some students and faculty entering the New School undergo a similar period of initial frustration and disenchantment when the accustomed structure suddenly proves to be nonexistent.

Second, each child comes equipped with behavior norms which have been internalized through several years of interaction with and reinforcement by teachers, parents, and peers. Most children will go along with whatever new scheme the adults in authority come up with, especially in middle-class schools. Their conceptions of what constitutes acceptable behavior conform so closely to those of the adults that few conflicts arise in any classroom situation. These children move easily, if passively, through a variety of classroom environments ranging from the permissiveness of kindergarten to the rigidity of military training.

With these children, the major task of the teacher is simply to reinforce the efforts the children make to conform to the new system. Our . . . elementary students and . . . undergraduates find that their anxiety in open educational situations is dispelled over a period of time, largely because they have been reinforced by their teachers for adopting such desired new behaviors as independent action in choosing and attempting to complete their own school experiences.

Some new teachers in open classrooms attempt a more passive role in which they offer a variety of attractive and interesting activities without giving children any sense of direction from above. These teachers refuse to use reinforcement because they view it as an imposition upon the students' freedom to pursue activities for their own intrinsic satisfaction. Unfortunately, the result is often chaotic classroom behavior. The children may respond to this situation by turning elsewhere in the environment for gratification, often to peers who tend to reward playing or similar behavior which provides instant and continuous reinforcement.

A common reaction of such teachers, who as students were often the most strenuous advocates of the right of children to be free and self-directed in the classroom, is despair and anger at what they come to regard as ingratitude on the part of the children to respond positively to the experience offered them. Several supervisors of interns . . . have noted that teachers who were extremely open during training have become markedly rigid and structured when confronted with the behavior of the children in their classroom. Faith Weinstein Dunne, in her review of Kevin Ryan's book *Don't Smile until Christmas*,[1] reported that Harvard interns often have a similar experience, which she termed the "call me Bill syndrome."

What these teachers apparently failed to understand was that control is not a process to be avoided but a tool which must be exercised in either a positive or a negative way. Having refused to systematically help children adapt to change through supportive means of control like positive reinforcement, they eventually had to regress to the traditional forms of structure and punishment, or negative reinforcement.

As Skinner noted, a major problem for any society, whether nation or classroom, is dealing with individuals who do not behave in accordance with the society's need for cooperative, or at least nondestructive, behavior. School psychologists find that approximately 10 per cent of most school populations need special attention from teachers or consultants. Many of these children are unable to engage in mutually rewarding cooperative classroom activity because of some handicap or disability. The remainder are simply unwilling to do so, becoming what Skinner calls "counter-control" individuals. In any case, special means are usually required to educate or contain these children.

Advocates of freedom, says Skinner, have traditionally dealt with these individuals by stating that they have the right to behave in any manner they wish *if* they are willing to abide by the consequences of their actions. Proponents of dignity add that to take away an individual's option to behave as he wishes if he will be held accountable infers that he loses the right to be "good" of his own accord. However, almost no one feels that freedom and dignity can or should be allowed to operate without accountability. For this reason, all the traditional aversive rituals and punishments are maintained despite their lack of effectiveness in dealing with individuals who abuse others in society while exercising their own freedom.

Thus, the test of any educational approach comes when teachers have to deal with the small number of countercontrol students in their classrooms. The rest of the students tend to have internalized enough conforming behavior standards and identify with the teacher to a degree that they will go along with whatever the school seems to demand of them this year. The 10 per cent figure has recurred rather frequently in my own conversations with interns and teachers who often report, "I could *really* open up my room if I could just find some way to deal with those three or four students who ruin everything I try!"

Traditional classroom teachers have generally relied on punishments and aversive techniques to maintain control of this dissident minority. Open classroom teachers who attempt to avoid using control or reinforcement tend to find themselves forced eventually to adopt similar methods as the result of pressure exerted by students, parents, administrators, or their own anxiety. The only viable alternative I can see is to recognize that every society requires some form of control. There seems to be no escape.

By examining the propositions that true freedom may be much more illusion than fact, while dignity may require punishment and degradation as an alternative, Skinner may have done educators a valuable service. Once we recognize the futility of completely discarding controls and creating absolute freedom, we can begin to maximize freedom and make controls less aversive and more humane. Skinner suggests that a greatly increased, well-organized use of positive reinforcement techniques may be the only way to reconcile any society's need for control with the individual's desire for freedom from aversive or punishing contingencies.

In the schools, this means a virtual abandonment of the kinds of threats and punishments so familiar to every teacher and student. Teachers must develop new powers of observation and learn to note, record, and reward the good things children do rather than swoop down with vengeance upon their errors. The classroom atmosphere must become positive and loving, drawing out desired behavior with encouragement and rewards rather than stressing and punishing failure. While this sounds idyllic, it is a mere technical skill, part of Skinner's "technology of behavior." After learning how to operate this way, teachers often respond, "Why, that is nothing more than common sense." Positive reinforcement may be merely common sense but in few classrooms today is it common practice!

By exerting control and direction in positive ways, open classroom teachers find two beneficial results. First, it becomes possible to co-opt the countercontrol student into at least superficial cooperation so the rest of the class can learn and develop in individual, meaningful directions. Theories of freedom notwithstanding, it has been my experience that given a humane environment, children who habitually act out or disrupt a class tend to be unhappy, unpopular, and low in self-esteem. Positive reinforcement offers these children a chance to find academic and peer-group success in a friendly, open environment. The fact that the teacher creates and controls that environment must seem to such children a negligible factor in view of their opportunity to grow.

The other benefit is derived by that cooperative but passive group which constitutes the majority of most classrooms. These children also tend to give superficial cooperation to innovative classroom practices but close examination often reveals that they have only a limited understanding of what they are doing, with no genuine preference for any particular method. These children, like the dissident minority, can be taught to become independent, creative, active participants in an open classroom setting.

If teachers view freedom of choice and self-direction as skills to be learned in small, sequential, reinforced steps rather than as the natural condition of American schoolchildren today, they find the path to creating and maintaining an open classroom much easier. Once these teachers realize that freedom and creativity are personal values which they as teachers are building into their classroom structure, they can begin to be much more effective in helping children reach those goals. The result can be that children interact cooperatively, think creatively, behave in a non-destructive manner, and work independently because they have *learned* to want to do those things, not because they may be punished or downgraded for their failure to do them.

As Skinner notes, the power of positive reinforcement is both vast and neutral. While we may not be able to avoid control, we can and must consistently examine the values and goals of the controllers. Teacher education programs which offer this skill must also provide students with a grounding in humanities and philosophy that will give them a sense of values. Broad-based education in social and human values . . . and . . . open classroom goals and settings . . . seem to me to be the best guarantee that the power of positive reinforcement will not be abused in their teaching.

The effect is circular in operation. Positive reinforcement techniques will make possible the creation of an open classroom while the operation of the open classroom will, in itself, minimize the negative effects of control. The result can and should be development of a humane classroom culture in which each child can learn not only to be free and independent but how to reconcile the demands of social living upon freedom.

NOTE

1. *Harvard Educational Review,* 41:3 (August, 1971): 401–8.

CHAPTER THREE

Cognitive Development

BEHAVIORISM HAS DOMINATED PSYCHOLOGY during the last few decades. A major concern has been with observable environmental causes and their effect on overt behavior. However, in the last few years, there has been a resurgence of concern for internal psychological processes, represented in the area of cognitive psychology by Neisser; the information-processing theorists, such as Haber; the Russian psychologists Anokhin, Sokolov, and Zaporozhets; and some of the developmental theorists, especially Jerome Bruner and Jean Piaget.

According to Neisser (1967), cognitive psychology focuses on the way in which "sensory input is transformed, reduced, elaborated, stored, recovered, and used. . . . Such terms as *sensation, perception, imagery, retention, recall, problem-solving,* and *thinking,* among others, refer to hypothetical stages or aspects of cognition" (p. 4). Cognition is thus concerned with how a person uses and manipulates the stimulus information he receives from the environment or reconstructs from memory. According to this psychological model, the human acts upon and manipulates stimulus information; he is not solely a passive receptor and respondent. Thus, cognition refers to the mental processes a person employs to learn from and adapt to the environment.

One of the most widely respected authorities on children's cognitive development is Jean Piaget. Whether one agrees or disagrees with Piaget's child-centered emphasis, there is no question that he deserves admiration for the impressive structure of theory and empirical data that he has built during his long and productive life, and in fact is still building.

A cornerstone of Piaget's theory is the concept of adaptation. It is interesting that Piaget began his career as a marine biologist and soon became interested in the survival-adaptation mechanisms of the undersea world. To learn is to adapt; to adapt is to survive and reproduce. All creatures must continually solve problems of adaptation in order to survive.

During his youth, Piaget worked in Paris with Theophile Binet, who was then engaged in developing the first Binet scale for the measurement of intelligence. Piaget became interested in why children made certain errors while taking the test. He noticed that there were characteristic patterns of correct and incorrect responses to intelligence-test problems. This observation led him to the study of mental processes in children. Turning away from conventional laboratory experimentation techniques, Piaget came to rely on his own powers of questioning, observation, and analysis. The result was a theory of the nature of intelligence that involves biological adaptation, equilibrium between the individual and his environment, and a set of mental operations that maintain this balance. Piaget's works are fascinating to read because his theories probe the labyrinths of the child's mind.

Ginsburg and Opper explain Piaget's most significant concepts, often within the context of the evolution of his career. Their book, *Piaget's Theory of Intellectual Development: An Introduction* (from which our selection was taken), provides an appropriate next step for those interested in further reading on Piaget.

Kise, Borucki, and Schmerber offer some suggestions for classroom applications of Piaget's concepts. Their article contains useful speculations regarding the nature of the child's mental processes as he develops language skills, which are so crucial to his adaptation. These speculations can help the teacher in many ways—for example, in choosing among various psycholinguistic approaches to teaching reading. It can also help him to understand one of Piaget's major contributions: the principle of conservation, which describes the ability of a child to grasp the permanence of physical phenomena, regardless of their movement or changes in shape.

Other cognitive psychologists, notably Jerome Bruner and David Ausubel, have also developed theories regarding the intellectual development of the child, but it is reasonable to say that Piaget has largely created the standards by which cognitive psychology is judged today. His work has challenged practitioners to become students of the mentality of children.

Good research theory does not necessarily result in solutions; it often leads to better questions. Piaget's thought not only can lead the teacher to a basic understanding of cognitive behavior but also can generate new questions about the processes of thought in the child.

RECOMMENDED READING

M. Brearly and E. Hitchfield. 1966. *A Guide to Reading Piaget* (New York: Schocken Books). The application of Piagetian concepts to the teaching of basic thinking skills in elementary schools.

S. Farnham-Diggory. 1972. *Cognitive Processes in Education: A Psychological Preparation for Teaching and Curriculum Development* (New York: Harper & Row). An ambitious effort to bring together theory and teaching methods by one of the major authorities in cognitive psychology.

H. G. Furth. 1970. *Piaget for Teachers* (Englewood Cliffs, N.J.: Prentice-Hall). A readable and interesting version of Piaget intended for the beginner.

H. Ginsburg and S. Opper. 1969. *Piaget's Theory of Intellectual Development: An Introduction* (Englewood Cliffs, N.J.: Prentice-Hall). A scholarly, yet readable, treatment of Piaget, from biographical data to the implications of his findings for education.

U. Neisser. 1967. *Cognitive Psychology* (New York: Appleton-Century-Crofts).

E. M. Segal and R. Lachman. 1972. "Complex Behavior or Higher Mental Processes: Is There a Paradigm Shift?" *American Psychologist* 27(1), 46–55. A thorough and well-documented discussion of the shift of research from traditional theories of mental behavior to the concept of thinking as a complex cognitive process.

7. HERBERT GINSBURG AND SYLVIA OPPER

JEAN PIAGET: BASIC IDEAS

Early in his life Piaget developed two major intellectual interests: biology, the study of life, and epistemology, the study of knowledge. After devoting a number of years to each of these disciplines, Piaget sought a way to integrate them. In the course of his work at the Binet Laboratory in Paris, he came to the conclusion that psychology might provide the link between biology and epistemology. Piaget decided to spend a few years on the study of the evolution of knowledge in the child and then to apply the fruits of this research to the solution of the theoretical problems which initially motivated him. Fortunately for child psychology the few years became many, and in their course Piaget has produced over thirty volumes

From Herbert Ginsburg and Sylvia Opper, *Piaget's Theory of Intellectual Development: An Introduction*, © 1969, pp. 13–25. Reprinted by permission of Prentice-Hall, Inc., Englewood Cliffs, New Jersey.

reporting his investigations into such matters as the child's moral judg-ment, the infant's patterns of behavior, and the adolescent's solution of scientific problems. Only in the 1950's was Piaget able to return to the-oretical issues in epistemology. Today, even at the age of more than seventy years, Piaget continues his contributions to psychology, as he has recently published works on mental imagery, memory, and other matters.

Piaget's research and theory have been guided by a framework which can be defined as a set of orienting attitudes. His definition of intelligence is not restrictive, but states that intelligence involves biological adaptation, equilibrium between the individual and his environment, and a set of mental operations which permit this balance. Piaget's research activities also have increasingly come to focus on the growth of the child's under-standing of the basic concepts of science, mathematics, and similar disci-plines. Piaget is less interested in studying the contents of the child's thought than the basic processes underlying it.

*   *   *

A scientist usually employs a theoretical framework to guide his experi-mentation and theorizing. The framework is not a detailed theory but a point of view or a set of attitudes which orient the scientist's activities. A psychologist, for example, may be basically committed both to Freudian ideas and to the personality-test approach, and these attitudes will then be likely to give direction to his research and analysis. For example, these ideas may influence him to choose to study the familial causes of neurosis rather than the physical bases of the disorder. Such an orientation would almost certainly lead him to investigate the matter by giving paper and pencil tests which might lead to different results from those which could be obtained by the direct observation of the child in his home. This is not to deny, of course, that scientists do change their opinions as a result of conflicting research evidence. However, it is . . . true that orienting attitudes can be influential; the scientist does not begin his work without any preconceptions.

Piaget's orienting attitudes, stated quite explicitly, have to do with the nature of intelligence and with its structure and functions.

INTELLIGENCE

First, how does Piaget define the nature of intelligence? The reader should be aware that Piaget had almost complete freedom in this regard. Previous to the 1920's, when he began his investigations, there had been little research or theorizing on intelligence. The mental-testing approach was in evidence, as exemplified by the Binet-Simon IQ test; and there were also scattered experimental investigations of intellectual processes like memory in the adult. However, neither of these approaches had been developed extensively, and psychologists had hardly agreed, and do not concur even today, on the proper subject matter for the psychology of intelligence. Does intelligence refer to rote memory, to creativity, to IQ-test performance, to the child's reasoning, or to other matters? Because Piaget began his studies during a pioneering era he was free to conceive of intelligence in terms of his unique perspective. He was careful not to begin by proposing too rigid or precise a definition of intelligence. Piaget did not want to fall into the trap of too narrowly circumscribing the subject matter when so little was known about it. To lay down an overrestrictive definition at the outset would have been to curtail investigation and impede discovery. In fact, the major aim of Piaget's research was to discover what actually constitutes intelligence.

Desiring to avoid premature restrictions, Piaget offered several definitions of intelligence, all couched in general terms. These definitions reflect Piaget's biological orientation. For example, "Intelligence is a particular instance of biological adaptation." [1] This states quite clearly that human intelligence is one kind of biological achievement, which allows the individual to interact effectively with the environment at a psychological level. Another definition states that intelligence "is the form of equilibrium toward which all the [cognitive] structures . . . tend." [2] The use of the term "equilibrium," borrowed from physics, implies a balance, a harmonious adjustment between at least two factors; in this case between the person's mental actions (the cognitive structures) and his environment. Although the environment may disturb the equilibrium, the individual can perform mental actions to restore the balance. The definition also states that equilibrium is not immediately achieved: the cognitive structures only gradually "tend" toward equilibrium. It is of special interest to the biologist to study this evolution and the dynamic processes underlying it. Piaget's primary goal, then, could be defined as the study of children's gradual attainment of increasingly effective intellectual structures. Another definition stresses that intelligence is "a system of living and acting operations." [3] Piaget is interested in mental activity, in what the individual *does* in his interaction with the world. Piaget believes that knowledge is not given to a passive observer; rather, knowledge of reality must be discovered and constructed by the activity of the child. As we shall see later, this position is at odds with the essentially passive-mechanistic view held by American behaviorists.

Thus far, we have seen that intelligence involves biological adaptation, equilibrium between the individual and the environment, gradual evolution, and mental activity. These definitions are quite general. It is also instructive to take note of what the definitions do *not* stress. They do not emphasize individual differences in intelligence. While such an emphasis would be quite consonant with a biological approach, Piaget is not concerned with whether one person is more intelligent or more clever than another, or why. Piaget, of course, recognizes that differences in intellectual ability do exist, but he is not particularly interested in this analysis; instead, he seeks to abstract from the various idiosyncratic manifestations of behavior a description of the general form of thought. Piaget's theories do not describe the average level of cognitive functioning; rather they depict the optimum capability of thought at a given period in development.

It is important to note that the definitions place little emphasis on the emotions. However, Piaget recognizes that the emotions influence thought, and in fact, he repeatedly states that no act of intelligence is complete without emotions. They represent the energetic or motivational aspect of intellectual activity. Nevertheless, Piaget's empirical investigations and detailed theories substantially ignore the emotions in favor of the structure of intellect.

Piaget has chosen one of several available strategies with which to investigate the psychology of intelligence. He de-emphasizes individual differences and the effects of emotions on thought, and instead focuses on the optimum level of functioning. Many psychologists, particularly English and American, have concentrated on individual differences by means of the test approach in order to investigate intellectual activity. Others have attempted from the outset to consider the influence of the emotions, especially anxiety, on intellectual performance. Which strategy is best? The answer seems to be that all are of interest. All view the problem of intelligence from different angles and deal with somewhat different issues. Since a man cannot study everything, he usually settles on one approach if he is to accomplish anything at all. As we shall see in the pages to follow, Piaget's approach seems to have amply demonstrated its merits.

In addition to proposing general definitions, Piaget has structured the psychology of intelligence by the selection of the particular subject matter he has investigated. . . . Piaget's early works were concerned with such matters as verbal communication and moral judgment. With the passage of time Piaget has come to stress the child's understanding of various scientific and mathematical ideas like velocity and one-to-one correspondence. This emphasis reflects Piaget's focus on epistemological problems. To understand Piaget's conception of intelligence, therefore, we must not only consider his definitions, but the nature of his research activities. The latter, especially in recent years, reveal rather unique epistemological concerns.

In conclusion, we have seen how Piaget's two major interests—biology and epistemology—have shaped his approach to the psychology of intelligence. The biological concern resulted in definitions of intelligence in general terms of growth, stages, adaptation, equilibrium, and similar factors. The epistemological focus has resulted in the empirical investigation of the child's understanding of space, time, causality, and similar notions.

In essence, Piaget looks at intelligence in terms of content, structure, and function. We will consider aspects of these in the following sections.

CONTENT

One simple aspect of thought is its manifest content. This refers to what the individual is thinking about, what interests him at the moment, or the terms in which he contemplates a given problem. For instance, suppose a mechanic is asked what makes a car go. He gives an answer in terms of the explosion of gas, the movements of pistons, the transfer of power from one point to another. These statements reflect the contents of his thought. If a young child were posed the same question, his response would be quite different. Ignorant of the workings of the motor, he might suppose that the car's movement results from all the horses inside. Obviously, the content of his thought is quite different from that of the adult.

During the early portion of his career, Piaget's research focused on the contents of the child's thought. *The Child's Conception of the World* and *The Child's Conception of Physical Causality*, both written in the 1920's, paid particular attention to the child's views of the physical world. The clinical method was used to obtain the child's answers to such questions as, where do shadows come from, what causes rivers to flow, or the clouds to move? Despite these initial investigations, Piaget felt that the study of content was only a minor goal for the psychology of intelligence. While descriptions of content may have some interest, they do not get at the heart of the matter; they do not explain why thought takes the form it does. For Piaget, therefore, the primary goal of the psychology of intelligence is not the mere description of the content of thought but the basic processes underlying and determining the content. Piaget has therefore devoted the greater part of his career in psychology to the study of the structures and functions of intelligence.

HEREDITARY STRUCTURES

It should come as no surprise that Piaget's theoretical framework deals with the role of biological factors in the development of intelligence. These factors operate in several ways: one of them is defined as the *heredi-*

tary transmission of physical structures. Different species are, of course, endowed by heredity with different physical structures. The nervous system, for example, varies considerably from worm to man. It is immediately obvious that the inherited physical structures both permit certain intellectual achievements and prohibit others. The human eye is one example of a physical structure. It is constructed in such a way that human beings are able to perceive three-dimensional space. It is conceivable, however, to think of eyes created that would perceive two-dimensional space, and the existence of such a physical structure would undoubtedly affect intelligence.

Another type of structure transmitted by heredity is the *automatic behavioral reaction*. For example, from birth members of many species possess various *reflexes*. When a specified event in the environment (a *stimulus*) occurs, the organism automatically responds with a particular behavior. No learning or training or other experience with the environment is usually necessary for the reflex response to occur. Moreover, all members of the species, unless they are in some way defective, possess the reflex. The basis for this automatic behavior is an inherited physical mechanism. When the stimulus occurs it activates this mechanism, which produces the response. One example of this behavior is the sucking reflex, which is necessary for survival. When any object (the stimulus) touches an infant's lips, the automatic response is to suck. The newborn does not need to be taught to suck. A further example is the ability to cry. The newborn's physical structure is such that when hungry he automatically signals his discomfort with a wail. Often the reflexes are adaptive: they help the organism in its interaction with the environment.

Piaget feels that in the case of human intelligence, reflexes and other automatic patterns of behavior play only a minor role. It is only the infant, and more specifically the newborn, whose behavior is heavily dependent on the elementary behavioral structures of the type described. Piaget's research has shown that after the first few days of life, the reflexes are modified by the infant's experience and are transformed into a new type of mechanism—the psychological structure—which is not directly and simply provided by heredity. As we shall see, psychological structures form the basis for intellectual activity and are the product of a complex interaction between biological and experiential factors.

GENERAL PRINCIPLES OF FUNCTIONING

We have seen that heredity affects intelligence in two ways. Inherited physical structures set broad limits on intellectual functioning. Inherited behavioral reactions have an influence during the first few days of human life but afterward are extensively modified as the infant interacts with his environment. Piaget's theoretical framework postulates that biological factors affect intelligence in a third way: all species inherit two basic tendencies or "invariant functions": *adaptation* and *organization*.

Let us first consider organization. This term refers to the tendency for all species to systematize or organize their processes into coherent systems which may be either physical or psychological. In the former case, fish possess a number of structures which allow functioning in the water— for example, gills, a particular circulatory system, and temperature mechanisms. All these structures interact and are coordinated into an efficient system. This coordination is the result of the organization tendency. It should be emphasized that organization refers not to gills or the circulatory structure in particular, but to the tendency observed in all life to integrate their structures into a composite system (or higher-order structure).

At a psychological level, too, the tendency to organize is present. In his interaction with the world, the individual tends to integrate his psychological structures into coherent systems. For example, the very young infant has available the separate behavioral structures of either looking at objects or . . . grasping them. He does not initially combine the two. After a period of development, he organizes these two separate structures into a higher-order structure which enables him to grasp something at the same time he looks at it. Organization, then, is the tendency common to all forms of life to integrate structures, which may be physical or psychological, into higher-order systems or structures.

The second general principle of functioning is *adaptation*. All organisms are born with a tendency to adapt to the environment. The ways in which adaptation occurs differ from species to species, from individual to individual within a species, or from stage to stage within any one individual. Nevertheless, the tendency to adapt in some way or another is an invariant function and therefore considered an aspect of biology. Adaptation may be considered in terms of two complementary processes: *assimilation* and *accommodation*.

We will illustrate these processes first by means of a simple physiological example, namely, digestion. When a person eats something, his digestive system reacts to the substances incorporated. In order to deal with the foreign substance, the muscles of the stomach contract in various ways, certain organs release acids, and so on. Putting the matter in general terms, we may say that the person's physical structures (the stomach and related organs) *accommodated* to the environmental event (the food). In other words, the process of accommodation describes the individual's tendency to change in response to environmental demands. The functional invariant of *assimilation* is the complementary process by which the individual deals with an environmental event in terms of his current structures.

In the case of digestion the acids transform the food into a form which the body can use. Thus the individual not only modifies his structures in reation to external demands (accommodation), he also uses his structures to incorporate elements of the external world (assimilation).

For Piaget intellectual adaptation is also an interaction, or an exchange, between a person and his environment and involves the same two processes—assimilation and accommodation—as are found in biology. On the one hand the person incorporates or assimilates features of external reality into his own psychological structures; on the other hand he modifies or accommodates his psychological structures to meet the pressures of the environment. Consider an example of adaptation in infancy. Suppose an infant of 4 months is presented with a rattle. He has never before had the opportunity to play with rattles or similar toys. The rattle, then, is a feature of the environment to which he needs to adapt. His subsequent behavior reveals the tendencies of assimilation and accommodation. The infant tries to grasp the rattle. In order to do this successfully he must accommodate in more ways than are immediately apparent. First, he must accommodate his visual activities to perceive the rattle correctly; then he must reach out and accommodate his movements to the distance between himself and the rattle; in grasping the rattle he must adjust his fingers to its shape; in lifting the rattle he must accommodate his muscular exertion to its weight. In sum, the grasping of the rattle involves a series of acts of accommodation, or modifications of the infant's behavioral structures to suit the demands of the environment.

Grasping the rattle also involves assimilation. In the past the infant has already grasped things; for him, grasping is a well-formed structure of behavior. When he sees the rattle for the first time he tries to deal with the novel object by incorporating it into a habitual pattern of behavior. In a sense he tries to transform the novel object into something that he is familiar with; namely, a thing to be grasped. We can say, therefore, that he assimilates the object into his framework.

Adaptation, then, is a basic tendency of the organism and consists of the two processes of assimilation and accommodation. How do the two relate to one another? First, it is clear that they are complementary processes. Assimilation involves the person's dealing with the environment in terms of his structures, while accommodation involves the transformation of his structures in response to the environment. Moreover, the processes are simultaneously present in every act. When the infant grasps the rattle his fingers accommodate to its shape; at the same time he is assimilating the rattle into his framework, the grasping structure.

In sum, Piaget postulates that there are two general principles of functioning which affect intelligence: *organization* and *adaptation* (assimilation and accommodation). These are biological factors in the sense that they are common to all species. While organization and adaptation are inherited, they are not structures (like reflexes) but *tendencies*. The particular ways in which an organism adapts and organizes its processes depend also on its environment, and its learning history. In Piaget's view, the human being does not inherit particular intellectual reactions; rather, he does inherit a tendency to organize his intellectual processes, and to adapt to his environment, in some way.

PSYCHOLOGICAL STRUCTURES

We have seen that man tends to organize his behavior and thought and to adapt to the environment. These tendencies result in a number of psychological structures which take different forms at different ages. The child progresses through a series of stages each characterized by different psychological structures before he attains adult intelligence. From birth to about two years the infant is unable to think; he can only perform overt action. For example, if a toy falls apart he cannot first think how it might best be put together again; instead, he might immediately act on the toy and try to reassemble it. His activities, however, are not random, but display order and coherence. Almost immediately after birth the infant shows organized behavior. As we have seen, some of these patterns of action, like the reflex, are due mainly to hereditary factors. However, specific heredity cannot explain all of the orderliness in the infant's behavior. For example, the two-month-old infant usually sucks his thumb or a finger. When put in the crib he regularly brings his hand to [his] mouth in a relatively quick and efficient way. In the common language we would probably say that he has acquired the "habit" of thumb-sucking. The word "habit" implies a regularity, a coherence, in the infant's actions. It is clear that thumb-sucking is not based entirely on inherited physical structures. While there is a reflex to suck any object touching the lips, there is no innate tendency to bring the hand to the mouth; this activity must be learned. In Piaget's theory, such an organized pattern of behavior is termed a *scheme*.* The concept of scheme is used in a very broad way. It can refer to the reflexes and other kinds of innate behavior already discussed. It is in this way that Piaget speaks of the "sucking scheme." But the vast majority of schemes are not innate; instead they are in some way based on experience as in the case of the thumb-sucking scheme.

* Piaget's French term *scheme* has usually been translated into English as *schema* (plural, *schemata*). We do not follow this practice since Piaget has lately been using the French word *schema* for another purpose. Also, the reader should be aware that *scheme* need not refer only to behavior; there are mental schemes too.

Thus far we have spoken of the scheme only as a pattern of behavior, or as an action which displays coherence and order. However, there are a number of additional aspects of the scheme. First, it involves activity on the part of the child; the concept is used to describe things he *does*. Most often, use of the term in this way presents no difficulties. Occasionally, however, scheme is used to describe actions which are not immediately obvious. For example, Piaget speaks of the "looking scheme." The use of "scheme" here is quite deliberate since he means to imply that vision is an active process; the child's eyes move as they actively *search* the environment. Second, scheme refers to the basic structure underlying the child's overt actions. Scheme is used to designate the essence of the child's behavior. Let us take thumb-sucking as an example. If we examine the infant's behavior in detail, we will see that no two acts of thumb-sucking performed by one child are precisely the same. On one occasion the activity starts when the thumb is 10 inches from the mouth; on another when it is 11 inches away. At one time the thumb travels in almost a straight line to the mouth; at another time its trajectory is quite irregular. In short, if we describe behavior in sufficient detail, we find that there are no two identical actions. There is no one act of thumb-sucking, but many; in fact as many as the number of times the child brings the thumb to the mouth. At first glance this situation might seem to pose insurmountable difficulties for the psychologist. How can he describe and explain behavior if each act is different from every other? Fortunately, the difficulty is only apparent, since most psychologists are not really interested in the fine details of behavior. What is important, especially for Piaget, is the structure of behavior, that is, an abstraction of the features common to a wide variety of acts which differ in detail. In the case of thumb-sucking, whether or not the act starts from a distance of 10 or 11 inches is of no significance. What is crucial is that the infant has acquired a regular way of getting the thumb into the mouth. This "regular way" is an abstraction furnished by the psychologist. The infant puts his hand into his mouth in many particular ways, no two being identical, and the psychologist detects in these specific actions a certain regularity which he then calls a scheme.

Let us now consider another type of psychological structure: that of the classifying *operations* of the older child from about seven to eleven years. Suppose an examiner presents him with a collection of red and blue beads mixed together. Confronted with this situation the older child first thinks of the objects as being members of classes. There is the class of red beads and the class of blue ones. Further, unlike the younger child, he realizes that the class of red beads is included in a larger class, that of beads in general. Another way of putting the matter is to say that he groups the red beads into one class and conceives of it as being a part of a hierarchy of classes. The class immediately "above" the red beads (that is, the more inclusive class) is that of beads-in-general. Of course, the class of beads-in-general may also be located in a classification hierarchy. The class of solid objects will contain the class of beads.

Obviously the older child's operational schemes are quite different from the infant's behavioral schemes. The latter involve patterns of behavior because the infant acts overtly on the world. Although the older child's schemes also involve acting on the world, this is done intellectually. He considers, for example, the relatively abstract problem of whether given classes are contained in others. Piaget describes this aspect of the older child's thought in terms of the operations of classification. What is important for Piaget is not that the child can answer questions about beads (that, of course, is trivial), but that his activities reveal the existence of a basic structure; namely, the operations of putting things together, of placing them in classes, of forming hierarchies of classes, and so on. Classification, then, is composed of a series of intellectual activities which constitute a psychological structure. Of course, the child does not realize that he has such a structure and may not even know what the word "classification" means. The classification structure and "schemes" both describe an observer's conception of the basic processes underlying the child's activities; the child himself is certainly not aware of these structures.

THE DESCRIPTION OF STRUCTURES

If we accept that Piaget's theoretical framework is based on the concept of psychological structures, how can we go about describing them? One way to describe them is by using common language. We can say that the child classifies objects or that his moral judgment is "objective," and so forth. Sometimes the common language adequately conveys meaning, but sometimes it does not. Unfortunately, there are occasions when an ordinary word means different things to different people. When this occurs the scientist is in danger of being misunderstood. Consequently, the sciences have tended to develop various formal languages in order to guarantee precise communication. The physicist does not say that objects "fall very fast" or "pick up speed as they go along." Instead, he writes a formula in which each term is precisely defined and in which the relations among the terms are completely specified by the formal language of mathematics. If the reader of the formula knows what the terms mean and understands the requisite mathematics, then the physicist's meaning can be accurately transmitted without the danger of misinterpretation.

Piaget feels that psychology too should attempt to use formal languages in describing the structures underlying thought. Psychological words in particular are quite ambiguous. While the theorists may intend a particular meaning for words like "habit," or "thought," or "classification," it is extremely probable that these terms will signify to others a wide variety of alternative interpretations. Consequently, Piaget has attempted to use formal languages—particularly terms of logic and of mathematics—to describe the structures underlying the child's activities. . . .

FUNCTIONS, STRUCTURES, AND EQUILIBRIUM

We cannot emphasize sufficiently the extent to which Piaget believes that the functional invariants—organization and adaptation (assimilation and accommodation)—and the psychological structures are inextricably intertwined. As we have seen, assimilation and accommodation, although complementary, nevertheless occur simultaneously. A balance between the two is necessary for adaptation. Moreover, adaptation is not separate from organization. In the process of organizing his activities the individual assimilates novel events into pre-existing structures, and at the same time he accommodates pre-existing structures to meet the demands of the new situation. Furthermore, the functional invariants (organization and adaptation) are closely related to the structures of intelligence.

As a result of the tendencies toward adaptation and organization, new structures are continually being created out of the old ones which will be employed to assist the individual in his interaction with the world. Looking at the matter in another way, structures are necessary for adaptation and organization. One could neither adapt to the environment nor organize one's processes if there were no basic structures available at the outset. On the other hand, the very existence of a structure, which by Piaget's definition is an organized totality, entails the necessity for organization and adaptation. There are, however, important differences between the invariant functions and the structures. As the individual progresses through the life-span, the functions will remain the same but the structures will vary, and appear in a fairly regular sequence. Another way of saying this is that intellectual development proceeds through a series of *stages* with each stage characterized by a different kind of psychological structure. An individual of any age must adapt to the environment and must organize his responses continually, but the instruments by which he accomplishes this—the psychological structures—will change from one age level to another. For example, both the infant and adult will organize and adapt, but the resulting psychological structures are quite different for the two periods.

Piaget further proposes that organisms tend toward equilibrium with the environment. The organism—whether a human being or some other form of life—tends to organize structures into coherent and stable patterns. His ways of dealing with the world tend toward a certain balance. He tries to develop structures which are effective in his interaction with reality. This means that when a new event occurs he can apply to it the lessons of the past (or assimilate the events into already existing structures), and he will easily modify his current patterns of behavior to respond to the requirements of the new situation. With increasing experience he acquires more and more structures and therefore adapts more readily to an increasing number of situations.

SUMMARY

The individual inherits physical structures which set broad limits on his intellectual functioning. He also inherits a few automatic behavioral reactions or reflexes which have their greatest influence on functioning in the first few days of life. These reflexes are rapidly transformed into structures which incorporate the results of experience. The third kind of inheritance—the general principles of functioning—is another biological aspect of intelligence. One general principle of functioning is organization; all species have the tendency to organize their processes.

A second aspect of general functioning is adaptation, which may be further subdivided into assimilation and accommodation. Accommodation refers to the organism's tendency to modify its structures according to the pressures of the environment, while assimilation involves using current structures which can deal with the environment. The result of the principles of functioning is a series of psychological structures which differ qualitatively from one another throughout a person's lifetime. For example, the infant employs behavioral schemes or patterns of action, while the child from about seven to eleven uses mental operations. What is important for Piaget is not the child's behavior in all its detail but the structure underlying his activities. For the purpose of clarity Piaget has made an attempt to describe these structures in terms of formal languages—logic and mathematics. The general tendencies—adaptation and organization—and the structures are all related to one another.

Assimilation and accommodation are complementary, whereas organization and adaptation are interwoven. For instance, one assimilates an environmental event into a structure, and one accommodates a structure to the demands of the environment. Eventually the organism tends toward equilibrium. He aims toward a balance between his structures and the requirements of his world. In this balance the structures are sufficiently developed so that he need exert little effort either to accommodate them to reality or to assimilate events into them.

NOTES

1. [Jean Piaget,] *Origins of Intelligence*, pp. 3–4.
2. [Jean Piaget,] *Psychology of Intelligence*, p. 6.
3. *Ibid.*, p. 7.

8. LEONARD KISE, DIANE BORUCKI, AND RONALD SCHMERBER

ENHANCING COGNITIVE GROWTH IN THE CLASSROOM

The literature relating cognitive development to classroom teaching practices has been varied and profuse. The theories of Jean Piaget have made a decided contribution to our understanding of cognitive development, reading, and language development, but as yet very little of this knowledge has been applied to practices in the classroom. The purpose of this article is to combine Piaget's major concepts with practical classroom ideas.

Piaget has focused on three basic theoretical concerns that are relevant to a discussion of cognitive development in the classroom: (1) the mechanisms by which children internalize and act upon the world in which they live, (2) the developmental stages of cognition for three- to eight-year-old children and (3) the functions of children's language during this period.

THE CHILD'S INTELLECTUAL PROCESSES

The application of Jean Piaget's work to classroom practices requires some knowledge of his view of the child. Piaget describes the child as one who actively seeks to adapt to the environment, basically by means of his intelligence. Intelligence is defined by Piaget as (p. 14) the "ability to interact effectively with the environment at the psychological level." This interaction is, in Piaget's view, an adaptation of the organism's schemata —that is, the mental structures underlying its overt actions—to the environment. Adaptation occurs through two processes: assimilation—adding environmental data to one's existing schemata of the environment without changing the existing schemata—and accommodation—restructuring one's schemata of the universe because they are inappropriate to this new knowledge. Through assimilation and accommodation, the child continually seeks an equilibrium between what he understands and what he experiences.

From Piaget's view of the child and his intelligence, several key concepts can be derived for implementation in teaching-learning behavior. First, if the child actively seeks to understand and control his environment by acting upon it, he learns by doing, that is, by an intellectual experiencing of the world in which he lives. Classroom environments that do not provide for "action experiences" deprive the child of the opportunity to grow intellectually. Children do not learn by dealing with words and other symbols or with vicarious experiences. They need to manipulate, act upon, and have personal experiences with the world. Unhurried field trips and opportunities to play, to imitate, and to examine reality in its total setting become the means by which the child develops intellectually.

COGNITIVE DEVELOPMENT OF THE CHILD
FROM THREE TO EIGHT

While Piaget recognizes that different hereditary and environmental conditions make each child's cognitive development unique, all children from three to eight years will move from the preconceptual stage of development (typically at three years old) into a transitional phase of intuitive development (from approximately four to seven years of age) and finally into the stage of concrete operations, which ultimately terminates in adult logical thought processes.

As Piaget describes intellectual growth and development, it is readily apparent that the preschool-kindergarten educational programs should differ considerably from those at the primary and intermediate levels.

The child of approximately two years of age has just moved from the sensorimotor stage, during which he has developed his neurophysical capacity to act. As he evolves the capacity to represent action—that is, to use language or body action to illustrate meaning rather than having to perform the action itself in order to communicate—the child is ready to begin the preoperational stage of development. The preoperational period, as conceived by Jean Piaget is divided into two parts: the preconceptual stage (two to four years) and the intuitive stage (four to seven years).

The preconceptual stage of intellectual development is characterized by imagery, language facilitation, and symbolic play. The relationships between elements of similar classes are not perceived by the child. To the child in this stage, dogs are dogs and cats are cats. He tends to focus on a single feature of the total object for differentiation. For example, dogs bark; therefore, if it barks, it is a dog. If a parent should bark in playing with the child, he is as alluring or as frightening to the child as if he were indeed a dog. This tendency to focus on a single attribute for classifying and interpreting the world produces some distorted conclusions about the environment. The language and play of the child reflect both the development of concepts based on gross perceptual characteristics and the child's tenacious egocentrism. Because signs and symbols are the general means by which conceptual thought is mediated, language is important to the child as the means by which to name the world around him and thus to understand his relationship to that world.

These principles offer teachers some directions for working with two-, three-, and four-year-old children. Experiences should be familiar to the child so that he is capable of personalizing them through his direct sensory association with them. In addition, the child should be able to attach names to these experiences and re-experience them in pantomime, imitation, and other forms of symbolic play. Thus, the preconceptual stage of development should be rich in personal and sensory experiences that facilitate the child's understanding of his relationship to the world. The child's interactions with the real world and his vicarious re-experiencing of them through symbolic play lead him into the stage of intuitive thought characteristic of four- to seven-year-olds.

The stage of intuitive thought is a transitional stage during which the child emerges from his egocentric characterization of the world to deal with the world in a more concrete, objective way. It is during the intuitive years from four to seven that the child first forms concepts (relationships) and attaches meaningful symbols (language) to his understanding of the world. As the child begins to focus on more than one attribute of an object—for instance, the dog's bark becomes only one characteristic that differentiates it from cats or horses—fewer distorted conclusions are drawn. Thus, concepts become more varied and elaborate. For example, the concept of family is extended to include aunts, uncles, cousins, and so forth. The ability to assimilate rather than to accommodate is readily apparent in this above example. The child at the intuitive stage of intellectual development has greater potential to classify related elements than he did at the preconceptual stage, when accommodation was more essential to his existence as he separated elements into single-variable classes.

Despite this more advanced intellectual potential, the child in the intuitive stage is still illogical. His egocentrism has not been removed. He interprets his world through perceptions that are loaded with egocentric explanations. His cause-effect understandings are more likely to be contiguous events or relationships than true cause-effect relationships. That is, objects and events that occur together are assumed to have causal relationship. For example, the child may discard his former belief that the moon follows him around in the car at night, but he cannot understand the relationship of his being in a moving car to the perceived movement of the moon. This inability to remove the self from a cause-effect relationship is typical of the child in the intuitive stage of intellectual development.

The child's thought tends to be static and irreversible. Things are what they are perceived to be. Piaget has illustrated this idea by making two equal-weight clay balls in front of the child. One of the balls is transformed into a sausage shape. The child tends to believe that this ball is larger (has more clay) because it appears longer to him. He knows that no more clay was added to the ball but, when confronted with the logic, will still rely upon his perception. The child at the intuitive stage will trust what he perceives over what logic seems to be telling him. When he begins to use logic as a basis for his reasoning, the child moves from the intuitive stage of development to the concrete-operations stage.

Educationally, the child of four to seven is in a very important intellectual-growth period. He still trusts his perceptions over logic, and he still is the most important element of his life. But his egocentrism is on trial, and, therefore, he is more vulnerable than he was, less certain about life, and less secure in himself than he was at the preconceptual stage, when egocentric reasoning ruled, or than he will be later, when he attempts to interpret the real world in a one variable form of logic.

To teachers and others who work with four- to seven-year-old children, certain facts seem relevant to facilitation of their intellectual growth. Experiences should still be personalized, still be real-life conditions. The child's world begins to be one in which things make sense to him in relation to other things. Greater opportunity to express understandings, to talk about the world, and to deal with his relationships with the world become significant intellectual-growth conditions. Less closure on abstract events is of paramount importance in teaching. Learning environments should be rich in experiences and in language related to those experiences. What are significant to the child are what he perceives and how he intuitively understands his experience. What are not terribly significant, in that they cannot be understood by the child, are such educational relationships as that of addition to subtraction, attempts to find *the* answer in science, and the rules of phonics and beginning reading. These things are better left to the concrete stage of intellectual development, when logical rules, cause-effect relationships, and systematic ordering of things are significant factors for intellectual growth.

Some children at the later primary levels are entering the concrete stage of intellectual operations, which is characterized by the child's ability to deal only with the concrete, real-life world. It is during this period (approximately seven to eleven years) that reasoning processes begin to appear logical, concepts become reversible, and the ability to classify and order the universe into hierarchies emerges. The child is capable of thinking logically about things without the intervention of the egocentric traits of the preoperational phase. The concept of reversibility—that is, what can be done can be undone—is also mastered. Objects can fit into more than one classification; thus dogs, cats, and horses can be classified independently and also as members of a single class—vertebrates. The ability to order the concrete world is facilitated by the child's emerging intellectual ability to serialize, extend, subdivide, differentiate, associate, generalize, specify, or combine structures into new relationships and groupings. The child can now focus on all attributes of objects and events. Judgment and moral reasoning become coherent and realistic. Language development has evolved to the point where the child can explain his thought processes. His understanding, however, is limited to the real and immediate events of his environment. Abstract thought is not fully comprehensible except in terms of gross generalizations to possible or hypothetical situations that approximate the real world of the child.

For the child at this stage, education is real, an exciting opportunity to know, if it is kept in the form of concrete experiences from which he can draw or upon which he can act. Learning is a vigorous ordering of the child's universe into a logical system on which operations can be performed. The child is in the process of accommodating his intellectual structures into an orderly system. As this intellectual operation becomes complete, he moves into the final stage of intellectual development, that of deductive reasoning and abstract thought.

LANGUAGE DEVELOPMENT

During the years from three to eight, the child is passing from one phase of language development to another. Piaget states that these phases closely parallel or follow the child's intellectual development in that thought precedes language. That is, language is an expression of the child's thought in symbolic form and, therefore, evolves only when thought is sufficiently resolved for language to be attached to the understanding.

During the preconceptual stage of intellectual development the roots of conceptual thought are put down. Language patterns are evolving.

Language is the key means by which the child establishes social communication. To Piaget, a word is a social signifier. The word "doll" communicates a common meaning in that it stands for an object that others can agree is a "doll." In addition, the word "doll" is an intellectual construction of the real object. Language thus represents one's knowledge of objects and their relationships in the world as well as being a common social signifier.

The intellectual thought of the child during the preconceptual stage is centered on personal experience. It is the child's personalized experiences (schemata) of the world that he uses to understand others' language. Thus, while two or more children can agree about what a "doll" is, the word has different meanings for each child, based on his experiences and the mental constructs he gives to it. The child's egocentric thought causes him to believe that everyone "thinks" as he does and that everyone shares his "feelings" and his desires.

From this discussion, it should be apparent that language reflects two types of speech: egocentric and socialized. Egocentric speech is used for its own sake—for example, to obtain pleasure by speaking or to think aloud to oneself (Piaget, pp. 32–33). It is divided into three basic categories:

1. Repetition—repeating words for the pleasure of saying them: Nonsense words and singing a word or phrase over and over are significant elements of repetitive egocentric speech.
2. Monologue—talking aloud to hear oneself: The child does not talk to others even though they may be present. This talk is sometimes heard only in snatches, as parts of it may drop to below auditory levels.
3. Collective monologue—speaking in the presence of others with no attempt to get them to understand or to listen: Others serve only as social stimulants to speech. Often we may hear several children seemingly playing and talking together, but upon careful inspection it becomes clear that each is talking with no interest in being heard or in listening to what others are saying.

Egocentric speech patterns dominate the language of the child even after seven or eight years of age. At six and a half, speech is still primarily egocentric (Piaget, p. 52). At seven and eight years of age, "egocentric talk loses some of its importance" (Piaget, p. 42). The child begins to understand others from spoken words (social speech) rather than from gestures, body movement, and other physical forms of expression associated with egocentric speech.

In socialized speech, the child is moving from the preoperational stage toward the concrete stage of intellectual development, during which he will begin to formalize experience into an orderly intellectual structure. Socialized speech is the process by which the child establishes a common ground or equivalent frame of reference between his thought and language and the thought and language of others. According to Piaget (p. 42), socialized speech is characterized by five phases of development: adapted information; criticism; commands, requests, threats; questions; and answers.

While collective monologue is primarily characterized by the egocentric desire to hear oneself talk in the presence of others, *adapted information* is characterized by the ability to communicate successfully with others, to take the point of view of the audience, to make others listen to one, and to influence others. In essence, the child intends to communicate with others. He wishes to be understood and to understand others. Whenever the child collaborates with the hearer in such a manner as to be understood, he is using the form of socialized speech that Piaget (p. 43) calls adapted information.

Adapted information obviously falls outside of the egocentric speech patterns described previously and is perhaps the first true communication of the socialized child. It is a most significant change of language pattern in the educational sense, because it requires communication, comprehension, and cooperation. Teachers should be capable of identifying adapted information as a separate form of speech because it can produce change in educational practice. Classroom experiences that encourage this level of communication should evolve. Typically, much learning should revolve around cooperative enterprises rather than collective enterprises. The child desires to be heard; thus he hears. Contrived listening experiences promoted at an earlier age to encourage egocentric attending will be discouraging to the child who is entering socialized speech through the use of adapted-information protocol. The teacher should encourage learning experiences that can be shared through language. Stauffer (p. 205), discussing the language-experience approach, describes several activities in which children can be encouraged in the use of adapted-information speech. In one example, children cooperate in developing an orderly story from pictures. It is not only sequencing of pictures that is important; each child must build upon the words of the previous speakers in turn. The children not only talk but must also listen and communicate to be heard.

"Adapted information and questions and answers constitute the categories of children's language whose function is to communicate intellectual process" (Piaget, p. 47). Criticisms, commands, requests, and threats, while dominant patterns of socialized speech, are not significant for intellectual development and processing. Piaget distinguishes the role of questions and answers from that of adapted information. Answers fall in the category of socialized speech when their purpose is to respond to the questioner. They are not spontaneous speech, as adapted information is, but are forced. Piaget, in his discussion of answers as a form of socialized speech (p. 50), states that children may be unnecessarily harassed by questions from adults. He commits the role of questions and answers to the natural, rather than coerced, form of teacher-pupil discussion and interaction. Thus, teachers who wish to enhance the child's socialized speech through a greatly increased question-answer environment may be limiting the intellectual processing associated with socialized speech.

If they are to be significant contributors to socialized speech, questions must come from the child, not from others. In fact, they form a relatively large portion of the child's speech (Piaget, p. 51). Questions serve two purposes: (1) self-interrogation—to think aloud to oneself—and (2) to elicit responses from others. In the latter form they are socialized speech. In both forms they represent intellectual processing on the part of the child. The child who asks questions of other children generally seeks descriptive or factual information. When he questions himself or adults, he may be seeking cause-effect relationships.

Interpreting the role of questions and answers as a form of socialized speech and of intellectual processing seems an appropriate teacher activity. Children obviously need opportunities to ask questions and to give answers, both with adults and with other children. Educational experiences should provide ample opportunity for social discourse in a natural, rather than coerced, environment. Children learn both from questioning and from giving and receiving answers. Piaget indicates the significant role that questions play as a means of intellectual processing. Often children may not want answers but wish only to question themselves to induce reflection. Teachers should be aware of this tendency and not be provoked when a child does not listen to the answer to the question he has asked.

In summary, thought is essential to language development. Egocentric speech is as significant to maturation as socialized speech is. Children from three to eight years of age pass through three stages of cognitive development. They are actively pursuing knowledge for particular reasons, depending upon their stage of development. Teachers can enhance and facilitate intellectual growth and maturity but they cannot shorten its maturational time. To understand the child is to know where he is in his intellectual growth. To teach the child is to enhance his understanding of his environment by providing him with ample experiences with that environment.

REFERENCES

Jean Piaget. *The Language and Thought of the Child.* Cleveland: World Publishing, 1966.
Russell G. Stauffer. *Directing Reading Maturity as a Cognitive Process.* New York: Harper and Row, 1969.

CHAPTER FOUR

Language Development and Reading

IT IS COMMON KNOWLEDGE AMONG AUTHORITIES in reading that although thousands of research studies have been done in the past several decades, the nature of the reading process remains to a large extent a mystery. Theories of reading describe what reading involves, but they have had relatively little value as a basis for specific reading techniques. Reading experts generally agree that decoding and perception are vital to the process, but they do not know how to ensure that a given child will become an excellent reader. A chief reason for this is that reading is not just a simple skill but involves the whole thinking process.

Reading and verbal behavior in general were one of the early interests of psychologists. In 1920, J. B. Watson defined language and thought as a learned repertoire of sensory images and symbolic language. Therefore, behavior-learning theory could be applied to the process of learning to speak and read as well as think. The hypothesis that a child's speech is shaped by reinforcement from his environment makes sense, for the totally deaf child rarely progresses much beyond the infantile sounds made at birth. Reading, too, is shaped by the environment, but the process is not so readily explainable by conventional learning theory. In fact, most children learn the basic patterns of adult speech with little formal instruction; yet many of them have great difficulty learning to read first-grade material. The comprehension of thought expressed in printed form involves mental processes of considerable complexity.

Nila Banton Smith, an outstanding authority on reading, notes that "we do not have clear and concise concepts of the different faces of comprehension which deal with the higher mental processes, nor do we have adequate procedures to serve us in providing practice on these specific processes in connection with reading content." Behaviorism was considered inadequate as an explanation of the reading process because it failed to account for the developmental characteristics of the child's mind and the nature of the language itself as major factors in learning to read. As a consequence, the study of psycholinguistics and the application of linguistic principles became the major focus of research in reading. Marianne Hall provides seven statements of the linguistic rationale for the language-experience approach, a pupil-centered method based on the existing verbal patterns of the child. The method begins with the child's oral language and therefore has a built-in factor of reading readiness. The level of the child's own oral-language development indicates his capability for abstract, symbolic. thought.

When a child reads material that is close to his own level of language development in both vocabulary and concepts, he is most likely to succeed and thus to develop positive feelings about himself. Success is both motivating and therapeutic. It helps the child to build a strong, academic self-concept. Beretta maintains that the self-concept is the core of the child's progress in reading. In other words, the key to reading is not so much the *skill* to read but the *will* to read. Thus, the teacher must be concerned with the child's self-concept while he is engaged in the complex task of reading, a formidable mission for the classroom teacher.

Techniques for teaching reading are usually a major part of the preparation of elementary-school teachers, but not in the preparation of most subject-matter teachers at middle-school and senior-high-school levels. Yet such subjects as social studies and English require that the student can read passably well. Science and even math require considerable reading skill because they involve many difficult concepts. Business courses emphasize all aspects of communication. The three articles in this section can sensitize the prospective teacher to the importance of reading and perhaps can help to prepare the would-be science or history teacher for that inevitable day when he realizes that his difficulties in teaching subject matter stem from the children's difficulties in reading. He may very well find himself teaching reading skills.

RECOMMENDED READING

A. R. Binter, J. Dlabal and L. Kise (eds.). 1969. *Readings in Reading* (Scranton, Pa.: International Textbook Co.). A comprehensive collection of articles on major areas of reading, from psycholinguistic theory to the mechanics of teaching basic reading skills.

J. Chall. 1967. *Learning to Read: The Great Debate* (New York: McGraw-Hill). A review of the major findings and conclusions of research in reading; authoritative and widely quoted.

K. S. Goodman. 1972. "The Key Is in the Children's Language," *The Reading Teacher* 25, 505–9. Psycholinguistics for elementary classroom and reading teachers.

L. C. Hunt, Jr. 1969. "Decoding or Meaning? It's More Than a Matter of Method," *Today's Education* 58(4), 21–22, 62. Further discussion of psycholinguistically based reading instruction for the practitioner.

National Society for the Study of Education. 1968. *Innovation and Change in Reading Instruction. Sixty-seventh Yearbook, Part II* (Chicago: University of Chicago Press). A summary of the best research findings on reading up to that time. The section entitled "The Next Decade," by Helen Robinson, is especially relevant to current developments in reading.

R. G. Stauffer. 1965. "Concept Development and Reading," *The Reading Teacher* 19, 101. A major authority in reading discusses concept formation as the major ingredient in building reading power.

9.   NILA BANTON SMITH

THE MANY FACES OF READING COMPREHENSION

Confucius, the famous Chinese scholar and teacher, once wrote: "Learning without thought is labor lost; thought without learning is perilous."

It has been more than two thousand years since Confucius expressed these ideas about the relationships of thought and learning. Other great philosophers have expressed similar ideas throughout the ages. Yet the implementation of their recommendation has scarcely been discernible in the teaching of reading even as century after century has passed by.

At the present moment we have one era of reading instruction that is in full bloom, another that is well on the way, and a third that is in the embryonic stage. Those who are helping to push the new era that is on its way are urging vigorously that we couple thought and reading, that we go far beyond the stage of picking up what the book *says* and use our higher mental processes in *thinking* about what it says. Contemporary

From *The Reading Teacher*, 23:3 (December, 1969), 249–59, 291. Reprinted with permission of the author and The International Reading Association.

educators are expressing themselves in dramatic and concrete ways in their attempts to spur us on in this direction.

Edgar Dale says it dramatically in this way:

We suffer from hardening of the categories. Our mental filing system, filled with arid, unrelated facts, becomes rigid and inflexible. Further, the movement from concrete to abstract learning requires . . . a concern with the higher mental processes. Instead of accepting and learning what the book *says*, students must analyze what the author meant, compare and contrast it with their own experiences—synthesize, evaluate, apply.

Jacques Barzun in urging an emphasis on thinking in education explains the process of thinking in this very concrete way. "Thinking is doing to a fact or an idea what we do to beefsteak when we distribute its parts throughout our body. We are presumably stronger and better for it, readier for attack and defense, as well as more competent to assimilate more of the same protein without strain."

So it is that the thinking skills are being stressed by educators in all fields and we are being told repeatedly that our present students, who are facing the vicissitudes of a changing, uncertain world, cannot rely on the accumulated experience of mankind; nor will it do them any good to ignore situations, shrink from decisions or retreat in confusion. We as teachers in general know full well that we should be teaching children to *think*, that we should be providing practice to develop *thinking skills* higher than those involved in memorization. We as *reading* teachers know that communication is the best medium for developing thinking skills and that reading content is the richest and most rewarding of all the communication media to use for this purpose. Reading content reposes in a bed of details not present in mass communication media, and these details offer stepping stones to the reader in aiding him to go over, beyond and above what the mere words may say. Teachers of reading truly have the best medium in the world to use as a vehicle in developing the higher intellectual processes. As yet, however, possibilities of doing this have not been adequately explored. We do not have clear and concise concepts of the different faces of comprehension which deal with the higher mental processes, nor do we have adequate procedures to serve us in providing practice on these specific processes in connection with reading content.

THE NEED FOR EMPHASIS ON HIGHER MENTAL PROCESSES

Several needs must be met if we are . . . to implement the thinking-skills objective of this emerging period. Some of these needs will be enumerated.

Research

It is regrettable that more research is not being conducted in regard to the development of the thinking skills in connection with reading content. We are going all out in research on decoding, the disadvantaged, perception, etc. These are important areas for investigation but the thinking processes in reading are also important. It is discouraging to find that during the last few years comprehension has dropped to a new low in terms of number of studies reported.

As an example of reduced current research in this area we might refer to the . . . summaries of reading research appearing in the March, 1969, *Journal of Educational Research* and the February, 1969, *Reading Research Quarterly*. In the *Quarterly*, Robinson *et al.* reported 374 researches, only 2 of which had to do with "interpretation," which term of course connoted comprehension. In the *Journal*, Harris *et al.* summarized only 3 studies dealing with comprehension out of a total of 194. Hence, the proportion of the number of studies reported on comprehension is pitifully small in comparison with that dealing with other topics.

Comprehension is the very heart of the reading act. There is no use of reading unless one understands the meanings. Could it be that investigators think that comprehension has already been researched to its limits, that there is very little new to be explored in this area? If so, I, personally, cannot agree with them. With the strong present movement in education toward the development of inquiry, questioning, reasoning, and evaluating we in the field of reading have an entirely new horizon opened up to us. We must find out how better to use the content of reading in developing ability to think in depth. An exciting frontier beckons to those who would like to ascertain which of the higher mental processes best lend themselves to development in reading, and what procedures are most effective in developing these processes with different students at all levels.

Stimulating Depth Reading

Teachers' questions are probably used more than any other technique in attempts to develop comprehension.

What kinds of questions are teachers asking? A study by Guszak reported in the *Journal of Educational Research* provides some insight that helps to answer this question. Guszak visited and recorded teachers' questions on assigned reading in second-, fourth- and sixth-grade classrooms. He concluded: (1) that literal questions were most frequently asked across grade levels, (2) that more incorrect answers to questions were accepted as correct by teachers in the fourth and sixth grade than in the second, and (3) that the dominant pattern of interaction at all grade levels was a teacher's question followed by a single congruent response.

According to this study plus our own common knowledge, teachers of reading generally are asking *literal* comprehension questions and devoting little or often no attention to discussion. Under this condition how can we expect to develop use of the higher thinking processes in connection with reading content?

Understanding Reading

A third need for greater emphasis on depth in reading is found in results of studies showing that children are not doing well in grasping meanings in reading.

I will refer to one of the . . . most comprehensive investigations in regard to this matter. Bormuth conducted a study designed to ascertain students' ability to comprehend at different levels—primary, intermediate, junior high, and high school levels. In his conclusion he makes these statements:

For many years reading experts and educators in general have maintained that the ultimate objective of reading instruction was to enable the child to understand what he read and not just to enable him to call the words on the page. And they have argued that this is the objective upon which we should expend our major efforts, since it is only through the child's use of these skills that he is able to acquire much of the knowledge he will need throughout his life. On the whole, this argument seems well reasoned.

But when we examine how well this goal is being accomplished we find a rather discouraging situation. Children are not able to read their instructional materials well enough to gain much information from them until they reach high school. Even in high school a large proportion of the materials remain essentially incomprehensible to a large proportion of the students. Furthermore, the apparently improved ability of the high school student may, in fact, have resulted merely because the less able students, the students who were unable to read well enough to learn the content of their instruction, have failed in school, dropped out, and are no longer present to pull down the average performance to its true level.

A more detailed analysis of children's comprehension skills showed that in the fourth grade a great many of the children were unable to exhibit comprehension of even the simplest structures by which language signals information.

In discussing his study, Bormuth says further:

An analysis of the materials used to teach comprehension skills and of the curriculum guides and textbooks which instruct the teacher in how to teach the skills tends to suggest instead that there is no clear concept of what skills are to be taught. Furthermore, the teaching procedures described are described only in the vaguest terms.

In the final analysis, we cannot, at present, definitely reject or disapprove procedures for teaching reading comprehension, but we must voice grave doubts about their efficacy. And we can definitely say that they do not produce sufficient results to enable children to profit from much of their reading.

I have now indicated some of the urgent needs in developing thinking skills in reading. Comprehension is a complex process, and its faces are multiple and divergent. Research on reading in depth is much too scant; the thinking skills involved are not as specifically delineated as we would like to have them; effective methodology in this area is limited. With these thoughts in mind I shall devote the remainder of this article to an attempt to sort out and label the thinking skills in the language of teachers, and to give constructive suggestions for developing these skills in the classroom.

RECOGNIZING THE MANY FACES OF COMPREHENSION

First we must realize that reading instruction had no comprehension face at all until about fifty years ago. The corpus of reading instruction up until 1915 to 1925 was that of teaching word recognition. When a child had learned to pronounce the words in reading, the teaching objective had been met.

Then rather suddenly a change took place. Standardized tests were developed. In order to use these tests in reading it was now necessary to ask questions on content rather than have children read orally. They did so poorly in answering questions that everyone became excited about teaching them to get the thought, and the term "comprehension" came into our reading vocabulary for the first time. We have used this terminology indiscriminately ever since, and in my opinion this omnibus term of "comprehension" has stood in the way of developing true depth in reading, which makes use of the many different thinking processes. In general, "comprehension" has meant to most people literal comprehension —giving back what the book says.

With the emergence of the present new period in reading instruction under the general educational influence of placing emphasis on the thinking skills, comprehension, which first stuck its head above the surface in the 1920's, seems to have developed many faces, at least vocabulary-wise, and it appears to be revolving . . . so fast that all of the faces are blurred and merging and overlapping, and the features of none are clear-cut or distinct. We hear of literal comprehension, factual reading, close reading, inferences, interpretation, critical reading, creative reading, etc., etc. Comprehension has indeed become a many splendored, many-faced thing.

It is good that we have advanced beyond our first concept of comprehension. Many people at present, however, seem to be taking just one step in extending their concept of this process. They recognize only two faces of comprehension. They teach the literal comprehension face in which the child gives back what the book says. Then they make some effort to recognize a second face, which they call "inferences." This term is altogether too broad. There are many different kinds of inferences that make use of different thinking skills. This inference face should be broken down into other faces.

By the way, I would like to say a word about the shibboleth of using the *wh* words *who, what, why, when* as a sure-fire means of giving practice on inferences or any other aspect of depth reading. Answers to all of these questions usually are given in the text and require only literal comprehension. Developing the thinking processes in reading isn't so easy that we can get results by using a trick so simple as this.

I have spoken of people who recognize only the two faces of comprehension which they call "literal comprehension" and "inferences." Others, and probably a larger group, recognize two faces only, which they call "literal comprehension" and "critical reading." This phrase, "critical reading," has come to be a sort of . . . slogan. Many are using this term about as indiscriminately as the broad term of "comprehension" has been used in the past. Critical reading is used very generally to include all of the thinking skills.

If we are to break down these big "lump-sum" concepts into a variety of thinking processes in order to distribute practice over different ones of them, we need to know what the thinking skills are. Some people have analyzed the thinking processes into separate skills and listed them. Here is one such list according to Bloom:

1. *Memory*: The pupil recalls or recognizes information.
2. *Translation*: The pupil changes information into a different symbolic form or language.
3. *Interpretation*: The pupil discovers relationships between facts, generalizations, definitions, values, and skills.
4. *Application*: The pupil solves a lifelike problem that requires the identification of the issue and the selection and use of appropriate generalizations and skills.
5. *Analysis*: The pupil solves a problem through his conscious knowledge of the parts and forms of thinking.
6. *Synthesis*: The pupil solves a problem that requires original, creative thinking.
7. *Evaluation*: The pupil makes a judgment of good or bad, or right or wrong, according to designated standards.

I know of a situation in which teachers are given this list and told to ask questions in each of these categories in their reading lessons. The list has the advantage of presenting a diversity of skills to be developed. The teachers tell me, however, that they can't remember this long list; that they can't clearly distinguish between some of the categories; that they can't think of questions for some of them; and that some of the items are rarely, perhaps never, applicable to the reading that the children are doing.

I am giving this example to indicate that a long list of higher mental processes does not seem to be very helpful to teachers in providing practice on depth skills in reading. In the interest of attempting to offer some practical, down-to-earth assistance to the classroom teacher I would like to suggest some models for reference in conducting meaning-getting discussion of reading content. The four models or categories of skills which I shall suggest are broad enough to include all of the thinking skills usually listed by psychologists, each category covering a cluster of these skills; the categories are clearly differentiated one from the other; they are applicable to most any selection in any book; and teachers can easily grasp and apply them. These four categories are (1) literal comprehension, (2) interpretation, (3) critical reading, and (4) creative reading. Many teachers with whom I have been working have used these models in formulating questions and making statements designed to stimulate discussion which would give practice on a planned variety of thinking skills rather than just asking questions hit or miss which may give practice on one or two thinking skills over and over again at the neglect of the others.

Literal Comprehension

The first category is labeled "literal comprehension," the term which I have mentioned several times before. This category does not include the *thinking* skills. Teachers do not need special help on this. I include it, however, as a contrast to the other categories which I shall describe and because after all it does have a place in meaning gathering.

I like to define literal comprehension as the skill of getting the primary, direct literal meaning of a word, idea, or sentence in context. There is no depth in this kind of reading. It is the lowest rung in the meaning-getting ladder, yet it is the one on which teachers of the past have given the most practice, and to which most still are devoting the preponderance of their comprehensive efforts. A teacher gives practice in literal comprehension when she asks, "With what was Johnny playing?" and the pupil answers, "With his red fire engine"; these are the exact words given in the book. Giving this answer requires no thinking. Such a question simply demands the pupil to recall from memory what the book says, simply asks him to repeat parrot-like the words that are in the book.

Throughout the elementary grades and high school, practice in literal comprehension dominates practice in the meaning-getting skills because the following techniques are so widely used: (1) fact questions based directly on the text, (2) true-false statements, (3) completion sentences, (4) multiple-choice exercises. These objective techniques used in standardized tests, informal tests, discussions, and assignments give practice in literal comprehension, but they do little or nothing to develop the ability to use the thinking skills in obtaining deeper meanings.

Interpretation

"Interpretation" is the label for a very usable category of thinking skills which should be emphasized in reading. This term could be used in a sense broad enough to cover all of the thinking skills. But teachers of reading need something more definitive; they need categories which are sharply differentiated from one another. If the whole set of thinking skills were included under the term of "interpretation" or "inferences," some of the most distinctive and desirable skills would probably become smothered and obscured.

In general, it may be said that interpretation probes for greater depth than literal comprehension. It is concerned with supplying meanings not directly stated in the text.

For example, in a third grade class the children were reading a ship story. Among other things there was a sentence saying, "The captain swung himself up onto the roof of the cabin." The teacher asked, "Where did the captain swing himself?" This was a literal comprehension question. Instead she might have used a question which would have given the children a chance to think. She might have said, "Can you give a reason why he went up on the roof?" or, "The sentence says he swung himself up on the roof. Can you tell just how he got up there?"

This is a very simple example. As children progress through the grades and secondary school, text becomes more complex and opportunities for interpretation experiences may increase rapidly if teachers of all subjects are watching for chances to stimulate their students in the use of their thinking skills.

Interpretation involves a cluster of several different kinds of thinking skills, such as: (1) supplying additional information by "reading between the lines," (2) making generalizations, (3) reasoning cause and effect, (4) anticipating endings, (5) making comparisons, (6) sensing motives, (7) discovering relationships.

These are important skills that the teacher should have in mind in teaching students to read in depth. [She] should raise the level of understanding far above literal comprehension, guiding it and directing it into interpretation of deeper meanings.

Critical Reading

A third cluster of thinking skills is involved in critical reading, skills that are over, above, and apart from those in interpretation as I see it. The critical-reading skill category is the one most direly in need of development in American life at the present time, and I deplore the fact that many are using the term as a general heading under which to classify all of the thinking skills ever used by human beings. Critical reading in my opinion should be singled out for its own area of development and for practice on its own specific thinking skills.

Critical reading is the third level in the hierarchy of reading-for-meaning skills. According to my thinking it includes literal comprehension and interpretation as defined above, but it goes farther than either of these in that the reader *evaluates, passes personal judgment on the quality, the value, the accuracy*, and *the truthfulness* of, what is read. These skills should not be included under interpretation. They belong specifically to critical reading.

The distinction indicated above is appropriate in terms of the meaning of the word *critical*, an adjective derived from the noun *critic*, which in turn has as one of its foreign sources the Greek word *krinein*, meaning "to judge, discern."

One dictionary definition of *critical* is "exercising or involving careful judgment; exact; nicely judicious as a critical examination." Another dictionary defines to be *critical* as "to judge with severity."

Critic is defined as "one who expresses a reasoned opinion . . . on any matter . . . involving a judgment of its value, truth or righteousness." *Criticism* is defined as "A critical observation or judgment," and *criticize* is defined thus: "To examine and judge as a critic."

According to the established meaning of the word then, critical reading would seem to be the kind of reading in which the reader gives his personal reaction to the text, passes his personal judgment upon it.

Critical thinking and critical reading can be cultivated in very young children. For example, Susan and other first graders were reading a story in their primers about a dog riding downhill in a cart. The accompanying picture showed the dog riding down the steep hill all by himself in the cart. A girl standing at the top of the hill had evidently given the cart a push. Susan blurted out, "This is foolish. A dog wouldn't sit in a cart and ride downhill like this. He'd jump out. My dog won't even sit in a cart and let me pull him around." Susan was doing critical reading. She was evaluating in terms of personal experience.

Throughout the elementary grades, students giving such evidences of critical thinking and reading should be warmly commended and other students encouraged to do likewise.

In later grades planned experience in critical reading may be provided, for example, developing with the class criteria in regard to the author's background, position, experience with the subject, prejudices; holding panel discussions, supported by reference to readings, etc. Evaluating ads, news items, editorials, cartoons, etc., in terms of propaganda is important. There is a very fertile field for critical reading at the higher levels.

Creative Reading

The term "creative reading" is frequently used in as broad a sense as "inferences," "critical reading," and other current popular terms which many have fallen into the habit of employing as one label to cover all thought processes in reading. Creative reading accompanies and grows out of literal comprehension, interpretation, or critical reading but it is different from any one of these. As is the case with these other kinds of reading, how is the teacher going to stimulate or encourage this thing called creative reading if she doesn't know what it is?

Creativity is a pretty involved subject with roots deep down in psychology. An adequate discussion of the creative art is quite complicated. It is a fascinating subject, though, and if some of you would like to read more about it I have listed some good references. I recommend that you delve into these (Knell, Stauffer, Torrance, Vinacke).

As a starting point, however, I would like to describe creative reading in such very simple terms that a teacher can immediately see the difference between this kind of reading and the other kinds that I have mentioned. First by way of contrast we should consider that in literal comprehension the student tries to get the direct meaning of the author who wrote the text; in interpretation he tries to supply meanings to complete the author's text; in critical reading he evaluates, passes judgment on the author's text. In creative reading, however, the individual leaves the author's text and goes out on his own beyond the author's text to seek out or express new ideas, to gain additional insights, to find the answer to a question or the solution to a lifelike problem. (Incidentally, I include problem-solving in creative reading because in processing this mental activity the individual goes beyond the text to think toward a solution creatively.)

Creative reading in its higher form starts with a question . . . which arises in the mind of the reader, . . . and is usually carried forward with high motivation, often a sense of urgency. We cannot expect this higher type of creative reading to happen in the classroom very often unless the teacher does something to develop it. Since inquiry is the starting point of creative reading, the teacher may ask questions which cause children to go beyond direct implications gathered from the text, at least calling for creative thinking, and she can encourage children, themselves, to ask questions. Once she develops the process of inquiry within children themselves, concerning reading content, creative reading is apt to follow, and when it does follow it should be praised warmly.

SUMMARY

I have . . . tried to describe four different faces of comprehension which together include all of the thinking processes listed by psychologists, and to offer them as models to assist teachers in differentiating between the various kinds of reading, thus resulting in an increased possibility at least of providing children experiences in the use of the many different thinking skills in reading.

Here is one short and extremely simple example of how a teacher might give a class experience in using thinking skills involved in all four categories that I have discussed.

The children were reading a story about a little girl named Ruth who was left at home to take care of her younger brother while her mother went away somewhere. The youngster wanted a cooky to eat. The cooky jar was kept on the basement steps. Ruth opened the door to the basement and stepped down to get a cooky. At that moment little brother slammed the door shut. It had a snap lock, so Ruth was locked in the basement when she was supposed to be upstairs taking care of little brother. She began to puzzle over her predicament. Finally she asked little brother to take the receiver off the phone and say "16 Wood Street" over and over again. This he did. The operator hearing a child's voice repeating this address suspected trouble and sent a policeman to the address and he let Ruth out of the basement.

Now for the four different types of meaning questions:

Literal comprehension: "What did little brother want to eat?"
Interpretation: "Why was the cooky jar kept on the basement steps?"
Critical reading: "Did mother do the right thing in leaving the children alone?"
Creative thinking: "How would you have solved this problem?"

Some printed materials are very helpful in giving practice in thinking in reading, and this is good. The development of the many different thinking processes in reading, however, depends to a large extent upon the teacher who knows and recognizes these different processes. Thinking is a personal matter. It varies with different groups and different individuals within groups. The best guarantee for development of the thinking skills is an informed, understanding teacher of reading to guide and encourage students to invent questions as well as to answer them; to reflect, infer, and predict; to string together beads of information in arriving at generalizations; to aid independence in thinking; to foster creativity; to nourish values; and to refine sensitivities. The major responsibility rests with the teacher during her daily interactions with her students.

REFERENCES

J. Barzun, quoted from J. E. Russell. *Change and Challenge in American Education*. Boston: Houghton Mifflin, 1969, p. 103.

B. S. Bloom (ed.). *Taxonomy of Educational Objectives*. New York: David McKay, 1956, pp. 186–87.

J. R. Bormuth. "The Effectiveness of Current Procedures for Teaching Reading Comprehension." Paper presented at fifty-eighth annual meeting of National Council of Teachers of English, Milwaukee, November 29, 1968.

E. Dale. "Things to Come. *The Newsletter*, 1960, 34, 3.

J. J. Guszak. "Teacher Questioning and Reading." In T. Harris *et al.*, *The Journal of Educational Research*, 1969, 62, 306.

T. Harris, W. Otto, and T. Barrett. "Summary and Review of Investigations Relating to Reading, July 1, 1967 to June 30, 1968." *The Journal of Educational Research*, 1969, 62, 306.

G. F. Knell. *The Art and Science of Creativity*. New York: Holt, Rinehart and Winston, Inc., 1965.

Helen M. Robinson, S. Weintraub, and Helen Smith. "Summary of Investigations Relating to Reading, July 1, 1967 to June 30, 1968." *Reading Research Quarterly*, 1969, 4 (2), 193–94.

R. G. Stauffer. *Teaching Reading as a Thinking Process*. New York: Harper and Row, 1969.

P. E. Torrance. "Developing Creative Readers." In R. Stauffer (Comp.), *Proceedings of the Annual Education and Reading Conference, 1963 and 1964*. Newark, Del.: University of Delaware, 1964.

W. E. Vinacke. *The Psychology of Thinking*. New York: McGraw-Hill, 1952.

10.
MARYANNE HALL

LINGUISTICALLY SPEAKING, WHY LANGUAGE EXPERIENCE?

The language experience approach has increasingly been employed for initial reading instruction in the last decade. In recent years, there has been growing interest in the implications of linguistic study for the teaching of reading. The term "linguistics" as related to reading instruction often signifies a beginning approach based on phoneme-grapheme correspondence through the presentation of a carefully controlled vocabulary illustrating selected spelling patterns. However, linguistics is used here with a broader application. Since reading is communication through written language, all reading . . . is linguistic. Knowledge about language supplied by linguists should lead to reading instruction based on accurate information about the reading process.

The relationship of reading to spoken language is basic to a linguistic definition of reading. This relationship is also basic to teaching reading through the language experience approach. Seven statements of the linguistic rationale for the language experience approach are expressed below in terms of the beginning reader.

The beginning reader must be taught to view reading as a communication process. Language experience reading is communication-centered. Attention is on communication through the medium of print just as in speaking and listening the emphasis is on communication through the medium of speech. In beginning reading, children should feel a need to communicate naturally through print just as before learning to read they had felt the need to communicate through speech. A creative and competent teacher must provide the stimuli and opportunities for children to communicate in reading and writing.

The content of personally composed stories involves concepts within the scope of children's background knowledge and interests. Communication is present as children react while discussing their ideas, as they write or watch the teacher write those ideas, and as they then read their ideas.

From *The Reading Teacher*, 25:1 (January, 1972), 328–31. Reprinted with permission of the author and the International Reading Association.

Comprehension is present since children do understand that which they first wrote.

The beginning reader is a user of language (Goodman, 1969). The spoken language which the child possesses is his greatest asset for learning written language. The normal child from an adequate home environment has mastered the patterns of his native language by the time of school entrance. This is not to overlook the fact that his linguistic facility is by no means complete. He has much to absorb in language flexibility and elaboration; still, he has more than sufficient linguistic ability to learn to read.

In discussions of reading readiness, great attention has been given to the experience background of children, and less to their language background. When attention has been given to language factors, usually that attention has been to the extent of vocabulary and general language facility in expressing and understanding spoken language instead of how this facility operates in learning to read. The child who learned spoken language in the preschool years displayed an amazing feat of linguistic performance. We should make it possible for him to learn to read with equal ease and to draw upon his existing linguistic background in doing so.

The beginning reader should understand the reading process as one of consciously relating print to oral language. As the beginning reader works with print he changes the unfamiliar graphic symbols to familiar oral language. Goodman (1968) defines reading as the processing of language information in order to reconstruct a message from print.

In the language experience approach the child finds translating print into speech greatly simplified since he is reading that which he first said. The message is easily reconstructed when the reader is also the author. In the beginning stages reading instruction must be geared to ensure success for the learner. The ease with which children can read their language should be capitalized on in language experience instruction.

Downing reports in studies of five- and six-year-olds' views of reading that their conceptions of language are different from those of their teachers. Terminology such as "word," "sentence," "sound," and "letter" was unclear to the children in his research. He comments on the need to provide "language experiences and activities which (a) *orient* children correctly to the true purposes of reading and writing and (b) enable children's natural thinking processes *to generate understanding* of the technical concepts of language."

The beginning reader should incorporate the learning of writing with the learning of reading. Relating the written language code to the spoken code was discussed earlier as the task of the beginning reader. Learning the written code involves decoding—going from print to speech—and encoding—going from speech to print. In the language experience approach, writing is a natural corollary of reading as a child first watches the recording of thought he has dictated and as he progresses gradually to writing independently.

The integration of decoding and encoding should provide reinforcement in both processes. In studies of preschool readers, Durkin reported that interest in writing often preceded interest in reading. Dykstra reported in the National First Grade Studies that a writing component added to reading programs enhanced achievement in reading.

The beginning reader should learn to read with materials written in his language patterns. The language experience approach does use materials written with the language of the reader for whom they are intended. Reading materials should always convey meaning to a child in natural language phrasing which sounds right and familiar to him—not necessarily "right" to the ears of a standard-English speaker. For children who do not speak standard English, the language of standard materials does not match their spoken language. While there are special materials written in nonstandard dialects, these materials are not available to all teachers of nonstandard-speaking children. Also, these materials may not fit all children in a group where they are being used. An often overlooked fact is that the limited preprimer language is also unlike the oral language of a child who does use standard English.

The point to be remembered here is that the nonstandard speaker is a user of language. The absence of mastery of standard English need not delay the beginning reading instruction when language experience materials are used. The teaching of oral standard English will be another part of the total language program.

It is recommended that the teacher record the syntactical patterns of the children as spoken but using standard spelling. For example, if the child says "des' " for "desk," the word will be written "desk," but if the child says, "My brother, he . . . ," this pattern will be written. The language communicates, and there is sufficient language to be used for teaching beginning reading.

The beginning reader should learn to read meaningful language units. In language experience reading, children are dealing with thought units from the flow of their speech. They are not dealing with a phoneme-grapheme unit or a word unit, but with a larger piece of language. From the total running flow of speech of others in their environment they learned to talk. The child gradually learned to pick words of very high meaning: "Mommy," "Daddy," "me," and others. From one-word utterances the child progressed to two-word patterns and built his linguistic knowledge from hearing natural speech around him.

In reading from language experience, children learn to read using the meaning-bearing patterns of language. They will be exposed to reading material which is not controlled in vocabulary and which does not distort language in an effort to limit vocabulary or to emphasize phoneme-grapheme relationships. They gradually acquire a reading vocabulary by identifying words from stories which represent the natural flow of written language. Perhaps with the first experience story, children learn to read one [word,] perhaps two or three from the next one, and so on until their word banks represent a respectable stock of known words. These words were presented and learned, not in isolation, but in meaningful sentence and story units.

The beginning reader should learn to read orally with smooth, fluent, natural expression. The language experience approach provides oral reading situations in which children can truly "make it sound like someone talking." In the language experience approach, word-by-word emphasis in oral reading should not be permitted to occur. The teacher's model is important in illustrating fluent natural reading in the first pupil-dictated stories. In their concern that children learn vocabulary, some teachers may tend to distort the reading of experience stories with overemphasis on separate words.

Lefevre maintains that "single words, analyzed and spoken in isolation, assume the intonation contours of whole utterances. Single words thus lose the characteristic pitch and stress they normally carry in the larger constructions that comprise the flow of speech and bear meaning." He emphasizes that the sentence is the minimal unit of meaning, and that children should develop "sentence sense" in reading. In the language experience way of learning to read, the beginner does learn to supply the "melodies of speech" as he reads.

The relationship of oral and written language can also be shown as punctuation signals are pointed out incidentally, with emphasis on function and meaning. For example, after a number of experience stories have been written, the teacher may casually say, "This is the end of your idea—so we put a period. The next word goes with the next idea—so we start this part with a capital letter."

SUMMARY

The linguistic rationale for the language experience approach gives theoretical support to the teacher who is concerned with the implementation of this approach in teaching beginning reading. Language experience reading is truly a linguistically based method since the relationship of oral and written language is the key to teaching children to read through the recording and reading of their spoken language. The beginning reader is a user of language who must relate graphic symbols to the oral language code he already knows. Understanding the process of language communication through language experience reading should enable the teacher to facilitate the task of learning to read for the beginner through use of relevant material which reflects *his* [the pupil's] language. The most important consideration is how language communicates meaning—in language experience reading, *communication is the central focus.*

REFERENCES

John Downing. "How Children Think About Reading," *The Reading Teacher*, 23, December, 1969, 217–30.

Dolores Durkin. "A Language Arts Program for Pre-First-Grade Children: Two Year Achievement Report," *Reading Research Quarterly*, 5, Summer, 1970, 534–65.

Robert Dykstra. "Summary of the Second-Grade Phase of the Cooperative Research Program in Primary Reading Instruction," *Reading Research Quarterly*, 4, Fall, 1968, 49–70.

Kenneth S. Goodman. *The Psycholinguistic Nature of the Reading Process.* Detroit: Wayne State University Press, 1968.

———. "Pro-Challenger Answer to 'Is the Linguistic Approach an Improvement in Reading Instruction?'" *Current Issues in Reading.* Conference Proceedings of 13th Annual Convention, ed. Nila B. Smith, pp. 268–76. Newark, Del.: International Reading Association, 1969.

Carl A. Lefevre. *Linguistics and the Teaching of Reading.* New York: McGraw-Hill, 1964.

11.

SHIRLEY BERETTA

SELF-CONCEPT DEVELOPMENT
IN THE READING PROGRAM

Aware teachers have probably always known that emotional factors play an important part in a child's success in learning to read. [In 1941,] Arthur Gates estimated from his clinical experience that 75 per cent of the chil-

From *The Reading Teacher*, 24:3 (December, 1970), 232–38. Reprinted with permission of The International Reading Association.

dren with severe reading disabilities showed personality maladjustment. Since that time the relationship between reading failure and various personality maladjustments has been explored in a number of research studies.

Of all the areas of personality correlated with reading achievement, one factor, self-concept, seems to be particularly useful for reading teachers. It may be worthwhile to look at the meaning of self-concept before exploring ways in which the reading teacher may help in the development of positive self-concept.

THE INFLUENCE OF SELF-CONCEPT ON READING

According to Sullivan, the self is made up of "reflected appraisals." These reflected appraisals come from the child's parents, teachers, and significant others. A child who, for whatever reason, develops negative self-perceptions may see himself as an inadequate reader, incapable of learning, or just generally inadequate. Children with negative self-images may be filled with fear of failure and terrified of new experiences. Some may be restless, unable to concentrate, and anxious under pressure of time limits. Others may be quiet and withdrawn. Failure in reading may be among these behavioral manifestations of poor self-concepts.

There are carefully designed studies that clearly show the relationship between self-concept and reading. One study that indicates a cause-effect relationship between self-concept and reading achievement is the doctoral dissertation of Mary Lamy. In this study, measurements of self-perception were made during kindergarten prior to reading instruction and during the first grade. Self-perception scores correlated as highly with reading achievement as did intelligence scores. Together the two scores were found to be better predictors of reading success than either score taken separately. Because Lamy's study shows a positive relationship between reading achievement and self-perceptions that were inferred during kindergarten —*before reading instruction*—it gives strong support to the idea that self-perceptions are causal factors in reading success and failure.

Other research has also supported the relationship between self-concept and reading achievement. Wattenberg and Clifford found that measures of self-concept during kindergarten are predictive of reading achievement. Giuliani found self-concept as well as verbal-mental ability significantly related to reading readiness. Toller compared self-evaluations of achieving readers with those of retarded readers. She found significant differences in favor of achievers on acceptance, adequacy, personal and social self, security, number of problems, and consistency of view of self.

SELF-CONCEPT DEVELOPMENT IN THE READING PROGRAM

Research supports the idea that an adequate self-concept is an important component of successful reading. The self-concept, then, may be thought of in the same way as basic skills, such as vocabulary building, recognition skills, and word-attack techniques, each of which is an important element of successful reading. In order to explore methods of promoting adequate self-concepts, it is necessary to relate these methods to an integrated reading approach.

The methods of developing self-concept will be set in the context of an individualized approach to reading. However, these methods need not be confined to the individualized approach. They may be used easily in a nongraded organization or even adapted for use in a more traditional reading program.

Rationale for the Individualized Approach

The objective of the individualized approach to reading is the fullest development of the student's skills and capacities. This approach is unique in that skills are developed by the flexible use of methods adapted to the learning style of the individual child. It also aims at developing greater and more lasting interest in reading than some traditional reading approaches. "The healthy child is naturally active and he is engaged almost continually while awake in an active exploration of his environment. He seeks from that environment those experiences that are consistent with his maturity and his needs" (p. 89). Discussing self-selection, Olson wrote, "Throughout nature there is a strong tendency for life to be sustained by the self-selection of an environment appropriate to the needs of the plant, animal, or human being" (p. 90). Olson described pacing as "the acts on the part of the teacher which insure that each child is provided with the materials upon which he can thrive and also . . . the attitude which expects from the child only that which he can yield at his stage of maturity" (p. 94).

Self-Concept Development and the Sensitive Teacher

What can the teacher do to promote adequate self-concepts in children? The reading teacher is not in a position to provide psychotherapy for severely disturbed children. However, she must consider personality factors as one influence on reading achievement. Some children may require help from outside the school before any reading program can be effective. However, there are many children within the normal range who have self-perceptions that limit their success in reading. It is the child who sees himself as inadequate or in inconsistent ways that is a concern of the reading teacher who uses an individualized approach.

The sensitive teacher is the most important element in helping the child with negative self-perceptions. The reading teacher must be highly skilled in the area of sensitive relating to the child as well as in reading instruction. Sensitive relating is experiential in nature and cannot be captured in words on paper. Writing about sensitivity is like writing about the skill of sailing. One can describe the skills involved in sailing, but there is a certain sensitivity that a person develops to the wind and the adjusting of his sails that cannot be adequately described. It is possible, however, to describe some attitudinal and behavioral aspects of the sensitive teacher.

The attitudes, personality, and skill of the teacher are the most important factors in the individualized approach. Barbe quoted Jacobs as saying, "Individualized reading starts not with procedures but with a creative, perceptive teacher—one who believes that children want to learn; who thinks with children rather than for them; who basically respects the individual behavior of every youngster; who works with children in orderly but not rigid ways" (p. 19).

THE EXPERIENCE OF SUCCESS AND MEANING. The sensitive teacher knows that experience of success and a sense of meaning in learning are essential for the growing child. Successful experience is one of the surest ways of achieving positive self-perceptions. It is unnecessary for a child to experience failure in reading. An aware teacher once said, "It's not where you are that counts in this class, it's where you go from where you are now that's important." It seems that with this kind of attitude every individual can go someplace.

The flexibility and variety of books used in the individualized approach allow the teacher to modify the learning material to fit the individual level of the child. By selecting from a range of books and activities, the teacher can help a child have experiences in which he can succeed. Each child may be challenged, not overwhelmed with threat. As a child develops his reading ability he realistically comes to see himself as one who can do things, as one who can be successful. Consistent communication of confidence from the teacher helps him to see that what he does is valued. This attitude helps the child to clarify his particular goals in reading and to start work toward them. It helps him to fulfill his learning potentialities.

In addition to meeting the level of ability of a child, it is important that tasks have meaning for him. When a child does not see any personal meaning in something, it becomes very difficult for him to learn it. Repeated experiences of this nature may cause him to see himself as lacking in ability to learn. New skills come to have meaning for a child when he can see these skills as consistent with his perceptions of self.

In order to provide experiences that have personal meaning, the teacher should be concerned with the child's interests. In some instances this is simply a matter of allowing the child freedom to select his own reading material. Other times the teacher may need to help a child learn to make choices and help him become aware of what is available for him to choose. Some children see themselves in such a helpless way that they are unable to make decisions about anything. Such a child might be helpless to answer the question "What are you interested in reading today?" But offered a choice between two stories briefly described he can probably select one. A sensitive teacher would have done some ground work to learn some of the child's interests. As time goes on, the teacher offers more choices and moves toward helping the child to learn to select and assume responsibility for his own activities. Learning to make satisfying choices in reading may help him to see himself as capable of decisions in other areas of his life.

In addition to helping children follow their own interests, the teacher may stimulate new interests through a wide variety of books and activities. The scope of activities which may be used is virtually unlimited. A display, report, or oral reading by one child may stimulate other students to read. A panel can be a springboard for class discussion. Children may use puppets or dolls for making book reviews interesting. Many aids such as those suggested by Brogan and Fox can be used to make the learning experience vital:

The classroom must be set up primarily as a place for active learning, with the focus on "doing centers, not just looking centers" [with] bulletin boards that truly communicate, the Work Table, painting and clay centers, the Make-It Table, toys and gadgets, science materials, radio and television, the Writer's Table, the puppet theater, the house, the cooking center, the victrola, filmstrips and films, and . . . the Library Corner or Reading Center [pp. 219–20].

Within a classroom such as this, students may prepare materials for their conferences with the teacher or the sharing period with other students and conduct group projects and self-expressive activities.

THE INDIVIDUAL CONFERENCE. A sensitive teacher can use the individual conference to help develop positive self-perceptions as well as develop reading skills. Using the individual conference does not imply that the teacher discard her role of reading instructor. In fact, the individualized program demands an extremely thorough knowledge of all skills so the teacher will be prepared to help with any skill at the appropriate time for the child.

The individual conference may take the place of the traditional reading circle. The child usually meets individually with the teacher and reads something that he has selected. The teacher observes both oral and silent reading skills to check the child's understanding of word meanings as well as sight vocabulary. She checks his comprehension by questions or by discussion and instructs in the necessary skills. Through the teacher's guidance the child gains awareness of his strengths and weaknesses and makes plans for developing skills. With opportunity for practice and correction in the privacy of a conference with his teacher, a child progresses at his own rate.

Each child is encouraged to select, from the range of materials, those books which he wants to read. The teacher may suggest ways in which the child can share his reading with others in the class. Sometimes the students are scheduled for their conferences once a week. Other times they ask for individual time as they feel a need.

Barbe has recognized the potentiality of the individual conference as something more than reading instruction. He wrote, "The individual conference is essentially a counseling session. The classroom teacher who has no formal training in counseling, as such, would do well to examine some of the literature on counseling techniques, as well as spend some time in in-service training developing this particular skill" (p. 48).

The individual conference provides the teacher with an opportunity to establish a warm and accepting relationship with the student. Through the individual conference the teacher and the child can develop a mutual trust and respect. It gives her an opportunity to relate to the child in a way that will help him develop a positive self-image. Rogers stated that it is the quality of the helping relationship that is most growth-producing.

In the individual conference the teacher is in a position to listen attentively to what the child is saying. This is not only a strong reinforcement for his reading, but it communicates some positive things to him. It says that he is a valuable person, that he is worthy of being heard, that what he has to say is important. Many children, when trying to verbalize, have been neglected or rejected by busy parents and come to think of themselves as not having anything worthwhile to contribute. A child with a negative self-concept may find that his teacher is the first person who listens to him.

SMALL GROUPS. Another aspect of the individualized reading program that adapts itself to development of positive self-perception is the small group. Grouping in the individualized program differs from the skill-oriented ability groups of other approaches. Small groups are important, not only in helping students with their skills and sharing their reading, but also for helping children gain positive perceptions of themselves—as social selves and learners. In a small group the teacher is a key to how well the group functions. Her role is that of facilitator of discussion rather than that of lecturer. Along with stimulating discussion of reading, the teacher may encourage students to relate reading to their personal experiences. It is very important that the teacher serve as a model of acceptance and warmth so that the children may emulate this attitude and develop a climate in which each child can express himself and feel valued.

The small group experience provides a lifelike situation for children to gain feedback about self and to learn to fulfill needs in socially accepted ways. As children interact with their classmates they may become aware of many choices and alternate ways of behaving.

CONCLUSION

For years the word "individual" has been taught, yet many programs are designed for administrative convenience. We realize the importance of good mental health, yet emotional development is rarely an intentional part of a curriculum. Self-concept is as much a factor in reading success as intelligence or mastery of basic skills. A program integrating reading instruction and development of positive self-perceptions is exciting because it offers the promise of meeting individual needs for learning and for good emotional development.

REFERENCES

W. Barbe. *Educator's Guide to Personalized Reading Instruction.* Englewood Cliffs, N.J.: Prentice-Hall, 1961.

Peggy Brogan and Lorene Fox. *Helping Children Read.* New York: Holt Rinehart and Winston, 1961.

A. Gates. "The Role of Personality Maladjustment in Reading Disability." *Journal of Genetic Psychology,* 1941, 59, 77–83.

G. Giuliani. "The Relationship of Self-Concept and Verbal-Mental Ability to Levels of Reading Readiness Amongst Kindergarten Children." *Dissertation Abstracts,* 1968, 28, 3866B.

Mary Lamy. "Relationship of Self-Perceptions of Early Primary Children to Achievement in Reading." *Dissertation Abstracts,* 1963, 24, 628–29.

W. Olson. "Seeking, Self Selection, and Pacing in the Use of Books by Children." In Jeannett Veatch (ed.), *Individualizing Your Reading Program.* New York: G. P. Putnam's Sons, 1959.

C. Rogers. "The Interpersonal Relationship: The Core of Guidance." *Harvard Educational Review,* 1962, 32, 416–29.

Gladys Toller. "Certain Aspects of the Self Evaluations Made by Achieving and Retarded Readers of Average and Above Average Intelligence." *Dissertation Abstracts*, 1968, 28, 976A.

W. Wattenberg and Clare Clifford. "Relation of Self-Concepts to Beginning Achievement in Reading." In W. Durr (ed.), *Reading Instruction: Dimensions and Issues*. Boston: Houghton Mifflin, 1967.

PART 2

Psychology and the Child

CHAPTER FIVE

The Perceptual
World of the Child

PERCEPTUAL PSYCHOLOGY is a body of interrelated theories that attempt to describe internal psychological processes. It is concerned with the ways in which the individual interprets his environment and the ways in which he views himself. It begins with the premise that the individual is not a mechanism that is pushed and pulled by his environment but has the potential to generate and direct his own psychological growth and development. From a perceptual point of view, the task of the teacher is to provide an accepting and supportive classroom atmosphere. As the child becomes increasingly self-confident, he grows to be a better learner.

Perceptual psychology provides a contrast to the behavioral emphasis on environmental cues, responses, and reinforcement. William Hitt has carefully marshalled the arguments for and against the behaviorist (realist) position and the phenomenological, or perceptualist (idealist), conception of man's nature. He presents the two positions with equal weight, concluding that "there appears to be truth in both views of man"—that each model has its uses, depending on the problem under study. The behaviorist model is useful in the analysis of environmental factors in learning, while the phenomenological model is appropriate for the investigation of internal processes, such as the process of creativity.

The theoretical principles of perceptual psychology as applied to teaching and learning are stated by Arthur Combs, just as B. F. Skinner stated the principles of behaviorism in Chapter 1 (pp. 12–21). Combs's analysis of the self-concept is at the heart of his system of perceptualism. He claims that the individual's self-concept—how he feels about himself in terms of self-worth—determines his level of growth and productivity. As

Combs and other such theorists have pointed out, the individual's level of self-actualization, or "personal quota" of achievement, appears to be related mostly to his beliefs about himself rather than to objective considerations. An entire research literature has developed on the theory of the self-concept, showing its relationship to motivation, vocational aspiration, and stereotypes of race and sex roles.

Probably the central premise of perceptual psychology is that self-awareness and self-acceptance are necessary preconditions for awareness and positive acceptance of others. When students feel that they are perceived by teachers as individuals of worth and dignity, they grow emotionally and intellectually. The essence of teaching, then, is not applying control techniques, but arranging the conditions in which the learner can "teach himself." As Moustakas states, "We cannot teach another person directly and we cannot facilitate real learning in the sense of making it easier," but when the self is free from threat, "the person is free to explore the materials and resources which are available to him in the light of his own interests and potentiality." In other words, the learner has to feel secure and accepted. Without that feeling, he can still be "taught," but the result will be compliance, not personal commitment.

A major issue in perceptual psychology concerns the nature of behavioral research. Opponents maintain that perceptualism is a "soft" psychology based mostly on opinion, not on scientific evidence. Combs agrees that perceptual, humanistic objectives are difficult to assess because they are largely a matter of personal, subjective meaning. Yet he believes that human judgment and inference are valid practices in research in perceptual psychology (although the researcher should not abandon the rigor of scientific methods and standards because of the difficulties involved). Although human judgment is fallible, "it can also be highly reliable when subjected to the same tests of credibility as in the physical sciences. Among these are tests such as internal and external reliability, predictive power, internal consistency, the test of fit in mental manipulation, and agreements with expert judgment" (Combs, 1973, p. 7).

One of the interesting aspects of perceptual psychology is that it is also *intrinsically* valid. It provides a very believable description of human behavior, which could also be rigorously tested as described above. It has commonsense value, and relatively little knowledge of specialized terminology is required to grasp its basic principles. It also provides a solid foundation for understanding current trends in popular psychology, such as the transactional, "I'm-OK/You're-OK" approach.

But the chief value of perceptual psychology is that it helps to sensitize the teacher to the needs and feelings of each child.

RECOMMENDED READING

D. Baumrind. 1972. "From Each According to Her Ability," *School Review* 80(2), 161–97. A well-substantiated analysis of one of the major conflicts that confront the adolescent girl: the feminine nurturant role *vs.* the role of competitor in traditionally male-dominated career fields.

A. W. Combs. 1973. "Educational Accountability from a Humanistic Perspective," *Educational Researcher* 2, 9, 19–21. An attempt to close the gap between the need for a supportive, pupil-centered classroom atmosphere and the growing pressures on teachers to provide clear evidence that subjct-matter objectives are being met.

G. Garner. 1974. "Modifying Pupil Self-Concept and Behavior," *Today's Education*, 63(1), 26–28. A description of an experiment with elementary school children, which used pupil self-appraisal as a means of improving self-concept and classroom behavior.

J. C. Jones and P. H. Mussen. 1958. "Self-Conceptions, Motivations, and Interpersonal Attitudes of Eearly- and Late-maturing Girls," *Child Development* 20, 491–501. A classic study of the maturational problem that affects the behavior of many adolescents; useful and thought-provoking research for veteran teachers and beginners alike.

C. E. Moustakas (ed.). 1956. *The Self* (New York: Harper & Row). A book of readings that provides illustrations of perceptual psychology both in and out of the classroom setting.

C. R. Rogers. 1961. *On Becoming a Person* (Boston: Houghton-Mifflin). One of the finest books to come out of the helping professions; topnotch reading for the teacher who wants to begin building strong, supportive relationships with children and other adults.

T. N. Saario, C. N. Jacklin and C. K. Tittle. 1973. "Sex-Role Stereotyping in the Public Schools," *Harvard Educational Review* 43(3), 386–416. Excellent source for citations of research data relating to all aspects of sex-role stereotyping in school curricular organization, instructional content, and achievement tests.

D. Snygg and A. W. Combs. 1959. *Individual Behavior* (New York: Harper & Row). A very readable text on perceptual psychology, free of jargon and obtuse research; brings together the best ideas and principles of perceptualism applied to teaching and counseling.

L. M. Soares, A. T. Soares and P. Pumerantz. 1973. "Self-Perception of Middle-School Pupils." *The Elementary School Journal* 73(7), 381–89. A comparative study of self-concepts of children in middle-schools *vs.* those in traditional middle-grade organizations, indicating that the greater academic demands of middle schools may result in a lowering of self-concepts.

12.

WILLIAM D. HITT

TWO MODELS OF MAN

A symposium sponsored by the Division of Philosophical Psychology of the American Psychological Association clearly pointed up the cleavage in contemporary theoretical and philosophical psychology. The symposium was held at Rice University to mark the inception of the Division of Philosophical Psychology as a new division of the APA. Participants included Sigmund Koch, R. B. MacLeod, B. F. Skinner, Carl R. Rogers, Norman Malcolm, and Michael Scriven. The presentations and associated discussions were organized in the book *Behaviorism and Phenomenology: Contrasting Bases for Modern Psychology*, edited by T. W. Wann.

THE ARGUMENT

As indicated by the title of the book, the main argument of the symposium dealt with phenomenology versus behaviorism. This argument also could be described as one between existential psychology and behavioristic psychology. The presentations dealt with two distinct models of man and the scientific methodology associated with each model. The discussions following each presentation may be described as aggressive, hostile, and rather emotional; they would suggest that there is little likelihood of a reconciliation between the two schools of thought represented at the symposium.

To illustrate the nature of the argument, some of the statements made by the participants are presented below.

In Support of Behaviorism

- Skinner (1964, p. 84):

An adequate science of behavior must consider events taking place within the skin of the organism, not as physiological mediators of behavior, but as part of behavior itself. It can deal with these events without assuming that they

From the *American Psychologist*, 24:7 (1969), 651–58. Originally presented at the meeting of the American Psychological Association, San Francisco, August, 1968. Copyright © 1969 by the American Psychological Association and used by permission.

110

have any special nature or must be known in any special way. . . . Public and private events have the same kinds of physical dimensions.

• Malcolm (p. 152):

Behaviorism is right in insisting that there must be some sort of conceptual tie between the language of mental phenomena and outward circumstances and behavior. If there were not, we could not understand other people, nor could we understand ourselves.

Attacks on Behaviorism

• Koch (p. 6):

Behaviorism has been given a hearing for fifty years. I think this generous. I shall urge that it is essentially a role-playing position which has outlived whatever usefulness its role might once have had.

• Rogers (p. 118):

It is quite unfortunate that we have permitted the world of psychological science to be narrowed to behavior observed, sounds emitted, marks scratched on paper, and the like.

In Support of Phenomenology

• MacLeod (p. 71):

I am . . . insisting that what, in the old, prescientific days, we used to call "consciousness" still can and should be studied. Whether or not this kind of study may be called a science depends on our definition of the term. To be a scientist, in my opinion, is to have boundless curiosity tempered by discipline.

• Rogers (p. 125):

The inner world of the individual appears to have more significant influence upon his behavior than does the external environmental stimulus.

Attacks on Phenomenology

• Malcolm (p. 148):

I believe that Wittgenstein has proved this line of thinking (introspectionism) to be disastrous. It leads to the conclusion that we do not and cannot understand each other's psychological language, which is a form of solipsism.*

• Skinner (1964, p. 106):

Mentalistic or psychic explanations of human behavior almost certainly originated in primitive animism [p. 79]. . . . I am a radical behaviorist simply in

---

* Solipsism is defined as the theory that only the self exists, or can be proved to exist.

the sense that I find no place in the formulation for anything which is mental.

This appears to be the heart of the argument:

The behaviorist views man as a passive organism governed by external stimuli. Man can be manipulated through proper control of these stimuli. Moreover, the laws that govern man are essentially the same as the laws that govern all natural phenomena of the world; hence, it is assumed that the scientific method used by the physical scientist is equally appropriate to the study of man.

The phenomenologist views man as the *source* of acts; he is free to choose in each situation. The essence of man is *inside* of man; he is controlled by his own consciousness. The most appropriate methodology for the study of man is phenomenology, which begins with the world of experience.

These two models of man have been proposed and discussed for many years by philosophers and psychologists alike. Versions of these models may be seen in the contrasting views of Locke and Leibnitz (see Allport), Marx and Kierkegaard, Wittgenstein and Sartre, and, currently, Skinner and Rogers. Were he living today, William James probably would characterize Locke, Marx, Wittgenstein, and Skinner as "tough-minded," while Leibnitz, Kierkegaard, Sartre, and Rogers would be viewed as "tender-minded." Traditionally, the argument has been one model versus the other. It essentially has been a black-and-white argument.

The purpose of this article is to analyze the argument between the behaviorist and the phenomenologist. This analysis is carried out by presenting and discussing two different models of man.

CONTRASTING VIEWS OF MAN

The two models of man are presented in terms of these contrasting views:

1. Man can be described meaningfully in terms of his behavior; or man can be described meaningfully in terms of his consciousness.
2. Man is predictable; or man is unpredictable.
3. Man is an information transmitter; or man is an information generator.
4. Man lives in an objective world; or man lives in a subjective world.
5. Man is a rational being; or man is an arational being.
6. One man is like other men; or each man is unique.
7. Man can be described meaningfully in absolute terms; or man can be described meaningfully in relative terms.

8. Human characteristics can be investigated independently of one another; or man must be studied as a whole.
9. Man is a reality; or man is a potentiality.
10. Man is knowable in scientific terms; or man is more than we can ever know about him.

Each of these attributes is discussed below.

SUPPORT FOR BOTH MODELS

The evidence offered below in support of each of the two models of man is both empirical and analytical. Perhaps some of the evidence is intuitive, but it at least seems logical to the author of this article.

Man Can Be Described Meaningfully in Terms of His Behavior; or Man Can Be Described Meaningfully in Terms of His Consciousness

According to John B. Watson, the founder of American behaviorism, the behavior of man and animals was the only proper study for psychology. Watson strongly advocated that

Psychology is to be the science, not of consciousness, but of behavior. . . . It is to cover both human and animal behavior, the simpler animal behavior being indeed more fundamental than the more complex behavior of man. . . . It is to rely wholly on objective data, introspection being discarded [Woodworth and Sheehan, p. 113].

Behaviorism has had an interesting, and indeed productive, development since the time of Watson's original manifesto. Tolman, Hull, and a number of other psychologists have been important figures in this development. Today, Skinner is the leading behaviorist in the field of psychology. Skinner (1957, p. 449) deals with both overt and covert behavior; for example, he states that "thought is simply *behavior*—verbal or nonverbal, covert or overt."

As a counterargument to placing all emphasis on behavior, Karl Jaspers, an existential psychologist and philosopher, points up the importance of consciousness on self-awareness. According to Jaspers (1963, p. 121), consciousness has four formal characteristics: (a) the feeling of activity—an awareness of being active; (b) an awareness of unity; (c) awareness of identity; and (d) awareness of the self as distinct from an outer world and all that is not the self. Jaspers (1957, p. 4) stresses that "Man not only exists but knows that he exists."

It is apparent from this argument that psychologists over the years have been dealing with two different aspects of man—on the one hand, his actions, and, on the other, his self-awareness. It seems reasonable that man could be described in terms of either his behavior *or* his consciousness or both. Indeed, behavior is more accessible to scientific treatment, but the systematic study of consciousness might well give the psychologist additional understanding of man.

Man Is Predictable; or Man Is Unpredictable

Understanding, prediction, and control are considered to be the three objectives of science. Prediction and control are sometimes viewed as evidence of the scientist's understanding of the phenomenon under study. The objective of prediction rests on the assumption of determinism, the doctrine that all events have sufficient causes. Psychological science has traditionally accepted the objective of predicting human behavior and the associated doctrine of determinism.

Indeed, there have been some notable successes in predicting human behavior. Recent predictions of the number of fatalities resulting from automobile accidents on a given weekend, for example, have been within 5–10% of the actual fatalities. College administrators can predict fairly accurately the number of dropouts between the freshman and sophomore years. Further, a psychometrician can readily predict with a high degree of accuracy the distribution of scores resulting from an achievement test administered to a large sample of high school students. As another example, the mean reaction time to an auditory stimulus can be predicted rather accurately for a large group of subjects. All of these examples lend support to the doctrine of determinism.

There also have been some notable failures in attempts to predict human behavior. For example, the therapist has had little success in predicting the effectiveness of a given form of therapy applied to a given patient. Similarly, the guidance counselor has had relatively little success in predicting the occupation to be chosen by individual high school students. Such failures in predicting human behavior sometimes prompt one to question the basic assumption of determinism.

To illustrate the complexity associated with predicting the behavior of man—as contrasted with that of other complex systems—consider the following illustration. Suppose that a research psychologist has made a detailed study of a given human subject. He now tells the subject that he predicts that he will chose Alternative A rather than Alternative B under such and such conditions at some future point in time. Now, with this limited amount of information, what do you predict the subject will do?

The evidence suggests that there is support for both sides of this issue. It is difficult to argue with the deterministic doctrine that there are sufficient causes for human actions. Yet these causes may be unknown to either the observer or the subject himself. Thus, we must conclude that man is both predictable and unpredictable.

Man Is an Information Transmitter; or Man Is an Information Generator

The information theorist and cyberneticists have formulated a model of man as an information transmitter. W. Ross Ashby (p. 280), the cyberneticist, has proposed a basic postulate that says that man is just as intelligent as the amount of information fed into him.

Intelligence, whether of man or machine, is absolutely bounded. And what we can build into our machine is similarly bounded. The amount of intelligence we can get into a machine is absolutely bounded by the quantity of information that is put into it. We can get out of a machine as much intelligence as we like, if and only if we insure that at least the corresponding quantity of information gets into it.

Ashby believes that we could be much more scientific in our study of man if we would accept this basic postulate and give up the idea that man, in some mysterious manner, generates or creates new information over and above that which is fed into him.

The information-transmitting model of man is indeed very compelling. It promises considerable rigor and precision; it is compatible with both empiricism and stimulus-response theory; and it allows the behavioral scientist to build on past accomplishments in the fields of cybernetics, systems science, and mechanics.

But, alas, man does not want to be hemmed in by the information-transmitting model. Man asks questions that were never before asked; he identifies problems that were never before mentioned; he generates new ideas and theories; he formulates new courses of action; and he even formulates new models of man. Now to say that all of these human activities are merely a regrouping or recombining of existing elements is an oversimplification, a trivialization of human activity. Further, the assumption that all information has actually been in existence but hidden since the days of prehistoric man is not intuitively satisfying.

Considering the evidence in support of man both as an information transmitter and as an information generator, would it be reasonable to view man as both a *dependent* variable and an *independent* variable?

Man Lives in an Objective World; or Man Lives in a Subjective World

Man lives in an objective world. This is the world of facts and data. This is a reliable world; we agree that this or that event actually occurred.

This is a tangible world; we agree that this or that object is actually present. This is the general world that is common to all.

But man also lives in a subjective world. This is the individual's private world. The individual's feelings, emotions, and perceptions are very personal; he attempts to describe them in words but feels that he can never do complete justice to them.

In making this comparison between the objective world and subjective world, it is important to distinguish between two types of knowledge. We can know *about* something, or we can personally *experience* something. These two forms of knowledge are not the same.

We conclude that man is both object and subject. He is visible and tangible to others, yet he is that which thinks, feels, and perceives. The world looks at man, and he looks out at the world.

Are both the objective world and the subjective world available to the methods of science? Empiricism in general and the experimental method in particular can be applied to the objective world; phenomenology can be applied to the subjective world. In his efforts to understand man, perhaps the psychologist should attempt to understand both worlds.

Man Is a Rational Being; or Man Is an Arational Being

Man is sometimes referred to as a rational animal. He is intelligent; he exercises reason; he uses logic; and he argues from a scientific standpoint. Indeed, man is considered by man to be the *only* rational animal.

An individual's action or behavior, of course, is sometimes considered irrational. This is the opposite of rational. The irrational person defies the laws of reason; he contradicts that which is considered rational by some particular community of people.

But man also is arational. This characteristic transcends the rational-irrational continuum; it essentially constitutes another dimension of man's life. As an example of man being arational in his life, he makes a total commitment for a way of life. This commitment may be for a given faith, a religion, a philosophy, a vocation, or something else. It may be that any analysis of this decision would reveal that it was neither rational nor irrational—it merely was.

Man's actions are guided by both empirical knowledge and value judgment. Empirical knowledge belongs to the rational world, whereas value judgment often belongs to the arational world. According to Jaspers (1967, p. 60), "An empirical science cannot teach anybody what he ought to do, but only what he can do to reach his ends by statable means."

To achieve greater understanding of man, it would seem essential that the psychologist investigate man's arational world as well as his rational world.

One Man Is like Other Men; or Each Man Is Unique

A major goal of science is to develop general laws to describe, explain, and predict phenomena of the world. These laws are frequently based upon the study of one sample of objects or events and are then expected to be valid for a different sample of objects or events. It then follows that a major goal of psychology is to formulate general laws of man. In fact, without the possibility of developing general laws of human behavior, can psychology even be considered a science?

There is a considerable amount of evidence to support the possibility of developing general laws of human behavior. For example, the results of the reaction-time experiments have held up very well over the decades. Moreover, the many conditioning experiments conducted over the past several decades—either classical or operant—certainly suggest that man is governed by general laws applicable to all. Further, the cultural anthropologist and social psychologist have clearly pointed up the similarity of people in a given culture, suggesting that they might be taken from the same mold.

On the other hand, there is considerable evidence to support the concept of individual uniqueness. For example, there are thousands of possible gene combinations and thousands of different environmental determinants, all of which bring about millions of different personalities. Further, it is apparent that no two people ever live in exactly the same environment. As someone once said about two brothers living in the same house, with the same parents, and with the same diet, "Only one of the boys has an older brother." Then, too, we might reflect on a statement made by William James (1925, pp. 242–43): "An unlearned carpenter of my acquaintance once said in my hearing: 'There is very little difference between one man and another; but what little there is, *is very important.*'"

Our conclusion from this brief analysis is that the evidence appears to support both models of man: (a) that he is governed by general laws that apply to all of mankind, and (b) that each individual is unique in a nontrivial way.

Man Can Be Described Meaningfully in Absolute Terms; or Man Can Be Described Meaningfully in Relative Terms

If we believe that man can be described in absolute terms, we view such descriptions as being free from restriction or limitation. They are independent of arbitrary standards. Contrariwise, if we believe that man can be described in relative terms, we see him as existing or having his specific nature only by relation to something else. His actions are not absolute or independent.

If the concept of absoluteness is supported, we must accept the idea of general laws for all of mankind, and we also must accept the related idea that man is governed by irrefutable natural laws. On the other hand, if the concept of relativism is supported, we probably can have no general laws of man; we must realize that everything is contingent upon something else; and we can be certain of nothing.

It would appear that there is evidence to support the concept of absoluteness in psychology. The basic psychophysical laws, for example, might be characterized as irrefutable natural laws. Similarly, the basic laws of conditioning seem to be free from restriction or limitation. This evidence might lead us to conclude that man can be described in absolute terms.

But before we can become smug with this false sense of security, the relativist poses some challenging questions. For example: What is considered intelligent behavior? What is normal behavior? What is an aggressive personality? What is an overachiever? At best, it would seem that we could answer such questions only in relative terms. The answers would be contingent on some set of arbitrary standards.

What can we conclude? Perhaps man can be described meaningfully in either absolute terms or relative terms, depending on what aspect of man is being described.

Human Characteristics Can Be Investigated Independently of One Another; or Man Must Be Studied as a Whole

The question here is: Can man be understood by analyzing each attribute independently of the rest, or must man be studied as a whole in order to be understood? Another way of phrasing the question is: Can we take an additive approach to the study of man, or is a holistic or Gestalt approach required?

There is some evidence to support an additive approach to the study of man. Consider the following areas of research: psychophysics, physiological psychology, motor skills, classical and operant conditioning, and sensation. All of these areas have produced useful results from experimentation involving the manipulation of a single independent variable and measuring the concomitant effects on a single dependent variable. Useful results have been produced by investigating a single characteristic independently of other characteristics.

Other areas of research, however, point up the value of a holistic point of view. Research in the area of perception, for example, has demonstrated the effect of individual motivation on perception. Similarly, studies of human learning have shown the great importance of motivation and intelligence in learning behavior. Further, as one more example, research in the area of psychotherapy has revealed that the relation between the personality of the therapist and that of the patient has a significant influence on the effectiveness of the therapy. All of these examples illustrate the importance of the interactions and interdependencies of the many variables operating in any given situation.

Support for a holistic view of man is seen in the works of Polanyi and Teilhard de Chardin, to mention only two. Polanyi (p. 47) gives this example: "Take a watch to pieces and examine, however carefully, its separate parts in turn, and you will never come across the principles by which a watch keeps time." Teilhard de Chardin (p. 110) says:

In its construction, it is true, every organism is always and inevitably reducible into its component parts. But it by no means follows that the sum of the parts is the same as the whole, or that, in the whole, some specifically new value may not emerge.

What can be concluded from this discussion? First, it would seem that a detailed analysis of man is essential for a systematic understanding. Yet, synthesis also is required in order to understand the many interactions and interdependencies. We can conclude that the most effective strategy for the behavioral scientist might be that used by the systems analyst —a working back and forth between analysis and synthesis.

Man Is a Reality; or Man Is a Potentiality

Is man a reality? If so, he exists as fact; he is actual; he has objective existence. Or is man a potentiality? If so, he represents possibility rather than actuality; he is capable of being or becoming. The question here is: Can we study man as an actually existing entity—as we would study any other complex system—or must we view man as a completely dynamic entity, one that is constantly emerging or becoming?

There is support for the view of man as an actuality. The numerous results from the many years of research in the area of experimental psychology, for example, suggest that man is definable and measurable, and is capable of being investigated as an actually existing complex system. Further, the many current studies in the area of cybernetics, which point up similarities between man and machine, lend credence to the concept of man as an existing system.

There also is evidence to support the view of man as a potentiality. For example, case studies have revealed that long-term criminals have experienced religious conversions and then completely changed their way of life. Further, complete personality transformations have resulted from psychoanalysis and electroshock therapy. Indeed, man is changeable, and any given individual can become something quite different from what he was in the past.

Maslow (p. 59) has stressed the importance of human potentiality:

I think it fair to say that no theory of psychology will ever be complete that does not centrally incorporate the concept that man has his future within him, dynamically active at this present moment.

What can we conclude? Only that man is both a reality and a potentiality. He represents objective existence, yet he can move toward any one of many different future states that are essentially unpredictable.

Man Is Knowable in Scientific Terms; or Man Is More than We Can Ever Know About Him

This final issue is basic to the entire study of man, and is closely tied to all the previous issues discussed. Is man knowable in scientific terms, or is man more than we can ever know about him?

There are many centuries of evidence to support the idea that man is scientifically knowable. Aristotle, for example, applied the same logic to his study of man as he did to other phenomena in the world. Further, volumes of data resulting from psychological experiments since the time of Wundt's founding of the first experimental psychology laboratory in 1879 indicate that man is scientifically knowable. Then, too, the many laboratory experiments and fields studies recently conducted by the different disciplines included in the behavioral and social sciences certainly suggest that man is scientifically knowable.

Yet, there also is support for the idea that man is more than we can ever know about him. Man has continued to transcend himself over the past million or so years, as demonstrated by the theory of evolution. Further, on logical grounds, it can be demonstrated that man becomes something different every time he gains new knowledege about himself, which would suggest that man is truly an "open system."

It is apparent that we know very little about man. William James (1956, p. 54) says, "Our science is a drop, our ignorance a sea." Erich Fromm (p. 31) believes that "Even if we knew a thousand times more of ourselves, we would never reach bottom."

What can we conclude? We must conclude that man is scientifically knowable—at least to a point. Yet there is no evidence to support the idea that man is—or ever will be—*completely* knowable.

CONCLUSIONS

This paper has presented two models of man:

1. The behavioristic model: Man can be described meaningfully in terms of his behavior; he is predictable; he is an information transmitter; he lives in an objective world; he is rational; he has traits in common with other men; he may be described in absolute terms; his characteristics can be studied independently of one another; he is a reality; and he is knowable in scientific terms.

2. The phenomenological model: Man can be described meaningfully in terms of his consciousness; he is unpredictable; he is an information generator; he lives in a subjective world; he is arational; he is unique alongside millions of other unique personalities; he can be described in relative terms; he must be studied in a holistic manner; he is a potentiality; and he is more than we can ever know about him.

This analysis of behaviorism and phenomenology leads to these conclusions:

1. The acceptance of either the behavioristic model or a phenomenological model has important implications in the everyday world. The choice of one versus the other could greatly influence human activities (either behavior or awareness) in such areas as education, psychiatry, theology, behavioral science, law, politics, marketing, advertising, and even parenthood. Thus, this ongoing debate is not just an academic exercise.

2. There appears to be truth in both views of man. The evidence that has been presented lends credence to both the behavioristic model and the phenomenological model. Indeed, it would be premature for psychology to accept either model as the final model.

3. A given behavioral scientist may find that both models are useful, depending upon the problem under study. The phenomenological model, for example, might be quite appropriate for the investigation of the creative process in scientists. On the other-hand, the behavioristic model might be very useful in the study of environmental factors that motivate a given population of subjects to behave in a certain manner.

4. Finally, we must conclude that the behaviorist and the phenomenologist should listen to each other. Both, as scientists, should be willing to listen to opposing points of view. Each should endeavor to understand what the other is trying to say. It would appear that a dialogue is in order.

REFERENCES

G. W. Allport. *Becoming: Basic Considerations for a Psychology of Personality*. New Haven: Yale University Press, 1955.

W .R. Ashby. "What Is an Intelligent Machine?" *Proceedings of the Western Joint Computer Conference*, 1961, 19, 275–80.

P. T. de Chardin. *The Phenomenon of Man*. New York: Harper and Row, 1961 (Harper Torchbook Edition).

E. Fromm. *The Art of Loving*. New York: Harper and Row, 1956.

W. James. "The Individual and Society." In *The Philosophy of William James*. New York: Modern Library, 1925. (Orig. publ. 1897).

———. *The Will to Believe and Other Essays on Popular Philosophy*. New York: Dover, 1956 (Orig. publ. 1896).

K. Jaspers. *Man in the Modern Age*. New York: Doubleday, 1957 (Orig. publ. in Germany, 1931).

———. *General Psychopathology*. Manchester, England: Manchester University Press, 1963 (Pub. in the United States by University of Chicago Press).

———. *Philosophy Is for Everyman*. New York: Harcourt, Brace and World, 1967.

S. Koch. "Psychology and Emerging Conceptions of Knowledge as Unitary." In T. W. Wann (ed.), 1964.

R. B. MacLeod. "Phenomenology: A Challenge to Experimental Psychology." In T. W. Wann (ed.), 1964.

N. Malcolm. "Behaviorism as a Philosophy of Psychology." In T. W. Wann (ed.), 1964.

A. H. Maslow. "Existential Psychology: What's in It for Us?" In R. May (ed.), *Existential Psychology*. New York: Random House, 1961.

M. Polanyi. *The Study of Man*. Chicago: University of Chicago Press, 1963 (First Phoenix Edition).

C. R. Rogers. "Toward a Science of the Person." In T. W. Wann (ed.), 1964.

B. F. Skinner. *Verbal Behavior*. New York: Appleton-Century-Crofts, 1957.

———. "Behaviorism at Fifty." In T. W. Wann (ed.), 1964.

T. W. Wann (ed.). *Behaviorism and Phenomenology: Contrasting Bases for Modern Psychology*. Chicago: University of Chicago Press, 1964.

R. S. Woodworth and M. R. Sheehan. *Contemporary Schools of Psychology*. New York: Ronald Press, 1964.

13.

ARTHUR W. COMBS

SEEING IS BEHAVING

How effective we are in dealing with the great human problem of any generation will depend in large measure upon the accuracy and scope of the ideas we hold about what people are like and why they behave as they do. This is particularly true for what we do as educators. People can only behave in terms of what seems to them to be so. Hence, the methods we use to solve our problems of curriculum will depend upon what we believe about the nature of the people we seek to teach. Whenever, therefore, science changes our ideas of what people are like, it must have far-reaching implications for our profession.

In recent years, the social sciences have been discovering some fascinating and exciting new ways of looking at human behavior, and these discoveries seem to me to have vast implications for the whole field of education. In this article I would like to state just two of these principles and point out some of the things it seems to me they mean for education.

BEHAVIOR IS A PERSONAL MATTER

The first principle is this: *People do not behave according to the facts as others see them; they behave in terms of what seems to them to be so.* The psychologist expresses this technically as: Behavior is a function of perception. What affects human behavior, we are beginning to understand, is not so much the forces exerted on people from without as the meanings existing for the individual within. It is feelings, beliefs, convictions, attitudes and understandings of the person who is behaving that constitute the directing forces of behavior. In an election, for example, people who vote for the Democrats believe that the Democrats will save the nation while the Republicans will certainly ruin it. The reverse is true of the people who vote the other way. Each side behaves in terms

From *Educational Leadership* 16 (October, 1958), 21–26. Reprinted with permission of the Association for Supervision and Curriculum Development and Arthur W. Combs. Copyright © 1958 by the Association for Supervision and Curriculum Development.

of what seems to it to be so. But what is *really* the fact of the matter we shall never know, for only one party gets elected! In order to understand the behavior of people we must understand how things seem to them.

Our failure to understand this simple and "obvious" fact about behavior is one of the most potent causes of misunderstanding and failure in dealing with human problems. A good example may be seen in the case of the child who feels that people do not like him. Feeling that he is unliked and unwanted, the child is likely to make himself obnoxious in his attempts to get the attention of adults who surround him. When company comes, for example, he is likely to make a nuisance of himself in his attempts to attract attention. Parents seeking to put a stop to this kind of annoying behavior may say, "For goodness sake, Jimmy, stop annoying Mr. Jones and go to your room!" Such behavior on the part of adults simply serves to prove what the child already believes —"People don't like me very well!"

When we fail to understand how things seem to people with whom we are working, we may make serious errors in our efforts to deal with them. The moment, however, we understand an individual's behavior as it seems to him, our own behavior can be much more accurate, realistic, precise and effective. If a child *thinks* his teacher is unfair, it doesn't make much difference whether the teacher is *really* unfair or not. If a child thinks his teacher is unfair, he behaves as though she were. Whether she is *really* unfair or not is, as the lawyers say, "irrelevant and immaterial information" as far as the child is concerned. In this sense, seeing is not only believing; seeing is behaving! To understand behavior we need to understand the personal meanings existing for the people who are behaving.

THE EFFECT OF THE CONCEPT OF SELF

The second important point we are currently discovering is this: *The most important ideas which affect people's behavior are those ideas they have about themselves.* This, the psychologist refers to as the *self concept.* The beliefs we hold about ourselves, we are learning, are among the most important determinants of behavior. People who see themselves as men behave like men; people who see themselves as women, behave like women. Our self concepts even affect the things we see and hear. If you don't think so, try going window shopping with a member of the opposite sex.

The self concept, we are finding, is so tremendously important that it affects practically everything we do. We are discovering that a child's success in school depends in very large measure upon the kind of self concepts he has about himself. Some years ago, Prescott Lecky observed that children often made about the same number of errors in spelling per page when they were writing free material, despite the difficulty of the material! One would normally expect more errors on harder material, but these children spelled as though they were responding to a built-in quota. It occurred to Lecky that they were behaving more in terms of their beliefs about spelling than in terms of their actual skills. Accordingly, he arranged to have a group of these children spend some time with a counselor who helped them to explore themselves and their feelings about their abilities to spell. As a consequence of these discussions an amazing thing happened. Despite the fact that these children had no additional work in spelling whatever, their spelling improved tremendously, and several of the children took up spelling as a hobby!

We are finding a similar phenomenon in the field of reading. Nowadays we catch children's visual difficulties fairly early so that it is rare these days to find a child coming to the reading clinic with anything very wrong with his eyes. More often than not, when a child is unable to read, the difficulty seems to lie in the fact that he has developed *an idea about himself* as a person who cannot read. Having developed such an idea, he gets caught in a vicious circle that goes something like this: Believing he cannot read, the child avoids reading and thus avoids the very practice which might make it possible for him to learn. Furthermore, believing that he does not read very well, he reads poorly when asked to do so. His teacher, in turn, observing this weakness, says, "My goodness, Johnny, you don't read very well!" which proves what he already thinks! Once having developed the idea that he cannot read, a child's experience confirms his belief, and his teacher, who should know, corroborates it. Just to make sure that the lesson is well learned, moreover, we may also send home a failing grade on his report card so that his parents can tell him too!

We are beginning to discover that the self concept acts very much like a quota for an individual. What a person believes about himself establishes what he can and will do. Once a self concept is established, furthermore, it is a very difficult thing to change, even if we would like to change it in a positive direction. The young man coming to the university believing that he is not very bright, for example, who is told by the test administrator that he has done very well, responds: "Are you sure? There must be some mistake!"

We are even discovering that the question of adjustment or maladjustment is very largely a question of the self concepts people have about themselves. Well-adjusted people, we now observe, are those who see themselves as liked, wanted, acceptable, able—as people of dignity and integrity. People who see themselves so are no trouble to anybody. They get along fine in our society. They are essentially happy people who work efficiently and effectively, and rarely cause difficulty in school or out. The people who cause us difficulty in our society are, almost without exception, those who see themselves as unliked, unwanted, unacceptable, unable, undignified, unworthy, and the like. These are the frustrated people of our generation who frustrate us. They are the maladjusted, unhappy ones who fill our jails, our mental hospitals and institutions.

Some Implications for Education

We have now stated two modern principles of behavior:

1. That people behave according to how things seem to them.
2. That the most important ideas any of us ever have are those ideas we hold about ourselves.

These two very simple ideas have vast implications for education. In some ways they corroborate things we educators have been feeling all along. They also raise questions about some of the things we have been doing. And, finally, they seem to point to some new ways of solving old problems. In the remainder of this article I would like to point out two or three of the important implications these ideas seem to have for me.

EDUCATION MUST DEAL WITH MEANINGS

If it is true that behavior is a function of how things seem to people, then education to be effective must deal with people's *meanings*—not just facts. As educators, we have done pretty well in gathering information and in making information available to people. Where we get into difficulty, however, is in helping people to discover the meaning of information in such a way that they will *behave differently* as a result of the process. When people misbehave it is rarely because they do not know what they should do. Most of us already know a great deal better than we behave. We are like the old farmer who said when they asked him why he wasn't using modern methods, "Heck, I ain't farming now half as well as I know how!"

It is over a failure to understand this problem that we sometimes get into communication difficulties with the public. The public wants the same thing we do. They want kids who *know* something, who *under-*

stand something, but most of all, who *behave* as though they know something. So do we. When the public, however, sees children behaving inadequately, it is likely to assume that the reason they behave so is because they don't *know* any better. But you and I as teachers are aware that this is not the problem. We know that it is very rare that teachers fail because of their lack of knowledge of subject matter. When teachers fail it is almost always because they are unable to bring about the third step we have been talking about—namely, how you get information translated into behavior.

Modern psychology tells us that it is only when knowledge becomes meaning that behavior is affected. If it is meanings that affect human behavior, then it is meanings with which we educators must deal. We will need to concern ourselves with different kinds of facts. We will have to deal with convictions, beliefs, attitudes, feelings, ideas, concepts and understandings. I suspect that we have not always done this in our zeal to "get the facts" from books. Sometimes we have failed to understand that people's behavior is not the result of objective facts, but of *personal* facts, the meaning things have for the behaver himself. I am afraid we have too often said to the child, "George, I am not interested in what you think; what are the facts?" Small wonder that some children conclude that what goes on in school has nothing to do with life in a meaningful way at all.

Since personal meanings lie inside people, they are not open to direct manipulation. To change meanings we must find effective ways of helping students explore and discover for themselves. We have to let personal meanings become an integral part of the curriculum. Many schools and many teachers have already learned to do this with great skill. We need now to push the movement forward.

One of the most exciting implications of these new principles is this: If it is true that behavior is a function of perception, then the causes of behavior lie fundamentally in the present and not in the past. Psychologists for several generations have told us that in order to understand an individual we need to know all that has happened to him in the past. As a result many teachers have often felt helpless to deal with a child because for one reason or other they were unable to acquire knowledge of all his past experiences. Many educators have never been entirely happy with this point of view. We have often felt, as Gordon Allport once expressed it, that "people are busy living their lives forward while psychologists busily trace them backwards!" We are now finding that many modern psychologists are providing support for our suspicion that this preoccupation with the past may not always be essential.

If it is true that behavior is a function of perception, then behavior is a result of how people are perceiving right now, *today, as of this moment!* This understanding opens a whole new world for education. This is not to say that behavior is not *also* the result of what has happened in the past. We can look at the causes of behavior in two ways. A person's behavior is *historically* the result of all the things that have happened to him in the past. It is *immediately* the result of how things seem to him at this moment. For example, a child who has been badly rejected in his youth may come to feel about himself that he is unliked, unwanted, unacceptable, that the world is a pretty tough place, almost too much for what he has to offer. These feelings he has acquired, of course, because of the things that have happened to him. But his behavior today, now, as of this moment, is the result of how he is *feeling* today. This way of looking at behavior opens a whole new frontier for educational practice.

When we believed that behavior was entirely a function of the past, there was, of course, very little we could do. It had all been done. Such a belief leads to preoccupation with the child's history instead of what is going on at the moment. The historical view of causation also encourages the old army game of passing the buck. The college says, "What can you do with youngsters who come so badly prepared from high school?" The high school says, "What can you do for the child who comes to you like this from elementary school?" and the elementary school teachers say, "What can you do with a child from a home like that?" The poor parent in our society is low man on the totem pole. He's stuck with it; he doesn't have anybody he can pass the blame to, except maybe to say, "Well, he gets it from the father's side of the family!"

If we believe that a child's behavior is solely the result of the forces working upon him, there is very little we can do to help, and we are always able to charge off our failures to other people. If, however, behavior is a function of perception, then there are tremendous things we can do in the present. We can help a person to see differently now, even if we cannot change his past. It means that you and I can help children in school without the necessity of having to change their environments. It means that there is something we can do for *every* child no matter what kind of background he comes from. Although we can rarely do much about the past, there are important things we can do about the present.

This new understanding also lifts a great weight from the teacher's shoulders. It means that we do not have to be social workers or psychiatrists, we can just be teachers! It means we do not have to pry, we do not have to know all about a child's background in order to be able to deal with him effectively. This is not to say that knowledge of his past and of his home situation might not be helpful. It does mean that we *do not have to have it* as an absolute essential. I don't know how you feel about this, but this sets me free to do a lot of things I was never able to do before. This simple idea has already caused revolutions in the field of social work, in psychotherapy and in the field of human relations. It seems equally promising in what it may offer to education.

For one thing, teachers do not have to feel defeated. If behavior is a function of perception, then no matter what goes on elsewhere in the child's life, it is still important what you and I do as teachers. People get their perceptions from those who surround them, and that means us. It may be that there are some children with whom we have to deal who are so sick that we cannot make *all* the difference. We may not be able to change a child completely, but neither are we helpless. Fritz Redl once said in a speech, "You know, the difference between a good child and a naughty child is not very great. The difference, however, between a naughty child and a real tough delinquent is a very great distance. Wouldn't it be wonderful if we could just keep them naughty?" I find this sentiment very reassuring. I think that what Redl is trying to tell us is that none of us need feel defeated. That whatever we do is *always* important even though for a particular child it may not be enough to produce immediate results.

Finally, if the self concept is as important as modern psychology tells us, this fact has vast importance of curriculum construction and design. One of the great tragedies of our time is that we have literally hundreds of thousands of people in our society who are the prisoners of their own perceptions. Believing they can only do x well, they only do x much. The rest of us, seeing them do only x much, say, "Well, that's an x much person," and this just proves what these people have thought in the first place! Such people are the victims of their own self concepts. Everyone loses as a result of this great waste of human potential.

But people get their self concepts from the ways they have been treated by the persons who surround them during their growing up. From the minute the child is born we begin to teach him who he is and what he is. Whether we are helpful, or hindering, or of no account at all in the development of children's self concepts will depend upon ourselves. We *can* behave in ways that don't count, ways that have nothing to do with meanings, and they will quickly disregard us. Or, we *can* behave in ways that are important in helping them discover who they are and what they are—in a positive fashion. We are, in a sense, the architects of children's self concepts.

Society needs adequate, well-adjusted, informed people as never before in history. What, then, shall we do to develop these kinds of people? I think the answer lies in the above definitions of the kinds of people we want. Earlier in this article we stated that whether or not an individual was likely to be well adjusted was largely a matter of his self concept. We observed that people who see themselves as liked, wanted, acceptable, able, dignified, worthy, etc., are the kinds who make effective, efficient citizens. People, on the other hand, who see themselves as unliked, unwanted, unacceptable, unable . . . are the ones who cause us trouble. If this is true, we do not have to be psychiatrists to help children grow.

To be effective in these terms, we need teachers who can understand and perceive how a child is thinking and feeling. We need teachers who can understand the impact of the ways they are behaving and the things they are doing on the perception of children. We need teachers skilled in helping children explore and discover themselves and their relationship to the world in which they live. In the final analysis, the question of curriculum construction boils down to this: How can a child feel liked, unless somebody likes him? How can a child feel wanted, unless somebody wants him? How can a child feel acceptable, unless somebody accepts him? And how can a child feel able, unless somewhere he has some success? In our answers to these questions related to the kinds of self concepts we seek lie the basic criteria for curriculum change and improvement.

14.

CLARK E. MOUSTAKAS

TRUE EXPERIENCE AND THE SELF

Experience is true to the person when he is himself alone. In such experience perception is unique and undifferentiated. The individual is free to discover and express his potentialities. In true experience every expression

"True Experience and the Self" by Clark E. Moustakas from *The Self* edited by Clark E. Moustakas. Copyright © 1956 by Clark E. Moustakas. By permission of Harper & Row, Publishers.

is creative, the creation of the person one is and is becoming. There is only the exploring, spontaneously expressing self, finding satisfaction in personal being.

There are no goals to pursue, directions to follow, or techniques to use. There is the growing, experiencing self, significance and meaning in personal experience, and exploration and discovery. True experience may be understood through empathy in communal living or in self-expression or utterance. But it cannot be communicated. To communicate the self is to abstract from it, speak of its aspects or parts and thus do violence to it. Communication represents or symbolizes the self. It distinguishes, compares, and characterizes. Communication is used to influence and often to change. Communication requires explanation, analysis, description, and clarification. It must make what is known by one person common to be understood. The self is not its symbol or external behavior. The self is itself alone existing as a totality and constantly emerging. It can be understood only as unique personal experience. Self-expression is not persuasive and is without special purpose or function. The self is undifferentiated in time and space. It is being, becoming, moving, undivided from the world of nature or the social world.

True being is self and other, individual and universal, personal and cultural. It cannot be understood by comparison, evaluation, diagnosis, or analysis. Such an approach breaks up an experience and violates its nature.

From the beginning the human person wants to feel that his who-ness is respected and his individuality is treasured. Too often the person is respected for what he represents in intelligence, achievement, or social status. This distorts the real nature of the person and interferes with human understandingness. It blocks the potential forces that exist within the person for creativity, for unique, peculiar, and idiosyncratic expression.

True growth, actualization of one's potential, occurs in a setting where the person is felt and experienced as sheer personal being. In such an atmosphere the person is free to explore his capacities and to discover for himself meanings and values of life consistent with the self.

In spite of all the advances in tests and measurements and in analyzing human behavior, understanding the person from his own point of view, in the light of his own unique experience, is the most real way of knowing him. More and more we are realizing that the self-expression of the individual in true experience is complete in itself. To see the person as he sees himself is the deepest way to know him and respect him.

Even the growing evidence, however, has not helped us to feel more trust in individual self-expression. The tendency remains to rely heavily on external measures. Recently Allport (1953) reported a series of studies in which the great need for food among men on a starvation diet failed to be uncovered on tests given these men. The number of food associations actually declined with longer periods of fasting. No one would question the importance of strong hunger in motivating behavior, yet it could not be determined without approaching the men directly and asking them to tell about this important need.

Adler (1927) once wrote that the only people who really know human nature are those who have experienced the worth and value of others through their own empathy. Correspondence of perceptual experience is perhaps the best basis for understanding what an experience means to another individual, but without such similarity of perception we can still know the meanings that experiences have for others through listening with objectivity and warmth, through attempting to understand the essence of the experience through the perceptions of the other person. Objectivity as used here refers to seeing what an experience is for another person, not how it fits or relates to other experiences, not what causes it, why it exists, or for what purpose. It is an attempt to see attitudes and concepts, beliefs and values of an individual as they are to him, not what they were or will become. The experience of the other person as he perceives it is sufficient unto itself, true and of value as itself, understood in terms of itself.

Knowing the content of individual experience does not explain the unique meaning or totality any more than knowing that a tree has a trunk and branches tells how it will be perceived by the different people who see it. The "facts" regarding human behavior have little meanings in themselves. It is the manner in which they are perceived and known that tells how they will be expressed in behavior. Experiments at the Hanover Institute (Kelley, 1947) have shown that we do not get our perceptions from the things around us, but that our perceptions come from us. There is no reality except individual reality and that is based on a background of unique experience.

It sometimes requires complex and thorough examination to diagnose tuberculosis, cancer, or a heart ailment in an individual, but knowing the presence of such a serious illness does not tell what it will mean in the life of an individual or his family. A group of physicians may find it easy to communicate with each other regarding the nature of an illness, but difficult to talk to patients when they have not taken into account the perceptions the patient has of his illness. To the extent that physicians fail to consider the personal experiences and meanings of the individual, they do not understand the full nature of the illness and often talk in authoritative terms disclosing their lack of real knowledge. These physicians show complete faith in the object or the part which has medical significance but little recognition of the person as a unique, special individual who in some ways is unlike any other person who has had a painful disease. When the physician doubts the impact of the individual's self-perception on his illness, he distrusts the potential curative powers within the person and his striving for health. This threatens the strength of being and self-confidence of the individual.

Facts regarding human living gain their full value when examined in the context of unique individual experience. Most experts are expert in pointing out facts, in making evaluations and diagnoses, but when they fail to recognize that facts gain their meaning in a personal context and these meanings differ for different individuals, then they fail to understand fully the true nature of the fact. When experts discard the individual's discrete experiences as insignificant, they often make generalizations about human growth and development which contradict the true nature of the person. Or they give recommendations which are inconsistent with the individual's purposes and values and interfere with his growth. These recommendations based on "facts" cannot be accepted and utilized and sometimes frighten and disturb the person.

In the final analysis the individual must know for himself the totality that he is. He alone has had touch with all his experiences. He alone knows his feelings and thoughts and what his experiences mean to him. The meaning depends on the values involved in the situation, event, or experience and these values come from the person's personal background. The individual alone can tell the true meaning of his experience.

There is a tendency among analytic people to see an individual in terms of someone else—his father, mother, or siblings. This approach distorts the real nature of the person and interferes with valid understandings of him. One does not recognize the otherness of a person as a reality by projecting into him someone else or by abstracting out of him transferred feelings and attitudes. And when one sees in a person his father or mother or anyone else, one ignores the person as he really is. Angyal (1951) regards this as a fundamental disregard for and destructive attitude toward the other person. He points out that real understanding of the other person is not some sort of shrewd analysis which has a keen eye for the weaknesses of of people but a deep perception of the core, of the essential nature of the other person as he is.

All psychological phenomena can be understood as illustrative of the single principle of unity or self-consistency (Lecky, 1951). When the individual is free to be himself his acts are always consistent with his values. No matter what we are told, our own perceptions of ourselves will always seem substantial and solid to us. Resistance is a way for the individual to maintain consistency of self in the light of external pressure. It is a healthy response, a sign that the will of the individual is still intact.

It is an effort by the individual to sustain the integrity of the self. When the individual submits without wanting to submit, he is weakened and unable to function effectively. Conformity blocks creativity while freedom and spontaneity foster growth.

Rank stressed the importance of positive will expression. He believed that the denial of will expression is the essence of neurosis. His aim was to strengthen will, not weaken it. In the light of external pressures (attempts to frighten and even terrify the person, to force him to submit to symbols, standards, and values outside himself) which, yielded to, may mean disintegration of self and destruction of will, the individual must often call upon the forces within himself, follow his internal cues, awareness, and direction, maintain his position and assert himself in order not to seriously distort his essence, his being. When the individual submits while the very core of his existence cries out against submission, the health and stability of the person is seriously impaired and he is often unable to think, decide, or act. Sometimes he becomes the expectations, convictions, and values of others.

It is within the nature of the individual to actualize himself and become whatever he is meant to be, to explore his individual potential as fully as possible (Goldstein, 1940, Horney, 1950). He will resist all attempts to change him that threaten his perception of self, and will respond favorably to situations which permit him to express and explore his potentials. The individual will not respond to stimuli which are inadequate to him. Such stimuli can be effective only if they are very strong and force themselves upon him. Then the person is driven into a catastrophic situation not only because he is unable to react adequately but also because he is shocked and disturbed, sometimes so severely he is unable to react at all. Thus when we force an individual to behave according to external values, when we impose our convictions on the other person, we impair his creativity and his will to explore and actualize.

Maintenance of the real self is of primary significance for the individual. It is the most stable consistent value in his life. The real self is the central core within each individual which is the deep source of growth. To operate in terms of the persons we are is natural, comforting, and satisfying. It permits us to be creative, to utilize our capacities.

It is not possible to accept the other person and at the same time openly reject his values and ideas. Such a concept is antithetical to the consistency of self. We cannot separate the individual from his behavior and say we accept him but do not accept his behavior. This type of distinction is possible when the self is viewed in terms of categories instead of holism or unity. Individuals do not see themselves in categories. Behavior is self.

Sometimes people are forced to reject the behavior of another person and, therefore, to reject the person. This rejection may be less severe if one focuses on the behavior itself. However, by rejecting the behavior of the person, one cannot escape a rejection of the person himself. Even though this is so, if the rejection occurs only occasionally in a relationship and it is limited to the behavioral act while at the same time the feelings are recognized and accepted, a general attitude of acceptance can still exist and be conveyed.

In the face of drastic action that will markedly affect the behavior of the person, can the individual continue to be silent and objective or must he express his own convictions? Must he live by whoever he is? Integrity of the self is the main source of strength in the individual. To be untrue to oneself, dishonest, or insincere may result in self-impairment. When the self is threatened and endangered, continued attempts completely to accept the other might eventuate in a disorganization of oneself. Two teachers may be able to listen and accept one another's opposing approaches within the same school system as long as administrative changes which will affect their work are not contemplated. Two teachers with varying philosophies and ideas may be able to work effectively in adjacent rooms, but if they had to work with the same group of children at the same time, it would be difficult for them to accept one another's methods and work harmoniously.

The following principles summarize the basic approach and recognition of the self in true experience and the creation of human understandingness.

1. The individual knows himself better than anyone else.
2. Only the individual himself can develop his potentialities.
3. The individual's perception of his own feelings, attitudes, and ideas is more valid than any outside diagnosis can be.
4. Behavior can best be understood from the individual's own point of view.
5. The individual responds in such ways as to be consistent with himself.
6. The individual's perception of himself determines how he will behave.
7. Objects have no meaning in themselves. Individuals give meanings and reality to them. These meanings reflect the individual's background.
8. Every individual is logical in the context of his own personal experience. His point of view may seem illogical to others when he is not understood.
9. As long as the individual accepts himself, he will continue to grow and develop his potentialities. When he does not accept himself, much

of his energies will be used to defend rather than explore and to actualize himself.

10. Every individual wants to grow toward self-fulfillment. These growth strivings are present at all times.

11. An individual learns significantly only those things which are involved in the maintenance or enhancement of *self*. No one can force the individual to permanent or creative learning. He will learn only if he wills to. Any other type of learning is temporary and inconsistent with the self and will disappear as soon as threat is removed.

12. Concepts, ideas, symbols, and events can be denied or distorted but experience is experienced in the unique reality of the individual person and cannot be untrue to itself. If it threatens the maintenance or enhancement of self, the experience will be of little relevance or consequence to the individual though it may temporarily stifle further growth.

13. We cannot teach another person directly and we cannot facilitate real learning in the sense of making it easier. We can make learning for another person possible by providing information, the setting, atmosphere, materials, resources, and by being there. The learning process itself is a unique individualistic experience. It may be a difficult experience for the individual person even if it has significance for the enhancement of self.

14. Under threat the self is less open to spontaneous expression; that is, is more passive and controlled. When free from threat the self is more open, that is, free to be and to strive for actualization.

The educational situation which most effectively promotes significant learning is one in which (a) the threat to the self of the learner is at a minimum while at the same time the uniqueness of the individual is regarded as worthwhile and is deeply respected, and (b) the person is free to explore the materials and resources which are available to him in the light of his own interests and potentiality.

Most research studies on the self have been highly structured and intellectualized. An increasingly narrow definition is emerging. Descriptions imply and sometimes clearly state that a definition of self is self. Statements an individual can make about himself or that someone else makes about him are tabulated and the score an individual receives is interpreted as an expression of the individual's self. These reports abstract the self into such parts as "self-concept," "negative-self," "inferred-self," and "ideal-self." The self finally becomes limited to verbal statements and categories. Viewing the self as categories, characteristics, and in other abstractive ways makes such studies possible, but they do not enrich our understanding of the experience of self. Thus conceptions of self are shared, communicated, and conveyed in words but the natural, spontaneous immanence of self is somehow lost.

The self is not its definition or description but rather the central being of the individual person. The self is not definable in words. Any verbal analysis tends to categorize or segment the self into communicable aspects or parts. The self can only be experienced. Any attempt to convey its meaning verbally must be based on function or structure and on language which can be partially understood. Therefore comparison, relatedness, and association to situations and events are required in a communicable definition of self. When the self is understood only in words the experience of the self is lost. The self as experienced involves the totality of the individual. It is a natural, automatic, and complete expression, only partially available to verbal communication. Understanding of self is possible through unqualified perception and empathy, that is, human presence and being.

When the focus is placed on words of the self rather than on the self itself, the unique perception of the individual person as expressed in the totality of his behavior is not really understood. In such a setting the opportunity for fuller expression of uniqueness and individuality is threatened. When we attempt to abstract from our experience facts, knowledge, and information we tend to focus on limited aspects of experience which will have relevance to another person, which can be conveyed in precise words. In that way, we tend to close the possibility for fuller impact, meaning, and significance of experience as it influences us naturally and automatically in the pursuit and exploration of our potentialities.

Fromm (1947) has emphasized that the duty to be alive is the same as the duty to become oneself. Somehow we do not have faith that if we simply permit a person to explore his interests in his own way he will become a truly human person. We fear that the individual will develop antisocial tendencies, emerge as inadequate, or become socially destructive. Autonomy is regarded with suspicion or distrust or simply interpreted and categorized as resistant behavior. We feel we have to condition the person, teach him directly, keep after him to socialize him and make him behave like others. We do not trust ourselves or have enough confidence that our own personal experiences with children will provide a healthy basis for social growth. We do not accept our own being, we do not own the self, when we act on external standards, judgments, and expectations. We seem satisfied when the child is like others and troubled when he turns out to be different.

Individuality must be encouraged, not stifled. Only what is true and therefore of value to society can emerge from individual interests, that is, expressions of one's true nature. All children may need love, safety, belongingness, acceptance, and respect as basic conditions to their growth, and when these conditions are provided by the human environment, growth will occur naturally through the person's potential. Adults may offer resources, make available opportunities, and give information and help when it is meaningful to the child, but to force standards, social values, and concepts on the child is to stifle his potential creativity and difference.

Relations must be such that the person is free to affirm, express, actualize, and experience his own uniqueness. Adults help to make this possible when they show they deeply care for him, respect his individuality, and accept the child's being without qualification. To permit the person to be and become is not to promote selfishness, but to affirm the person's truly human self.

Somehow we must remove the beliefs that make men mistrust themselves and each other. Being given the opportunity to grow and to actualize one's self provides the best basis for interacting with others, and within the framework of groups and society. When individuals are free to operate in terms of their real selves, they do not violate the trust that is conveyed to them. Under such an atmosphere, individual integrity is maintained and fostered and society is enriched. We must not accept as intrinsic an antagonism between individual interests and social interests. Maslow (1954) has strongly emphasized that this kind of antagonism exists only in a sick society. But it need not be true. Individual and social interests are synergetic, *not* antagonistic. Creative individual expression, that is, expression of one's own intrinsic nature, results in social creativity and growth which in turn encourage and free the individual to further self-expression and discovery.

REFERENCES

Alfred Adler. *Understanding Human Nature.* New York: Greenberg Publishers, Inc., 1927.

Gordon W. Allport. "The Trend in Motivational Theory." *American Journal of Orthopsychiatry*, 23:107-19 (1953).

Andras Angyal. "A Theoretical Model for Personality Studies." *Journal of Personality*, 20:131-41 (1951).

Erich Fromm. *Man for Himself: An Inquiry into the Psychology of Ethics.* New York: Rinehart and Company, Inc., 1947.

Kurt Goldstein. *Human Nature: In the Light of Psychotherapy.* Cambridge: Harvard University Press, 1940.

Karen Horney. *Neurosis and Human Growth.* New York: W. W. Norton & Company, Inc., 1950.

Earl C. Kelley. *Education for What Is Read*. New York: Harper & Brothers, 1947.

Prescott Lecky. *Self-Consistency: A Theory of Personality*. Frederick C. Thorne, ed. New York: Island Press, 1951.

A. H. Maslow. "The Instinctoid Nature of Basic Needs." *Journal of Personality*, 22:326-47 (March 1954).

Otto Rank. *Will Therapy*. New York: Alfred A. Knopf, 1936.

Carl R. Rogers. *Client-centered Therapy*. Boston: Houghton Mifflin Company, 1951.

CHAPTER SIX

Intelligence and Creativity

WHAT IS THE NATURE of intelligence and creativity? Are they inborn gifts and therefore not subject to change in the schooling process? Are they unitary traits, or is each a composite of many facets?

Nineteenth- and early-twentieth-century investigators tended to think of intelligence as an innate characteristic, predetermined by genes in the same way that eye or skin color is determined. Galton (1914), for example, wrote:

. . . a man's natural abilities are derived by inheritance, under exactly the same limitations as are the form and physical features of the whole organic world. Consequently, as it is easy, notwithstanding those limitations, to obtain by careful selection a permanent breed of dogs or horses gifted with peculiar powers of running, or of doing anything else, so it would be quite practical to produce a highly gifted race of men by judicious marriages during several consecutive generations.

A contemporary advocate of similar views is Arthur Jensen, who perceives racial differences in performance as reflections of genetic endowment rather than results of differences in environment. His views have engendered lively and occasionally acrimonious debate. (See, for example, *Harvard Educational Review*, 1969, and *Psychology Today*, December, 1973.)

In the early part of this century a school of thought arose which maintained that intelligence has its source entirely in the environment. When the Communists took control of Russian schools they attempted to create a system based on the postulate that environment is all-important in determining man's nature. Probably the contemporary school of thought described as behaviorist most closely reflects this position.

The "nature-nurture" conflict raged for many years, but today most educators and psychologists would agree that "both heredity and environmental factors enter into all behavior. The reacting organism is a product of its genes and its past environment, while present environment provides the immediate stimulus for current behavior" (Anastasi, 1958). Piaget's theory of intellectual development (see pp. 57-60) also postulates an interactive relationship between biological endowment and environmental stimuli and demands.

Alfred Binet, originator of the first successful intelligence test, saw intelligence as a unitary trait that expresses itself in various competencies. This view is still widely held. Wechsler, for example, describes intelligence as "the aggregate or global capacity of the individual to act purposefully, to think rationally, and to deal effectively with his environment." Although Wechsler contends that there are various qualitatively different features of intelligence, his theory is still a general-aptitude model (Matarazzo, 1972, p. 79).

Others see intelligence as a composite of many discrete skills. Guilford's "Three Faces of Intellect" has become a classic exposition of this position. Beginning with the proposition that there are many ways to be intelligent, he has constructed a three-dimensional paradigm of human intellect, incorporating results of factor analysis. His concept of intellectual operations, classified as cognition, memory, divergent thinking, convergent thinking, and evaluation, has had a profound effect on our notions of intelligence and creativity.

As Anastasi (1961, Chap. 10) points out, it is practically impossible to determine why two subgroups respond differently to an IQ test. For example, if women and men achieve different scores, is it because of a sex-linked genetic difference, or is it because society teaches boys and girls to think differently? Lynn considers the differences between men and women in intellectual functioning and finds that males are superior in problem tasks while females excel in lesson tasks. He relates these differences to biological predispositions, different parent-child relationships, and cultural reinforcements. He concludes with suggestions for increasing the utilization of the intellectual capacities of women in our society.

We have learned much about the nature of human intellect during the past eighty years. We have now a considerable body of knowledge about the learning process and the learner. We have developed group and individual intelligence tests for assessing students' likelihood of succeeding in school and for developing educational programs to challenge differing abilities. We are more aware of the need to adapt curricula to children's levels of intellectual development. We know something about the factors that raise or lower intelligence. Finally, we have some understanding of how cultural differences affect performance on intellectual tasks.

However, our knowledge about creativity is not nearly so extensive as our knowledge about intelligence. We are still seeking ways in which to describe, measure, and predict creativity. Haimowitz and Haimowitz consider the lives of creative people in an attempt to discover some of the environmental and experiential factors that have distinguished them from others. They attempt to provide a view of research and thinking on creativity today and some suggestions for the teacher who wants to encourage flexibility and imagination in the classroom. They urge us to make creative thinking a major objective of learning.

RECOMMENDED READING

A. Anastasi. 1958. "Heredity, Environment, and the Question *How?*" *Psychological Review*, 65, 197–208. An authoritative analysis of the nature-nurture issue that provides valuable additional reading to the complex subject of theories and measurement of intelligence.

R. J. Armstrong and R. F. Mooney. 1971. "The Slossen Intelligence Test: Implications for the Reading Specialist," *Reading Teacher* 24, 336–40, 368. Information on the short-form verbal intelligence test that is now widely used by many reading specialists and elementary and middle-school teachers.

M. P. Honzik, J. W. Macfarlane and L. Allen. 1949. "The Stability of Mental-Test Performance Between Two and Eighteen Years," *The Journal of Experimental Education* 17, 309–24. An objective study of the predictive value of intelligence test scores during the school years when I.Q. tests are most frequently used.

J. McV. Hunt. 1970. "Learning Ability, Intelligence, and Educability." In V. A. Allen (ed.), *Psychological Factors in Poverty* (Chicago: Mark). The nature of intellectual functioning discussed within the context of the teaching of culturally and socially deprived children.

A. R. Jensen. 1973. "The Differences Are Real," *Psychology Today* 7(7), 79–86. Reports of recent research on the relationship of heredity to intelligence test scores. This issue also contains articles on the subject by Rice and Dobshansky, in layman's language.

J. D. Matarazzo. 1972. *Wechsler's Measurement and Appraisal of Adult Intelligence* (Baltimore: Williams & Wilkins Co.). A scholarly analysis of the nature of adult intelligence, theoretical developments, and the measurement of intelligence, with primary focus on the Wechsler I.Q. test.

15.

J. P. GUILFORD

THREE FACES OF INTELLECT

My subject is in the area of human intelligence, in connection with which the names of Terman and Stanford have become known the world over. The Stanford Revision of the Binet intelligence scale has been the standard against which all other instruments for the measurement of intelligence have been compared. The term IQ or intelligence quotient has become a household word in this country. This is illustrated by two brief stories.

A few years ago, one of my neighbors came home from a PTA meeting, remarking: "That Mrs. So-And-So thinks she knows so much. She kept talking about the 'intelligence *quota*' of the children—'intelligence *quota*,' imagine. Why, everybody knows that IQ stands for 'intelligence *quiz*.' "

The other story comes from a little comic strip in a Los Angeles morning newspaper, called "Junior Grade." In the first picture a little boy meets a little girl, both apparently about the first-grade level. The little girl remarks, "I have a high IQ." The little boy, puzzled, said, "You have a what?" The little girl repeated, "I have a high IQ," then went on her way. The little boy, looking thoughtful, said, "And she looks like such a nice little girl, too."

It is my purpose to speak about the analysis of this thing called human intelligence into its components. I do not believe that either Binet or Terman, if they were still with us, would object to the idea of a searching and detailed study of intelligence, aimed toward a better understanding of its nature. Preceding the development of his intelligence scale, Binet had done much research on different kinds of thinking activities and apparently recognized that intelligence has a number of aspects. It is to the lasting credit of both Binet and Terman that they introduced such a great variety of tasks into their intelligence scales.

From J. P. Guilford, "Three Faces of Intellect," *American Psychologist*, 14 (1959), 469–79. Copyright © 1959 by the American Psychological Association and reproduced by permission. "Three Faces of Intellect" was originally given as the Walter V. Bingham Memorial Lecture at Stanford University on April 13, 1959.

Two related events of very recent history make it imperative that we learn all we can regarding the nature of intelligence. I am referring to the advent of the artificial satellites and planets and to the crisis in education that has arisen in part as a consequence. The preservation of our way of life and our future security depend upon our most important national resources: our intellectual abilities and, more particularly, our creative abilities. It is time, then, that we learn all we can about those resources.

Our knowledge of the components of human intelligence has come about mostly within the last 25 years. The major sources of this information in this country have been L. L. Thurstone and his associates, the wartime research of psychologists in the United States Air Force, and more recently the Aptitudes Project at the University of Southern California. . . . The results from the Aptitudes Project that have gained perhaps the most attention have pertained to creative-thinking abilities. These are mostly novel findings. But to me, the most significant outcome has been the development of a unified theory of human intellect, which organizes the known, unique or primary intellectual abilities into a single system called the "structure of intellect." It is to this system that I shall devote the major part of my remarks, with very brief mentions of some of the implications for the psychology of thinking and problem solving, for vocational testing, and for education.

The discovery of the components of intelligence has been by means of the experimental application of the method of factor analysis. It is not necessary for you to know anything about the theory or method of factor analysis in order to follow the discussion of the components. I should like to say, however, that factor analysis has no connection with or resemblance to psychoanalysis. A positive statement would be more helpful, so I will say that each intellectual component or factor is a unique ability that is needed to do well in a certain class of tasks or tests. As a general principle we find that certain individuals do well in the tests of a certain class, but they may do poorly in the tests of another class. We conclude that a factor has certain properties from the features that the tests of a class have in common. I shall give you very soon a number of examples of tests, each representing a factor.

THE STRUCTURE OF INTELLECT

Although each factor is sufficiently distinct to be detected by factor analysis, in very recent years it has become apparent that the factors themselves can be classified because they resemble one another in certain ways. One basis of classification is according to the basic kind of process or operation performed. This kind of classification gives up five major groups of intellectual abilities: factors of cognition, memory, convergent thinking, divergent thinking, and evaluation.

Cognition means discovery or rediscovery or recognition. Memory means retention of what is cognized. Two kinds of productive thinking operations generate new information from known information and remembered information. In divergent-thinking operations we think in different directions, sometimes searching, sometimes seeking variety. In convergent thinking the information leads to one right answer or to a recognized best or conventional answer. In evaluation we reach decisions as to goodness, correctness, suitability, or adequacy of what we know, what we remember, and what we produce in productive thinking.

A second way of classifying the intellectual factors is according to the kind of material or content involved. The factors known thus far involve three kinds of material or content: the content may be figural, symbolic, or semantic. Figural content is concrete material such as is perceived through the senses. It does not represent anything except itself. Visual material has properties such as size, form, color, location, or texture. Things we hear or feel provide other examples of figural material. Symbolic content is composed of letters, digits, and other conventional signs, usually organized in general systems, such as the alphabet or the number system. Semantic content is in the form of verbal meanings or ideas, for which no examples are necessary.

When a certain operation is applied to a certain kind of content, as many as six general kinds of products may be involved. There is enough evidence available to suggest that, regardless of the combinations of operations and content, the same six kinds of products may be found associated. The six kinds of products are: units, classes, relations, systems, transformations, and implications. So far as we have determined from factor analysis, these are the only fundamental kinds of products that we can know. As such, they may serve as basic classes into which one might fit all kinds of information psychologically.

The three kinds of classifications of the factors of intellect can be represented by means of a single solid model, shown in Figure 1. In this model, which we call the "structure of intellect," each dimension represents one of the modes of variation of the factors. Along one dimension are found the various kinds of operations, along a second one are the various kinds of products, and along the third are various kinds of content. Along the dimension of content a fourth category has been added, its kind of content being designated as "behavioral." This category has been added on a purely theoretical basis to represent the general area sometimes called "social intelligence." More will be said about this section of the model later.

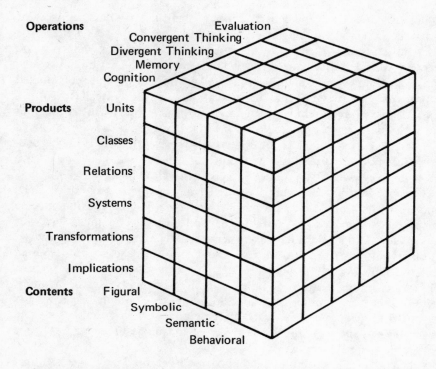

Figure 1. A cubical model representing the structure of intellect.

In order to provide a better basis for understanding the model and a better basis for accepting it as a picture of human intellect, I shall do some exploring of it with you systematically, giving some examples of tests. Each cell in the model calls for a certain kind of ability that can be described in terms of operation, content, and product, for each cell is at the intersection of a unique combination of kinds of operation, content, and product. A test for that ability would have the same three properties. In our exploration of the model, we shall take one vertical layer at a time, beginning with the front face. The first layer provides us with a matrix of 18 cells (if we ignore the behavioral column for which there are as yet no known factors), each of which should contain a cognitive ability.

The Cognitive Abilities

We know at present the unique abilities that fit logically into 15 of the 18 cells for cognitive abilities. Each row presents a triad of similar abilities, having a single kind of product in common. The factors of the first row are concerned with the knowing of units. A good test of the ability to cognize figural units is the Street Gestalt Completion Test. In this test, the recognition of familiar pictured objects in silhouette form is made difficult for testing purposes by blocking out parts of those objects. There is another factor that is known to involve the perception of auditory figures—in the form of melodies, rhythms, and speech sounds—and still another factor involving kinesthetic forms. The presence of three factors in one cell (they are conceivably distinct abilities, although this has not been tested) suggests that more generally, in the figural column, at least, we should expect to find more than one ability. A fourth dimension pertaining to variations in sense modality may thus apply in connection with figural content. The model could be extended in this manner if the facts call for such an extension.

The ability to cognize symbolic units is measured by tests like the following:

Put vowels in the following blanks to make real words:

P_____W_____R
M_____RV_____L
C_____RT_____N

Rearrange the letters to make real words:

R A C I H
T V O E S
K L C C O

The first of these two tests is called Disemvoweled Words, and the second Scrambled Words.

The ability to cognize semantic units is the well-known factor of verbal comprehension, which is best measured by means of a vocabulary test, with items such as:

GRAVITY means _____
CIRCUS means _____
VIRTUE means _____

From the comparison of these two factors it is obvious that recognizing familiar words as letter structures and knowing what words mean depend upon quite different abilities.

For testing the abilities to know classes of units, we may present the following kinds of items, one with symbolic content and one with semantic content:

Which letter group does not belong?
XECM   PVAA   QXIN   VTRO

Which object does not belong?
clam   tree   oven   rose

A figural test is constructed in a completely parallel form, presenting in each item four figures, three of which have a property in common and the fourth lacking that property.

The three abilities to see relationships are also readily measured by a common kind of test, differing only in terms of content. The well-known analogies test is applicable, two items in symbolic and semantic form being:

JIRE : KIRE : : FORA : KORE   KORA   LIRE   GORA   GIRE

poetry : prose : : dance : music   walk   sing   talk   jump

Such tests usually involve more than the ability to cognize relations, but we are not concerned with this problem at this point.

The three factors for cognizing systems do not at present appear in tests so closely resembling one another as in the case of the examples just given. There is nevertheless an underlying common core of logical similarity. Ordinary space tests, such as Thurstone's Flags, Figures, and Cards, or Part V (Spatial Orientation) of the Guilford-Zimmerman Aptitude Survey (GZAS), serve in the figural column. The system involved is an order or arrangement of objects in space. A system that uses symbolic elements is illustrated by the Letter Triangle Test, a sample item of which is:

$$
\begin{array}{llll}
 & & d & \overline{\quad\quad} \\
 & b & e & \underline{\quad\quad} \\
 a & c & f & ?
\end{array}
$$

What letter belongs at the place of the question mark?

The ability to understand a semantic system has been known for some time as the factor called general reasoning. One of its most faithful indicators is a test composed of arithmetic-reasoning items. That the phase of understanding only is important for measuring this ability is shown by the fact that such a test works even if the examinee is not asked to give a complete solution; he need only show that he structures the problem properly. For example, an item from the test Necessary Arithmetical Operations simply asks what operations are needed to solve the problem:

A city lot 48 feet wide and 149 feet deep costs $79,432. What is the cost per square foot?	A. add and multiply B. multiply and divide C. subtract and divide D. add and subtract E. divide and add

Placing the factor of general reasoning in this cell of the structure of intellect gives us some new conceptions of its nature. It should be a broad ability to grasp all kinds of systems that are conceived in terms of verbal concepts, not restricted to the understanding of problems of an arithmetical type.

Transformations are changes of various kinds, including modifications in arrangement, organization, or meaning. In the figural column for the transformations row, we find the factor known as visualization. Common measuring instruments for this factor are the surface-development tests, and an example of a different kind is Part VI (Spatial Visualization) of the GZAS. A test of the ability to make transformations of meaning, for the factor in the semantic column, is called Similarities. The examinee is asked to state several ways in which two objects, such as an apple and an orange, are alike. Only by shifting the meanings of both is the examinee able to give many responses to such an item.

In the set of abilities having to do with the cognition of implications, we find that the individual goes beyond the information given, but not to the extent of what might be called drawing conclusions. We may say that he extrapolates. From the given information he expects or foresees certain consequences, for example. The two factors found in this row of the cognition matrix were first called "foresight" factors. Foresight in connection with figural material can be tested by means of paper-and-pencil mazes. Foresight in connection with ideas, those pertaining to events, for example, is indicated by a test such as Pertinent Questions:

In planning to open a new hamburger stand in a certain community, what four questions should be considered in deciding upon its location?

The more questions the examinee asks in response to a list of such problems, the more he evidently foresees contingencies.

The Memory Abilities

The area of memory abilities has been explored less than some of the other areas of operation, and only seven of the potential cells of the memory matrix have known factors in them. These cells are restricted to three rows: for units, relations, and systems. The first cell in the memory matrix is now occupied by two factors, parallel to two in the corresponding cognition matrix: visual memory and auditory memory. Memory for series of letters or numbers, as in memory span tests, conforms to the conception of memory for symbolic units. Memory for the ideas in a paragraph conforms to the conception of memory for semantic units.

The formation of associations between units, such as visual forms, syllables, and meaningful words, as in the method of paired associates, would seem to represent three abilities to remember relationships involving three kinds of content. We know of two such abilities, for the symbolic and semantic columns. The memory for known systems is represented by two abilities very recently discovered (Christal). Remembering the arrangement of objects in space is the nature of an ability in the figural column, and remembering a sequence of events is the nature of a corresponding ability in the semantic column. The differentiation between these two abilities implies that a person may be able to say where he saw an object on a page, but he might not be able to say on which of several pages he saw it after leafing through several pages that included the right one. Considering the blank rows in the memory matrix, we should expect to find abilities also to remember classes, transformations, and implications, as well as units, relations, and systems.

The Divergent-Thinking Abilities

The unique feature of divergent production is that a *variety* of responses is produced. The product is not completely determined by the given information. This is not to say that divergent thinking does not come into play in the total process of reaching a unique conclusion, for it comes into play wherever there is trial-and-error thinking.

The well-known ability of word fluency is tested by asking the examinee to list words satisfying a specified letter requirement, such as words beginning with the letter "s" or words ending in "-tion." This ability is now regarded as a facility in divergent production of symbolic units. The parallel semantic ability has been known as ideational fluency. A typical test item calls for listing objects that are round and edible. Winston Churchill must have possessed this ability to a high degree. Clement Attlee is reported to have said about him . . . that, no matter what problem came up, Churchill always seemed to have about ten ideas. The trouble was, Attlee continued, he did not know which was the good one. The last comment implies some weakness in one or more of the evaluative abilities.

The divergent production of class ideas is believed to be the unique feature of a factor called "spontaneous flexibility." A typical test instructs the examinee to list all the uses he can think of for a common brick, and he is given eight minutes. If his responses are: build a house, build a barn, build a garage, build a school, build a church, build a chimney, build a walk, and build a barbecue, he would earn a fairly high score for ideational fluency but a very low score for spontaneous flexibility, because all these uses fall into the same class. If another person said: make a door stop, make a paper weight, throw it at a dog, make a bookcase, drown a cat, drive a nail, make a red powder, and use for baseball bases, he would also receive a high score for flexibility. He has gone frequently from one class to another.

A current study of unknown but predicted divergent-production abilities includes testing whether there are also figural and symbolic abilities to produce multiple classes. An experimental figural test presents a number of figures that can be classified in groups of three in various ways, each figure being usable in more than one class. An experimental symbolic test presents a few numbers that are also to be classified in multiple ways.

A unique ability involving relations is called "associational fluency." It calls for the production of a variety of things related in a specified way to a given thing. For example, the examinee is asked to list words meaning about the same as "good" or to list words meaning about the opposite of "hard." In these instances the response produced is to complete a relationship, and semantic content is involved. Some of our present experimental tests call for the production of varieties of relations, as such, and involve figural and symbolic content also. For example, given four small digits, in how many ways can they be related in order to produce a sum of eight?

One factor pertaining to the production of systems is known as expressional fluency. The rapid formation of phrases or sentences is the essence of certain tests of this factor. For example, given the initial letters:

W____c____e____n____

with different sentences to be produced, the examinee might write "We can eat nuts" or "Whence came Eve Newton?" In interpreting the factor, we regard the sentence as a symbolic system. By analogy, a figural system would be some kind of organization of lines and other elements, and a semantic system would be in the form of a verbally stated problem or perhaps something as complex as a theory.

In the row of the divergent-production matrix devoted to transformations, we find some very interesting factors. The one called "adaptive flexibility" is now recognized as belonging in the figural column. A faithful test of it has been Match Problems. This is based upon the common game that uses squares, the sides of which are formed by match sticks. The examinee is told to take away a given number of matches to leave a stated number of squares with nothing left over. Nothing is said about the sizes of the squares to be left. If the examinee imposes upon himself the restriction that the squares that he leaves must be of the same size, he will fail in his attempts to do items like that in Figure 2. Other odd kinds of solutions are introduced in other items, such as overlapping squares and squares within squares, and so on. In another variation of Match Problems the examinee is told to produce two or more solutions for each problem.

A factor that has been called "originality" is now recognized as adaptive flexibility with semantic material, where there must be a shifting of meanings. The examinee must produce the shifts or changes in meaning and so come up with novel, unusual, clever, or farfetched ideas. The Plot Titles Test presents a short story, the examinee being told to list as many appropriate titles as he can to head the story. One story is about a missionary who has been captured by cannibals in Africa. He is in the pot

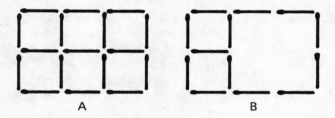

A   B

Figure 2. A sample item from the test Match Problems. The problem in this item is to take away four matches in A, leaving three squares. The solution is given in B.

and about to be boiled when a princess of the tribe obtains a promise for his release if he will become her mate. He refuses and is boiled to death.

In scoring the test, we separate the responses into two categories, clever and nonclever. Examples of nonclever responses are: African Death, Defeat of a Princess, Eaten by Savages, The Princess, The African Missionary, In Darkest Africa, and Boiled by Savages. These titles are appropriate but commonplace. The number of such responses serves as a score for ideational fluency. Examples of clever responses are: Pot's Plot, Potluck Dinner, Stewed Parson, Goil or Boil, A Mate Worse Than Death, He Left a Dish for a Pot, Chaste in Haste, and A Hot Price for Freedom.

The number of clever responses given by an examinee is his score for originality, or the divergent production of semantic transformations.

Another test of originality presents a very novel task so that any acceptable response is unusual for the individual. In the Symbol Production Test the examinee is to produce a simple symbol to stand for a noun or a verb in each short sentence, in other words to invent something like pictographic symbols. Still another test of originality asks for writing the "punch lines" for cartoons, a task that almost automatically challenges the examinee to be clever. Thus, quite a variety of tests offer approaches to the measurement of originality, including one or two others that I have not mentioned.

Abilities to produce a variety of implications are assessed by tests calling for elaboration of given information. A figural test of this type provides the examinee with a line or two, to which he is to add other lines to produce an object. The more lines he adds, the greater his score. A semantic test gives the examinee the outlines of a plan to which he is to respond by stating all the details he can think of to make the plan work. A new test we are trying out in the symbolic area presents two simple equations such as $B - C = D$ and $z = A + D$. The examinee is to make as many other equations as he can from this information.

The Convergent-Production Abilities

Of the 18 convergent-production abilities expected in the three content columns, 12 are now recognized. In the first row, pertaining to units, we have an ability to name figural properties (forms or colors) and an ability to name abstractions (classes, relations, and so on). It may be that the ability in common to the speed of naming forms and the speed of naming colors is not appropriately placed in the convergent-thinking matrix. One might expect that the thing to be produced in a test of the convergent production of figural units would be in the form of figures rather than words. A better test of such an ability might somehow specify the need for one particular object, the examinee to furnish the object.

A test for the convergent production of classes (Word Grouping) presents a list of 12 words that are to be classified in four, and only four, meaningful groups, no word to appear in more than one group. A parallel test (Figure Concepts Test) presents 20 pictured real objects that are to be grouped in meaningful classes of two or more each.

Convergent production having to do with relationships is represented by three known factors, all involving the "education of correlates," as Spearman called it. The given information includes one unit and a stated relation, the examinee to supply the other unit. Analogies tests that call for completion rather than a choice between alternative answers emphasize this kind of ability. With symbolic content such an item might read:

pots   stop   bard   drab   rats   ?

A semantic item that measures education of correlates is:

The absence of sound is _____.

Incidentally, the latter item is from a vocabulary-completion test, and its relation to the factor of ability to produce correlates indicates how, by change of form, a vocabulary test may indicate an ability other than that for which vocabulary tests are usually intended, namely, the factor of verbal comprehension.

Only one factor for convergent production of systems is known, and it is in the semantic column. It is measured by a class of tests that may be called ordering tests. The examinee may be presented with a number of events that ordinarily have a best or most logical order, the events being presented in scrambled order. The presentation may be pictorial, as in the Picture Arrangement Test, or verbal. The pictures may be taken from a cartoon strip. The verbally presented events may be in the form of the various steps needed to plant a new lawn. There are undoubtedly other kinds of systems than temporal order that could be utilized for testing abilities in this row of the convergent-production matrix.

In the way of producing transformations of a unique variety, we have three recognized factors, known as redefinition abilities. In each case, redefinition involves the changing of functions or uses of parts of one

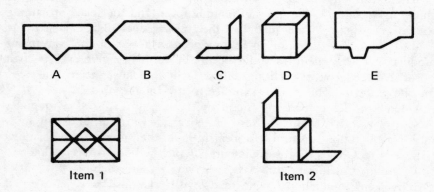

Figure 3. Sample items from the test Hidden Figures, based upon the Gottschaldt figures. Which of the simpler figures is concealed within each of the two more complex figures?

unit and giving them new functions or uses in some new unit. For testing the ability of figural redefinition, a task based upon the Gottschaldt figures is suitable. Figure 3 shows the kind of item for such a test. In recognizing the simpler figure within the structure of a more complex figure, certain lines must take on new roles.

In terms of symbolic material, the following sample items will illustrate how groups of letters in given words must be readapted to use in other words. In the test Camouflaged Words, each sentence contains the name of a sport or game:

> I did not know that he was ailing.
> To beat the Hun, tin goes a long way.

For the factor of semantic redefinition, the Gestalt Transformation Test may be used. A sample item reads:

> From which object could you most likely make a needle?
> A. a cabbage
> B. a splice
> C. a steak
> D. a paper box
> E. a fish

The convergent production of implications means the drawing of fully determined conclusions from given information. The well-known factor of numerical facility belongs in the symbolic column. For the parallel ability in the figural column, we have a test known as Form Reasoning, in which rigorously defined operations with figures are used. For the parallel ability in the semantic column, the factor sometimes called "deduction" probably qualifies. Items of the following type are sometimes used.

> Charles is younger than Robert.
> Charles is older than Frank.
> Who is older, Robert or Frank?

Evaluative Abilities

The evaluative area has had the least investigation of all the operational categories. In fact, only one systematic analytical study has been devoted to this area. Only eight evaluative abilities are recognized as fitting into the evaluation matrix. But at least five rows have one or more factors each, and also three of the usual columns or content categories. In each case, evaluation involves reaching decisions as to the accuracy, goodness, suitability, or workability of information. In each row, for the particular kind of product of that row, some kind of criterion or standard of judgment is involved.

In the first row, for the evaluation of units, the important decision to be made pertains to the identity of a unit. Is this unit identical with that one? In the figural column we find the factor long known as "perceptual speed." Tests of this factor invariably call for decisions of identity, for example, Part IV (Perceptual Speed) of the GZAS or Thurstone's Identical Forms. I think it has been generally wrongly thought that the ability involved is that of cognition of visual forms. But we have seen that another factor is a more suitable candidate for this definition and for being in the very first cell of the cognitive matrix. It is parallel to this evaluative ability but does not require the judgment of identity as one of its properties.

In the symbolic column is an ability to judge identity of symbolic units, in the form of series of letters or numbers or of names of individuals.

Are members of the following pairs identical or not:

825170493_____825176493
dkeltvmpa_____dkeltvmpa
C. S. Meyerson_____C. E. Meyerson

Such items are common in tests of clerical aptitude.

There should be a parallel ability to decide whether two idea are identical or different. Is the idea expressed in this sentence the same as the idea expressed in that one? Do these two proverbs express essentially the same idea? Such tests exist and will be used to test the hypothesis that such an ability can be demonstrated.

No evaluative abilities pertaining to classes have as yet been recognized. The abilities having to do with evaluation where relations are concerned must meet the criterion of logical consistency. Syllogistic-type tests involving letter symbols indicate a different ability from the same type of test involving verbal statements. In the figural column we might expect that tests incorporating geometric reasoning or proof would indicate a parallel ability to sense the soundness of conclusions regarding figural relationships.

The evaluation of systems seems to be concerned with the internal consistency of those systems, so far as we can tell from the knowledge of one such factor. The factor has been called "experiential evaluation," and its representative test presents items like that in Figure 4 asking "What is wrong with this picture?" The things wrong are often internal inconsistencies.

A semantic ability for evaluating transformations is thought to be that

**Figure 4. A sample item from the test Unusual Details.
What two things are wrong with this picture?**

known for some time as "judgment." In typical judgment tests, the examinee is asked to tell which of five solutions to a practical problem is most adequate or wise. The solutions frequently involve improvisations, in other words, adaptations of familiar objects to unusual uses. In this way the items present redefinitions to be evaluated.

A factor known first as "sensitivity to problems" has become recognized as an evaluative ability having to do with implications. One test of the factor, the Apparatus Test, asks for two needed improvements with respect to each of several common devices, such as the telephone or the toaster. The Social Institutions Test, a measure of the same factor, asks what things are wrong with each of several institutions, such as tipping or national elections. We may say that defects or deficiencies are implications of an evaluative kind. Another interpretation would be that seeing defects and deficiencies are evaluations of implications to the effect that the various aspects of something are all right.*

SOME IMPLICATIONS OF THE STRUCTURE OF INTELLECT

For Psychological Theory

Although factor analysis as generally employed is best designed to investigate ways in which individuals differ from one another, in other words, to discover traits, the results also tell us much about how individ-

---

* For further details concerning the intellectual factors, illustrative tests, and the place of the factors in the structure of intellect, see Guilford (1959).

uals are alike. Consequently, information regarding the factors and their interrelationships gives us understanding of functioning individuals. The five kinds of intellectual abilities in terms of operations may be said to represent five ways of functioning. The kind of intellectual abilities distinguished according to varieties of test content and the kinds of abilities distinguished according to varieties of products suggest a classification of basic forms of information or knowledge. The kind of organism suggested by this way of looking at intellect is that of an agency for dealing with information of various kinds in various ways. The concepts provided by the distinctions among the intellectual abilities and by their classfications may be very useful in our future investigations of learning, memory, problem solving, invention, and decision making, by whatever method we choose to approach those problems.

For Vocational Testing

With about 50 intellectual factors already known, we may say that there are at least 50 ways of being intelligent. It has been facetiously suggested that there seem to be a great many more ways of being stupid, unfortunately. The structure of intellect is a theoretical model that predicts as many as 120 distinct abilities, if every cell of the model contains a factor. Already we know that two cells contain two or more factors each, and there probably are actually other cells of this type. Since the model was first conceived, 12 factors predicted by it have found places in it. There is consequently hope of filling many of the other vacancies, and we may eventually end up with more than 120 abilities.

The major implication for the assessment of intelligence is that to know an individual's intellectual resources thoroughly we shall need a surprisingly large number of scores. It is expected that many of the factors are intercorrelated, so there is some possibility that by appropriate sampling we shall be able to cover the important abilities with a more limited number of tests. At any rate, a multiple-score approach to the assessment of intelligence is definitely indicated in connection with future vocational operations.

Considering the kinds of abilities classified as to content, we may speak roughly of four kinds of intelligence. The abilities involving the use of figural information may be regarded as "concrete" intelligence. The people who depend most upon these abilities deal with concrete things and their properties. Among these people are mechanics, operators of machines, engineers (in some aspects of their work), artists, and musicians.

In the abilities pertaining to symbolic and semantic content, we have two kinds of "abstract" intelligence. Symbolic abilities should be important in learning to recognize words, to spell, and to operate with numbers. Language and mathematics should depend very much upon them, except that in mathematics some aspects, such as geometry, have strong figural involvement. Semantic intelligence is important for understanding things in terms of verbal concepts and hence is important in all courses where the learning of facts and ideas is essential.

In the hypothesized behavioral column of the structure of intellect, which may be roughly described as "social" intelligence, we have some of the most interesting possibilities. Understanding the behavior of others and of ourselves is largely nonverbal in character. The theory suggests as many as 30 abilities in this area, some having to do with understanding, some with productive thinking about behavior, and some with the evaluation of behavior. The theory also suggests that information regarding behavior is also in the form of the six kind of products that apply elsewhere in the structure of intellect, including units, relations, systems, and so on. The abilities in the area of social intelligence, whatever they prove to be, will possess considerable importance in connection with all those individuals who deal most with other people: teachers, law officials, social workers, therapists, politicians, statesmen, and leaders of other kinds.

For Education

The implications for education are numerous, and I have time just to mention a very few. The most fundamental implication is that we might well undergo transformations with respect to our conception of the learner and of the process of learning. Under the prevailing conception, the learner is a kind of stimulus-response device, much on the order of a vending machine. You put in a coin, and something comes out. The machine learns what reaction to put out when a certain coin is put in. If, instead, we think of the learner as an agent for dealing with information, where information is defined very broadly, we have something more analogous to an electronic computer. We feed a computer information; it stores that information; it uses that information for generating new information, either by way of divergent or convergent thinking; and it evaluates its own results. Advantages that a human learner has over a computer include the step of seeking and discovering new information from sources outside itself and the step of programing itself. Perhaps even these steps will be added to computers, if this has not already been done in some cases.

At any rate, this conception of the learner leads us to the idea that learning is discovery of information, not merely the formation of associations, particularly associations in the form of stimulus-response connections. I am aware of the fact that my proposal is rank heresy. But if we are to make significant progress in our understanding of human learning and particularly our understanding of the so-called higher mental processes of thinking, problem solving, and creative thinking, some drastic modifications are due in our theory.

The idea that education is a matter of training the mind or of training the intellect has been rather unpopular, wherever the prevailing psychological doctrines have been followed. In theory, at least, the emphasis has been upon the learning of rather specific habits or skills. If we take our cue from factor theory, however, we recognize that most learning probably has both specific and general aspects or components. The general aspects may be along the lines of the factors of intellect. This is not to say that the individual's status in each factor is entirely determined by learning. We do not know to what extent each factor is determined by heredity and to what extent by learning. The best position for educators to take is that possibly every intellectual factor can be developed in individuals at least to some extent by learning.

If education has the general objective of developing the intellects of students, it can be suggested that each intellectual factor provides a particular goal at which to aim. Defined by a certain combination of content, operation, and product, each goal ability then calls for certain kinds of practice in order to achieve improvement in it. This implies choice of curriculum and the choice or invention of teaching methods that will most likely accomplish the desired results.

Considering the very great variety of abilities revealed by the factorial exploration of intellect, we are in a better position to ask whether any general intellectual skills are now being neglected in education and whether appropriate balances are being observed. It is often observed these days that we have fallen down in the way of producing resourceful, creative graduates. How true this is, in comparison with other times, I do not know. Perhaps the deficit is noticed because the demands for inventiveness are so much greater at this time. At any rate, realization that the more conspicuously creative abilities appear to be concentrated in the divergent-thinking category, and also to some extent in the transformation category, we now ask whether we have been giving these skills appropriate exercise. It is probable that we need a better balance of training in the divergent-thinking area as compared with training in convergent thinking and in critical thinking or evaluation.

The structure of intellect as I have presented it to you may or may not stand the test of time. Even if the general form persists, there are likely to be some modifications. Possibly some different kind of model will be invented. Be that as it may, the fact of a multiplicity of intellectual abilities seems well established.

There are many individuals who long for the good old days of simplicity, when we got along with one unanalyzed intelligence. Simplicity certainly has its appeal. But human nature is exceedingly complex, and we may as well face that fact. The rapidly moving events of the world in which we live have forced upon us the need for knowing human intelligence throughly. Humanity's peaceful pursuit of happiness depends upon our control of nature and of our own behavior; and this, in turn, depends upon understanding ourselves, including our intellectual resources.

REFERENCES

R. E. Christal. "Factor Analytic Study of Visual Memory." *Psychological Monographs*, 1958, 72, No. 13 (Whole No. 466).

J. P. Guilford, "The Structure of Intellect." *Psychology Bulletin*, 1956, 53, 267–93.

———. *Personality*. New York: McGraw-Hill, 1959.

16.   DAVID B. LYNN

DETERMINANTS OF INTELLECTUAL GROWTH IN WOMEN

This paper postulates that the intellectual development of women is based on an interaction of: (1) biologically rooted potentials which predispose women toward some roles more than others; (2) parent-child relationships, seemingly inherent in the typical family pattern, which predispose toward certain cognitive styles; and (3) both blatant and subtle cultural reinforcement of traditional feminine-role prescriptions. It also suggests areas of research for improving the quality of the education of girls and women.

But why should the education of females be singled out for special consideration when girls average higher grades than boys throughout the school years? [1] True, the gap in grades between boys and girls gradually narrows toward high school graduation; even so, if grades were the only criterion there would be little justification for giving special attention to the education of females.

From *School Review*, 80:2 (Feb., 1972), 241–57. Copyright © 1972 by The University of Chicago. All rights reserved.

Nevertheless, there are a number of reasons for concern. Grades are not always a valid measure of actual scholastic achievement: girls receive better grades than boys even in subjects in which boys score higher on standard achievement tests.[2] For another, males, on the average, score higher than females in measures of comprehension, verbal reasoning, mathematical reasoning, mechanical aptitude, and analytic and problem-solving ability. There is small comfort in the superiority of females in measures of verbal fluency, correct language use, spelling, articulation, manual dexterity, perceptual speed, clerical skills, and rote memory.[3]

Most people would agree that the skills in which males surpass females are those essential to scientific, technical, professional, and administrative excellence. On all measures of abilities there is considerable overlap in distribution of scores between the two sexes, but sex differences are substantial in some aspects of analytic ability, in mathematical reasoning, and in mechanical aptitude. In addition to surpassing females in measures of high-level intellectual operations, males also surpass them in almost every aspect of actual intellectual achievement—books and articles written, artistic productivity, and scientific achievement.

Why should the lesser intellectual achievement of women be reason for alarm? Do not the maternal and domestic roles fulfill the needs of both women and society? Margaret Mead wrote that cultures find it difficult to motivate women to seek anything more than motherhood, that both men and women implicitly consider the role of women superior to that of men because they perform the biological function of producing babies. (The male contribution to reproduction does not receive comparable recognition.) Because of her capacity to bear children, Norman Mailer considers woman "a step, or a stage, or a move or a leap nearer the creation of existence." Since the significance of the lives of women is assured through this biological function, there has been no need to confer status on women's work. The work of men, Mead writes, must be given status by the culture to fortify artificially their frail egos and make them think that life is worthwhile. Consequently, the same work will receive prestige when done by men in one culture, but not when done by women in another. My position, to be discussed in more detail later, is that conditions have changed, that producing and rearing children can no longer be the sole basis for the meaningful existence of women.

Certainly women are superbly qualified by nature and reinforced by nurture to produce and care for babies. If such functions were not bred into the species and supported by social institutions, this animal would not have survived. In addition to the obvious biological capacities to give birth and to nurse, there appear to be other potentials which predispose women toward some roles more than others, potentials not only biologically rooted but reinforced and institutionalized by cultural prescriptions. There are sex differences, seemingly biologically based (e.g., they appear in earliest infancy), that should contribute to keeping the female closer to the nest than the male. Staying near the nest seems functional both for child care and for protecting against attrition of females, the less-expendable sex for the survival of the species. Her small size, lesser muscle mass, lower metabolism and energy level, and less restless and vigorous overt activity should make her more likely than the male to remain near the nest. The greater restless and vigorous overt activity of the male occurs in such early infancy that it seems clearly biologically based. Moreover, the assumption of a biological foundation is supported by recent evidence that male-hormone treatment of pregnant primates increased the incidence of rough-and-tumble play among female offspring and decreased their tendency to withdraw from the initiation, threats, and approaches of others. In humans, too, girls affected by male hormones *in utero* showed more of a developmental tendency toward vigorous activity ("tomboyish behaviour") than did other girls. The lower pain threshold and greater tactile sensitivity of the female from birth on should discourage her from venturing out where she might expose herself to painful stimuli. Her lesser interest in novel or highly variable stimuli, evident as early as five months of age, should also reduce the temptation to explore. A woman's interest in people, essential for raising babies, had its origin when she herself was in the cradle. At the age of 12 weeks, girls looked longer at *photographs* of faces than at schematic line drawings of normal or distorted faces, whereas boys failed to discriminate between these stimuli. By 24 weeks, boys paid more attention to geometric forms than to faces, whereas girls preferred photographs or drawings of human faces.[4] Girls also vocalized more to the faces than to the forms; boys vocalized equally to each.[5]

The greater interest that young females show in others, which should have implications for later child rearing, is also found in other primates. In rhesus monkeys, the juvenile female is more interested in an infant rhesus than is the juvenile male, and she is also gentler with it.[6] With humans, even in infancy, girls may stay closer to the nest than boys. This is suggested by unpublished work of Kagan, reported by Maccoby, on infants during the first year of life. This study showed that when baby girls are set down on the floor in a strange room they cling to the mother's leg longer than baby boys and are more upset when placed behind a barrier where they can see mother but not reach her.

Most cultures reinforce those potentials which would keep females at home—by training in nurturance, responsibility, and obedience, and allotting women tasks at or near home that minister to the needs of others and involve responsible discharge of established routines rather than high-level skills.[7] In the past it may have been functional for survival of the species to keep women docile, subservient, at home, and pregnant. Today, however, a new adaptation may be demanded for the species to thrive. With the population explosion, having more children than needed for simple replacement of one generation by the next may stigmatize a woman rather than symbolize biological fulfillment. As a result of medical progress, a woman should have many vigorous years ahead after she has produced and raised those children necessary for replacement. By the time they are 35 or 40, for many women the responsibilities of motherhood consume only a fraction of their energies, leaving them relatively free for other pursuits. Our society has generated few (if any) roles for either men or women that offer prestige and fulfillment other than vocational ones, barren as work can sometimes be. So it would seem that society must confer prestige on women as well as men for work, since women can find only partial fulfillment through producing and rearing children. It also seems obviously unfunctional to restrict opportunities for productive contributions to society for women who are prepared to contribute, want to, and *need* to.

Society has a long way to go in adapting to these new demands. There are biases in vocational counseling, prejudice against hiring women for responsible positions, discriminatory promotion practices, lower pay for women doing the same jobs as men, and many other barriers, including inflexible schedules and inadequate day-care facilities which make it difficult for women with children to further their education or to work. Even if the nation were not legally and morally committed to equal opportunity for all its people, it could be damaging to the fabric of society itself, not simply unsatisfying to women, for them to face years without a meaningful role. One can imagine all kinds of mischief resulting in addition to an unwelcome and destructive overinvestment of mothers in their children.[8] If the Women's Liberation movement did not exist, society would have to invent one to help awaken the nation to the necessity of undertaking the new adaptations demanded of it.

FEMININE IDENTIFICATION AND LEARNING STYLE

Let us hypothesize ways in which nature contributes to the process of acquiring feminine identification to produce a style of thinking and learning for females which differs measurably from that of males. We have already described sex differences appearing early in infancy, suggesting a biological origin. That biological differences could, in theory, underlie sex differences in style of thinking and learning is suggested by the fact that differences have been reported in almost every physical variable, including body build, anatomical characteristics, physiological functioning, biochemical composition,[9] and even in the structure and function of areas of the brain itself. But postulating biological differences underlying at least some of the sex differences in style of thinking and learning is not meant to minimize the powerful forces operating in family interaction, and in the culture as a whole, to foster masculine and feminine role differentiation. Sex differences in style of thinking are postulated as multi-determined.

An almost universal experience in the human condition is that of the mother as the primary caretaker of the infant. The first and principal person to whom the baby forms an attachment is usually the mother.[10] *It is hypothesized that both male and female infants also usually establish their initial and principal identification (as contrasted with attachment) with the mother.* Initially, she is the principal person on whom they model themselves, so that they internalize some of her characteristics and often react in a fashion similar to her without being aware of doing so. This almost universal condition of the mother as the major caretaker demands that the boy make a shift from his initial identification with her to identification with the masculine role, while no shift is demanded of the girl. In our culture, certainly, the girl has the same-sex parental model for identification (the mother) with her more than the boy has the same-sex model (the father) with him. Much incidental learning which she can apply directly in her life results from the girl's contact with her mother. We tend to assimilate characteristics of those with whom we associate, whether motivated to do so or not. In the absence of his father and male models, a masculine role is spelled out for the boy, often by his mother and women teachers. Through reinforcement of the culture's highly developed system of rewards for typical masculine-role behavior and punishment for signs of femininity, the boy's early-learned identification with the mother weakens. The later-learned identification with a culturally defined, stereotyped masculine role is impressed upon this weakened mother identification. This leads to another hypothesis: *Males tend to identify with a culturally defined masculine role, whereas females tend to identify with their mothers.*

We suggest that the task of achieving these separate kinds of identification for each sex requires separate methods of learning. These separate identification tasks seem to parallel the two kinds of learning tasks differentiated by Woodworth and Scholsberg—the *problem* and the *lesson.*[11] With a problem to master, the learner must explore the situation and determine the goal before his task becomes clear; with a lesson, exploration and goal seeking are omitted or minimized, as when someone is instructed to memorize a poem or a list of nonsense syllables or to examine pictures and recognize them later. The female's task of achieving mother identification is considered roughly parallel to the learning *lesson*, and the task of achieving masculine-role identification for the male is considered roughly parallel to the learning *problem*.

We can assume that finding the goal *does* constitute a major problem for the boy in acquiring the masculine role. When the boy begins to be aware that he does not belong in the same sex category as the mother, he must then find the proper sex-role identification goal. Hartley [12] says of the boy's identification problem that the desired behavior is seldom defined positively as something he *should* do, but usually negatively, as something he should *not* do, and that includes any behavior that people regard as "sissy." The boy must learn to set the masculine role as his goal from these largely negative admonishments sometimes made by women and often without the benefit of the presence of a male model during most of his waking hours. He must also restructure the admonishments, often negatively made and given in many contexts, in order to abstract the principles defining the masculine role. He is assisted in his quest by his high energy level, his vigor, and his curiosity, all probably biologically rooted.

It is assumed, on the other hand, that finding the goal does not constitute a major problem for the girl in learning her mother-identification lesson. Since the girl, unlike the boy, need not shift from the initial mother identification, and since she typically has the mother with her a relatively larger proportion of the time, it is postulated that the question of the object of identification (the mother) seldom arises for the girl. Remember, we have postulated biologically based mechanisms which increase the likelihood that the girl will remain at home much of the time, increasing the probability of her modeling the mother. She learns the mother-identification lesson in the context of an intimate personal relation with the mother, largely by imitation but also through parental behavior selectively reinforcing her mother-similar tendencies. Similarly, abstracting the principles that define the mother role is not considered a problem for girls, since any bit of behavior on the mother's part is of potential importance in learning the mother-identification lesson. The girl needs to learn, not principles defining the feminine role, but, rather, an identification with her specific mother.

One of the basic steps in this formulation can now be taken. We assume that the process of learning appropriate identification habituates each sex to a different method of perceiving, thinking, and learning (cognitive style), which is subsequently applied to learning tasks generally. The boy acquires a cognitive style that primarily involves (1) defining the goal, (2) restructuring the situation, and (3) abstracting principles. In contrast, the girl acquires a cognitive style that primarily involves (1) a personal relationship, and (2) lesson learning.[13]

A number of hypotheses follow. It is in the context of a close personal relationship with the mother that the girl learns the mother-identification lesson. This process is reinforced by appropriate rewards for signs that she is learning this lesson. Since she is rewarded in the context of the personal relationship with her mother, she should become highly motivated to maintain this relationship. By generalization, a strong need for affiliation should develop in other learning situations. This need is thought to be superimposed on an existing preference for faces over other visual stimuli, which emerges in early infancy. The boy has fewer opportunities than the girl to receive rewards for modeling himself after the adult male in a close personal relationship. His rewards result from learning the appropriate principles of masculine-role identification as they are abstracted from many contexts. Therefore, the need for affiliation in learning situations does not become as strong for him. The lesser need for affiliation is consistent with his early failure to differentiate a preference for faces over other stimuli. What evidence supports the hypothesis that *females more than males are motivated to learn in a social context?*

It is supported by McClelland *et al.*[14] who found that the achievement-motive scores of college women were not increased by appealing to their leadership motivation and intelligence—an appeal which was effective for male college students. Women did obtain higher scores when the dimension of "achievement" was social acceptability. Sears found that the scholastic achievement of elementary school girls was consistently related to their affiliative motives,[15] but for boys scholastic achievement was related to their achievement motivation. In nursery school, girls who made more attempts to obtain recognition for achievement also made more attempts to obtain love and attention, while no such relationship obtained for achievement-oriented boys.[16] Achievement and approval seeking from adults were also related for girls of early elementary school age, but not for boys.[17] Thus the data are consistent with the hypothesis that females more than males are motivated to learn in a social context.

Since girls do not have to shift identification from the mother, they are not motivated by their identification task to assert themselves as vigorously as is necessary for boys. From the earliest age boys are described as more vigorous, restless, and aggressive than girls. It is not surprising, then, that *in learning situations females often show greater docility, passive acceptance, and dependence,*[18] and that in motor tasks, where one has to react with speed to various stimuli, *they show a "reactive response set" whereas males show an "active response set."* That is, women seem to wait for the appearance of a stimulus before they prepare to respond, whereas men seem to have a motor-response set available for instantaneous reaction prior to the appearance of a stimulus, whatever it may be.

In learning to identify with the mother, the girl may find that any bit of behavior on the mother's part might be of potential importance. The mother-identification lesson does not require the girl to restructure the situation or abstract principles of femininity, but, rather, to learn the lesson as presented. She is thereby gaining practice in lesson learning that is not available to the male, who is struggling to solve the masculine-role identification problem. Therefore *females surpass males in rote memory*. Indeed, females generally surpass males in rote memory demanding exact repetition of a group of digits, the copying of geometric figures or pictures from memory immediately after presentation, and the recitation of a story, a paragraph, or a poem read to or by them.[19]

Physiologically, girls mature faster than boys. There is an earlier maturation of the speech organs and probably an earlier maturation of the cortical structures relevant to speech, so it is not surprising that girls talk sooner than boys. There is much evidence that the amount of contact between a child and adults enhances the language development of the child. We have presented arguments supporting the proposition that girls spend more time with the mother than boys do and experience more verbal interaction with her. We have also developed the proposition that from an early age they have a greater interest in people than boys have. It follows that *females surpass males in verbal fluency and language use*. This is not to say that they surpass males in verbal reasoning and vocabulary; in fact, the reverse is true. Vocabulary is related to curiosity and a wide range of experiences, both more common among males. Verbal reasoning relates to problem-solving skills, which we have postulated to favor males also. Females do surpass males in verbal fluency, correct language use, sentence complexity, grammatical structure, spelling, and articulation. Their verbal skills seem to be utilized more in the service of affiliative motives than in the solution of problems other than interpersonal ones. Their more personal use of speech was found in a study showing that women used more words implying feeling, emotion, or motivation, and made more references to the self, whereas men used a greater number of words implying time, space, quantity, and destructive action. These sex differences, however, tended to disappear in the higher ranges of intelligence.[20]

The term "analytic ability" has several meanings, one of which is to be able to respond to one aspect of a stimulus situation without being greatly influenced by the background. Witkin and his associates label as field-dependent those individuals who cling to the external context of a perceptual situation and hesitate to deviate from the given data. (Field-dependent people are readily influenced by misleading cues and have more trouble than field-independent ones in discovering an embedded figure hidden in a complex design.) They concluded that there are consistent though small differences in field dependence between women and men.[21] These findings have been generalized to children as young as eight years and to populations in Europe and in Hong Kong.

A second aspect of analytic ability concerns the mode of grouping diverse arrays of objects or pictures. People who group analytically put objects with each other on the basis of some selected element they have in common (e.g., all those lying down). In a study of this ability, Kagan, Moss, and Sigel found that girls in the second to fourth grades used fewer analytic groupings than boys.[22] A third aspect is judgment of category width (i.e., how widely something can deviate from the standard and still be judged as falling into the same category as the standard). Those who judge analytically use broad categories, ignoring irrelevant features and focusing on the common characteristics. Wallach and Caron gave sixth-grade children a concept-attainment session in which to establish criteria concerning geometric forms with certain characteristics. A test session followed in which the subjects judged whether figures of varying deviation from the standard were similar to it. It was found that girls tolerated less deviation than males by every index, thus agreeing with the hypothesis that females use narrower categories than males. Pettigrew found that females typically use narrower category estimates than males when asked to classify a variety of phenomena susceptible to quantitative or numerical classification.[23]

In learning the mother-identification lesson, girls have had little practice in ignoring irrelevant cues and isolating significant ones, whereas boys have had much practice in doing so while solving the masculine-role identification problem. Even during infancy boys look longer at geometric forms and show more curiosity than do girls, both of which abilities may be related to later analytic ability. Thus it is not surprising that *females are less analytic than males.*

In the process of solving the masculine-role identification problem, the male acquires a cognitive style that should be applicable in solving other problems. It is hypothesized that he is thereby accumulating practice in problem solving. On the other hand, the feminine cognitive style deriving from the process of learning the mother-identification lesson, is not well geared to problem solving. Consequently, *females are surpassed by males in problem-solving skills.* Sweeny reported studies that support this proposition, including experiments of his own demonstrating that men solve certain classes of problems with greater facility than women do, even when differences in intellectual aptitude, special knowledge or training, and special abilities are controlled. In general, the results confirmed the hypothesis that sex differences will favor men in problems that involve difficulties in restructuring (i.e., discarding the first approach and reorganizing the task in a new way), but not in similar problems that involve no such difficulties. Another study found that female college students were surpassed by male students in problem solving even when the characteristics of the problems were altered so that they were inappropriate for the male but appropriate for the female role (e.g., cooking or sewing). Moreover, the male superiority was not reduced by giving both males and females a chance to warm up and become familiar with material. On the other hand, Milton had previously found that altering the content to make it more feminine did reduce male superiority but did not eliminate it.[24]

Another study by Milton with college students is pertinent to sex differences in problem-solving skills. In this study the Terman-Miles M-F test was the primary index of sex-role typing, although other M-F questionnaires were also employed. In general, the results indicate that there is a positive relation between the degree of masculine sex-role typing and problem-solving skill, both across sexes and within a sex. When this relation is accounted for, the difference between men and women in problem-solving performance is diminished. Thus, the data are consistent with the proposition that males generally surpass females in problem-solving skills.[25]

CULTURAL REINFORCEMENT OF TRADITIONAL FEMININITY

Remember, we postulated that the intellectual development of women is determined by an interaction of (1) biologically rooted potentials that predispose women toward some roles more than others; (2) parent-child relationships, seemingly inherent in the typical family pattern, which predispose toward certain cognitive styles; and (3) both blatant and subtle cultural reinforcement of traditional feminine-role prescriptions.

The pervasive patriarchal foundation of society is an example of a cultural reinforcement of traditional feminine-role prescriptions. Brown noted that the superior position and privileged status of the male permeates nearly every aspect of our lives, from the prizes in boxes of breakfast cereal to God as "Father" rather than "Mother." [26] The double standard of sexuality has by no means disappeared, nor has lower pay for the same job, nor stereotypes about what is appropriate woman's work.[27] Advertising presents a demeaning image of a childishly sexy housewife, apprehensive lest husband reject her coffee, and the children her cookies.

It is not surprising that in one study [28] both men and women, *especially* the women, rated men as more worthwhile than women, and in another study [29] both boys and girls with increasing age had a better opinion of boys and a worse opinion of girls. Goldberg demonstrated women's contempt for their own capabilities when he asked them to rate the scholarship in an essay signed, alternately, John McKay and Joan McKay.[30] Women generally agreed that John's article was scholarly and Joan's was commonplace, although it was the same article.

Feminine-role prescriptions are reinforced in the family. Girls are treated less permissively than boys and more conformity is demanded of them. One cannot rule out a biological component in the mother's handling, however, since Mitchell found that rhesus mothers punish the male infant earlier and more often but restrain, protect, and have more physical contact with the female infant.[31] The American father, even more than the mother, encourages his daughter to behave in a feminine way, even when she is still a preschooler.[32]

Reinforcement of the traditional feminine role pervades our schools, from the image of females presented in school readers to discriminatory vocational counseling. When Child, Potter, and Levin analyzed the content of third-grade readers, they found that girls and women are shown as sociable, kind, and timid, but inactive, unambitious, and uncreative.[33] The person who is nurtured is usually female, and the person who supplies information is male. Seventy-three percent of the central characters are male, leaving only 27 percent female. Cursory perusal of current readers will substantiate these findings. Teachers also give girls differential treatment. They are likely to reward girls for dependence, friendliness, and conformity, while rewarding some boys at least for autonomy, independence, and creativity.[34] The vocational counselor may be tempted to encourage girls, whatever their talents, into traditional feminine fields for their own protection against future discrimination, or because they believe the girls will probably later change their minds and marry and raise a family. In addition, girls are genuinely difficult to counsel because, compared with boys, they are unrealistic in appraisal of their abilities, so that there is essentially no relation between their scholastic achievement and intelligence and their vocational aspirations.

SUGGESTIONS FOR RESEARCH

If social demands for conformity and passivity in girls contribute to any of the sex differences in intellectual functioning described above, research attempting to change such attitudes should result in improved intellectual performance. Surprisingly, little research of this sort has been done. One study found that men had a consistently more favorable attitude toward problem solving than women, and that group discussion aimed at improving this attitude increased the problem-solving performance of women but not of men.[35] In another study, Torrance observed that boys made many more suggestions than girls about how science toys might be used. He discussed with parents and teachers how misplaced emphasis on stereotyped sex roles could interfere with later potential and advised them to encourage girls to experiment more freely with science toys. After this, the girls demonstrated and explained as many ideas as the boys. Other experimental procedures for overcoming the narrow definition of femininity might be (1) introduce sections in social science on the changing role of women; (2) bring achieving women (professors, executives, scientists) into the schools in the early grades as resident scholars, leaders of seminars and workshops, etc.; (3) eradicate feminine stereotypes from school readers; and (4) have workshops geared to eliminating discrimination against females in vocational counseling.

Play for boys seems to be preparation for entering the objective, ordered, rule-regulated vocational and public life of a masculine-oriented adult world. Piaget could find not a single collective game played by girls with as many rules and with the fine and consistant organization and codification of these rules as the game of marbles for boys. Tyler observed that boys' recreational pursuits in the first grade were related to their mental ability, with brighter boys preferring paper-and-pencil games and activities. Brighter girls showed no such preference.[36] Young girls often play house; young boys engage in fantasy activities outside the house (e.g., flying airplanes and driving trains). Evidence has been accumulating that boys who want to become scientists crystallize their interest between the ages of 10 and 14, and one can only assume that their play often influences their choice. With all this in mind, research might be done to test the effects of encouraging changes in the play of girls to foster greater preparation for the vocational and public life of adults, including both broader interests and the objective reciprocity which comes from applying rules in collective games.

There are some changes which might be introduced into experimental classrooms to test their effectiveness in enhancing intellectual functioning in girls. Teachers could reward rote memorization and superficial language skills less and teach and construct tests so that grades depend more on thought. When the girl starts to school she is in advance of boys in many ways, including language development, and her greater success with rote responses and superficial language skills in the early grades may so habituate these responses that it is difficult for her to switch when more thought is required later. Why not demand thought at the appropriate level of complexity in every grade so that children do not become "spoiled by success" in superficial tasks? In addition, more attention might be given to classroom discussion on the cognitive styles of problem solving, such as breaking a set; that is, to approach a problem in a new way when the first approach proves unproductive.

Since there is considerable overlap between the distribution of scores of the two sexes in all measures of ability, a simple solution suggests itself: just group students by ability. Besides the problems inherent in such groupings, however, two people may score high on the same ability but approach it with different cognitive styles. So why not group by cognitive style, the different ways by which individuals approach intellectual tasks? This is difficult because so many elements are involved. An individual may resemble another in his approach to mathematical tasks but differ in approaching verbal reasoning and other tasks. Personality also enters into styles of tackling intellectual tasks. Grouping by cognitive style, disregarding sex, is difficult also because there are systematic sex differences in cognitive style in equally capable males and females. Even so, the possibility is still open to research on grouping by an interaction of cognitive style and ability (rather than sex). The first task would be to develop genuinely sensitive and meaningful tests of cognitive styles in approaching a variety of intellectual tasks.

I flinch at the thought of "Female Mathematics" or "Female Science" in parallel to "Black," "Native American," or "Chicano History," but experimentation along these lines should not be summarily ruled out. Perhaps a more practical solution would be to try Garai and Scheinfeld's suggestion of having textbooks and teachers present to mixed classes the approach considered to be most easily understood by males *and* that considered to favor females. Probably both sexes would gain, since presenting a variety of approaches to the solution of problems usually enhances learning.

There is some evidence that girls tend to be more timid and more confused by failure and criticism. A negative relationship has been found between anxiety and cognitive development in females. Experiments might be tried to raise frustration tolerance in girls, perhaps using behavior-modification approaches. Before frustration tolerance is built up, a relaxed learning atmosphere with reward for success rather than punishment for failure should facilitate learning for girls. Since impulsive, active, and even aggressive behavior may be associated with intellectual development in girls, testing the effectiveness of reinforcing (or at least not dampening) such behavior in girls seems appropriate.

In conclusion, I hope that women can add much that is uniquely theirs to our vocational public life. I join with Erik Erikson in the wish that when women gain full participation "they will add maternal concern to the cares of world governing." [37]

NOTES

1. Eleanor E. Maccoby, "Sex Differences in Intellectual Functioning," in *The Development of Sex Differences* (Stanford, Calif.: Stanford University Press, 1966), pp. 27–28.
2. E. S. Carter, "How Invalid Are Marks Assigned by Teachers?" *Journal of Educational Psychology* 43 (1952): 218–28; J. S. Coleman, *The Adolescent Society* (Glencoe, Ill.: Free Press, 1961); E. H. Hanson, "Do Boys Get a Square Deal in School?" *Education* 79 (1959): 597–98.
3. Josef E. Garai and Amram Scheinfeld, "Sex Differences in Mental and Behavioral Traits," *Genetic Psychology Monographs* 77 (1968): 169–299.
4. Michael Lewis, Jerome Kagan, and John Kalafat, "Patterns of Fixation in the Young Infant," *Child Development* 37 (1966): 331–41.
5. Jerome Kagan, "Continuity in Cognitive Development During the First Year," *Merrill-Palmer Quarterly* 15 (1969): 101–19.
6. A. Chamove, Harry F. Harlow, and Gary D. Mitchell, "Sex Differences in the Infant-directed Behavior of Preadolescent Rhesus Monkeys," *Child Development* 38 (1967): 329–35.
7. Herbert Barry III, Margaret K. Bacon, and Irving L. Child, "A Cross-cultural Survey of Some Sex Differences in Socialization," *Journal of Abnormal and Social Psychology* 55 (1957): 327–32.
8. Bruno Bettelheim, "Women: Emancipation Is Still to Come," *New Republic*, November 7, 1964, pp. 48–58.
9. Anne Anastasi, *Differential Psychology* (New York: Macmillan Co., 1958), p. 462.
10. H. Rudolph Schaffer and Peggy E. Emerson, "The Development of Social Attachments in Infancy," *Monographs of the Society for Research in Child Development*, vol. 29, no. 3 (1964).
11. Robert S. Woodworth and Harold Schlosberg, *Experimental Psychology* (New York: Henry Holt & Co., 1954), p. 529.
12. Ruth E. Hartley, "Sex-Role Pressures and the Socialization of the Male Child," *Psychological Reports* 5 (1959): 458.
13. David B. Lynn, *Parental and Sex-Role Identification: A Theoretical Formulation* (Berkeley, Calif.: McCutchan Publishing Corp., 1969), pp. 34–42.
14. David C. McClelland, J. W. Atkinson, R. A. Clark, and E. L. Lowell, *The Achievement Motive* (New York: Appleton-Century-Crofts, Inc., 1953).
15. Pauline S. Sears, "The Effect of Classroom Conditions on the Strength of Achievement Motive and Work Output on Elementary School Children" (final report, cooperative research project no. 873, Stanford University, 1963).
16. Forrest B. Tyler, Janet E. Rafferty, and B. B. Tyler, "Relationships among Motivations of Parents and Their Children," *Journal of Genetic Psychology* 101 (1962): 69–81.

17. Vaughn J. Crandall, Rachel Dewey, Walter Katkovsky, and Ann Preston, "Parents' Attitudes and Behaviors and Grade-School Children's Academic Achievements," *Journal of Genetic Psychology* 104 (1964): 53–66.
18. See Garai and Scheinfeld (n. 3 above); Laberta A. Hatwick, "Sex Differences in Behavior of Nursery School Children," *Child Development* 8 (1957): 343–55; Herman A. Witkin, H. B. Lewis, M. Hertzman, K. Machover, P. B. Meissner, and S. Wapner, *Personality Through Perception* (New York: Harper & Row, 1954).
19. Leona E. Tyler, *The Psychology of Human Differences* (New York: Appleton-Century-Crofts, Inc., 1965), p. 246.
20. Goldine C. Gleser, L. A. Gottschalk, and J. Watkins, "The Relationship of Sex and Intelligence to Choice of Words: A Normative Study of Verbal Behavior," *Journal of Clinical Psychology* 15 (1959): 182–91.
21. Herman A. Witkin, R. B. Dyk, H. F. Faterson, D. R. Goodenough, and S. A. Karp, *Psychological Differentiation* (New York: John Wiley & Sons, 1962).
22. Jerome Kagan, Howard A. Moss, and Irving E. Sigel, "The Psychological Significance of Styles of Conceptualization," *Basic Cognitive Processes in Children*, J. C. Wright and Jerome Kagan, eds., in *Monographs of the Society for Research in Child Development*, vol. 28, no. 2 (1963).
23. Samuel Roll, "Sex Differences in Problem Solving as a Function of Content and Order of Presentation," *Psychonomic Science* 19 (1970): 97.
24. G. Alexander Milton, "Sex Differences in Problem Solving as a Function of Role Appropriateness of the Problem Content," *Psychological Reports* 5 (1959): 705–8.
25. Milton, "The Effects of Sex-Role Identification upon Problem-solving Skill," *Journal of Abnormal and Social Psychology* 55 (1957): 208–12.
26. Daniel G. Brown, "Sex-Role Development in a Changing Culture," *Psychological Bulletin* 54 (1958): 232–42.
27. Kate Millett, *Sexual Politics* (Garden City, N.Y.: Doubleday & Co., 1970), pp. 39–40.
28. John P. McKee and Alex C. Sherriffs, "The Differential Evaluation of Males and Females," *Journal of Personality* 25 (1957): 356–71.
29. S. Smith, "Age and Sex Differences in Children's Opinion concerning Sex Differences," *Journal of Genetic Psychology* 54 (1939): 17–25.
30. Philip Goldberg, "Are Women Prejudiced Against Women?" *Trans-action* 5 (April 1968): 28–30.
31. Gary D. Mitchell, "Attachment Differences in Male and Female Infant Monkeys," *Child Development* 39 (1968): 612–20.
32. Evelyn W. Goodenough, "Interest in Persons as an Aspect of Sex Difference in the Early Years," *Genetic Psychology Monographs* 55 (1957): 287–323.
33. Irvin L. Child, Elmer H. Potter, and Estelle M. Levin, "Children's Textbooks and Personality Development: An Exploration in the Social Psychology of Education," *Psychological Monographs*, vol. 60, no. 3 (1946), whole no. 279; Betty Miles, "Harmful Lessons Little Girls Learn in School," *Redbook* (March 1971), p. 86.
34. See H. H. Davidson and G. Lang, "Children's Perception of Their Teachers' Feelings Toward Them Related to Self-Perception, School Achievement, and Behavior," *Journal of Experimental Education* 29

(1960): 107–18; Sears (n. 15 above); E. Paul Torrance, *Guiding Creative Talent* (Englewood Cliffs, N.J.: Prentice-Hall, Inc., 1962).

35. Gloria L. Carey, "Sex Differences in Problem-solving Performance as a Function of Attitude Differences," *Journal of Abnormal and Social Psychology* 56 (1958): 256–60.

36. See Jean Piaget, *The Moral Judgment of the Child* (New York: Free Press, 1965), p. 77; Leona Tyler, "The Relationship of Interests to Ability and Reputation Among First-Grade Children," *Educational and Psychological Measurement* 11 (1951): 255–64.

37. "Erik Erikson: The Quest for Identity," *Newsweek*, December 21, 1970, p. 87.

17.

NATALIE READER HAIMOWITZ
AND MORRIS L. HAIMOWITZ

WHAT MAKES THEM CREATIVE?

Today the world is seeking creative men and women to invent better solutions to problems and to help us live together more peacefully in a rapidly changing and increasingly complex world.

Creativity, often regarded as a magical, inborn quality, sometimes equated with intelligence and talent, is neither of these. Many people, though possessed of high intelligence and able to grasp and use established methods, cannot innovate or invent. Similarly, many are born with a congenital "facility" known as talent, a physiological predisposition for certain skills and abilities, but are nevertheless unable to create or invent, even in the areas in which they demonstrate talent.

Creativity has been defined as the capacity to innovate, to invent, to place elements in a way in which they have never before been placed, such that their value or beauty is enhanced. Contrasted with conformity, it is the capacity to transcend the usual ways of solving problems or seeing ideas, rules, or relationships.

Creative means not only original, it also includes the unpredictable, surprising, shocking, funny, or poetic—the not rational or not logical or not reasonable. The creative person puts things in new perspectives, performs an act of closure, finds a more elegant solution.

From *Human Development,* by M. L. Haimowitz and N. R. Haimowitz (eds.), 3d ed., (New York: T. Y. Crowell, 1973), pp. 197–207.

METHODS OF PROBLEM SOLVING

In problem solving, we may observe two different methods of approach, both of which have value in a complex culture. On the one hand there is "convergent" thinking, which integrates what is already known, unifying or harmonizing existing facts in a logical, well-organized, orderly manner; it is thinking which conforms to existing knowledge and exacting methods. "Divergent" thinking, on the other hand, reaches into the unknown. Its essence is not its orderliness but its originality. Gulford, having elaborated on these qualitatively dissimilar kinds of thinking, demonstrates that existing intelligence tests rest heavily on skills which are convergent, reflecting cultural values which reward and esteem existing knowledge more highly than they reward innovation and invention.

Obviously, both convergent and divergent thinking are important in the development of a science. A report of the Foundation for Research on Human Behavior at Ann Arbor, Michigan, which defines creativity as "looking at things in a new and different way," points out that divergent thinking occurs at the discovery phase, the insight phase, the intuitive phase of problem solving, and concludes that it is to be contrasted with the kind of restrained thinking concerned with validation of insights and testing of hypotheses. It is the former kinds of abilities, however, that are creative.

As in the world of physical objects and physical forces, creativity is often demonstrated in the interpersonal sphere by finding new ways to resolve interpersonal problems, by discovering new and more satisfying ways to interact with others. . . . Anyone who has observed sensitive and insightful handling of an interpersonal problem can testify that there is such a thing as inventiveness in social relationships. In marked contrast are formal, traditional relationships, in which everyone's behavior is pre-arranged, where everyone knows what is to be done and who will do it.

COMPONENTS OF CREATIVITY

The following components of creativity have been suggested in the literature: basic security, intelligence, flexibility, spontaneity, humor, originality, ability to perceive a variety of essential features of an object or situation, playfulness, competitiveness, radicalness, eccentricity. We would add freedom, marginality, and secularity to this list. Conversely, characteristics which would hypothetically correlate negatively with creativity would be neatness, rigidity, control, thoroughness, reason, logic, respect for tradition and authority, and a tendency to routinize and organize tasks.

DISCOVERING CREATIVE PERSONS

One type of test wherein creative people function differently from equally "intelligent" but less creative persons is the word association test; the more creative person associates a larger number of categories with each word. Another is a hidden-shapes test which requires that the subject find a given geometrical form in a complex pattern in which it is "hidden." Another presents the beginning of a story and asks the subjects to compose first a funny, then a sad, and finally a moralistic ending.

An interesting, simple test asks the subject to draw two parallel lines and to use these lines in making a design. If he makes a design inside the lines, he is restricting himself more than if his design goes outside the two lines:

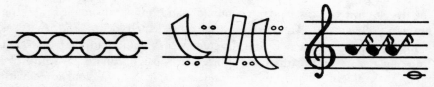

| Less creative, stays in bounds | More creative, transcends bounds, but holds close | Still more creative, adds lines, invents a melody |

Another test gives the subject a problem. "You are newly married. About a month after the wedding, your parents come to visit you for Sunday dinner. Your mother starts cleaning your house. You are angry about this. Let's act it out for 3 or 4 minutes. Now let's act it out again, you taking the part of your mother." The creative person finds new solutions to this stress situation.

Another test asks for a written story: "Here is a picture. Write a story about it." The creative person writes stories or endings to half-completed stories that few others imagine.

Still another test says: "Here is a newspaper. How many uses can you find for it?" The more creative can think of more and better uses than the less creative.

The Rorschach Test uses standardized ink blots. The subject is asked, "Tell me what you see." The creative person perceives objects, forms, and relationships others don't see.

In all these tests, it is assumed that the person who offers creative solutions in the test situation will be more creative in solving real life problems. This is a bold assumption, since many creative persons, being non-conformists, may not be willing to invest energy in the rather arbitrary test situation; they may not care at all about what a newspaper can be used for, nor will they necessarily find pleasure or even interest in making up stories about pictures or ink blots.

CREATIVITY AND OBSESSION

For some persons the act of creating is a most exhilarating experience, the grandest, most exciting event of their lives. Others seem to be driven obsessively, without rest or diversion, until completing the task they had set for themselves. Einstein spoke of being driven by an obsession; the Curies worked without reward for many years before they discovered radium. Edison, the Wright brothers, and Louis Daguerre, who worked for six years to discover a way to make photographs—all seemed to have a clear purpose in mind. Andrew Carnegie said the key to success was first a clear, concise mental picture of the thing one seeks, "A Definite Major Purpose grown or forced into the proportions of an obsession. . . . I knew I wanted to go into the making of steel. I whipped up that desire until it became a driving obsession with me . . . my desire drove me day and night." His second step was the development of "a Mastermind principle," which meant that he involved others in the obsession, others who possessed the qualities he lacked and needed. Carnegie said, "Jesus understood the principle of the Mastermind and made effective use of it in His alliance with His Disciples. That is where I got my first clue. . . ."

 . . . Carnegie felt very strongly that anyone could accomplish just about anything he really tried to accomplish. His biographer Napoleon Hill said to him, "I take it that most of the men who work for you have no Definite Major Purpose in life, for if they had, they, too, would be as rich as you. Is this correct?" To this, Carnegie replied, "You will find that the highest aim of a majority of the men working for me is to hold the jobs they have. They are where they are and they are drawing the wages they receive solely because of the limitations they have set up in their own minds. . . ."

 When Carnegie developed an idea, he used it conscientiously in all areas of his life. Thus, in his home his wife became the partner to the Mastermind: "There are but few marriages which do not need a new and improved plan of relationship at frequent intervals. . . . The time would be well spent if married people set aside a regular hour for a confidential Mastermind meeting at least once every week during which they would come to an understanding concerning every vital factor in their relationship. . . . Keep the fire of romance burning. Let it become a part of the

Mastermind ceremony and your marital relationship will yield priceless returns. . . . The force that is born of a combination of love and sex is the very elixir of life through which nature expresses all creative effort. . . ."

CREATIVITY AND BASIC SECURITY

There are two conflicting views concerning the relationship between inner security and creativity. The reluctance of some talented people to seek psychological help for their emotional problems is supported by the belief that if the individual becomes more comfortable, he may become less creative. We hear this view also from individuals who are associated with minority political or religious movements. The belief is held that with increased security one becomes more satisfied, more conforming, and one loses his need for and interest in unpopular, deviant opinions and activities. According to this view, creativity emerges from dissatisfaction and neurosis.

The other view regards creativity as emerging only when the organism has solved its basic problems of biological and social survival. Maslow, for instance, holds that only when the individual has achieved some sense of basic security—being fed, clothed, safe from harm, achieving sexual satisfaction, being loved by others, esteeming himself—can he spare the energy for the more whimsical, relaxed capacity to innovate and improvise. Similarly Erikson, with his concepts of "autonomy" and "initiative," suggests that only when the individual has solved his more primitive, elemental problems in relating to his world, only when he feels secure enough to initiate, and realistic enough to build a stable sense of personal identity, do "higher" kinds of human activity emerge. In this view, frustration blocks creativity. Both theorists postulate that while the individual is experiencing insecurity in the gratification of the "lower level" of needs, he cannot really be creative.

Carefully conducted, longitudinal studies of creative and not-so-creative individuals and societies might help to clarify the conflicting evidence. Scattered evidence from biographies of famous creative individuals in the arts and sciences (evidence obtained and presented by students of literature rather than by social scientists) fails to support the notion that creativity can only emerge when basic needs have been satisfied. The childhood of such eminent innovators as Darwin, Schubert, Sarah Bernhardt, Brahms, Van Gogh, the Brontës, Gauguin do not stand out as models of security, love, and the satisfaction of basic needs. Darwin was shy, afraid of his successful father. Schubert lived in unbelievable poverty, loving music which his father denied him. Sarah Bernhardt was an illegitimate daughter of a milliner-courtesan with no home and no person to call her own. Alfred Nobel was a hunchback and Schiller reportedly an epileptic.

Of course, doting biographers often play up the Horatio Alger struggles of the impoverished, crippled child who by hard work and courage overcomes impossible obstacles and achieves greatness and immortality. When we attempt, as social scientists, to re-create the lives of those who are no longer living from biography, we must wonder whether what we read is factual or partly the inventiveness of the biographer.

When we study highly creative persons, we often find poverty or physical defects. We also find broken homes, suggesting that the individuals must certainly have experienced loss of parental love through death, rejection, or desertion, and we often notice minority group status in political, religious, or racial groups such that the individual must have experienced some sense of insecurity in his "belongingness" to the larger society. If biography is enough rooted in fact, then we know that factors other than basic security are equally crucial.

CREATIVITY AND INTELLIGENCE

The observation has been made that the more creative are not necessarily the more intelligent. Creativity appears to be in some way associated with intelligence, but the two do not refer to the same dimensions of behavior. Just as creativity is measured operationally, that is, is defined as being what the creativity test measures, so is intelligence measured operationally, as what the intelligence test measures. We assume that the person who shows intelligence in an intelligence test will also show intelligence in other aspects of his life. Yet the intelligence test may fail to tap the devices used by a general planning a campaign or those of a young lady seeking a husband or the behavior of an architect planning a new school or a hostess at a party. The kinds of intelligence valued on intelligence tests are verbal, memory, or convergent—organizing, logical *skills*—rather than divergent, original kinds of *talents*. Creative talents may be penalized or missed in typical intelligence tests. While those who seem to innovate successfully are apparently also those with high intelligence, it is quite possible to discover highly intelligent persons who do not innovate and discover, and to find highly creative persons who do not show superiority on intelligence tests.

Getzels and Jackson did just that. They gave both intelligence tests and tests of creativity to 449 adolescents. As might be expected, many scored high in both intelligence and creativity tests, others low in both kinds of tests. From the 449 subjects, two special groups were selected out: one of 24 individuals who scored in the highest 20 per cent in intelligence, but not highest in creativity; and the second group of 28 who scored in the top 20 per cent in creativity, but did not excel in intelligence.

Comparing these two groups showed that "despite striking differences in mean IQ the creative and intelligent groups were equally superior to the total population in school performance as measured by the standardized achievement tests." Yet, from teachers' ratings, they found that teachers preferred the intelligent group rather than the creative. They also found that the need for achievement was no different in either group from the total population. Most striking differences were found when comparing the fantasy materials of the two groups. Judges, working blindly, could with high accuracy place authors of fantasy productions in the correct group—either "high intelligence" or "highly creative." The creative subjects consistently used more stimulus-free, humorous, and playful themes. Intelligent subjects' fantasy productions were orderly, logical, but "bound."

Other studies indicate that original people prefer certain types of intellectual tasks, prefer the complex to the simple problem or solution—they delay coming to conclusions until most of the pieces can be fitted together —and that creative people have more energy and are more impulsive and responsive to emotion, even when solving problems.

In *The Creative Process*, a study of 38 geniuses, including the introspective reports of such men as Einstein, Henry James, D. H. Lawrence, and Van Gogh, Ghiselin suggests that those who are creative have passion and skill for their work and, when concerned with major problems which they cannot solve, appear to "forget" the problem for a time. But they would suddenly, while asleep, taking a walk, reading a book, or talking about something else, be struck with the solution. The idea would appear to be coming from their own unconscious, which had been working on the problem all the time. . . .

CREATIVITY AND FREEDOM

. . . The very act of creating something new and different involves the courage to go beyond cultural limits. When we study the childhood biographies of creative artists, scientists, inventors, such as the Brontës, Fermi, Thomas Jefferson, Shaw, Whitney, Edison, Robert Burns, we are impressed with the apparent freedom they experienced in their early lives, even though it may have been associated with parental neglect, death, or desertion. They seemed to live in the midst of broad areas in which to roam, with freedom to explore, with privacy to contemplate. In many biographies, we find the absence of the parent of the same sex. Perhaps the trauma of the loss had its compensations in freedom, absence of parental coercion, and less oedipal competition, and an absence of "a mold into which to fit oneself and with which to identify."

Such hypotheses arise as we recognize the fact that so many well-known persons have come from broken homes: Washington, Jefferson, Lincoln, Herbert Hoover, Bach, Beethoven, Schubert, Schumann, Stalin, Hitler, Stonewall Jackson, the Brontës, Robert Burns, Robert Fulton, Sibelius, Debussy, Andrew Johnson, Tchaikowsky, Gauguin, Leonardo da Vinci, James Garfield, Joseph Conrad, Michelangelo, Andrew Jackson, and hundreds of others.

No statistical study has been made to determine whether such a hypothesis as this would be true: the fathers of eminent men and women died or left the family before the child reached puberty in greater proportions than the fathers of the noneminent. . . . Some sons without fathers become more creative; others become more delinquent.

Certainly the death of a parent in the child's infancy may so shatter basic security as to make creativity impossible. However, losing a parent in middle or late childhood may give the child more freedom and more responsibility. A number of studies by Watson, Baldwin, Lafore, Hattwick, Symonds, and Carpenter indicate that children from permissive homes, where considerable personal freedom is permitted, are much more likely to be creative than children from restrictive homes.

Imagine the courage it takes to tackle the proposition that the world is composed of atoms and that these atoms are made up of neutrons and electrons. One cannot see an atom or an electron or neutron; one cannot even demonstrate them easily, as one can the invisible forces of gravity or electricity. The same is true for concepts in psychology. One cannot see motivation of the superego, and they are very difficult to demonstrate. If it takes courage to try to understand these concepts, think how much more courage would be required to imagine the concept, to create it. When developing new concepts, one is leaving the culture, leaving the traditional, taking off for a new world, in the manner of Columbus. . . .

Creativity thus appears to be associated with freedom in the self which arises from freedom in the family, in the committee, the club, the social gathering, or any small group. By "freedom" here is meant the absence of a domineering group member or leader and the absence of felt status differences. In our experiments with small groups we have noted more willingness of members to explore, to suggest wild ideas, to joke about the purposes or methods of the group when the designated leader is quietly receptive to such behavior. Very often a leader may encourage group participation, but his domineering ways block participation and creativity. For example, he may ask the group to make suggestions but, instead of waiting patiently for them, would go ahead and make his own. Later he may report, "I tried to get them to open up, but they wouldn't. They just don't have ideas." The leader who tries to impose standards against the wishes of the group will evoke more apathy or rebellion than creativity.

Studies in group dynamics suggest leadership is essential for a creative atmosphere. Leadership may be defined as any act of any member which helps the progress of the group. Thus, if two members are blocking each other's actions and dividing the group into two anxious and opposing camps, progress may be blocked. An act of leadership might be to point this situation out to the group or it might be a suggestion for a five-minute break or a suggestion that the collection of some data would settle the differences or a joke about how much we all hate each other. Every class-room needs creative ideas for the optimum advancement of the class. Thus, the best teacher is not only one skilled in the content of the subject matter, but also one skilled in group leadership.

Some children learn better working alone; others work better in pairs or in small groups; still others do best in large groups. Some children are aware of their peculiar needs in this respect, but others are not. In our own classes we have often asked for volunteers for a committee job. When the job calls for six persons on one committee, different people will respond than when the task calls for three committees of two each. When we ask the students about this, some say, "I like to work with only one other person" or "I like to work in a larger group." Recognition, acceptance, and use of individual differences in such matters greatly benefits the teacher as well as the students; and leadership in the home, school, church, camp, or factory is a major factor in creativity.

CREATIVITY AND MARGINALITY

Some students of civilization, such as Hume, Teggart, Bucher, William James, and Robert Park, have described a catastrophic theory of progress. Park points out that races are the product of isolation and inbreeding, while civilization is a consequence of contact and communication. The decisive events in man's history have been those which brought men together through the catastrophes of mass migration. The collisions, conflicts, and fusions of peoples and cultures incidental to these migrations cause both tragedy and creativity. Bucher writes that every advance in culture commences with a new period of wandering.

Somewhere in his own wanderings over the earth, Robert Park invented the term "marginal man" to indicate what Simmel had called "the stranger." The stranger is one who stays but is a potential wanderer; he is thus not bound, as others are, by the local proprieties and customs. He is the freer man. He is less involved with others, and he can be more objective in his judgment since he is not confined by one set of customs, pieties, or precedents. The stranger is the man of the cities, where division of labor and increased production have emancipated him from the age-old struggle against starvation and have given him freedom from ancient customs as well as leisure to create.

. . . In his autobiography *Upstream*, Ludwig Lewisohn wavers between the warm security of the ghetto which he has left and the cold freedom of the outer world where he is a stranger. Heine had the same problem, struggling to be a German and also a Jew. He was both, and being both he was not fully either. He was a marginal man, and he was creative.

The marginal man is the Okie in California, the Puerto Rican in New York, the southern white migrant in Chicago, the European in America and the American in Europe, the mulatto who mingles with whites, the white man in Africa, the Irishman in England, the Catholic in Asia or in the Protestant South.

Marginality, while personally costly, also sets a man free, makes it possible for him to be creative, to see aspects of a culture in a new light because he comes from another culture. When we study the highly esteemed creative men of our culture, it seems that marginality is far more the rule than the exception.

George Bernard Shaw, for example, was born a Protestant in Catholic Ireland. Economically and socially on the fringes of the middle class, his social position was continually threatened by the economic embarrassment and alcoholism of his father. He was personally neglected by his parents. Shaw departed from the home of his childhood to live and work as an Irishman in London, clearly an outgroup position. His circumstances can be easily said to have led to his cynicism. And his cynicism about his father, his religion, his economic and social order, and most of the institutions of his day is the essence of his creativity.

. . . Freud was a Jew in a non-Jewish society, as was Karl Marx. Joseph Conrad was the orphan of Polish nationals exiled in Russia. Sarah Bernhardt was the child of unmarried parents of different religions. Mme. Curie was Polish, living in France; Gershwin was the son of immigrants. Stalin was a Georgian; Hitler an Austrian; Napoleon a Corsican; and Churchill, half-American. Their marginality led to creativity or to other intense effort—the pursuit of political power. It may be that the outcast position of marginality enables the individual to get diverse, multidimensional views of values and customs that those thoroughly "in" society or class fail to achieve or do not need. It may be this very multidimensionality, and perhaps the insecurity and defensiveness that goes with marginality, which prevents the individual from "swallowing" wholeheartedly the traditional values, practices, and beliefs of the dominant society. The marginal man can innovate, partly because he does not accept the cultures as he sees them (his isolation creates resistance) and partly because he sees divergent possibilities where "belongers" see only one way, the way to which they are accustomed.

The group most responsible for emotionalized attitudes is the primary group. If the individual is fairly secure in his early family relationships and if the values of the family place great emphasis on the family traditions, we would expect the individual to carry on the family traditions. If, however, he is marginal in his family (feels "left out" emotionally, physically, or psychologically), originality may emerge. It may also emerge when a person is thoroughly entrenched in a family which honors innovation and change as important values.

Although marginality may be a precondition of creativity, it may produce the reverse. No one can be so uncreative, so rigid as the marginal man. The new convert, for example, is typically the most conforming. The 100 per cent American is often a European who just got here, or his child. The *nouveaux riches* are the most careful about their clothes, carpets, and coiffures. What makes the creative marginal man different from the one who is an extreme conformist? We suggest that one major difference is his sense of humor, which accepts one's own playful, childish, spontaneous, loving, hating, stingy, and generous impulses. (Aristotle, St. Augustine, Newton, Galileo, and Freud are striking exceptions.) Watson suggests that a permissive home atmosphere is most important in the development of creativity.

CREATIVITY AND RIVALRY

The pressure to win over a rival appears to be an important element in creativity. Studies of the lives of great scientists show they were tremendously concerned about receiving recognition for their achievements. After all, most great discoveries or inventions were made by several persons at about the same time. Intense rivalries as to who was first—the question of *priority*—occupied a great deal of their time and energy. Darwin was ashamed of this preoccupation, but Newton and Galileo seemed only angry that others might dare say, "I found it first."

Newton was not merely concerned with establishing his priority for the law of universal gravitation and for his work on optics and the calculus; he also was occasionally obsessed by this. His manuscripts contain twelve versions of a defense of his priority against Leibniz in the invention of the calculus. When president of the Royal Society, Newton appointed a committee to adjudicate the rival claims of Leibniz, and packed the committee with his adherents.

Alfred Nobel engaged in a long, continuing battle with Frederick Abel and James Dewar over the invention of smokeless gunpowder. The Nobel Foundation library holds many yards of shelves documenting Nobel's arguments that he perfected it first.

Merton and Barber examined a sample of 264 multiple discoveries in the history of science. They found of the 36 multiples before 1700, 92 per cent were strenuously contested.

Per Cent of Multiple Discoveries Strenuously Contested (n=264)

Before 1700 (n=36)	92
18th century	72
First half 19th century	72
Second half 19th century	59
20th century	33

Adoring biographers of great men frequently claim their idols were above such interests. Ernest Jones, in his excellent biography of Sigmund Freud, wrote that "Freud was never interested in questions of priorities, which he found merely boring." Merton calls this "an extraordinarily illuminating statement by a scholar who had devoted his own life to penetrating the depths of the human soul. For, of course, no one could have known better than Jones . . . how very often Freud turned to matters of priority. . . . Freud expressed an interest in this matter on more than 150 recorded occasions."

Similarly, we find the following concerned with priority: Descartes, Pascal, Lister, Michelangelo, Galileo, and the men striving to be first to reach the South Pole, or the Moon, to transplant a heart, or to find a cure for cancer, pollution, or a disease-resistant corn.

SACRED AND SECULAR VALUES

In a sacred or folk society, creativity is discouraged. The late Robert Redfield defined a folk society as a relatively stable, small, homogeneous, isolated community, where unchanging traditions guide behavior. This kind of society does not seek change and tends to reject innovations. Most traditions have religious meaning. To alter them is sacrilegious. Wankel is receiving millions of dollars for his design for a simple gasoline engine. Priority means fame and fortune.

Redfield contrasted the folk society with the secular society, which is rapidly changing, large, heterogeneous, in communication with distant lands; its values favor the new, the different, where nothing is more worthless than yesterday's newspaper or last season's styles, and nothing so valuable as a new cloth for men's shirts or a new spray for mosquitoes. A child reared in such a society, assimilating his culture, learns to value the novel, to adopt new fads with pleasurable expectations, and perhaps he begins to look forward to setting the pace himself. If his innovations or inventions should strike the popular fancy, he is a great man, for a moment at least.

Thus, if the group has a favorable attitude toward change, a milieu is created in which creativity is favored. In interviews with 200 scientists and artists, we asked, "Were you ever seriously encouraged by a teacher?" Nearly all said "Yes."

In an analysis of the childhood of 1,400 great men and women, we repeatedly found the overwhelming importance of an outstanding teacher. We believe the single most crucial step in increasing creativity in our society would be to recruit and hold the best teachers.

Children appear to lose much of their creative ability at age five and again at age ten. Whether this is a developmental or imposed loss is not yet known for certain, but the small evidence collected supports the possibility that children stop being creative because obedience, conformity, and discipline are expected by the family, school, and neighborhood more than creativity is expected. Those classes with teachers skilled in developing creativity probably will not suffer the usual fourth-grade slump in creativity.

The creative process involves several stages:

A. Becoming deeply involved in a task with no clear or immediate solution.
B. Forgetting about the problem while becoming engaged in other tasks for a few hours or days.
C. Suddenly, without reason or explanation, understanding the solution in a more or less exciting *Hooray! I've got it!* experience.
D. Further work in developing the solution.

A teacher can encourage students in each stage of the process. At Stage A he or she asks, depending on class, age, and so on, such questions as:

1. What are your interests?
2. How much should a child love a parent?
3. How can our neighborhood be improved?
4. What can be done about poor housing, pollution, unemployment?

5. How can geologists dig more efficiently?
6. Listen to this music, then paint a picture and tell a story about it.
7. Role play our class, making fun of teacher, school, subject matter.
8. List all the signs you can think of that show that creative learning is going on.
9. Write your own songs, poems, stories, plays.
10. Divide into groups of three, and talk about what you like and don't like about friends.
11. Seated in groups of six or eight, discuss how you would go about making friends, or settling an argument with someone.

At Stages B, C, and D, time is provided in the class, especially for Stage D. Creativity can be encouraged by asking students to observe reality in detail by looking at, handling, and describing a simple object—a leaf, a fingernail, or pencil—drawing it, or making up a story or song about it; showing appreciation for their accomplishments by praising the children publicly; and by urging them to examine problems and new ideas in some systematic way to find out how true they are. Creativity is also encouraged by providing opportunities for working together as well as alone, in active as well as silent daydream sessions, in times to imitate and times to express their own feelings and ideas and times to play games of their own invention with their own rules.

Books that stimulate imagination and fantasy and thinking processes have been written by Bruno Munari, Janet Wolff, Bernard Owelt, Alastair Reed, Lenore Klein, and many others. "Guess what animal is so big it would take a whole room to stand up in?" "The butterfly wishes it could be stronger. What do you think it would like to be?" "Let's go for a make-believe walk on the mountain." The teacher tells the story and the children act it out. "Look at the pretty blue flowers. Watch out! There's a deep ravine! Let's walk around it. See the big bear. Who wants to be the bear? Who will be the pretty blue flowers? Oh, there is a cardinal! Who will be the cardinal?"

Creative children tend to have strong drives to act without regard for the group. They may become dominant and thus be isolated or criticized by their age-mates. They can pose quite a problem in the classroom. Creative teachers can sometimes identify the more creative children by observing their wide range of interests or unconventional vocational choices and can encourage creativity, while also teaching such children human relations skills: how to be assertive as well as friendly, how to work alone effectively without becoming withdrawn.

SUMMARY

In exploring some of the environmental and experiential factors in creativity, the following have been considered: enough feeling of security to risk venturing beyond social norms; intelligence involving divergent rather than convergent thinking, which seems to be related to a highly developed sense of humor; freedom to explore, to think, to feel, to roam; enough pressure from marginality to push the person outside his family or social group; and a secular social climate which favors innovation. Such a social climate is fostered by good teachers, informality, freedom for all to participate, skilled but not domineering leadership, opportunity to rotate roles, and a feeling of trust and equality among group members.

1. Creative ideas come to those persons who are looking intensely for solutions to problems.
2. Creative solutions may be systematically developed in classrooms from kindergarten through graduate school.
3. Creative solutions are found when the problem has no immediate "right answer." Teaching problems with "right answers" develops imitation and memory skills but retards creativity.
4. Tasks can be designed for students which require less imitation and more creative solutions.

REFERENCES

S. J. Beck. *Rorschach's Test*, Vols. I and II (New York: Grune and Stratton, 1946).

Foundation for Research on Human Behavior. *Creativity and Conformity* (Ann Arbor, Mich.: The Foundation, 1958).

J. W. Getzels and P. W. Jackson. "The Highly Creative and the Highly Intelligent Adolescent: An Attempt at Differentiation." A paper presented at the American Psychological Association Convention, Washington, D.C., August, 1958.

Brewster Ghiselin. *The Creative Process* (Berkeley: University of California Press, 1952).

J. C. Goway. *Creativity* (New York: Wiley, 1967).

J. P. Guilford, *et al.*, "A Factor-Analytic Study of Creative Thinking," Report from Psychological Laboratory, University of Southern California, 1951–52.

Napoleon Hill. *How to Raise Your Salary* (Chicago: Combined Registry Co.).

L. Lewisohn. *Upstream* (New York: Boni & Liveright, 1922).

Robert R. Merton. "Behavior Patterns of Scientists," *The American Scholar* (Spring 1969): 197–225.

R. E. Park. *Race and Culture* (Glencoe, Ill.: The Free Press, 1950).

Robert Redfield. *The Folk Culture of Yucatán* (Chicago: University of Chicago Press, 1941).

Georg Simmel. *Soziologie* (Leipzig: Duncker und Humblot, 1908).

CHAPTER SEVEN

The Dynamics of School Adjustment

THE REPORT of the Joint Commission on Mental Health of Children (1970) emphasized the importance of children's psychological well-being. This has become a primary concern for education, since the schools have the responsibility to try to prevent the development of mental health problems, which tend to expand and rigidify with age, and also to make education a positive experience in terms of the child's over-all growth.

A child's adjustment to school is related to the problems and pressures that confront him and to the coping behaviors he is able to muster in a given situation. Estimates of the extent of mental-health problems vary considerably, for objective criteria as to who is mentally ill and who is not are difficult to specify. Nevertheless, teachers and administrators agree that a substantial number of children simply do not adjust very well to the pressures of school life. Whether the central cause of adjustment difficulties is in the school environment, the home, or the community, the school can have a significant effect in helping a child develop healthy ways of coping with his emotional and behavioral difficulties. There are many basic principles and practices of mental-health assessment that are important aspects of preparation of a teacher. The teacher is a major component of the child's total mental-health environment.

Achievement itself is therapeutic, especially if the child has achieved little in the past. Therefore, successful academic experiences can be a large step toward emotional growth. The teacher must, first of all, present classroom materials and tasks that are appropriate for the child's ability level and motivation and thus must maximize the likelihood of his having successful experiences. A second classroom variable under the teacher's control is the kind of management techniques employed in the classroom. A generally punitive environment may lead to the apparent suppression of problem behaviors, which often reappear, compounded by harmful emotional sideeffects resulting from pervasive punishment. A third aspect of the classroom relevant to a child's mental health is how much personal acceptance and recognition as an individual the child receives. In each of these three areas, the teacher is the key element.

Research indicates that teachers today are more sophisticated about mental health in the classroom than teachers were in the 1930s and 1940s. Also, today's teachers have access to more information about mental-health problems in children and their relationship to school than the teachers of twenty to thirty years ago. In addition, many more schools have support services such as guidance counselors, social workers, psychologists, and other community agencies to which the teacher can refer a child having adjustment difficulties in the school situation. These professionals may also function in a preventative mental-health role by working with student groups, families, and community groups.

Morse's article analyzes the problems of emotional disturbance. It was written explicitly for the teacher—beginner and veteran alike—and should sensitize the reader to the reality of mental illness. Morse implies that special planning may be needed to help the teacher to cope with the problem child in the regular classroom setting. Sometimes the teacher is part of the problem the child is manifesting—for example, he may inadvertently be reinforcing a behavior that is a source of difficulty in the classroom setting.

As we have seen earlier, the quality of the relationship between teacher and pupil is of great importance. One facet of the relationship is built on verbal transactions that influence perceptions and behavior. Mueller and Baker analyze specific aspects of verbal transactions that frequently occur between teacher and student in middle and senior high school. In this context, it must be stated that most children take what teachers say to them quite seriously—most of the time, anyway—although it may not seem so to teachers. Since communication is so vital, teachers need to be aware of the effects their words have on young people.

Finally, Levine's article on transcendental meditation touches on a topic of growing interest, self-actualization in the affective area. It may not necessarily become accepted in the form in which it is now practiced, but it is reasonable to predict that one version or another of personal meditation or bio-feedback training will be tried out in the schools. Research indicates that, unlike sensitivity training, TM has no negative side-effects; the participant either experiences an improved emotional state, or else nothing happens—he simply doesn't profit from it.

But the research is not yet complete. TM needs to be tried out by teachers as well as by professionally trained personnel. Any technique for the betterment of children in school can be useful only if it can be implemented by teachers. Today, however, the outlook appears promising.

RECOMMENDED READING

Association for Supervision and Curriculum Development. 1966. *Learning and Mental Health in the Classroom* (Washington, D.C.: National Education Association). A practical guide that will help teachers to diagnose referral cases and to develop preventive techniques in the classroom.

J. B. Dusek. 1974. "Implications for Developmental Theory for Child Mental Health," *American Psychologist* 29(1), 19–24. The ways that developmental theories of growth and development can be utilized to meet the objectives of the 1970 Joint Commission on Mental Health of Children.

E. H. Erikson. 1968. *Identity: Youth and Crisis* (Norton & Co.). The "identity crisis"—a major emotional hurdle of adolescents—is discussed by one of today's major authorities in developmental psychology.

J. Holt. 1964. *How Children Fail* (New York: Ditman). A widely quoted description of the ways by which children become alienated and rejected during the process of schooling; shows how teachers themselves sometimes cause mental health problems in the classroom.

Joint Commission on Mental Health of Children. 1970. *Digest of Crisis in Child Mental Health: Challenge of the 1970's.* Authoritative data on national trends in mental health problems of young people, with recommendations for the future.

S. B. Sarason. 1960. *Anxiety in Elementary School Children* (New York: Wiley). Still a fresh and useful resource book for the practitioner.

18.   WILLIAM C. MORSE

DISTURBED YOUNGSTERS IN THE CLASSROOM

John can make a shambles of my classroom. The only way I can get anyplace talking with him is away from the group. Then he explains very clearly why he does various things. He usually admits that they were dumb things to do, but there is no carryover. He already has a court record.

"And then there are Beth and George. Beth is so quiet and dreamy

From *Today's Education*, 58:4 (1969), 30–37.

that she seems here only when I press her with questions and then she drifts away. George is another story. His conversations are non sequiturs. He asks the strangest questions—and always with a worried look. The psychologist has referred him for intensive treatment, but there is a long waiting list. Most of the time I can almost keep on top of the situation, but there are days when I don't seem to be getting anywhere."

An experienced teacher was describing her classroom. Almost any teacher in almost any school could paint a similar picture, and although the percentage of Johns, Beths, and Georges in the typical classroom is small, it does not take huge numbers of disturbed youngsters to create a critical mass that can confound a teacher and convert a classroom to chaos.

What can a teacher do that will be helpful to the disturbed children in the classroom and at the same time will keep them from disrupting the rest of the class? Source books are not available for teaching attitudes, values, identification, or empathic behavior. Advice ranges from the assured behavior modifiers who direct the teacher to "train" the pupils to the proponents of a leave-them-alone-and-they'll-all-come-home-to-Summerhill philosophy.

These answers are too simple. If the schools are to meet their responsibility toward all children, teachers and schools must change. Teachers need to understand what causes the disturbed children in their classes to be that way. They need to develop new teaching skills and to find new ways of using resources. School systems need to look for new ways to use the resources—the time, space, techniques, and personnel—now available and to add new resources.

UNDERSTANDING DISTURBED PUPILS

Some children are disturbed both in their home-community life and in school. Their difficulties are pervasive—with them wherever they go. For example, many a youngster who is rejected and unwanted in his family feels the same way in school.

In other children, disturbance shows up at home or at school but not in both situations. Ralph, for instance, is a skilled leader on the playground and in his neighborhood and gets along reasonably well in his fatherless home. He chafes under the pressure of school routines, however. He is in constant contest with conformity demands and has no interest in school learning. Generally speaking, he is happy-go-lucky and forgets a school disciplinary episode almost before it is over.

Other children who feel supported and do very well in school have difficulties elsewhere. The school is sometimes central in problem behavior and sometimes peripheral, but the aim is to make the school compensatory whenever possible.

The behavior symptoms a child displays are not an automatic revelation of the causes of that behavior. To plan effectively for a disturbed child, the teacher needs not only to see accurately what the youngster does but to understand why he does it. This requires the teacher to do some diagnostic thinking and to gain the ability to see life through the eyes of the pupil.

Let us apply diagnostic thinking first to pupils who are aggressive toward peers, perhaps toward the teacher, and even toward school requirements—pupils who display what is called "acting-out behavior." Children with this broad range of symptoms are the most frequent referrals to special services and special classes. They may provoke fights, break rules, and generally defy the teacher. Older youngsters often turn sullen and hostile. Acting-out children prevent others from working, may react with an outburst if required to conform, and are ready to rebel at a moment's notice.

Since this type of behavior can make conducting classes impossible, no one should be surprised that teachers find it the most vexing difficulty.

When teachers explore beyond the generalized acting-out symptoms, they find some common patterns.

Sometimes aggressiveness results from a lack of adequate socialization. Our culture is producing increasing numbers of children who have never developed social concerns for others, who still function on an impulse basis, doing what they want to do when they feel like it. For one reason or another they lack a suitable prototype for basic identification. Sometimes they take on an omnipotent character—"No one can make me." At best they are narcissistic, bent on following their own desires; at worst they are without the capacity to feel for others. They practice a primitive hedonism.

Sometimes, these children come from indulgent, protective families and become embittered when crossed. When one is asked why he did something, he is likely to say, "I felt like it," until he learns it goes over better to say that he doesn't know why.

Because his delinquent and destructive behavior may stem from a lack of incorporated norms and values, the child with a defect in socialization needs a benign but strong surveillance, so that he is held accountable for misbehavior. He requires clear and specific limits, enforced without anger or harshness. At the same time, he needs models, such as a "big brother," teachers, and older youths, to set an example of proper behavior.

The process of rehabilitation of the unsocialized child is slow and rough, with many periods of regression, because the school is asking the child to give up immediate gratification for long-term goals and to replace self-seeking with consideration for the rights of others. Frequently these youngsters make their first attachment to a single strong teacher and will comply only with his demands. Generalized trust builds slowly. Substantial correction, especially at adolescence, is most difficult. Since the school is the major conformity agent of society, it becomes the natural battle-ground.

A subgroup among the aggressive children is composed of youngsters who lack social skills but have the capacity to learn them because they have been cared about and loved at home, even though their families have been too disorganized to teach adequate behavior. They are not so much anticonforming as they are untutored in social skills. Role playing and demonstrations by models are useful to show such children the behavior expected of them.

While the reduction of acting-out behavior through teaching basic socialization is difficult, teachers still must try. Learning to value the rights of others is essential for members of a democratic society and recent follow-up studies indicate that neither individual treatment nor institutional custody is a satisfactory approach for such youth.

Another common cause of acting-out behavior is alienation. Estrangement from the educational establishment is occurring more and more frequently. Sometimes, from their very first day, these students find no gratification in the school experience, and their disinterest turns to hostility. The teacher sees these youngsters as problems in motivation. "They just don't seem to care about anything they should be doing."

For the most part, these are not weak children, and they are often well-accepted by peers outside of school. Having found life engaging elsewhere, they can't wait to get at it. One sixth grader had already figured out the number of days until he could quit school. Cars, money, the opposite sex, jobs—these are high demands of the alienated adolescent.

Youngsters like this are usually first admonished, then suspended to "shape them up." Suspension actually works in reverse, since they want out in the first place. If the youngsters are not suspended, too many teachers handle the problem by demanding nothing and letting them do just about as they please.

The better way of resolving the difficulty would be to undertake a thorough examination of the curriculum to see what could be altered. A junior high school pupil, already conducting a profitable business of his own, found nothing in classes with any meaning to him. With visions of establishing himself as an adult, he finally ran away with his girl friend.

Education is turning off an increasing number of able and intellectual youths. Such disenchantment was evidenced first at the college level, but it has already seeped down to the junior high. Many young people feel that school is a meaningless scramble for grades and graduation instead of the authentic education experience they seek. What often needs to be done is to make over the school rather than the pupil, but some teachers still rigidly follow the current curriculum as though it were sacred.

In some children, acting-out behavior in school is reaction to failure. No one wants to fail or even be in a marginal position, and yet thousands get failure messages every school day. The child comes to hate the establishment that makes him a failure, so he strikes back. Some failed first at home, where nothing they did was as good as what a sibling did—where no matter how hard they tried, they failed. The hatred such children feel for adults at home may transfer to their teachers, who may never have been in the least unfair.

The amount of defiling and belittling, to say nothing of direct abuse, that children suffer in our supposedly child-favoring culture comes as a shock to many a protected teacher. If the cause of acting-out behavior is in the home, then acting out in school is merely a displacement, but the acting-out child gets a reputation that is passed along ahead of him and he lives up to it.

School can be too taxing for certain children, grading too severe, and teacher's help too scarce. Although they get along well at home, children with mild learning disabilities or limited academic ability frequently drift into frustration at school. Some of the slow-developing early primary pupils or late-blooming adolescents in junior high are too immature to meet expectations. The solution is for the school to adjust to the pupil by proper pacing. Many of these pupils change surprisingly when a perceptive teacher builds in success.

Still other children who act out are anxious about their lives in general. Often they are hyperactive, driven to release tension through physical activity. They are oversensitive, easily distracted, and given to disruptive behavior. After misbehaving, they feel guilty and promise never to repeat the offense, but in a subsequent period of anxiety they do repeat it, acting out in order to dissipate tension.

Some of this group actually seek punishment because they feel they are bad and should pay the penalty. This feeling of guilt may stem from wrong things they have done or merely thought of doing. For instance, one boy, who was being stimulated by a seductive mother, used to blow up in math class, where concentration was required. He could do the math, but not when he was upset. It took the social worker a long time to help him work this out.

A special category of anxiousness, found with increasing frequency in suburbia, is achievement neurosis. In order to meet overt or covert expectations, pupils who have this affliction feel compelled to be on top. They have lost the satisfaction of learning as its own reward; grades are to prove they are as good as their parents want them to be. These youngsters are frequently tense and driven and overvalue the academic. Their parents are forever inquiring, "How well is John doing?"

Children who are driven in this way need to be made to feel better about themselves. Some of them demand much attention, always seeking resubstantiation by adult approval. If the source of the damaged self-picture is an overdemanding home or neighborhood, it is often difficult to provide enough compensatory success in school to allay it. This is where counselors, psychiatrists, psychologists, school social workers, or referral agencies play their part.

By now it is easy to see why any two acting-out children may not need the same type of help from the teacher. But teachers' concerns are not limited to those who directly disrupt the educational process, for the profession is equally attuned to pupils who have given up. While withdrawn children may not cause the teacher managerial difficulty, they, too, are in need of special assistance.

Many unhappy, depressed youngsters are in school today. Basically, these youngsters have very low self-esteem; they have somehow been taught by life that they are good-for-nothing and important to nobody. Often, internal preoccupation takes over, and they drift into a world of fantasy. They absorb the support sensitive teachers give, but often this is not sufficient to strengthen them to a point where they can sustain themselves.

Sometimes students are confirmed losers. They just know they will fail and usually contrive to make their anticipations come true. Others come to rely on fate rather than on their own efforts. As one youngster put it: "Fifty-fifty, I pass or I flunk. It depends on the breaks." So why put forth any effort?

Another group of the withdrawn children are the lonely ones. The loner drifts by himself at recess or eats alone in the junior high cafeteria or has no one to talk to about his high school lessons. Because he feels that nobody would care, he sees no point in trying to make friends. Many youngsters who are scapegoats in their peer group come from among the lonely ones, especially if they have some physical problem such as overweight, a tic, or odd looks. In these cases, the way the teacher manages the group life in the classroom is just as important as individual attention and counseling.

DEALING WITH DISTURBED PUPILS

No magic, no single cure, no shortcut will solve the problems of disturbed children in the schools. The job demands an extension of the individualization that is the essence of good school practice. This calls for teacher time and specially planned curricular experiences. To provide these, many school systems will add a new resource—the psychological, social-work, or psychiatric consultant. Conflict between specialists and regular classroom teachers used to be commonplace, but teachers have now discovered a new way to use the specialists' help, replacing long discourses on "how Johnny got that way" with discussions of what can be done now, in the classroom.

Frequently, a curriculum expert and the principal should join the teacher and the special consultant in discussions about a disturbed child. Remedial action should be based on study of the deviant youngster's classroom behavior and of his basic personality. Clinical insights provide the backdrop for practical planning.

When the problem is caused not by the school but by the child's home situation, the remedial goal is to have the school provide a supportive environment that will compensate, in part, for what is lacking or negative. Referral services to agencies that can offer individual therapy are vital also. They are not enough, however. Group work agencies, boys' clubs, and big brothers can help the unsocialized child who does not have serious internal conflicts. Such a child is in dire need of basic identification building.

Many disturbed children who can function within normal bounds and utilize the regular classroom much of the time lapse occasionally into disruptive behavior that throws the classroom into chaos. Some schools —secondary as well as elementary—deal with this problem by having a special teacher, trained to work with the disturbed in both academic and behavioral spheres, to whom such a child goes during a crisis. This teacher works with him in a special classroom where he can receive assistance on both individual and small group bases.

While the issue is still current, the crisis teacher and the child discuss the matter, much after the fashion of crisis intervention in community mental health. Close liaison with the regular teacher is, of course, mandatory. Referrals to a school or community service for intensive individual work may be needed, but the crisis teacher is the key person to support the regular classroom teacher and the pupil and to coordinate the entire effort in time of stress. When the pupil has gained control and/or is able to do the task in question, he returns to the regular classroom.

NEEDED CHANGES

The task is to examine the classroom environment and the teacher's role. What changes will improve the helping index?

No one has any idea of making the teacher into a psychotherapist, although many disturbed students form a profound relationship with their teachers. The function of the teacher is to provide pupils with a reasonable human relationship (in itself therapeutic) and the opportunity to grow through academic accomplishment and social learning.

Achievement is therapeutic for a child, especially when he has achieved little or nothing in the past. Having an adult who cares about him and who helps him when he falters instead of getting angry and rejecting him is certainly helpful. Peer acceptance in the classroom has lasting significance for the lonely child.

In this sense, therapeutic intervention has always been a part of school, but some children need much more. Providing that more will require three things:

1. The schools will have to reexamine how the curriculum, methodology, and experiences can be bent to enhance growth and minimize failure.
2. Teachers will have to learn new skills.
3. Teachers will have to become more open about their feelings toward disturbed children, because externalizing attitudes is a necessary step in changing negative feelings.

Since the school operation itself provokes a considerable amount of school difficulty, what is taught and how it is taught will require adjustment. Pupils need short assignments that interest them and that they are capable of doing. Not only the level of difficulty but the rate of learning should be attuned to the child, with provision for remedial teaching of what he has missed.

Individualization for the alienated youngster requires new subject matter that is relevant rather than merely different. Some children with learning disabilities require the use of self-tutoring devices. Iconoclastic curriculums, such as cooperative work programs for older youths, are needed.

Although most behaviorists avoid considering disturbed children in any but symptomatic terms, they offer the teacher two most useful guidelines.

First, they tell teachers to study what the child actually does. Observation of how and to what the pupil responds often shows that much of what the teacher is doing is quite beside his intent. Many disturbed children are adept at controlling teachers by getting them to make inappropriate responses, thus reinforcing just what the teacher wishes to eliminate. If the pupil cares more about having *some* kind of relationship with the teacher than he does about *what* kind of relationship he has, he can get teacher attention by misbehavior. Thus, a teacher encourages repeat performances of an undesirable behavior even as he tells a pupil not to behave that way.

Second, behaviorists emphasize that many pupils do not operate on the basis of high-level gratifications, such as love of learning. Teachers must deal with them on their own motivational level. For example, the attention span and motivation of some who need concrete rewards suddenly improves when the teacher recognizes this need. Free time earned for work done or proper behavior may help get children started who have never had any real success before. They forget their "can't do" to earn free time. Behavior that approximates being acceptable is worth rewarding at first.

Punishment, the major reward many disturbed children receive, is a poor teaching device. Low grades seldom work as a challenge. Emphasis needs to be on accomplishments rather than on failures. Many teachers, wedded to the illusion of homogeneity, have a hard job learning to help these children achieve by accommodating to the special range they present in ability, rate, motivation, and interests. Sometimes the range can be narrowed. In junior and senior high, for example, a student can be assigned in every course for the teacher and the content best suited to him.

When nothing else works, something may be gained by asking a child to do only what interests him. One pupil studied nothing but the Civil War. Another drew pictures. This was no real solution, but the teacher survived and the other students could do their work. Desperate conditions require desperate measures, and it is better to have a student reading about the Civil War than conducting a war with the teacher.

Teachers of classes that include disturbed children need to be particularly skilled in group management. The capacity to establish a work orientation for the class as a whole that will provide psychological insulation is one of the most critical skills in a class that includes disturbed children. Jacob Kounin and his associates have found out that the same teachers are successful in managing both disturbed and normal students.

These teachers focus on the group and its learning activities, actively solicit feedback, concentrate on more than one thing at a time, and select the proper targets for their interventions. The high degree of involvement reduces negative contagion from the disturbed pupils and provides the needed reserve for the teacher to work out the marginal situations that develop.

The first questions a teacher needs to ask are, "How meaningful is the work to these pupils? Can they do it? Do I understand the various roles and relationships in the class well enough to be able to emphasize the things that will maintain stability instead of reacting in a haphazard way to everything that happens?"

The successful teacher knows how to use grouping itself as a tool.

- Some classroom groups are particularly stable and constitute a reservoir of peer help for the distraught pupil; other groups have such a thin shell of control that one acting-out pupil means a breakdown. If most members of a class offer support, they can calm down a lot of misbehavior as well as serve as models of proper action.
- Pupils whose behavior frightens their own age peers and makes them anxious may not bother slightly older children; so upgrouping a disturbed child may reduce negative group effects.
- Sometimes the size of the group is important. Classes with several disturbed pupils should be smaller than others. In fairly large schools, three or four teachers of the same grade or course can arrange to have one small class for those who need it by making the other classes somewhat larger.
- When a class needs relief from a pupil's disturbing antics, sending the offender to another class for a visit may be helpful. The teacher needs to make advance provisions for doing this. He also needs to know when to intervene in this way and to find out what the child does that makes his classmates anxious and angry.

Of course, any kind of exclusion must be used with extreme care. It would be ill-advised for a youngster who wanted out in the first place, or one who was so fearful as to be traumatized. Sometimes, however, planned exclusion can produce controls in a youngster.

Teachers need to develop skill in talking productively with children. They spend a great deal of time in verbal interaction with their students and, unfortunately, the typical verbal interplay is largely a waste. Fritz Redl has pioneered with what he calls "life-space interviewing," a technique that is particularly well suited to helping the teacher of disturbed children put an end to the undersirable behavior or at least to take steps in that direction.

The content of life-space interviewing focuses on the ego level and the behavior experience in the "life-space" shared by teacher and student. The technique provides an opportunity for diagnostic exploration, mild probing, and planning for the future on the basis of realistic appraisal. First the teacher asks the pupil for his perception of what happened, and then, step by step, examines what can be done to clarify reality. This leads to specific strategies which can serve to reduce recurrences. Of course, not all students will respond, but this style prevents moralizing on the one hand and passive acceptance on the other. The same principles can be used with groups for classroom problem solving.

Classroom problem solving brings up the concept of crisis intervention. Youngsters are most teachable at a time of conflict, when they are searching for a resolution. Being able to use the crisis at hand and knowing how to talk effectively to children are two skills basic to any classroom management of disturbed pupils. Behind this rests a new concept of acceptance. Psychological acceptance means responding to the student in order to facilitate his adopting more acceptable patterns of behavior. This may mean more strict enforcement of regulations, more listening to his concerns, or doing whatever is relevant to his self-concept and nature.

Three qualities seem to be critical in order for a teacher to develop the right interpersonal relationship with disturbed students: strength to stand testing without giving in or becoming hostile; a belief that the youngster can change (this eliminates the self-fulfilling prophesy of failure that many teachers imply, if only on the unconscious level); and a recognition that the classroom is a good place for helping youngsters. Of course, certain teachers seem to have natural talent with particular types of disturbed children. Definitive teachers, for example, are most successful with insurgent pupils, while a quiet teacher may get closer to frightened youngsters.

Disturbed children require an inordinate amount of teacher time, so there is never enough to go around. Several plans have been used to add teacher power. Frequently, children low in confidence and self-esteem benefit from one-to-one sessions, cause no disruptions during them, and focus on the task. Sometimes, with a mature class, a teacher can borrow a little special time for such students, but in most cases this is just not possible. Often the only feasible learning condition for them is a tutorial, manned by a community volunteer, a teacher aide, or an older student, with the teacher supervising and designing the lesson material.

Other means of stretching the busy teacher's time include the use of a self-tutoring device, task cards setting up individual projects, and prerecorded tapes with lessons and answers. A peer may serve as tutor-listener if proper pairing can be arranged.

Parents are a teacher's resource more often than we have believed. Programs for disturbed students, particularly the alienated ones, are reaching out to include the home. Rather than letting behavior difficulties continue to a point where a student must be excluded, the schools now, at an early stage of a difficulty, schedule conferences in which parents, student, teacher, and a mental health specialist participate. The assumption is that all parties really want to solve the difficulty, and the support of the home may be critical. When parents are hostile to the pupil, the hostility is less likely to provoke unfortunate behavior if the matter can be talked out and plans drawn up to meet the difficulties. While no punches are pulled, the issue is to teach the child what he *must* learn rather than revert to punitive handling.

Help may be needed outside the classroom. Here a "big brother" or "big sister" may be most important in providing not only reasonable recreation but identification as well. Assistance with homework, especially at the junior and senior high levels, may be the only road to survival.

A wise teacher keeps time flexible in planning for the disturbed youngster. Some children may be able to benefit from one hour of school but no longer. Some can make it through the morning but fall apart before the afternoon is under way.

Wise use of space is important. For example, some disturbed students benefit from having offices or study cubicles to reduce distraction. On the other hand, some need to see others and observe what is going on in order to feel less anxious.

The more flexible the concept of space in the teacher's mind, the more he can use this resource to serve the disturbed student. Dividing the room into work centers for various subgroups is one technique. Using the hall not as a punitive place but as a stimulus control may be appropriate. Some older youngsters can do their work better in the library, while others would roam the halls if not under surveillance.

Above all, the teacher and the school need to bear in mind that, for a disturbed child, being able to escape temporarily from group pressures is often the key to survival. Each school should have a place and, if possible, a person for a disturbed child to go to at a time of crisis.

Even with the most able consultation and highly skilled teaching it may not be possible to help a child in the regular school setting, and unless he can be helped—not merely contained—in the classroom, he should not be there. The teacher's survival and the other children's welfare, as well as his own, are at stake.

For children who still fail to respond in the regular classroom after everything feasible has been done, the next step is the special class. Such classes provide relief for the whole school system and, generally speaking, they offer the disturbed pupils more individualized planning, with the result that pupil behavior and achievement improve. Some recent research, however, suggests that the improvement tends to disappear when the pupil returns to the mainstream. Indeed, the special class is far from being a panacea. It often helps least the unsocialized youngster, who needs so much, and sometimes it includes very disturbed children, even though the general consensus is that psychotic children need more help than a special class can give.

The special class falls short of the mark for other reasons. Frequently, special class curriculums do not include individual work and family contacts, although classroom work alone is usually not enough. Further, many public school teachers do not have the assistants they need to conduct a special class successfully.

And the special class bears a stigma. Students seldom see the value of being "special" and attitude is a critical part of the impact. Particularly at the secondary level, they resist being set apart. To adolescents, the stigma is so oppressive to their whole quest for a self (and a normal self) that it generates a great deal of friction. The stigma is strengthened because teachers and school administrations are seldom eager to welcome back a "cured" student. Nevertheless, special class provisions, if properly handled and staffed, are part of the sequence of support needed in every school program.

When all is said and done, most disturbed children are, and will continue to be, in the regular classroom, and, like it or not, classrooms and teaching will have to change if the schools are to fulfill their ever increasing responsibility for the social and emotional development of children.

19.

RICHARD J. MUELLER
AND JAMES F. BAKER

GAMES TEACHERS AND
STUDENTS PLAY

Growth, like any ongoing function, requires adequate objects in the environment to meet the needs and capacities of the growing child, boy, youth, and young man, until he can better choose and make his own environment.—
PAUL GOODMAN, *Growing Up Absurd*

Research indicates that a great many teachers are concerned more about the discipline aspect of their teaching career, especially in the beginning years of experience, than any other area in their years of teaching in our public schools. It will be the purpose of this article to provide a working format, or structure, for a positive approach toward helping the teacher understand and control classroom discipline at the psychological verbal level.

Discipline is an important integral factor in the implementation of behavioral objectives as established by the public school. It will be a basic assumption in this paper that "good discipline," the establishing of control in an instructional situation, improves the learning situation and helps the students to develop independently—to walk by themselves in an increasingly complex society replete with "Future Shock" implications.

This description of discipline is not stated punitively; positive discipline control concerns promulgating a higher level of individual student awareness of destructive behavior, stimulated by teachers, so that individual students can react positively to directions and instructions without obvious and destructive coercion. At any rate, discipline here does not mean sending the miscreant to the Dean of Students.

A second basic assumption is, generally speaking, that the content material of any given class is not the basis of the typical dispute between the teacher and the student. Amidon and Flanders cite research indicating content-oriented teachers, who tend toward parental directive discipline, can and do effect less knowledge upon students when compared

Reprinted by permission from the April, 1972, issue of *The Clearing House*.

with teachers who are less knowledgeable in their area, but who tend toward nondirective interaction with their students.

One approach to a positive control of students in the learning situation can be likened to psychological verbal games played between teachers and students. Certainly there is no irreverence here. These games teachers and students play for control of the classroom are deadly serious. Teachers, however, who become effectively aware of student psychological verbal games can learn to sidestep them, or to deal with them within the areas of reality, rather than as a "game." The classroom teacher with good control techniques is free to work with his students in establishing positive interaction and interpersonal rapport so the real business of the classroom can be effected.

Verbalized communication within the classroom can be sorted into the following general categories:

1. Communications which flow from the student to the teacher in a child-parent manner.
2. Communications which flow from the teacher to the student in a directive, parent-oriented manner.
3. Positive communications which are autonomously and independently directed toward objective appraisal of the classroom problem at hand.

These three categories are simply labeled Child, Parent, and Adult (Berne). Communication between the teacher and the student constantly shifts from one of these positions to another. Each teacher is continually exerting verbal influence on the student and on the learning situation. It is assumed that communication occurs most smoothly when the communication between teacher and student is complementary—that is, adult to adult. When communications become crossed, child to parent and parent to child, negative feelings usually arise in both parties.

But in most instances secondary schools traditionally place particular emphasis upon the directive, or parent level, of communication between teacher and student: "You do what I say. You do what I say because I am the 'parent.'" Indeed, a basic tenet of control for the classroom teacher is reflected in the firmly established phrase *"in loco parentis."*

Teacher-student games are communications that ignore the reality of the classroom. For example, some student statements or inquiries may sound legitimate to the teacher, but in effect are not. When a student asks "Why do we have to do homework?" he may have a perfectly valid question, but his motive generally does not fit the question. This student usually wants the teacher to respond parentally: "Because homework is good for you," or "Because I tell you to." The student starts the game and the teacher finishes it in the traditional manner. The student already knows the answer.

This teacher was literally "set up" by the student to play the parent role. Nothing positive was accomplished by the verbal exchange because of the frustration and demeaning of the teacher with certain knowledge by the student of another conflict won. Perhaps, the teacher might have answered the query of why homework with the following: "Homework is for your benefit, not mine. Doing it is your responsibility. You make the decision. Not doing it, however, carries certain penalties of which you are well aware." Any retort by the student after this adult answer will be ineffective.

Another example might be "Why do you treat Negroes better than me?" or just the opposite, "Why do you treat white kids better than me?" Just as in the first example, the student is attempting to place the teacher in an uncompromising parental position. An answer by the teacher such as "I don't discriminate, you know that," really does not satisfy the inquiry. Instead, this question might be answered by asking the student, "In what specific ways do I do this?" This return is at the adult level asking for specific examples. If the student does not have any, then for the time being that question has been answered without loss of face by the teacher. If the student does have an example, or examples, adult level communication can continue until understanding is reached between teacher and student.

A final example: "Why should I study? You'll only fail me anyhow." Though an adult question, the student expects the teacher to tell him that study is good for the student—that studying is the good American way to win, when the student has more personal examples that there are other ways to win. And even if he does study, but fails to pass the test, he will, in all probability, fail anyway. So why study? Again the reason for study centers around value for the student. Whether the value be self-discipline or, more importantly, to prove to himself that he can win through his own effort, the student should be made to understand that he controls the pass-failing and not the personal whim of the teacher.

We should place particular emphasis on another assumption: that no level of communication described here is totally destructive in teacher-student relationships, but that there is a time and a place for each level. Certainly we are helping, rather than destroying, a child when we punish him for disregarding personal safety by letting gas escape from science lab jets. In addition, the child in us is a necessary condition for normal rebellion, and especially so in creative personalities. It is, however, the adult-to-adult communication which provides depth to the instructional situation. It permits both the teacher and the student to view their world without the anxiety of destructive aggressiveness.

In summary, students instinctively respect and interact positively with teachers who do not play games.

REFERENCES

Edmund J. Amidon and Ned Flanders. *The Role of the Teacher in the Classroom*. Minneapolis, Minn.: Pauls Amidon and Associates, 1963, pp. 56–62.
Eric Berne. *Games People Play*. New York: Grove Press, Inc., 1964, p. 22.
Paul Goodman. *Growing Up Absurd*. New York: Random House, 1960.
Alvin Toffler. *Future Shock*. New York: Random House, 1970.

20.   PAUL H. LEVINE

TRANSCENDENTAL MEDITATION AND THE SCIENCE OF CREATIVE INTELLIGENCE

The search for definition of basic goals which is so prominent a concern of the educational community echoes a similar quest for purpose within my own field of science and, indeed, within society at large. While educators are asking, "What are schools for?" [1] scientists are asking, "What is the significance of science?" [2] and political leaders still seek to define our "national purpose." The soul-searching is widespread, yet within each profession or field of activity the search is carried out within the boundaries of that field, solutions are sought in the framework of the problem perceived, and more fundamental aspects of the situation are consequently overlooked.

It seems clear that what is really being asked is, What should be the objectives of human activity? with specific reference in each of the examples cited to the activities of teaching, doing science, or running a nation. If we adopt the common-sense position that the principal objective

From *Phi Delta Kappan* 54:4 (Dec., 1972), 231–35.

of *any* activity is to promote the fulfillment of the individuals engaged in and influenced by that activity, then the real goal of education is seen to encompass nothing less than the *fulfillment* of the student.

In the sense we are using it here, fulfillment implies the actualization of the full potentialities for growth latent in the individual. Therefore, the measure of any educational system is first the breadth of its implicit *vision* of the range of these potentialities and second its *effectiveness* in providing every student with a practical means for achieving such full development. If a crisis is felt to exist in education, then it may logically be asked whether the fault lies in too narrow a vision of the possibilities and, in consequence, too restricted an armamentarium for achievement.

This article discusses a particular conception of the range of potential human development which, if further validated by a growing body of anecdotal and scientific evidence, must necessarily change our ideas about individual fulfillment and with this our views on the structure and responsibility of education. The conception is that of Maharishi Mahesh Yogi; it is being taught as part of a new discipline called the Science of Creative Intelligence.

CREATIVE INTELLIGENCE

The concept of creative intelligence arises from an examination of the structure of purposeful change in nature. No matter where we look, new forms and relationships are continually being created from lesser developed states. This evolution appears to be orderly, i.e., governed by intelligible laws. The intelligence displayed by nature in this process may be called creative intelligence. When we observe creation in action, whether it be in astronomy or biology—or even the growth of a rose—we encounter striking parallels in the structure of the creative process as it unfolds in each case. Through such interdisciplinary analyses, it comes to be appreciated that a fundamental significance can be accorded to creativity (and to the intelligence shaping its expression), a significance which transcends the particular sphere of activity in which the creativity is being manifested. Creative intelligence thus becomes a valid object of intellectual inquiry in its own right.

The relevance of such inquiry to education, and to practical life in general, stems from the circumstance that the creative impulse in man, as expressed in his progressive thoughts and actions, is found upon close examination to be structured along precisely the same lines as creative processes in the purely physical domain. This circumstance (not as remarkable as it may seem at first glance, since we are, after all, part of nature) immediately suggests a transcendental aspect to human creativity which necessarily casts consideration of the human condition into broader evolutionary contexts.

Fulfillment, for example, comes to mean full expression in an individual's life of the creative intelligence inherent in his nature. Lack of fulfillment (which we may call suffering) in this view is ascribed to some restriction of the flow of creative intelligence from its source at the core of one's being to the level of conscious awareness from which one perceives and acts. A practical consequence of this approach is the intriguing possibility that human problems can be attacked at a common fundamental level—without specific regard to the nature of the problem—much in the same way that a gardener simultaneously attends to deficiencies in the development of the many separate leaves of a plant by simply watering the root.

TRANSCENDENTAL MEDITATION

The existence of a simple natural technique called transcendental meditation lends substance to the above considerations, removing them from the realm of purely philosophical speculation. TM, as it is frequently abbreviated, is a systematic procedure of "turning the attention inwards towards the subtler levels of a thought until the mind transcends the experience of the subtlest state of the thought and arrives at the source of the thought. This expands the conscious mind and at the same time brings it in contact with the creative intelligence that gives rise to every thought." [3]

This technique for the direct *experience* of the field of creative intelligence at the root of one's being is apparently a universal human faculty not requiring any particular intellectual or cognitive facility other than the ordinary ability to think. It is easily learned by anyone in about six hours of instruction (spread out over four consecutive days) from a Maharishi-trained teacher.* Once learned, it can be continued without the necessity for additional instruction. It is primarily on the basis of this systematic and apparently universally applicable procedure for the empirical † verification of theoretical constructs involving creative intelligence

* A number of nonprofit tax-exempt organizations coordinate the activities of TM teachers. The educational community is served by the Students' International Meditation Society (SIMS), whose national headquarters is located at 1015 Gayley Avenue, Los Angeles, California 90024. Inquiries may be directed to the attention of the Science and Education Communications Coordinator.

† The customary view that subjective experience is ipso facto beyond the purview of science is undergoing change. See, for example, "States of Consciousness and State-Specific Sciences," by Charles T. Tart, in *Science*, June 16, 1972, pp. 1, 203.

that one may validly speak in terms of a *science* of creative intelligence, or SCI.

The rapidly expanding interest in SCI, both in and out of academia, and—surprisingly—both within the Establishment and the youth subculture, presently derives not so much from an appreciation of its inherent scope as from a desire for a fuller understanding of the immediate practical benefits of TM.* Notwithstanding the simplicity of the prac-

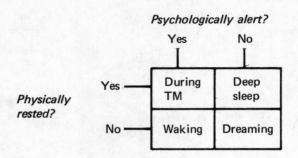

Figure 1. Relationship of TM to other states of consciousness.

tice, meditators unanimously report improvements in the energy and enthusiasm with which they approach their activities and in their clarity of mind, mental and physical health, and ability to interact harmoniously with their environment.† Marked reductions in tension and moodiness are frequently cited, even by those in particularly stressful occupations or family situations. The list goes on to include increased creativity, perceptiveness, self-confidence, productivity, reading speed, psychomotor facility, and learning ability. As one might expect, meditators report concurrent reductions in their use of tranquilizers, stimulants, and other prescribed

---

* The rate of instruction in TM has doubled each year since 1968. By the fall of 1972 over 150,000 Americans had learned TM. The broad base of this appeal can be gauged from the range of publications featuring articles on TM and SCI during the past year: *Time* (October 25, 1971), *Yale Alumni Magazine* (February, 1972), *Soldiers Magazine* (February, 1972), *Kentucky Law Journal* (1971–72, Vol. 60, No. 2), *Seventeen* (July, 1972), *Wall Street Journal* (August 31, 1972), *Today's Health* (April, 1972), *Science Digest* (February, 1972), and *Psychology Today* (March, 1972).

† TM is a purely mental technique practiced individually every morning and evening for 15 to 20 minutes at a sitting. It requires no alteration of life-style, diet, etc., and being a technique of direct experience (rather than a religion or philosophy), it does not require belief in the efficacy of the practice nor an understanding of the underlying theory.

drugs—and, most significantly, of nonprescription drugs as well.* The combined effect is succinctly expressed by a Yale biology instructor: "There's been a quantum increase in the quality of my life since I started meditating."

Experiences during meditation vary from individual to individual and from one meditation to the next. A common experiential denominator, observed even in the first meditation, is a unique blend of deep physical relaxation and expanded mental awareness. The relationship of this state of mind and body to the more familiar states of waking, dreaming, and deep sleep may be schematized as in the matrix shown in Figure 1.

Viewed in this context, TM can perhaps be accepted as just another natural albeit very useful style of functioning of the nervous system, to be alternated with the others on a regular daily basis. Since the dynamism of daily activity in large measure depends on the thoroughness of the psychophysiological rest achieved during the deep sleep and dreaming states, the additional profound rest claimed to occur during TM would account for the enlivened functioning in the waking state reported by meditators.

SCIENTIFIC RESEARCH

The anecdotal claims for TM, even when they are echoed by people of unquestioned objectivity and stature, must nevertheless be verified by the tools of science before they can be accepted by a society grappling with the very ills TM is purported to relieve so effortlessly. A unique aspect of TM vis-à-vis other techniques for mental or physical development is the depth of scientific investigation of its effects currently in progress throughout the world. Major research projects on TM are being carried out at over 40 universities and institutes, including the Harvard Medical School, Stanford Research Institute, and the Universities of Cambridge, Cologne, Rome, and Capetown. In great measure, this widespread research activity is made possible by the availability of large numbers of cooperative meditators at virtually every major university, as well as by the effortlessness of the technique itself, which permits experimentation to be performed without disturbing the meditation.

---

* The widely publicized efficacy of TM in promoting the voluntary reduction of drug abuse as documented, for example, in the retrospective study of 1,862 subjects by Drs. R. K. Wallace and H. G. Benson of the Harvard Medical School (see "Narcotics Research, Rehabilitation, and Treatment" in "Hearings Before the Select Committee on Crime, House of Representatives," Serial No. 92–1, Part 2, p. 682, U.S. Government Printing Office, 1971) tends to overshadow public understanding of the broader effects of the practice and particularly its utility for the nondrug abuser.

Much of the meditation research is still in its early phases, particularly the long-term clinical studies of TM's *possible* value for hypertensives (Harvard Medical School) and in the relief of mental illness (Hartford's Institute of Living). The research that has reached publication stage, however, is already sufficient to establish that the psychophysiological effects both during and after TM are real and unique in their degree of integration.

In the *American Journal of Physiology*, a team of Harvard and University of California researchers has reported on these integrated characteristics of mind and body during TM, calling it a "wakeful hypometabolic physiologic state," i.e., a state of restful alertness (see Figure 1).[4] They found that the degree of metabolic rest after 5-10 *minutes* of TM was characterized by an average decrease in oxygen consumption of 17%, deeper than that achieved after 6-7 *hours* of sleep. They found a reduction in heart rate of three beats per minute, which, when correlated with an earlier study reporting a drop in cardiac output of 25% during TM,[5] indicates a significant reduction in the workload of the heart. EEG (i.e., "brain wave") measurements showed a predominance of slow alpha wave activity in the central and frontal areas of the brain, thereby clearly distinguishing TM from the waking, dreaming, and sleeping states.*

Most significant were the observations of an approximately threefold increase in skin resistance during TM, indicating relaxation and a reduction of anxiety. Biochemical studies of the meditators' blood showed a remarkable reduction in lactate concentration both during and after meditation. Anxiety symptoms are believed to be correlated with high blood lactate levels. Thus, as reported in a recent *Scientific American* article, Robert K. Wallace and Herbert Benson are led to view TM as an integrated response or reflex which is opposite in its characteristics to the "fight or flight" response believed to be primarily responsible for the high incidence of hypertension and related diseases in today's fast-paced society.[6]

Psychological studies of personality changes attributable to TM have also begun to appear in the literature. In the *Journal of Counseling Psychology*, a University of Cincinnati team concluded that "the practice of meditation for a 2-month period would appear to have a salutary influence on a subject's psychological state as measured by the Personal Orientation Inventory."[7] Changes in the direction of increased "self-actualization" were found to occur for meditating subjects.

Another study, reported in the *Journal of Psychosomatic Medicine*, gives insight into a possible explanation for the wide variety of beneficial

---

* The psysiological measurements also show that TM is radically different from hypnotic states and other so-called altered states of consciousness.

results apparently following from the simple practice of TM.[8] It was found that meditators habituated more rapidly to a stressful environment than nonmeditators and, furthermore, that meditators' nervous systems displayed greater autonomic stability. This evidence, together with the lactate observations cited earlier, tends to substantiate the view (presented in SCI) that TM acts to reduce one's store of psychophysiological stress while simultaneously reducing the likelihood of further stress accumulation. When one considers the manifold deleterious effect of stress, it becomes apparent that any technique which can reduce stress—e.g., the twice-daily experience of a hypometabolic wakeful state—has the potential for simultaneous improvement of one's life on all those levels previously stress afflicted. A "quantum jump in the quality of life" suddenly becomes credible.

IMPLICATIONS FOR EDUCATION

In the broader vision of SCI, stresses are viewed as impediments to the spontaneous flow of creative intelligence from the inner being to the level of conscious awareness from which one perceives and acts. An integral component of fulfillment, therefore, becomes the progressive physiological refinement of the nervous system in the direction of a reduced accumulation of stress. Indeed, SCI associates such refinement with a "growth in consciousness" and delineates the remarkable potentialities of a fully stress-free, fully normalized nervous system. The attainment of higher states of consciousness, long thought to be incompatible with an active life, now is said to be within the reach of anyone through TM, and experiential evidence of this possibility seems to be one of the common cumulative effects of the practice.

The implications of all of this for education are quite exciting. At the most superficial level, the level of the problems, reduction of drug abuse among students and of social tension in the classroom is a likely concomitant of a widespread introduction of TM into the schools. The improved attitudes and behavior which generally are among the more immediate of TM's effects offer a chance for achieving affective goals without sacrificing performance goals. Indeed, preliminary reports of increased learning ability and reading speed with TM would seem to indicate that affective dispositions and cognitive resources grow hand in hand. Students at ease inside can be expected to respond more spontaneously and creatively to a learning environment.

On the other side of the desk, a meditating teacher (or administrator), being more at ease, energetic, healthy, clear-minded, creative, and perceptive, should naturally become more effective. Already . . . there is concrete evidence that these are all valid expectations if the implementation of a TM/SCI-based program is approached with proper planning.

On a deeper level, if further research continues to substantiate "growth in consciousness" as a pragmatically meaningful concept, can this dimension of human development be overlooked by an educational system whose goal is the actualization of the full potentialities for growth latent in the student? One of the most ancient expressions of man's wisdom, the Vedas (to which SCI traces its ancestry), hold that "knowledge is structured in consciousness," the implication being that the higher the level of consciousness the more profound the level of knowledge which can be owned.

This leads finally to the most fundamental possibility for educational fulfillment of all those opened through SCI. The holistic ideal of education is to provide a common basis for all branches of learning. Certainly, *knowingness*, that very intimate relationship between the knower and the object of knowledge, is this common basis. The science of creative intelligence is principally the study of this relationship, both through intellectual analysis and through the direct experience of the field from which all knowledge springs. The whole tree is captured by capturing the seed. In the fullest sense, therefore, creative intelligence may be said to be both the goal and the source of education.

A WORLD PLAN

Concrete programs are already under way for the widest diffusion of SCI and TM. Since its inauguration as an accredited course at Stanford in the 1970 winter quarter, SCI has achieved recognition from a rapidly growing number of universities and colleges around the world. The SCI course at Yale this past year, for example, explicitly demonstrated its integrative and interdisciplinary nature by bringing together psychologists, philosophers, political scientists, and artists in a common exploration of the potentialities of consciousness.

SCI is being taught at other educational levels, including junior and senior high schools and adult education, in industry, and even in the military. Indeed, the commandant of the U.S. Army War College, Major General Franklin M. Davis, speaking at the First International Symposium on the Science of Creative Intelligence,* said, "In military educa-

* Held at the University of Massachusetts, Amherst, July 18 through August 1, 1971. International symposia on SCI are now held regularly each year at a number of universities throughout the world. Participants in 1971 included Buckminster Fuller, Harvey Brooks (dean of engineering and applied physics, Harvard University, and president, American Academy of Arts and Sciences), Melvin Calvin (Nobel Laureate

tion, creative intelligence appears to have a definite potential, because it carries with it so much in the way of innovation, creative thinking, and what we in the military call 'challenging the assumption'!" To which Maharishi added, "When the military rises in creative intelligence, world peace will be a reality."

Educators at MIU (Maharishi International University), the institution founded in 1971 to formalize the training of SCI teachers, are now completing the preparation of syllabuses and teaching aids—including color video cassettes—for the teaching of SCI at all educational levels. MIU is currently embarked on an ambitious world plan to open 3,600 centers for the training of SCI teachers—one center per million population—throughout the world. Each center has as its goal the training of 1,000 teachers by means of a 33-lecture, video-based course prepared specially for this purpose by Maharishi. The stated objectives of the world plan include the development of the full potential of the individual and the "realization of the highest idea of education."

A utopian vision? Perhaps. But who would have imagined that a scant 14 years after a lone monk walked out of the Himalayas armed only with knowledge and his dedication to a long tradition of educators, the Illinois House of Representatives would formally resolve:

That all educational institutions, especially those under State of Illinois jurisdiction, be strongly encouraged to study the feasibility of courses in Transcendental Meditation and the Science of Creative Intelligence on their campuses and in their facilities; and be it further . . . resolved that a copy of this resolution be sent to: the Superintendent of Public Instruction, the deans of all state universities, the Department of Mental Health, State of Illinois, to inform them of the great promise of the program herein mentioned.[9]

And who would have thought that in this same "Year of the World Plan," the National Institute of Mental Health would award an initial grant of $21,540 to help train 120 secondary school teachers to teach SCI in American high schools?

Evidently, in the long war against the bondage of ignorance, a new and fascinating chapter is being written. Its outcome? In absolute earnest, Maharishi often tells his teachers-in-training, "Anything is possible, and anything means . . . anything."

---

in chemistry), and Willis Harman (director, Educational Policy Research, Stanford Research Institute). Symposia in 1972 featured Donald Glaser (Nobel Laureate in physics), Hans Selye, Marshall McLuhan, astronaut Rusty Schweickart, and the State Department China expert Alfred Jenkins.

NOTES

1. Robert L. Ebel. "What Are Schools For?" *Phi Delta Kappan*, September, 1972, p. 3.
2. Victor F. Weisskopf. "The Significance of Science," *Science*, April 14, 1972, p. 138.
3. Maharishi Mahesh Yogi. *Maharishi Mahesh Yogi on the Bhagavad-Gita: A New Translation and Commentary* (Baltimore: Penguin Books, 1969), p. 470.
4. Robert Keith Wallace, Herbert Benson, and Archie F. Wilson. "A Wakeful Hypometabolic Physiologic State," *American Journal of Physiology*, September, 1971, pp. 795–99.
5. Robert Keith Wallace. "The Physiological Effects of Transcendental Meditation: A Proposed Fourth Major State of Consciousness," Ph.D. Dissertation, University of California, Los Angeles, 1970; see also *Science*, March 27, 1970, p. 1,751.
6. Robert Keith Wallace and Herbert Benson. "The Physiology of Meditation," *Scientific American*, February, 1972, p. 84.
7. William Seeman, Sanford Nidich, and Thomas Banta. "Influence of Transcendental Meditation on a Measure of Self-Actualization," *Journal of Counseling Psychology*, May, 1972, pp. 184–87.
8. David W. Orme-Johnson. "Autonomic Stability and Transcendental Meditation," *Journal of Psychosomatic Medicine*, in press.
9. House Resolution No. 677, adopted May 24, 1972.

PART 3

Factors in Classroom Learning

CHAPTER EIGHT

Motivation

THE PSYCHOLOGY OF MOTIVATION SEEKS TO EXPLAIN the conditions that must be met in order for someone to be moved to do something. Depending on the theory in question, motivation is conceptualized as providing the general energy underlying all human behavior and/or a specific direction or goal for behavior. For example, hunger motivates people to seek food in one way or another. Other behavior might be energized by the desire to maintain one's self-esteem or social image. Motivation operates on three levels: first with primary and obvious drives, such as hunger; second, with the alertness and activity levels required for any behavior to be carried out; and third, with complex and abstract sources, such as self-esteem and self-actualization.

Abraham Maslow is concerned with self-actualization. Perhaps no single theory in psychology has gathered such ardent supporters as his "Theory of Human Motivation." Easy to understand and yet containing profound implications, Maslow's concept of a hierarchy of needs leading to a state of self-actualization has influenced theory and practice, not only in education, but also in humanistic and behaviorist psychology, mental health, industrial psychology, and even marketing. In addition, students of political science have applied the theory to the emerging nations, tracing their development from an early concern for immediate economic and safety needs to more advanced, secure stages of self-esteem and broader involvement in international affairs.

Maslow's needs hierarchy provides a convincing description of need development in a way that is also consistent with common sense. The pattern of the child's needs reflects many factors, such as the home, peer-group pressures, physical development—all interacting within a given child. These needs constitute the hidden agenda that he brings to the classroom. Unfortunately, there is as yet little empirical documentation of this theory. Indeed, a major problem with Maslow's theory is the difficulty of investigating it empirically.

The research report by Finger and Silverman focuses on the motivational development of children during the elementary and middle school years. They found that children who do well in the early grades and then decline in achievement never pull up again. Successful elementary school children who experience a slump in junior high school do not typically improve in senior high school. The article also includes an excellent discussion of motivational research.

Until very recently, the influence of societal factors on motivation among females has not been a major issue among educators, or with the public either. Perhaps one of the reasons is that girls have always done well in school, on the average, in competition with boys. In fact, even in such subjects as math and science, where boys' and girls' scores on achievement tests are nearly equal, girls get higher average grades. Yet, with time, females experience environmental pressures that appear to limit their aspirations. David Lynn, in Chapter 6 (pp. 161-76), has surveyed significant research to determine what is known about the factors influencing intellectual growth in women.

One of the most fascinating studies in the field of sex differences is Matina Horner's research on the aspirations of women as viewed by both men and women. The results of Horner's study are startling. Both males and females took it for granted that men do and should have high career aspirations, but correspondingly high aspirations among women who were at least equally qualified aroused fear and guilt among the women and were subject to social punishment. Intellectual competency was seen as aggressive behavior, a characteristic not appropriate for the traditionally defined woman's role. The standard of excellence by which women's performance was evaluated by peers was sex-based rather than competency-based. Subsequent studies corroborate Horner's conclusions.

This kind of research has thrown some light on the discrepancy between nearly equal if not superior academic performance of women as compared with men, but their substantially poorer occupational achievement. Teachers must recognize the long-term developmental nature of sex-role problems and analyze to what extent their behavior in the classroom contributes to these problems.

RECOMMENDED READING

J. S. Coleman. 1960. "The Adolescent Subculture and Academic Achievement," *The American Journal of Sociology* 337–47. A classic study of the relationship of adolescent attitudes and behavior to schoolwork.

W. D. Glasser. 1969. *Schools Without Failure* (New York: Harper & Row). Development of the belief that the elimination of failure in the classroom will both greatly reduce mental health problems and greatly increase the desire to learn.

D. C. McClelland. 1961. "Toward a Theory of Motivation." In D. C. McClelland (ed.), *The Achieving Society* (Princeton, N.J.: Van Nostrand). McClelland's oft-cited research on motivation, based on the Thematic Apperception test, as the means by which individuals express their aspirations toward getting ahead in life; also the basis for Matina Horner's investigation of the motivational attitudes of women.

H. A. Thelen. 1960. "The Triumph of Achievement over Inquiry in Education," *Elementary School Journal* 60, 190–97. The belief that individualizing instruction will stimulate motivation to learn.

C. Weinberg. 1965. "The Price of Competition," *Teachers College Record* 672, 106–14. A thorough and insightful look at the issue of competition in schools and its effects on the attitudes and motivation of young people.

21.

A. H. MASLOW

A THEORY OF HUMAN MOTIVATION

In a previous paper (1943) various propositions were presented which would have to be included in any theory of human motivation that could lay claim to being definitive. These conclusions may be briefly summarized as follows:

1. The integrated wholeness of the organism must be one of the foundation stones of motivation theory.
2. The hunger drive (or any other physiological drive) was rejected as a centering point or model for a definitive theory of motivation. Any drive that is somatically based and localizable was shown to be atypical rather than typical in human motivation.
3. Such a theory should stress and center itself upon ultimate or basic

From A. H. Maslow, "A Theory of Human Motivation," *Psychological Review, 50* (1943) pp. 370–96. Copyright © 1943 by the American Psychological Association, and reproduced by permission of The American Psychological Asscoiation and Mrs. Bertha G. Maslow.

goals rather than partial or superficial ones, upon ends rather than means to these ends. Such a stress would imply a more central place for unconscious than for conscious motivations.

4. There are usually available various cultural paths to the same goal. Therefore conscious, specific, local-cultural desires are not as fundamental in motivation theory as the more basic, unconscious goals.

5. Any motivated behavior, either preparatory or consummatory, must be understood to be a channel through which many basic needs may be simultaneously expressed or satisfied. Typically an act has *more* than one motivation.

6. Practically all organismic states are to be understood as motivated and as motivating.

7. Human needs arrange themselves in hierarchies of prepotency. That is to say, the appearance of one need usually rests on the prior satisfaction of another, more prepotent need. Man is a perpetually wanting animal. Also no need or drive can be treated as if it were isolated or discrete; every drive is related to the state of satisfaction or dissatisfaction of other drives.

8. *Lists* of drives will get us nowhere for various theoretical and practical reasons. Furthermore any classification of motivations must deal with the problem of levels of specificity or generalization of the motives to be classified.

9. Classifications of motivations must be based upon goals rather than upon instigating drives or motivated behavior.

10. Motivation theory should be human-centered rather than animal-centered.

11. The situation or the field in which the organism reacts must be taken into account but the field alone can rarely serve as an exclusive explanation for behavior. Furthermore the field itself must be interpreted in terms of the organism. Field theory cannot be a substitute for motivation theory.

12. Not only the integration of the organism must be taken into account, but also the possibility of isolated, specific, partial, or segmental reactions.

It has since become necessary to add to these another affirmation.

13. Motivation theory is not synonymous with behavior theory. The motivations are only one class of determinants of behavior. While behavior is almost always motivated, it is also almost always biologically, culturally, and situationally determined as well.

The present paper is an attempt to formulate a positive theory of motivation which will satisfy these theoretical demands and at the same time conform to the known facts, clinical and observational as well as experimental. It derives most directly, however, from clinical experience. This theory is, I think, in the functionalist tradition of James and Dewey, and is fused with the holism of Wertheimer, Goldstein, and Gestalt Psychology, and with the dynamicism of Freud and Adler. This fusion or synthesis may arbitrarily be called a "general-dynamic" theory.

It is far easier to perceive and to criticize the aspects in motivation theory than to remedy them. Mostly this is because of the very serious lack of sound data in this area. I conceive this lack of sound facts to be due primarily to the absence of a valid theory of motivation. The present theory then must be considered to be a suggested program or framework for future research and must stand or fall, not so much on facts available or evidence presented, as upon researches yet to be done, researches suggested, perhaps, by the questions raised in this paper.

THE BASIC NEEDS

The "Physiological" Needs

The needs that are usually taken as the starting point for motivation theory are the so-called physiological drives. Two recent lines of research make it necessary to revise our customary notions about these needs, first, the development of the concept of homeostasis, and second, the finding that appetites (preferential choices among foods) are a fairly efficient indication of actual needs or lacks in the body.

Homeostasis refers to the body's automatic efforts to maintain a constant, normal state of the blood stream. Cannon has described this process for (1) the water content of the blood, (2) salt content, (3) sugar content, (4) protein content, (5) fat content, (6) calcium content, (7) oxygen content, (8) constant hydrogen-ion level (acid-base balance), and (9) constant temperature of the blood. Obviously this list can be extended to include other minerals, the hormones, vitamins, etc.

Young (1941) has summarized the work on appetite in its relation to body needs. If the body lacks some chemical, the individual will tend to develop a specific appetite or partial hunger for that food element.

Thus it seems impossible as well as useless to make any list of fundamental physiological needs, for they can come to almost any number one might wish, depending on the degree of specificity of description. We can not identify all physiological needs as homeostatic. That sexual desire, sleepiness, sheer activity, and maternal behavior in animals are homeostatic has not yet been demonstrated. Furthermore, this list would not include the various sensory pleasures (tastes, smells, tickling, stroking) which are probably physiological and which may become the goals of motivated behavior.

In a previous paper (1943) it has been pointed out that these physiological drives or needs are to be considered unusual rather than typical because they are isolable, and because they are localizable somatically. That is to say, they are relatively independent of each other, of other motivations and of the organism as a whole, and secondly, in many cases, it is possible to demonstrate a localized, underlying somatic base for the drive. This is true less generally than has been thought (exceptions are fatigue, sleepiness, maternal responses) but it is still true in the classic instances of hunger, sex, and thirst.

It should be pointed out again that any of the physiological needs and the consummatory behavior involved with them serve as channels for all sorts of other needs as well. That is to say, the person who thinks he is hungry may actually be seeking more for comfort, or dependence, than for vitamins or proteins. Conversely, it is possible to satisfy the hunger need in part by other activities such as drinking water or smoking cigarettes. In other words, relatively isolable as these physiological needs are, they are not completely so.

Undoubtedly these physiological needs are the most prepotent of all needs. What this means specifically is that, in the human being who is missing everything in life in an extreme fashion, it is most likely that the major motivation would be the physiological needs rather than any others. A person who is lacking food, safety, love, and esteem would most probably hunger for food more strongly than for anything else.

If all the needs are unsatisfied, and the organism is then dominated by the physiological needs, all other needs may become simply non-existent or be pushed into the background. It is then fair to characterize the whole organism by saying simply that it is hungry, for consciousness is almost completely preempted by hunger. All capacities are put into the service of hunger-satisfaction, and the organization of these capacities is almost entirely determined by the one purpose of satisfying hunger. The receptors and effectors, the intelligence, memory, habits, all may now be defined simply as hunger-gratifying tools. Capacities that are not useful for this purpose lie dormant, or are pushed into the background. The urge to write poetry, the desire to acquire an automobile, the interest in American history, the desire for a new pair of shoes are, in the extreme case, forgotten or become of secondary importance. For the man who is extremely and dangerously hungry, no other interests exist than food. He dreams food, he remembers food, he thinks about food, he emotes only about food, he perceives only food, and he wants only food. The more subtle determinants that ordinarily fuse with the physiological drives in organizing even feeding, drinking, or sexual behavior may now be so completely over-whelmed as to allow us to speak at this time (but *only* at this time) of pure hunger drive and behavior, with the one unqualified aim of relief.

Another peculiar characteristic of the human organism when it is domi-nated by a certain need is that the whole philosophy of the future tends also to change. For our chronically and extremely hungry man, Utopia can be defined very simply as a place where there is plenty of food. He tends to think that, if only he is guaranteed food for the rest of his life, he will be perfectly happy and will never want anything more. Life itself tends to be defined in terms of eating. Anything else will be defined as unimportant. Freedom, love, community feeling, respect, philosophy, may all be waved aside as fripperies which are useless since they fail to fill the stomach. Such a man may fairly be said to live by bread alone.

It cannot possibly be denied that such things are true but their *gen-erality* can be denied. Emergency conditions are, almost by definition, rare in the normally functioning peaceful society. That this truism can be forgotten is due mainly to two reasons. First, rats have few motivations other than physiological ones, and since so much of the research upon motivation has been made with these animals, it is easy to carry the rat-picture over to the human being. Secondly, it is too often not realized that culture itself is an adaptive tool, one of whose main functions is to make the physiological emergencies come less and less often. In most of the known societies, chronic extreme hunger of the emergency type is rare, rather than common. In any case, this is still true in the United States. The average American citizen is experiencing appetite rather than hunger when he says "I am hungry." He is apt to experience sheer life-and-death hunger only by accident and then only a few times through his entire life.

Obviously a good way to obscure the "higher" motivations, and to get a lopsided view of human capacities and human nature, is to make the organism extremely and chronically hungry or thirsty. Anyone who at-tempts to make an emergency picture into a typical one, and who will measure all of man's goals and desires by his behavior during extreme phys-iological deprivation, is certainly being blind to many things. It is quite true that man lives by bread alone—when there is no bread. But what happens to man's desires when there *is* plenty of bread and when his belly is chronically filled?

At once other (and "higher") needs emerge and these, rather than physiological hungers, dominate the organism. And when these in turn are satisfied, again new (and still "higher") needs emerge and so on. This is what we mean by saying that the basic human needs are organized into a hierarchy of relative prepotency.

One main implication of this phrasing is that gratification becomes as important a concept as deprivation in motivation theory, for it releases the organism from the domination of a relatively more physiological need, permitting thereby the emergence of other more social goals. The physiological needs, along with their partial goals, when chronically gratified cease to exist as active determinants or organizers of behavior. They now exist only in a potential fashion in the sense that they may emerge again to dominate the organism if they are thwarted. But a want that is satisfied is no longer a want. The organism is dominated and its behavior organized only by unsatisfied needs. If hunger is satisfied, it becomes unimportant in the current dynamics of the individual.

This statement is somewhat qualified by a hypothesis to be discussed more fully later, namely that it is precisely those individuals in whom a certain need has always been satisfied who are best equipped to tolerate deprivation of that need in the future, and that furthermore, those who have been deprived in the past will react differently to current satisfactions from the one who has never been deprived.

The Safety Needs

If the physiological needs are relatively well gratified, there then emerges a new set of needs, which we may categorize roughly as the safety needs. All that has been said of the physiological needs is equally true, although in lesser degree, of these desires. The organism may equally well be wholly dominated by them. They may serve as the almost exclusive organizers of behavior, recruiting all the capacities of the organism in their service, and we may then fairly describe the whole organism as a safety-seeking mechanism. Again we may say of the receptors, the effectors, of the intellect, and the other capacities that they are primarily safety-seeking tools. Again, as in the hungry man, we find that the dominating goal is a strong determinant not only of his current world-outlook and philosophy but also of his philosophy of the future. Practically everything looks less important than safety (even sometimes the physiological needs which, being satisfied, are now underestimated). A man, in this state, if it is extreme enough and chronic enough, may be characterized as living almost for safety alone.

Although in this paper we are interested primarily in the needs of the adult, we can approach an understanding of his safety needs perhaps more efficiently by observation of infants and children, in whom these needs are much more simple and obvious. One reason for the clearer appearance of the threat or danger reaction in infants is that they do not inhibit this reaction at all, whereas adults in our society have been taught to inhibit it at all costs. Thus even when adults do feel their safety to be threatened we may not be able to see this on the surface. Infants will react in a total fashion and as if they were endangered, if they are disturbed or dropped suddenly, startled by loud noises, flashing light, or other unusual sensory stimulation, by rough handling, by general loss of support in the mother's arms, or by inadequate support.*

In infants we can also see a much more direct reaction to bodily illnesses of various kinds. Sometimes these illnesses seem to be immediately and per se threatening and seem to make the child feel unsafe. For instance, vomiting, colic or other sharp pains seem to make the child look at the whole world in a different way. At such a moment of pain, it may be postulated that, for the child, the appearance of the whole world suddenly changes from sunniness to darkness, so to speak, and becomes a place in which anything at all might happen, in which previously stable things have suddenly become unstable. Thus a child who because of some bad food is taken ill may, for a day or two, develop fear, nightmares, and a need for protection and reassurance never seen in him before his illness.

Another indication of the child's need for safety is his preference for some kind of undisrupted routine or rhythm. He seems to want a predictable, orderly world. For instance, injustice, unfairness, or inconsistency in the parents seems to make a child feel anxious and unsafe. This attitude may be not so much because of the injustice per se or any particular pains involved, but rather because this treatment threatens to make the world look unreliable, or unsafe, or unpredictable. Young children seem to thrive better under a system which has at least a skeletal outline of rigidity, in which there is a schedule of a kind, some sort of routine, something that can be counted upon, not only for the present but also far into the future. Perhaps one could express this more accurately by saying that the child needs an organized world rather than an unorganized or unstructured one.

The central role of the parents and the normal family setup are indisputable. Quarreling, physical assault, separation, divorce or death within the family may be particularly terrifying. Also parental outbursts of rage or threats of punishment directed to the child, calling him names, speaking to him harshly, shaking him, handling him roughly, or actual physical punishment sometimes elicit such total panic and terror in the child that we must assume more is involved than the physical pain alone. While it is true that in some children this terror may represent also a fear of

---

* As the child grows up, sheer knowledge and familiarity as well as better motor development make these "dangers" less and less dangerous and more and more manageable. Throughout life it may be said that one of the main conative functions of education is this neutralizing of apparent dangers through knowledge, *e.g.*, I am not afraid of thunder because I know something about it.

loss of parental love, it can also occur in completely rejected children, who seem to cling to the hating parents more for sheer safety and protection than because of hope of love.

Confronting the average child with new, unfamiliar, strange, unmanageable stimuli or situations will too frequently elicit the danger or terror reaction, as, for example, getting lost or even being separated from the parents for a short time, being confronted with new faces, new situations or new tasks, the sight of strange, unfamiliar or uncontrollable objects, illness or death. Particularly at such times, the child's frantic clinging to his parents is eloquent testimony to their role as protectors (quite apart from their roles as food-givers and love-givers).

From these and similar observations, we may generalize and say that the average child in our society generally prefers a safe, orderly, predictable, organized world which he can count on, and in which unexpected, unmanageable or other dangerous things do not happen, and in which, in any case, he has all-powerful parents who protect and shield him from harm.

That these reactions may so easily be observed in children is in a way a proof of the fact that children in our society feel too unsafe (or, in a word, are badly brought up). Children who are reared in an unthreatening, loving family do *not* ordinarily react as we have described above (Shirley, 1942). In such children the danger reactions are apt to come mostly to objects or situations that adults too would consider dangerous.*

The healthy, normal, fortunate adult in our culture is largely satisfied in his safety needs. The peaceful, smoothly running, "good" society ordinarily makes its members feel safe enough from wild animals, extremes of temperature, criminals, assault and murder, tyranny, etc. Therefore, in a very real sense, he no longer has any safety needs as active motivators. Just as a sated man no longer feels hungry, a safe man no longer feels endangered. If we wish to see these needs directly and clearly we must turn to neurotic or near-neurotic individuals, and to the economic and social underdogs. In between these extremes, we can perceive the expressions of safety needs only in such phenomena as, for instance, the common preference for a job with tenure and protection, the desire for a savings account, and for insurance of various kinds (medical, dental, unemployment, disability, old age).

---

* A "test battery" for safety might be confronting the child with a small exploding firecracker, or with a bewhiskered face, having the mother leave the room, putting him upon a high ladder, a hypodermic injection, having a mouse crawl up to him, etc. Of course I cannot seriously recommend the deliberate use of such "tests," for they might very well harm the child being tested. But these and similar situations come up by the score in the child's ordinary day-to-day living and may be observed. There is no reason why these stimuli should not be used with, for example, young chimpanzees.

Other broader aspects of the attempt to seek safety and stability in the world are seen in the very common preference for familiar rather than unfamiliar things, or for the known rather than the unknown. The tendency to have some religion or world-philosophy that organizes the universe and the men in it into some sort of satisfactorily coherent, meaningful whole is also in part motivated by safety-seeking. Here too we may list science and philosophy in general as partially motivated by the safety needs (we shall see later that there are also other motivations to scientific, philosophical or religious endeavor).

Otherwise the need for safety is seen as an active and dominant mobilizer of the organism's resources only in emergencies, *e.g.*, war, disease, natural catastrophes, crime waves, societal disorganization, neurosis, brain injury, chronically bad situation.

Some neurotic adults in our society are, in many ways, like the unsafe child in their desire for safety, although in the former it takes on a somewhat special appearance. Their reaction is often to unknown, psychological dangers in a world that is perceived to be hostile, overwhelming and threatening. Such a person behaves as if a great catastrophe were almost always impending, *i.e.*, he is usually responding as if to an emergency. His safety needs often find specific expression in a search for a protector, or a stronger person on whom he may depend, or, perhaps, a Fuehrer.

The neurotic individual may be described in a slightly different way with some usefulness as a grown-up person who retains his childish attitudes toward the world. That is to say, a neurotic adult may be said to behave "as if" he were actually afraid of a spanking, or of his mother's disapproval, or of being abandoned by his parents, or having his food taken away from him. It is as if his childish attitudes of fear and threat reaction to a dangerous world had gone underground and, untouched by the growing up and learning processes, were now ready to be called out by any stimulus that would make a child feel endangered and threatened.*

The neurosis in which the search for safety takes its clearest form is in the compulsive-obsessive neurosis. Compulsive-obsessives try frantically to order and stabilize the world so that no unmanageable, unexpected or unfamiliar dangers will ever appear (Maslow and Mittelmann, 1941). They hedge themselves about with all sorts of ceremonials, rules and formulas so that every possible contingency may be provided for and so that no new contingencies may appear. They are much like the brain injured cases, described by Goldstein, who manage to maintain their equilibrium by

---

* Not all neurotic individuals feel unsafe. Neurosis may have at its core a thwarting of the affection and esteem needs in a person who is generally safe.

avoiding everything unfamiliar and strange and by ordering their restricted world in such a neat, disciplined, orderly fashion that everything in the world can be counted upon. They try to arrange the world so that anything unexpected (dangers) cannot possibly occur. If, through no fault of their own, something unexpected does occur, they go into a panic reaction as if this unexpected occurrence constituted a grave danger. What we can see only as a none-too-strong preference in the healthy person, *e.g.*, preference for the familiar, becomes a life-and-death necessity in abnormal cases.

The Love Needs

If both the physiological and the safety needs are fairly well gratified, then there will emerge the love and affection and belongingness needs, and the whole cycle already described will repeat itself with this new center. Now the person will feel keenly, as never before, the absence of friends, or a sweetheart, or a wife, or children. He will hunger for affectionate relations with people in general, namely, for a place in his group, and he will strive with great intensity to achieve this goal. He will want to attain such a place more than anything else in the world and may even forget that once, when he was hungry, he sneered at love.

In our society the thwarting of these needs is the most commonly found core in cases of maladjustment and more severe psychopathology. Love and affection, as well as their possible expression in sexuality, are generally looked upon with ambivalence and are customarily hedged about with many restrictions and inhibitions. Practically all theorists of psychopathology have stressed thwarting of the love needs as basic in the picture of maladjustment. Many clinical studies have therefore been made of this need and we know more about it perhaps than any of the other needs except the physiological ones (Maslow and Mittelmann).

One thing that must be stressed at this point is that love is not synonymous with sex. Sex may be studied as a purely physiological need. Ordinarily sexual behavior is multi-determined, that is to say, determined not only by sexual but also by other needs, chief among which are the love and affection needs. Also not to be overlooked is the fact that the love needs involve both giving *and* receiving love.

The Esteem Needs

All people in our society (with a few pathological exceptions) have a need or desire for a stable, firmly based, (usually) high evaluation of themselves, for self-respect, or self-esteem, and for the esteem of others. By firmly based self-esteem, we mean that which is soundly based upon real capacity, achievement and respect from others. These needs may be classified into two subsidiary sets. These are, first, the desire for strength, for achievement, for adequacy, for confidence in the face of the world, and for independence and freedom.* Secondly, we have what we may call the desire for reputation or prestige (defining it as respect or esteem from other people), recognition, attention, importance or appreciation.† These needs have been relatively stressed by Alfred Adler and his followers, and have been relatively neglected by Freud and the psychoanalysts. More and more today, however, there is appearing widespread appreciation of their central importance.

Satisfaction of the self-esteem need leads to feelings of self-confidence, worth, strength, capability and adequacy of being useful and necessary in the world. But thwarting of these needs produces feelings of inferiority, of weakness and helplessness. These feelings in turn give rise to either basic discouragement or else compensatory or neurotic trends. An appreciation of the necessity of basic self-confidence, and an understanding of how helpless people are without it, can be easily gained from a study of severe traumatic neurosis (Kardiner, 1941).

The Need for Self-Actualization

Even if all these needs are satisfied, we may still often (if not always) expect that a new discontent and restlessness will soon develop, unless the individual is doing what he is fitted for. A musician must make music, an artist must paint, a poet must write, if he is to be ultimately happy. What a man *can* be, he *must* be. This need we may call self-actualization.

This term, first coined by Kurt Goldstein, is being used in this paper in a much more specific and limited fashion. It refers to the desire for self-fulfillment, namely, to the tendency for him to become actualized in what he is potentially. This tendency might be phrased as the desire to become more and more what one is, to become everything that one is capable of becoming.

The specific form that these needs will take will of course vary greatly from person to person. In one individual it may take the form of the

* Whether or not this particular desire is universal we do not know. The crucial question, especially important today, is "Will men who are enslaved and dominated inevitably feel dissatisfied and rebellious?" We may assume on the basis of commonly known clinical data that a man who has known true freedom (not paid for by giving up safety and security but rather built on the basis of adequate safety and security) will not willingly or easily allow his freedom to be taken away from him. But we do not know that this is true for the person born into slavery. The events of the next decade should give us our answer.

† Perhaps the desire for prestige and respect from others is subsidiary to the desire for self-esteem or confidence in oneself. Observation of children seems to indicate that this is so, but clinical data give no clear support for such a conclusion.

desire to be an ideal mother, in another it may be expressed athletically, and in still another it may be expressed in painting pictures or in inventions. It is not necessarily a creative urge; although in people who have any capacities for creation it will take this form.

The clear emergence of these needs rests upon prior satisfaction of the physiological, safety, love and esteem needs. We shall call people who are satisfied in these needs basically satisfied people, and it is from these that we may expect the fullest (and healthiest) creativeness.* Since, in our society, basically satisfied people are the exception, we do not know much about self-actualization, either experimentally or clinically. It remains a challenging problem for research.

The Preconditions for the Basic Need Satisfactions

There are certain conditions which are immediate prerequisities for the basic need satisfactions. Danger to these is reacted to almost as if it were a direct danger to the basic needs themselves. Such conditions as freedom to speak, freedom to do what one wishes so long as no harm is done to others, freedom to express one's self, freedom to investigate and seek for information, freedom to defend one's self, justice, fairness, honesty, orderliness in the group are examples of such preconditions for basic need satisfactions. Thwarting in these freedoms will be reacted to with a threat or emergency response. These conditions are not ends in themselves but they are *almost* so since they are so closely related to the basic needs, which are apparently the only ends in themselves. These conditions are defended because without them the basic satisfactions are quite impossible, or at least, very severely endangered.

If we remember that the cognitive capacities (perceptual, intellectual, learning) are a set of adjustive tools, which have, among other functions, that of satisfaction of our basic needs, then it is clear that any danger to them, any deprivation or blocking of their free use, must also be indirectly threatening to the basic needs themselves. Such a statement is a partial solution of the general problems of curiosity, the search for knowledge, truth and wisdom, and the ever-persistent urge to solve the cosmic mysteries.

We must therefore introduce another hypothesis and speak of degrees

---

* Clearly creative behavior, like painting, is like any other behavior in having multiple determinants. It may be seen in "innately creative" people whether they are satisfied or not, happy or unhappy, hungry or sated. Also it is clear that creative activity may be compensatory, ameliorative or purely economic. It is my impression (as yet unconfirmed) that it is possible to distinguish the artistic and intellectual products of basically satisfied people from those of basically unsatisfied people by inspection alone. In any case, here too we must distinguish, in a dynamic fashion, the overt behavior itself from its various motivations or purposes.

of closeness to the basic needs, for we have already pointed out that *any* conscious desires (partial goals) are more or less important as they are more or less close to the basic needs. The same statement may be made for various behavior acts. An act is psychologically important if it contributes directly to satisfaction of basic needs. The less directly it so contributes, or the weaker this contribution is, the less important this act must be conceived to be from the point of view of dynamic psychology. A similar statement may be made for the various defense or coping mechanisms. Some are very directly related to the protection or attainment of the basic needs, others are only weakly and distantly related. Indeed if we wished, we could speak of more basic and less basic defense mechanisms, and then affirm that danger to the more basic defenses is more threatening than danger to less basic defenses (always remembering that this is so only because of their relationship to the basic needs).

The Desires to Know and to Understand

So far, we have mentioned the cognitive needs only in passing. Acquiring knowledge and systematizing the universe have been considered as, in part, techniques for the achievement of basic safety in the world, or, for the intelligent man, expressions of self-actualization. Also freedom of inquiry and expression have been discussed as preconditions of satisfactions of the basic needs. True though these formulations may be, they do not constitute definitive answers to the question as to the motivation role of curiosity, learning, philosophizing, experimenting, etc. They are, at best, no more than partial answers.

This question is especially difficult because we know so little about the facts. Curiosity, exploration, desire for the facts, desire to know may certainly be observed easily enough. The fact that they often are pursued even at great cost to the individual's safety is an indication of the partial character of our previous discussion. In addition, the writer must admit that, though he has sufficient clinical evidence to postulate the desire to know as a very strong drive in intelligent people, no data are available for unintelligent people. It may then be largely a function of relatively high intelligence. Rather tentatively, then, and largely in the hope of stimulating discussion and research, we shall postulate a basic desire to know, to be aware of reality, to get the facts, to satisfy curiosity, or as Wertheimer phrases it, to see rather than to be blind.

This postulation, however, is not enough. Even after we know, we are impelled to know more and more minutely and microscopically on the one hand, and on the other, more and more extensively in the direction of a world philosophy, religion, etc. The facts that we acquire, if they are isolated or atomistic, inevitably get theorized about, and either analyzed or organized or both. This process has been phrased by some as the search for "meaning." We shall then postulate a desire to understand, to systematize, to organize, to analyze, to look for relations and meanings.

Once these desires are accepted for discussion, we see that they too form themselves into a small hierarchy in which the desire to know is prepotent over the desire to understand. All the characteristics of a hierarchy of prepotency that we have described above seem to hold for this one as well.

We must guard ourselves against the too easy tendency to separate these desires from the basic needs we have discussed above, *i.e.*, to make a sharp dichotomy between "cognitive" and "conative" needs. The desire to know and to understand are themselves conative, *i.e.*, have a striving character, and are as much personality needs as the "basic needs" we have already discussed.

FURTHER CHARACTERISTICS OF THE BASIC NEEDS

The Degree of Fixity of the Hierarchy of Basic Needs

We have spoken so far as if this hierarchy were a fixed order but actually it is not nearly as rigid as we may have implied. It is true that most of the people with whom we have worked have seemed to have these basic needs in about the order that has been indicated. However, there have been a number of exceptions.

1. There are some people in whom, for instance, self-esteem seems to be more important than love. This most common reversal in the hierarchy is usually due to the development of the notion that the person who is most likely to be loved is a strong or powerful person, one who inspires respect or fear, and who is self-confident or aggressive. Therefore such people who lack love and seek it may try hard to put on a front of aggressive, confident behavior. But essentially they seek high self-esteem and its behavior expressions more as a means to an end than for its own sake; they seek self-assertion for the sake of love rather than for self-esteem itself.

2. There are other, apparently innately creative people in whom the drive to creativeness seems to be more important than any other counterdeterminant. Their creativeness might appear not as self-actualization released by basic satisfaction, but in spite of lack of basic satisfaction.

3. In certain people the level of aspiration may be permanently deadened or lowered. That is to say, the less prepotent goals may simply be lost, and may disappear forever, so that the person who has experienced

life at a very low level, *i.e.*, chronic unemployment, may continue to be satisfied for the rest of his life if only he can get enough food.

4. The so-called psychopathic personality is another example of permanent loss of the love needs. These are people who, according to the best data available, have been starved for love in the earliest months of their lives and have simply lost forever the desire and the ability to give and to receive affection (as animals lose sucking or pecking reflexes that are not exercised soon enough after birth).

5. Another cause of reversal of the hierarchy is that when a need has been satisfied for a long time, this need may be underevaluated. People who have never experienced chronic hunger are apt to underestimate its effects and to look upon food as a rather unimportant thing. If they are dominated by a higher need, this higher need will seem to be the most important of all. It then becomes possible, and indeed does actually happen, that they may, for the sake of this higher need, put themselves into the position of being deprived in a more basic need. We may expect that after a long-time deprivation of the more basic need there will be a tendency to reevaluate both needs so that the more prepotent need will actually become consciously prepotent for the individual who may have given it up very lightly. Thus, a man who has given up his job rather than lose his self-respect, and who then starves for six months or so, may be willing to take his job back even at the price of losing his self-respect.

6. Another partial explanation of *apparent* reversals is seen in the fact that we have been talking about the hierarchy of prepotency in terms of consciously felt wants or desires rather than of behavior. Looking at behavior itself may give us the wrong impression. What we have claimed is that the person will *want* the more basic of two needs when deprived in both. There is no necessary implication here that he will act upon his desires. Let us say again that there are many determinants of behavior other than the needs and desires.

7. Perhaps more important than all these exceptions are the ones that involve ideals, high social standards, high values and the like. With such values people become martyrs; they will give up everything for the sake of a particular ideal, or value. These people may be understood, at least in part, by reference to one basic concept (or hypothesis) which may be called "increased frustration-tolerance through early gratification." People who have been satisfied in their basic needs throughout their lives, particularly in their earlier years, seem to develop exceptional power to withstand present or future thwarting of these needs simply because they have strong, healthy character structure as a result of basic satisfaction. They are the "strong" people who can easily weather disagreement or opposition, who can swim against the stream of public opinion and who can

stand up for the truth at great personal cost. It is just the ones who have loved and been well loved, and who have had many deep friendships who can hold out against hatred, rejection or persecution.

I say all this in spite of the fact that there is a certain amount of sheer habituation which is also involved in any full discussion of frustration tolerance. For instance, it is likely that those persons who have been accustomed to relative starvation for a long time are partially enabled thereby to withstand food deprivation. What sort of balance must be made between these two tendencies, of habituation, on the one hand, and of past satisfaction breeding present frustration tolerance, on the other hand, remains to be worked out by further research. Meanwhile we may assume that they are both operative, side by side, since they do not contradict each other. In respect to this phenomenon of increased frustration tolerance, it seems probable that the most important gratifications come in the first two years of life. That is to say, people who have been made secure and strong in the earliest years tend to remain secure and strong thereafter in the face of whatever threatens.

Degrees of Relative Satisfaction

So far, our theoretical discussion may have given the impression that these five sets of needs are somehow in a step-wise, all-or-none relationship to each other. We have spoken in such terms as the following: "If one need is satisfied, then another emerges." This statement might give the false impression that a need must be satisfied 100 per cent before the next need emerges. In actual fact, most members of our society who are normal are partially satisfied in all their basic needs and partially unsatisfied in all their basic needs at the same time. A more realistic description of the hierarchy would be in terms of decreasing percentages of satisfaction as we go up the hierarchy of prepotency. For instance, if I may assign arbitrary figures for the sake of illustration, it is as if the average citizen is satisfied perhaps 85 per cent in his physiological needs, 70 per cent in his safety needs, 50 per cent in his love needs, 40 per cent in his self-esteem needs, and 10 per cent in his self-actualization needs.

As for the concept of emergence of a new need after satisfaction of the prepotent need, this emergence is not a sudden, saltatory phenomenon but rather a gradual emergence by slow degrees from nothingness. For instance, if prepotent need A is satisfied only 10 per cent then need B may not be visible at all. However, as this need A becomes satisfied 25 per cent, need B may emerge 5 per cent, as need A becomes satisfied 75 per cent, need B may emerge 90 per cent, and so on.

Unconscious Character of Needs

These needs are neither necessarily conscious nor unconscious. On the whole, however, in the average person, they are more often unconscious rather than conscious. It is not necessary at this point to overhaul the tremendous mass of evidence which indicates the crucial importance of unconscious motivation. It would by now be expected, on a priori grounds alone, that unconscious motivations would on the whole be rather more important than the conscious motivations. What we have called the basic needs are very often largely unconscious, although they may, with suitable techniques, and with sophisticated people, become conscious.

Cultural Specificity and Generality of Needs

This classification of basic needs makes some attempt to take account of the relative unity behind the superficial differences in specific desires from one culture to another. Certainly in any particular culture an individual's conscious motivational content will usually be extremely different from the conscious motivational content of an individual in another society. However, it is the common experience of anthropologists that people, even in different societies, are much more alike than we would think from our first contact with them, and that as we know them better we seem to find more and more of this commonness. We then recognize the most startling differences to be superficial rather than basic, *e.g.*, differences in style of hairdress, clothes, tastes in food, etc. Our classification of basic needs is in part an attempt to account for this unity behind the apparent diversity from culture to culture. No claim is made that it is ultimate or universal for all cultures. The claim is made only that it is relatively *more* ultimate, more universal, more basic, than the superficial conscious desires from culture to culture, and makes a somewhat closer approach to common-human characteristics. Basic needs are *more* common-human than superficial desires or behaviors.

Multiple Motivations of Behavior

These needs must be understood *not* to be *exclusive* or single determiners of certain kinds of behavior. An example may be found in any behavior that seems to be physiologically motivated, such as eating, or sexual play, or the like. The clinical psychologists have long since found that any behavior may be a channel through which flow various determinants. Or to say it in another way, most behavior is multi-motivated. Within the sphere of motivational determinants any behavior tends to be determined by several or *all* of the basic needs simultaneously rather than by only one of them. The latter would be more an exception than the former. Eating may be partially for the sake of filling the stomach, and partially for the sake of comfort and amelioration of other needs. One may make love not only for pure sexual release, but also to convince one's self of one's masculinity, or to make a conquest, to feel powerful, or to win more basic affection. As an illustration, I may point out that it would be possible (theoretically if not practically) to analyze a single act of an individual and see in it the expression of his physiological needs, his safety needs, his love needs, his esteem needs and self-actualization. This contrasts sharply with the more naive brand of trait psychology in which one trait or one motive accounts for a certain kind of act, *i.e.*, an aggressive act is traced solely to a trait of aggressiveness.

Multiple Determinants of Behavior

Not all behavior is determined by the basic needs. We might even say that not all behavior is motivated. There are many determinants of behavior other than motives.* For instance, one other important class of determinants is the so-called field determinants. Theoretically, at least, behavior may be determined completely by the field, or even by specific isolated external stimuli, as in association of ideas, or certain conditioned reflexes. If, in response to the stimulus word "table," I immediately perceive a memory image of a table, this response certainly has nothing to do with my basic needs.

Secondly, we may call attention again to the concept of "degree of closeness to the basic needs" or "degree of motivation." Some behavior is highly motivated, other behavior is only weakly motivated. Some is not motivated at all (but all behavior is determined).

Another important point is that there is a basic difference between expressive behavior and coping behavior (functional striving, purposive goal seeking). An expressive behavior does not try to do anything; it is simply a reflection of the personality. A stupid man behaves stupidly, not because he wants to, or tries to, or is motivated to, but simply because he *is* what he is. The same is true when I speak in a bass voice rather than tenor or soprano. The random movements of a healthy child, the smile on the face of a happy man even when he is alone, the springiness of the healthy man's walk, and the erectness of his carriage are other examples of expressive, non-functional behavior. Also the *style* in which a man carries out almost all his behavior, motivated as well as unmotivated, is often expressive.

* I am aware that many psychologists and psychoanalysts use the term "motivated" and "determined" synonymously, *e.g.*, Freud. But I consider this an obfuscating usage. Sharp distinctions are necessary for clarity of thought and precision in experimentation.

We may then ask, is *all* behavior expressive or reflective of the character structure? The answer is "No." Rote, habitual, automatized, or conventional behavior may or may not be expressive. The same is true for most "stimulus-bound" behaviors.

It is finally necessary to stress that expressiveness of behavior and goal-directedness of behavior are not mutually exclusive categories. Average behavior is usually both.

Goals as Centering Principle in Motivation Theory

It will be observed that the basic principle in our classification has been neither the instigation nor the motivated behavior but rather the functions, effects, purposes, or goals of the behavior. It has been proven sufficiently by various people that this is the most suitable point for centering in any motivation theory.

Animal- and Human-Centering

This theory starts with the human being rather than any lower and presumably "simpler" animal. Too many of the findings that have been made in animals have been proven to be true for animals but not for the human being. There is no reason whatsoever why we should start with animals in order to study human motivation. The logic or rather illogic behind this general fallacy of "pseudo-simplicity" has been exposed often enough by philosophers and logicians as well as by scientists in each of the various fields. It is no more necessary to study animals before one can study man than it is to study mathematics before one can study geology or psychology or biology.

We may also reject the old, naive, behaviorism which assumed that it was somehow necessary, or at least more "scientific," to judge human beings by animal standards. One consequence of this belief was that the whole notion of purpose and goal was excluded from motivational psychology simply because one could not ask a white rat about his purposes. Tolman has long since proven in animal studies themselves that this exclusion was not necessary.

Motivation and the Theory of Psychopathogenesis

The conscious motivational content of everyday life has, according to the foregoing, been conceived to be relatively important or unimportant accordingly as it is more or less closely related to the basic goals. A desire for an ice cream cone might actually be an indirect expression of a desire for love. If it is, then this desire for the ice cream cone becomes extremely important motivation. If, however, the ice cream is simply something to cool the mouth with, or a casual appetitive reaction, then the desire is relatively unimportant. Everyday conscious desires are to be regarded as symptoms, as *surface indicators of more basic needs*. If we were to take these superficial desires at their face value we would find ourselves in a state of complete confusion which could never be resolved, since we would be dealing seriously with symptoms rather than with what lay behind the symptoms.

Thwarting of unimportant desires produces no psychopathological results; thwarting of a basically important need does produce such results. Any theory of psychopathogenesis must then be based on a sound theory of motivation. A conflict or a frustration is not necessarily pathogenic. It becomes so only when it threatens or thwarts the basic needs, or partial needs that are closely related to the basic needs (Maslow, 1943).

The Role of Gratified Needs

It has been pointed out above several times that our needs usually emerge only when more prepotent needs have been gratified. Thus gratification has an important role in motivation theory. Apart from this, however, needs cease to play an active determining or organizing role as soon as they are gratified.

What this means is that, *e.g.*, a basically satisfied person no longer has the needs for esteem, love, safety, etc. The only sense in which he might be said to have them is in the almost metaphysical sense that a sated man has hunger, or a filled bottle has emptiness. If we are interested in what *actually* motivates us, and not in what has, will, or might motivate us, then a satisfied need is not a motivator. It must be considered for all practical purposes simply not to exist, to have disappeared. This point should be emphasized because it has been either overlooked or contradicted in every theory of motivation I know.* The perfectly healthy, normal, fortunate man has no sex needs or hunger needs, or needs for safety, or for love, or for prestige, or self-esteem, except in stray moments of quickly passing threat. If we were to say otherwise, we should also have to aver that every man had all the pathological reflexes, *e.g.*, Babinski, etc., because if his nervous system were damaged, these would appear.

It is such considerations as these that suggest the bold postulation that a man who is thwarted in any of his basic needs may fairly be envisaged simply as a sick man. This is a fair parallel to our designation as "sick" of the man who lacks vitamins or minerals. Who is to say that a lack of love is less important than a lack of vitamins? Since we know the pathogenic effects of love starvation, who is to say that we are invoking value-questions in an unscientific or illegitimate way, any more than the

* Note that acceptance of this theory necessitates basic revision of the Freudian theory.

physician does who diagnoses and treats pellagra or scurvy? If I were permitted this usage, I should then say simply that a healthy man is primarily motivated by his needs to develop and actualize his fullest potentialities and capacities. If a man has any other basic needs in any active, chronic sense, then he is simply an unhealthy man. He is as surely sick as if he had suddenly developed a strong salt hunger or calcium hunger.*

If this statement seems unusual or paradoxical the reader may be assured that this is only one among many such paradoxes that will appear as we revise our ways of looking at man's deeper motivations. When we ask what man wants of life, we deal with his very essence.

SUMMARY

1. There are at least five sets of goals, which we may call basic needs. These are briefly physiological, safety, love, esteem, and self-actualization. In addition, we are motivated by the desire to achieve or maintain the various conditions upon which these basic satisfactions rest and by certain more intellectual desires.

2. These basic goals are related to each other, being arranged in a hierarchy of prepotency. This means that the most prepotent goal will monopolize consciousness and will tend of itself to organize the recruitment of the various capacities of the organism. The less prepotent needs are minimized, even forgotten or denied. But when a need is fairly well satisfied, the next prepotent ("higher") need emerges, in turn, to dominate the conscious life and to serve as the center of organization of behavior, since gratified needs are not active motivators.

Thus man is a perpetually wanting animal. Ordinarily the satisfaction of these wants is not altogether mutually exclusive, but only tends to be. The average member of our society is most often partially satisfied and partially unsatisfied in all of his wants. The hierarchy principle is usually empirically observed in terms of increasing percentages of non-satisfaction as we go up the hierarchy. Reversals of the average order of the hierarchy are sometimes observed. Also it has been observed that an individual may permanently lose the higher wants in the hierarchy under special conditions. There are not only ordinarily multiple motivations for usual behavior, but in addition many determinants other than motives.

---

* If we were to use the word "sick" in this way, we should then also have to face squarely the relations of man to his society. One clear implication of our definition would be that (1) since a man is to be called sick who is basically thwarted, and (2) since such basic thwarting is made possible ultimately only by forces outside the individual, then (3) sickness in the individual must come ultimately from a sickness in the society. The "good" or healthy society would then be defined as one that permitted man's highest purposes to emerge by satisfying all his prepotent basic needs.

3. Any thwarting or possibility of thwarting of these basic human goals, or danger to the defenses which protect them, or to the conditions upon which they rest, is considered to be a psychological threat. With a few exceptions, all psychopathology may be partially traced to such threats. A basically thwarted man may actually be defined as a "sick" man, if we wish.

4. It is such basic threats which bring about the general emergency reactions.

5. Certain other basic problems have not been dealt with because of limitations of space. Among these are (a) the problem of values in any definitive motivation theory, (b) the relation between appetites, desires, needs, and what is "good" for the organism, (c) the etiology of the basic needs and their possible derivation in early childhood, (d) redefinition of motivational concepts, i.e., drive, desire, wish, need, goal, (e) implication of our theory for hedonistic theory, (f) the nature of the uncompleted act, of success and failure, and of aspiration-level, (g) the role of association, habit and conditioning, (h) relation to the theory of inter-personal relations, (i) implications for psychotherapy, (j) implication for theory of society, (k) the theory of selfishness, (l) the relation between needs and cultural patterns, (m) the relation between this theory and Allport's theory of functional autonomy. These as well as certain other less important questions must be considered as motivation theory attempts to become definitive.

REFERENCES

A. Adler. *Social Interest*, London: Faber & Faber, 1938.

W. B. Cannon. *Wisdom of the Body*. New York: Norton, 1932.

A. Freud. *The Ego and the Mechanisms of Defense*. London: Hogarth, 1937.

S. Freud. *New Introductory Lectures on Psychoanalysis*. New York: Norton, 1933.

E. Fromm. *Escape from Freedom*. New York: Farrar and Rinehart, 1941.

K. Goldstein. *The Organism*. New York: American Book Co., 1939.

K. Horney. *The Neurotic Personality of Our Time*. New York: Norton, 1937.

A. Kardiner. *The Traumatic Neuroses of War*. New York: Hoeber, 1941.

D. M. Levy. "Primary Affect Hunger." *American Journal of Psychiatry*, 1937, 94, 643–52.

A. H. Maslow. "Conflict, Frustration, and the Theory of Threat," *Journal of Abnormal and Social Psychology*, 1943, 38, 81–86.

———. "Dominance, Personality and Social Behavior in Women," *Journal of Social Psychology*, 1939, 10, 3–39.

———. "The Dynamics of Psychological Security-Insecurity," *Character & Personality*, 1942, 10, 331–44.

———. "A Preface to Motivation Theory," *Psychosomatic Medicine*, 1943, 5, 85–92.

——— and B. Mittelmann. *Principles of Abnormal Psychology*. New York: Harper & Bros., 1941.

H. A. Murray *et al. Explorations in Personality*. New York: Oxford University Press, 1938.

J. Plant. *Personality and the Cultural Pattern*. New York: Commonwealth Fund, 1937.

M. Shirley. "Children's Adjustments to a Strange Situation," *Journal of Abnormal and Social Psychology*, 1942, 37, 201–17.

E. C. Tolman. *Purposive Behavior in Animals and Men*. New York: Century, 1932.

M. Wertheimer. Unpublished lectures at the New School for Social Research, 1939.

P. T. Young. *Motivation of Behavior*. New York: John Wiley & Sons, 1936.

———. "The Experimental Analysis of Appetite," *Psychological Bulletin*, 1941, 38, 129–64.

22.

JOHN A. FINGER, JR.,
AND MORTON SILVERMAN

CHANGES IN ACADEMIC PERFORMANCE IN THE JUNIOR HIGH SCHOOL

One does not have to undertake a scientific study to discover that academic underachievement constitutes a significant problem at all levels of the educational process. However, it is not clear whether academic failure is the same sort of phenomenon in both older and younger students. Conceivably, academic achievement could be a developmental process that starts in the early grades and follows its course through to college graduation or beyond. It is equally possible, however, to view an academic career as a series of events that entail varying demands upon a student's academic assets and liabilities. In an earlier study (Finger and Schlesser, 1965), it was shown that a preliminary edition of the Personal Values Inventory (PVI) (Schlesser and Finger, 1962) could identify the academic motivation factor as early as the seventh grade. The characteristics of academic motivation at the junior high school level are quite similar to those identified

Reprinted with permission of the authors and The American Personnel and Guidance Association from *Personnel and Guidance Journal* 45 (1966), 157–64. Copyright © 1966 The American Personnel and Guidance Association.

in secondary and college students. It would seem, then, that starting at levels as low as the seventh grade, academic motivation bears a continuous and significant relationship to academic success.

Things are less clear, however, with elementary school students. Some preliminary explorations with the PVI have suggested that academic motivation cannot be identified in elementary school students, that, at best, it bears but a weak relationship to elementary school grades. Whether these tentative findings are attributable to differences between older and younger students, the differing demands of their teachers or problems in test construction, they raise the question of discontinuity in academic motivation and performance.

In reviewing the school histories of a large number of students in the schools of New York State, Armstrong has demonstrated that the junior high school era is one of two periods in educational careers where abrupt changes in school performance occur. While some children earned good grades in junior high school after a history of poor elementary school marks, approximately 45 per cent of the boys and girls with good elementary school records went on to do only fair or poor work in junior high school. The indications of a significant discontinuity in educational career at the junior high school level were underscored by Armstrong's report of the frequent irreversibility of these changes. Relatively few of the students whose school grades deteriorated in junior high school went on to do good or even fair work at the high school level.

The influences shaping an academic career at the start of the junior high school period are obviously numerous and complex. This study was designed to explore one aspect of this complex period, the relationship between academic motivation as measured by the PVI, and changes in grades between elementary school and junior high school.

PROCEDURE

In the spring of 1964, the State of Rhode Island tested all sixth-grade students on a battery of intelligence and achievement tests. The students' scores on the California Test of Mental Maturity, the California Achievement Test in Reading, Language and Arithmetic and the Scholastic Testing Service Work-Study Skills Test were made available for this study. All available seventh-grade students in five junior high schools of two Rhode Island cities who had attended selected elementary schools were tested with the PVI in November, 1964. The PVI is an objective self-administered test that inquires into students' values and interests through frank questions. The test yields eleven scores, in the areas of home, persistence, self-control–deliberateness, self-views, school defenses, planning,

thinking process rather than some externally imposed time-schedule or body of content. It is a purposeful activity employing the strategy of incorporating more meaningful student input into the learning process, structured in a fashion that invites greater self-awareness through reflectively dealing with concerns that are psychologically significant. Scientific reflective thinking, as a cognitive process, is a key to any learning that is purposeful—as all learning is.

When teachers describe reflective teaching as non-directive, it indicates again how most teachers categorize techniques at either extreme. If a method advocates cooperative student-teacher planning of learning experiences, many teachers falsely assume that it implies almost total abdication of the teacher's responsibility and leadership. To plan cooperatively does not mean the students take over. This fear of a teacher's loss of control is further exaggerated when teachers assume that asking students to help plan learning activities means they will reject any formal study and simply want to mess around. The teacher must, therefore, dominate in order to get the students to cover the material assigned for that course.

Reflective inquiry is not laissez-faire teaching; nor is it entirely student centered. Reflective teaching is more client centered . . . than centered directly upon tasks prescribed for students by a teacher. Reflective teaching is based upon field psychology, comprising the principle of interaction between the person and his environment. In this interactive process, the person is not self-sufficient psychologically; rather, he seeks further clarity of outlook by purposefully interacting with elements in his cognitive field.

Because of this interaction with one's environment, the person becomes aware of perplexities and disharmonies that he feels psychologically. Simultaneously, internal motivation propels him toward solving his perplexity in a reflective manner. If the person does not "feel" some degree of cognitive tension due to his interaction with vectors in his field, then, in reference to meaningful learning, he may learn only at the rote or understanding level. Learning that is dictated by a teacher without being assimilated into one's field is meaningless learning. Planning learning activities that do not invite cooperative student-teacher input most frequently results in teacher-centered teaching that students "learn" because they must.

Cooperative teacher and student selection and planning of learning experiences best describes reflective teaching. Because content will probably remain rather meaningless when taught non-reflectively, the classroom teacher should incorporate a teaching strategy that includes the problem-raising, problem-solving stages of reflective teaching. In both of these phases, the teacher attempts to balance the emphasis on both the person and the content. Content cannot be divorced from the person; moreover, content should become a means for creating perplexity within any given field.

Beginning with student-expressed concerns and curiosities that overlap content or lead toward further consideration of material encourages immediate participation. For the reflective teacher content alone is meaningless, yet the students cannot select all of the learning experiences. By interacting, sometimes starting with content that is inconsisent or with expressed student outlooks that are inadequate, or sometimes beginning with a teacher-initiated experience or a student-initiated activity, the teacher and the students cooperatively come to know the interests and priorities that are significant for each other in this learning experience.

Just as reflective teaching is not entirely non-directive or student centered, neither is it concerned only with individualism. The individual person is certainly important, for he gives meanings to what he perceives and experiences. These meanings are indeed individual and personal: however, as the person continuously interacts he also seeks to further clarify his meanings; often, he alters or reconfirms his views. As he restructures his field of meanings, he necessarily looks outside of himself for additional experiences that influence his search for clearer meanings of his perceptions. In this process, the student simultaneously comes to know himself and his environment better.

In a social-psychological sense, a person interacts with his psychological environment as a means of self-development. This interaction must usually be consistent with terms of social convention that the larger society has imposed regarding acceptable behavior. Following this guideline individualism evolves into humanism.

The person, interacting with members of the larger group, both gives and receives perceptions that assist in the formulation of common understandings about aspects of reality, truth, governance, etc. This development of individual awareness and group consciousness is the goal of the reflective process.

Another aspect of reflective teaching that is frequently misinterpreted has to do with its relativism. If all knowledge is relative, some teachers aks, why learn anything at all? The extreme is again cited because so often teachers view reflective thinking as advocating that position. Reflective teaching is not based upon predetermined ends or prescribed behaviors, such as those identified by the so-called behavioral objectives school, but it does not deny the importance of content. Conclusions of static answer and absolute truth negate the principle of insight development in an evolving universe. While common agreement exists among persons who perceive phenomena in similar fashions, that agreement cannot be viewed as absolute truth for all times; even though it is a presently verifiable truth for those persons. As man's perceptions of evidence change due to his interaction with various data, his interpretation of truth changes. A person can hold for some time a belief that he rationalizes, but even his ideas do not remain absolutely static. As one's perceptions change, so do one's attitudes.

In order for man to communicate, common perceptions are accepted as a basis for language. Men find it convenient to have some agreed upon foundations which help to further the creation of knowledge. It seems appropriate to continue using certain data judged adequate such as a base ten numbering system, until it is perceived as inadequate and creates a need for new insighting. Thus, with some commonly perceived acceptable knowledge, the reflective teacher adopts a teaching strategy that is more an open process model for facilitating individual growth than the performance contracting model imposing minimum behavior levels on students.

Reflective teaching does anticipate that the student will approximate tentative outlooks commonly known to exist in any study, those the teacher knows from personal study as well as those held by experts in the field. However, most significant to reflective thinking is the anticipation of novel solutions that students suggest when engaged in reflective study. To teach students only those conclusions which already exist invites little reflective thinking. Rather, in planning a reflective learning strategy, the teacher ought to deliberately structure more open-ended learning activities inviting creative thinking and problem solving. This purposeful planning for some novel solutions as an outgrowth of reflective study is characteristic of creative thought that teaching for prescribed solutions restricts.

Reflective teaching is relative because man, psychologically, is relative. Perceived discrepancies create degrees of cognitive perplexity motivating a person to reflect toward a clearer awareness of the relationship between himself and perceived data. Because this process takes place in a constantly evolving field, new insights render previous information and solutions susceptible to revision. Reflective teaching encourages problem solving and the finding of solutions to inquiries; but these solutions are held adequate for the time being based on obtainable data, and not held absolute—an attitude that closes further reflective consideration. Conclusions are deemed tentative—available for reconsideration whenever warranted.

The reflective teacher regards solutions as tentative and open-ended, and designs teaching to make students aware of that attitude about content. Common agreement is reached on many solutions because communication is facilitated and evidence available, both to students and to members of the larger community of inquirers, indicates that this conclusion is the most adequate and harmonious based upon available data at this time.

Lastly, reflective teaching is not based on the teacher's selection of all of the content to be studied by a class. Nor is content to be imposed upon students by textbook publishers, school boards, state legislatures, curriculum guides, or community pressure groups. The imposition of content to such an extent that students have not time for either identifying with subject matter or identifying personal concerns within the subject matter area causes students to resort most often to rote learning rather than meaningful reflective learning.

Teacher selected and prescribed content, most of it foreign to students, violates the psychological principle which maintains that a student cannot abstract much beyond his knowledge and experiences. Yet, teachers present content which is usually much beyond students and expect them, in fact require them, to come up to the teacher's level or fail. Reflective teaching emphasizes that teachers engage in a strategy that helps them identify the students' level and interest in a topic or concept, then design learning experiences cooperatively which account for student interests and needs.

How can a teacher be aware of student interests? In place of immediate content exposition, reflective teaching advocates that both the teacher and the students interact in an exploratory manner to discover each other's feelings, interests, and needs related to elements of the subject at hand. Usually, the teacher initiates some exploration of a perplexity that he perceives to exist in the subject and invites some student identification with that concern. It is often necessary for the teacher to present directly, or through media, questioning, simulation, or whatever seems appropriate for initiating reflective study, a number of dichotomous views, conflicting reports, or relevant issues concerning the subject being studied. Not knowing which issue students will feel the greatest concern about, the teacher suggests a number of "problems" that individuals and small groups of students deem significant for their inquiry. Problem-raising is thus often the main function of the reflective teacher; once students have psychologically chosen a concern, problem-solving naturally follows.

Important in this process of cooperatively identifying "content" is that students are actively involved, as group members, in exploring, organizing, refining, and "solving" their concerns. Instead of the teacher selecting content and imposing it according to some "planned schedule," students and the teacher together engage in a group process characterized by cooperative and reflective investigations which assist in developing greater individual awareness about one's self, one's group, and the concerns of the group. The teacher's role is not one of explaining "content," but one of guiding the group inquiry process toward reflective self-awareness using perplexing subject matter as a means for developing clearer insights into the nature of whatever subject is under consideration.

To summarize, reflective teaching and reflective learning are not the far-out radical approaches to education that some would believe. Reflective teaching is indeed less structured than traditional education; it involves the students more meaningfully in the selecting and planning of learning experiences through cooperative teacher-small group interaction; it is organized around a strategy designed to propel students toward anticipated outcomes/solutions, or conclusions that are both relative and open to novel problem-solving rather than narrow and predetermined. Reflective learning is an exploratory process involving interaction that leads toward self-enhancement. Reflective teaching necessarily employs the method of reflective learning as its educational strategy.

26.

JAMES H. BLOCK

TEACHERS, TEACHING, AND MASTERY LEARNING

Mastery learning is both a philosophy about schooling and an associated set of instructional strategies whereby the philosophy can be implemented in the classroom. This philosophy asserts that under appropriate instructional conditions virtually *all* students can and will learn well most of what they are taught.

Actually, the roots of this philosophy go back several hundred years. For example, they can be found in the writings of the Jesuits, Comenius, Pestalozzi, and Herbart. But it was only in the latter part of the nineteenth century and in the early years of the twentieth that the mastery learning idea was applied to U.S. education by individuals such as Washburne at Winnetka and Morrison at the University of Chicago. And it was not until the late 1950s and early 60s that the technology required to sustain an efficient and effective mastery learning strategy became available. Only in roughly the last decade, therefore, have feasible mastery learning procedures become available to the American classroom teacher.

From *Today's Education* 63:7 (November-December, 1973), 30–36.

Two major types of mastery learning strategies are now in use. Both types attempt to better individualize instruction by (a) helping students when and where they have learning difficulties, (b) giving them sufficient time to learn, and (c) clearly defining what they will be expected to learn and to what level. But one type uses primarily an *individually based* instructional format where each student learns independently of his classmates. The other employs a *group-based* approach, where each student learns cooperatively with his classmates.

Since few schools may possess the resources required to implement an individually based approach to mastery learning, let us focus here on only one example of the group-based approaches: Bloom's "learning for mastery" strategy.[1]

BLOOM'S STRATEGY

The genesis for Bloom's mastery learning ideas was a conceptual model of school learning suggested by John B. Carroll.[2] This model rested on the observation that a student's aptitude for a particular subject predicted either the level to which he could learn the subject in a given time or the time he would require to learn it to a given level. Hence, rather than defining aptitude as an index of the level to which a student could learn, Carroll defined aptitude as a measure of learning rate: A student with high aptitude for a subject would learn it quickly, while one with a low aptitude would learn it more slowly.

In its simplest form, Carroll's model suggested that if each student were allowed the time he needed to learn some subject to some mastery criterion and if he spent the necessary time, then he would be likely to attain mastery. The time spent was determined either by the student's perseverance—i.e., the amount of time he was willing to spend actively engaged in learning—or by the time he was allowed to learn. The time needed, on the other hand, was determined by the student's aptitude for the topic, the quality of his instruction and the instructional materials, and his ability to understand the instruction and the materials.

If the quality of instruction and of the instructional materials was high, then the student would readily understand the instruction and would need little time to learn the topic beyond that required by his aptitude. If the quality of the instruction and of the materials was low, however, the student would then need much additional time.

Bloom transformed this conceptual model into a working model for mastery learning by the following logic. If aptitude were predictive of the *rate*, but not necessarily of the *level*, at which a student could learn, it should be possible to fix the degree of learning expected of each student at some mastery performance level. Then, by attending to the time allowed and the quality of instruction—the variables under teacher control in Carroll's model—the teacher should be able to ensure that each student attains this level.

Elaborating on this logic, Bloom argued that if students were normally distributed with respect to aptitude for some subject and were provided with *uniform* instruction as to time allowed and quality of instruction, then few of them would attain mastery, and the relationship between aptitude and achievement would be high. But if each student received *differential* instruction as to time allowed and quality of instruction, then a majority of students, perhaps 95 percent, could be expected to attain mastery, and there should be little or no relationship between aptitude and achievement.

The mastery learning strategy developed in accordance with this reasoning is designed for use in group-based instructional situations where the calendar time allowed for learning is relatively fixed. As noted above, Carroll's model of school learning proposed that each student can master a given topic if he is provided enough time. Consequently, Bloom's mastery learning strategy attempts to minimize the time a student needs to learn so that it is within the fixed amount of calendar time available. This is accomplished through two distinct sets of steps. One set occurs prior to the actual classroom instruction; the second takes place in the classroom.

PRECONDITIONS FOR MASTERY LEARNING

The teacher who wishes to achieve mastery learning begins with the assumption that most of his students can learn well and that he can teach so that most *will* learn well. Practically, this means that the teacher shifts from the belief that only a small percentage of his students can really learn to the belief that almost all of them can. It also means that the teacher decides to base each student's grade on his actual performance rather than on his rank in class.

The teacher then turns to the problem of formulating what he means by mastery of his course. Ideally, he would first define what material all students will be expected to learn. This entails the formulation of course objectives. He would next determine to what level or mastery performance standard they would be expected to achieve these objectives. Lastly, he would prepare a final or summative examination over all these objectives for administration at the course's close. He could then compare each student's score on this test against the predetermined mastery standard in order to test for mastery or nonmastery.

In actual practice, though, teachers have found it useful to use their old course achievement tests as working definitions of the material that each student will be expected to master. They have also found it convenient to administer one or more of these tests throughout the course for grading purposes. Finally, rather than grade the student's performance on a mastery/nonmastery basis, the teachers have found it useful to fix an absolute grading scale wherein mastery corresponds to a grade of A or B and nonmastery corresponds to a grade C, D, or F. The teacher forms this scale by determining the level of performance that students traditionally had to exhibit on the course examinations in order to earn an A, B, C, D, or F. All students who achieve to a particular level using mastery learning methods then receive the grade that corresponds to this level.

Now, the teacher breaks his course into a sequence of smaller learning units, each of which typically covers about two weeks' worth of material. In practice, these units correspond roughly to chapters in the course textbook or to a set of topics.

Next, for each unit he develops perhaps the single most important component of the Bloom-type mastery learning strategy: the unit feedback/correction procedures. The purpose of these procedures is to monitor the effectiveness of the group-based instruction so that it can be supplemented and/or appropriately modified to better suit the learning requirements of each student.

First, the teacher constructs a brief, ungraded diagnostic-progress test or formative evaluation instrument for each unit. The quizzes and homework that most teachers now use to determine how students are progressing ordinarily do not describe student learning in great enough detail to enable the teacher to prescribe what each student might do to overcome his particular learning problems. Mastery learning requires prescriptive evaluation instruments, such as these formative tests.

These tests are explicitly designed to be an integral part of each unit's instruction and to provide specific information or feedback to both the teacher and the student about how the student is changing as a result of the group-based instruction. Usually, a score of less than 80 to 85 per cent correct on these tests indicates that the student is having learning problems.

Second, the teacher now develops a set of alternative instructional materials or correctives keyed to each item on each unit formative test. All students cannot learn for mastery unless some students are provided with alternative ways of learning certain material in addition to group-based instruction.

To date, peer and cross-age tutoring and, especially, small-group study sessions in which each student has a chance to teach and be taught have proven highly effective. Alternative textbooks, workbooks, programmed instructional materials, academic games and puzzles, and selected "affective" educational exercises have also been tried.

These correctives teach the material tested by each item, but they do so in ways that differ from the group-based instruction. Typically, the correctives will attempt to present the material in a different sensory mode or modes or in a different form of the same mode than the group-based instruction. And/or they will involve the student in a different way and/or provide not only different types of encouragements for learning but also different amounts of each type.

Should a student encounter difficulty in learning certain material from the group-based instruction unit, he can then use the correctives to explore alternative ways of learning the unmastered material, select those correctives best suited to his particular learning requirements, and overcome his learning problems before they impair subsequent learning.

For the *individual* teacher, the construction of these feedback/correction procedures is time-consuming. However, if small groups of teachers in the same subject matter area work together, we find they can develop both the formative tests and the accompanying correctives for an entire year's work by working two to three hours a day for just a few weeks. The first formative test and the relevant correctives are much harder to develop than subsequent ones.

OPERATING PROCEDURES FOR MASTERY LEARNING

The teacher is now ready to teach. Since students are not accustomed to learning for mastery or to the notion that they all might earn As, the teacher usually must spend some time at the course's outset orienting them to the procedures to be used. During this period, teachers have stressed the following points:

1. The student will be graded *solely* on the basis of his summative examination performance.
2. The student will be graded against predetermined performance standards and not in relation to the performance of his peers.
3. All students who attain a particular level of performance will receive the corresponding grade (hopefully an A), and there will be no fixed number of As, Bs, Cs, Ds, or Fs.
4. Throughout the course, the student will be given a series of ungraded diagnostic-progress tests to promote and pace his learning.
5. Each student will receive all the help he needs in order to learn.

This orientation period—combined with continual encouragement, support, and positive evidence of learning success—should develop in most students the belief that they can learn and the motivation to learn.

Following the orientation period, the teacher teaches the first unit of the course using his customary group-based instructional methods. At the end of this instruction, rather than moving on to the next unit, he administers the unit formative test to determine how each student is achieving. Students score their own tests.

On the basis of the test results, the teacher certifies the progress of the students who achieved mastery of the unit (i.e., scored at or above about 80 to 85 per cent correct). He encourages the students who have not achieved mastery to use the unit's correctives to complete their learning of unmastered material. These students are then responsible for using the correctives to complete their learning of the unit as soon as possible, and preferably before the group-based instruction on the next unit begins.

Typically, the students will use the correctives on their own time, except that at the beginning of the course, class time is often set aside to get students into the habit of using the correctives.

With each learning unit, the teacher repeats this cycle of group-based instruction, formative testing, and certification or correction until the course is completed. He administers summative tests as required throughout the course, although, ideally, he need give only one final examination per quarter, term, or semester.

All students who score above a certain performance level over these tests earn As. All who perform at lower levels earn appropriately lower grades, though we usually find that when students learn by mastery methods, the number of Bs and Cs is small and there are virtually no Ds and Fs.

SOME STUDENT LEARNING OUTCOMES

In the years since publication of Bloom's learning for mastery strategy, extensive school-based mastery learning research has been carried out around the world, at all levels of education, in all types of schools, in an increasingly wide variety of basic and more specialized subjects, and in the physical and social sciences, the humanities, and the professions, especially medicine and dentistry.

Bloom-type mastery learning strategies have been successfully used for small samples of students in classrooms where the student-teacher ratios have ranged from 20 to 30 to 1 and for large samples of up to 500,000 students where the student-teacher ratios approach and exceed 70 to 1. The strategies have even been used effectively to teach the rudiments of such advanced topics as matrix algebra, probability theory, statistics, and mathematical proof to elementary school pupils.

There are some problems in interpreting the results of most of this research. First, most of it comes from the more structured subjects like mathematics and the sciences, from introductory and intermediate courses, and from schools in middle socioeconomic areas. Second, the research tends to be done in the classroom rather than in the laboratory and by teachers rather than experimenters.

Third, it may tend to paint too rosy a picture of the impact that mastery learning approaches can have on student learning. This is because the research is usually published, and published research tends not to report negative results. Fourth, the research sometimes comes from projects wherein it is difficult to determine whether mastery learning ideas have actually been applied. Finally, the research is so voluminous that one runs the risk of overinterpretation *or* underinterpretation simply because important studies might not have been unearthed.

Taking all the problems into account, however, the following statement seems fair:

In general, two to three times as many students who have learned a particular subject by mastery methods have achieved As, Bs, or their equivalent as have students who have learned the same subject by more conventional, group-based instructional methods.

Thus, if 25 per cent of a group of students earned As and Bs when learning by an ordinary, group-based nonmastery instructional method, then, typically, 50 to 75 per cent of a similar group earned As and Bs when learning by group-based mastery methods. The data also indicate that mastery approaches to instruction can drastically cut the number of those receiving Cs, Ds, and Fs.

So far, we have considered the effects of mastery learning strategies on the cognitive or intellectual aspects of student learning. There is also a growing body of evidence of the impact of these strategies on the affective or emotional aspects of student learning.

At least in the short run, mastery approaches to learning can yield greater student interest in and more positive attitudes toward the topics learned than can nonmastery approaches, although if students are asked to master a subject too well, this may eventually turn them off. Mastery approaches can also generate in students increased confidence in their ability to learn. Finally, students really enjoy learning by mastery approaches.

There have been no studies of the effects of mastery learning approaches on affective traits that develop over long periods of time, such as self-concept and mental health. Related research suggests, however, that the provision of repeated successful short-term learning experiences might help shape long-term constructive attitudes toward school and toward learning in general and might help develop a positive academic self-concept. More speculative research suggests that the provision of a long history of positive school learning experiences may even help to partially immunize students against school-induced mental and emotional disorders.

Last, but not least, mastery approaches to learning have yielded some evidence—primarily anecdotal and impressionistic—that they are helping students learn how to learn. This evidence is of at least three different types.

First, many students who have learned for mastery using a wide variety of correctives apparently become more accustomed to the notion that there are many ways to learn besides from lectures and textbooks. I have been especially intrigued with how often students turn to other students for aid and assistance and with how they come to exhibit increased co-operation and decreasing competition in their learning.

Second, students who have learned for mastery have been observed to become more careful and selective in their learning. On the one hand, they do more informal formative evaluation and, thereby, gain some measure of quality control over their learning and their study habits. On the other hand, they also spend more time actively engaged with the material to be learned rather than with extraneous material or with nonlearning activities.

Third, the students who have learned for mastery have been observed to generate their own learning rewards (e.g., the chance to tutor a peer) rather than relying only on those rewards the teacher might provide. Work is presently under way to study each of these phenomena in more detail. It may well be the case that this research will provide a far more compelling case for the classroom use of mastery learning than even the past research.

IMPLICATIONS FOR THE TEACHER

What, then, are the implications of mastery learning for the role of class-room teacher?

By adopting the view that all can learn and by defining mastery, the teacher is essentially determining what ought to be or to occur in his classroom. Similarly, by adopting the view that all will learn and then using feedback/correction procedures to reach mastery, the teacher is translating these "oughts" into concrete materials, plans, and actions.

Since we call such conceptions of what ought to be "values," the first implication of mastery learning for the teacher is that he get accustomed to explicit valuing. That is, the teacher must not only determine what ought to be so in his classroom, but he must also get used to making these oughts explicit in how and what he teaches.

To value something in the abstract or in private may be relatively easy; to make one's values concrete and public is much more difficult, because this opens one up to possible criticism by those who disagree with one's values. This is especially true where, as in mastery learning, many of the values (e.g., everyone can and will learn) to which the teacher explicitly ascribes may be at loggerheads with the values held by his colleagues and superiors.

Besides valuing, therefore, the mastery learning teacher must stand ready to justify the values represented in his instruction. The mastery learning teacher, for example, can expect to be required to defend his grading standards when perhaps 80 per cent of his students earn As.

Another implication of mastery learning is that the teacher needs to exercise a measure of quality control in his teaching.

One dimension of his responsibility in this area is the use of feedback/correction procedures to pinpoint and to overcome student learning problems. Time after time, when a mastery learning strategy fails, it fails not because the teacher has not prepared appropriate feedback/correction procedures but because he did not implement them. In particular, the teacher has a tendency to fail to induce students to correct the learning difficulties revealed by formative testing.

The second dimension of the teacher's quality control responsibility is the monitoring of the effectiveness of his instruction from one cycle of his course to the next. Often the teacher can improve the quality of his instruction during one cycle of his course by using the formative test results and other information from the previous cycle as his benchmarks. And by using one year's results as a quality control check on the next, the teacher can have a greater impact on more and more students' learning over the years.

For example, by noting which items on each unit formative test most students answered correctly and incorrectly, the teacher can determine the material for which the group-based instruction was generally effective and for which it was not. He can then tally the types of correctives to which the students turned for supplementary instruction on this material. After studying how these correctives present the material or involve the students or encourage their learning, the teacher can revise his original instruction accordingly to teach this material better in the future.

Regardless of the quality control procedure one adopts, not even the best mastery learning strategies will help all students earn As the first cycle. Only through the cycle-by-cycle exercise of some quality control procedures can the teacher eventually ensure that as many students as possible earn As.

The final implication of mastery learning for the role of classroom teacher is that the teacher must do more communicating and cooperating with his colleagues and students. In regard to colleagues, this increased communication and cooperation will yield at least two benefits. First, it can allay some of their misgivings and guard against the possibility that what one is doing will be misperceived. Second, as noted previously, it can cut the work load required to construct feedback/correction procedures.

In regard to the students, increased cooperation and communication can have several salutary effects. First, it can smooth the introduction of mastery learning ideas into the classroom. Students can provide invaluable feedback to the teacher about what they like and do not like about a particular mastery strategy and about how the strategy might be changed.

Second, it can help to implement a successful strategy. There is no reason why students in a mastery learning situation cannot be trusted to perform many activities that the teacher would ordinarily perform. Students might correct their own formative tests, construct their own correctives, and tutor each other.

Third, increased cooperation and communication can create a learning environment in which students see themselves as having a stake. I would hazard the guess that no learning environment can have a dramatic impact on students' learning unless they perceive themselves as belonging.

I hope that these implications do not convey the impression that mastery learning is difficult to achieve in the classroom. It is not. My point in broaching them is simply to suggest that mastery learning is not a painless panacea.

Associated with teaching by mastery learning methods are certain costs as well as manifold benefits for students and, most of all, for teachers. Each teacher will have to decide whether the chance to have a clear and consistent positive impact on most of his students' learning is worth the effort and energy that teaching for mastery requires.

REFERENCES

Benjamin S. Bloom, "An Introduction to Mastery Learning Theory," in James H. Block, ed., *Schools, Society, and Mastery Learning,* (New York: Holt, Rinehart, and Winston, 1974).

John B. Carroll, "A Model of School Learning." *Teachers College Record,* Vol. 64 (May 1963), pp. 723–33.

27.

PATRICK SUPPES

COMPUTER TECHNOLOGY AND THE FUTURE OF EDUCATION

Current applications of computers and related information-processing techniques run the gamut in our society from the automatic control of factories to the scrutiny of tax returns. I have not seen any recent data, but we are certainly reaching the point at which a high percentage of regular employees in this country are paid by computerized payroll systems. As another example, every kind of complex experiment is beginning to be subject to computer assistance either in terms of the actual experimentation or in terms of extensive computations integral to the analysis of the experiment. These applications range from bubble-chamber data on elementary particles to the crystallography of protein molecules.

As yet, the use of computer technology in administration and management, on the one hand, and scientific and engineering applications, on the other, far exceed direct applications in education. However, if potentials are properly realized, the character and nature of education during the course of our lifetimes will be radically changed. Perhaps the most important aspect of computerized instructional devices is that the kind of individualized instruction once possible only for a few members of the aristocracy can be made available to all students at all levels of abilities.

Because some may not be familiar with how computers can be used to provide individualized instruction, let me briefly review the mode of operation. In the first place, because of its great speed of operation, a computer can handle simultaneously a large number of students—for instance, 200 or more, and each of the 200 can be at a different point in the curriculum. In the simplest mode of operation, the terminal device at which the student sits is something like an electric typewriter. Messages can be typed out by the computer and the student in turn can enter his responses on the keyboard. The first and most important feature to add is the delivery of audio messages under computer control to the student. Not only children, but students of all ages learn by ear as much as by eye, and for

Phi Delta Kappan, 49:8 (April, 1968), 420–23.

293

tutorial ventures in individualized instruction it is essential that the computer system be able to talk to the student.

A simple example may make this idea more concrete. Practically no one learns mathematics simply by reading a book, except at a relatively advanced level. Hearing lectures and listening to someone else's talk seem to be almost psychologically essential to learning complex subjects, at least as far as ordinary learners are concerned. In addition to the typewriter and the earphones for audio messages, the next desirable feature is that graphical and pictorial displays be available under computer control. Such displays can be provided in a variety of formats. The simplest mode is to have color slides that may be selected by computer control. More flexible, and therefore more desirable, devices are cathode-ray tubes that look very much like television sets. The beauty of cathode-ray tubes is that a graphical display may be shown to the student and then his own response, entered on a keyboard, can be made an integral part of the display itself.

This is not the place to review these matters in detail; but I mean to convey a visual image of a student sitting at a variety of terminal gear —as it is called in the computer world. These terminals are used to provide the student with individualized instruction. He receives information from audio messages, from typewritten messages, and also from visual displays ranging from graphics to complex photographs. In turn, he may respond to the system and give his own answers by using the keyboard on the typewriter. Other devices for student response are also available, but I shall not go into them now.

So, with such devices available, individualized instruction in a wide variety of subject matters may be offered students of all ages. The technology is already available, although it will continue to be improved. There are two main factors standing in our way. One is that currently it is expensive to prepare an individualized curriculum. The second factor, and even more important, is that as yet we have little operational experience in precisely how this should best be done. For some time to come, individualized instruction will have to depend on a basis of practical judgment and pedagogical intuition of the sort now used in constructing textbook materials for ordinary courses. One of the exciting potentialities of computer-assisted instruction is that for the first time we shall be able to get hard data to use as a basis for a more serious scientific investigation and evaluation of any given instructional program.

To give a more concrete sense of the possibilities of individualized instruction, I would like to describe briefly three possible levels of interaction between the student and computer program. Following a current usage, I shall refer to each of the instructional programs as a particular system of instruction. At the simplest level there are *individualized drill-and-practice systems,* which are meant to supplement the regular curriculum taught by the teacher. The introduction of concepts and new ideas is handled in conventional fashion by the teacher. The role of the computer is to provide regular review and practice on basic concepts and skills. In the case of elementary mathematics, for example, each student would receive daily a certain number of exercises, which would be automatically presented, evaluated, and scored by the computer program without any effort by the classroom teacher. Moreover, these exercises can be presented on an individualized basis, with the brighter students receiving exercises that are harder than the average, and the slower students receiving easier problems.

One important aspect of this kind of individualization should be emphasized. In using a computer in this fashion, it is not necessary to decide at the beginning of the school year in which track a student should be placed; for example, a student need not be classified as a slow student for the entire year. Individualized drill-and-practice work is suitable to all the elementary subjects which occupy a good part of the curriculum. Elementary mathematics, elementary science, and the beginning work in foreign language are typical parts of the curriculum which benefit from standardized and regularly presented drill-and-practice exercises. A large computer with 200 terminals can handle as many as 6,000 students on a daily basis in this instructional mode. In all likelihood, it will soon be feasible to increase these numbers to a thousand terminals and 30,000 students. . . .

At the second and deeper level of interaction between student and computer program there are *tutorial systems,* which take over the main responsibility both for presenting a concept and for developing skill in its use. The intention is to approximate the interaction a patient tutor would have with an individual student. An important aspect of the tutorial programs in reading and elementary mathematics with which we have been concerned at Stanford in the past three years is that every effort is made to avoid an initial experience of failure on the part of the slower children. On the other hand, the program has enough flexibility to avoid boring the brighter children with endlessly repetitive exercises. As soon as the student manifests a clear understanding of a concept on the basis of his handling of a number of exercises, he is moved on to a new concept and new exercises. . . .

At the third and deepest level of interaction there are *dialogue systems* aimed at permitting the student to conduct a genuine dialogue with the computer. The dialogue systems at the present time exist primarily at the conceptual rather than the operational level, and I do want to emphasize that in the case of dialogue systems a number of difficult technical problems must first be solved. One problem is that of recognizing spoken speech. Especially in the case of young children, we would like the child to be able simply to ask the computer program a question. To permit this interaction, we must be able to recognize the spoken speech of the child and also to recognize the meaning of the question he is asking. The problem of recognizing meaning is at least as difficult as that of recognizing the spoken speech. It will be some time before we will be able to do either one of these things with any efficiency and economy.

I would predict that within the next decade many children will use individualized drill-and-practice systems in elementary school; and by the time they reach high school, tutorial systems will be available on a broad basis. Their children may use dialogue systems throughout their school experience.

If these predictions are even approximately correct, they have far-reaching implications for education and society. As has been pointed out repeatedly by many people in many different ways, the role of education in our society is not simply the transmission of knowledge but also the transmission of culture, including the entire range of individual, political, and social values. Some recent studies—for example, the Coleman report—have attempted to show that the schools are not as effective in transmitting this culture as we might hope; but still there is little doubt that the schools play a major role, and the directions they take have serious implications for the character of our society in the future. Now I hope it is evident from the very brief descriptions I have given that the widespread use of computer technology in education has an enormous potential for improving the quality of education, because the possibility of individualizing instruction at ever deeper levels of interaction can be realized in an economically feasible fashion. I take it that this potentiality is evident enough, and I would like to examine some of the problems it raises, problems now beginning to be widely discussed.

Three rather closely related issues are particularly prominent in this discussion. The first centers around the claim that the deep use of technology, especially computer technology, will impose a rigid regime of impersonalized teaching. In considering such a claim, it is important to say at once that indeed this is a possibility. Computer technology could be used this way, and in some instances it probably will. This is no different from saying that there are many kinds of teaching, some good and some bad. The important point to insist upon, however, is that it is certainly not a *necessary* aspect of the use of the technology. In fact, contrary to the expectations sometimes expressed in the popular press, I would claim that one of the computer's most important potentials is in making learning and teaching more personalized, rather than less so. Students will be subject to less regimentation and lockstepping, because computer systems will be able to offer highly individualized instruction. The routine that occupies a good part of the teacher's day can be taken over by the computer.

It is worth noting in this connection that the amount of paper work required of teachers is very much on the increase. The computer seems to offer the only possibility of decreasing the time spent in administrative routine by ordinary teachers. Let us examine briefly one or two aspects of instruction ranging from the elementary school to the college. At the elementary level, no one anticipates that students will spend most of their time at computer consoles. Only 20 to 30 percent of the student's time would be spent in this fashion. Teachers would be able to work with classes reduced in size. Also, they could work more intensely with individual students, because some of the students will be at the console and, more importantly, because routine aspects of teaching will be handled by the computer system.

At the college level, the situation is somewhat different. At most colleges and universities, students do not now receive a great deal of individual attention from instructors. I think we can all recognize that the degree of personal attention is certainly not less in a computer program designed to accommodate itself to the individual student's progress than in the lecture course that has more than 200 students in daily attendance. (In our tutorial Russian program at Stanford, under the direction of Joseph Van Campen, all regular classroom instruction has been eliminated. Students receive 50 minutes daily of individualized instruction at a computer terminal consisting of a teletype with Cyrillic keyboard and earphones; the audio tapes are controlled by the computer.)

A second common claim is that the widespread use of computer technology will lead to excessive standardization of education. Again it is important to admit at once that this is indeed a possibility. The sterility of standardization and what it implies for teaching used to be illustrated by a story about the French educational system. It was claimed that the French minister of education could look at his watch at any time of the school day and say at once what subject was being taught at each grade level throughout the country. The claim was not true, but such a situation could be brought about in the organization of computer-based instruction. It would technically be possible for a state department of education, for example, to require every fifth-grader at 11:03 in the morning to be subtracting one-fifth from three-tenths, or for every senior in high school to be reciting the virtues of a democratic society. The danger of the technology is that edicts can be enforced as well as issued, and many persons are rightly concerned at the specter of the rigid standardization that could be imposed.

On the other hand, there is another meaning of standardization that holds great potential. This is the imposition of educational standards on schools and colleges throughout the land. Let me give one example of what I mean. A couple of years ago I consulted with one of the large city school systems in this country in connection with its mathematics program. The curriculum outline of the mathematics program running from kindergarten to high school was excellent. The curriculum as specified in the outline was about as good as any in the country. The real source of difficulty was the magnitude of the discrepancy between the actual performance of the students and the specified curriculum. At almost every grade level, students were performing far below the standard set in the curriculum guide. I do not mean to suggest that computer technology will, in one fell stroke, provide a solution to the difficult and complicated problems of raising the educational standards that now obtain among the poor and culturally deprived. I do say that the technology will provide us with unparalleled insight into the actual performance of students.

Yet I do not mean to suggest that this problem of standardization is not serious. It is, and it will take much wisdom to avoid its grosser aspects. But the point I would like to emphasize is that the wide use of computers permits the introduction of an almost unlimited diversity of curriculum and teaching. The very opposite of standardization *can* be achieved. I think we would all agree that the ever-increasing use of books from the sixteenth century to the present has deepened the varieties of educational and intellectual experience generally available. There is every reason to believe that the appropriate development of instructional programs for computer systems will increase rather than decrease this variety of intellectual experience. The potential is there.

The real problem is that as yet we do not understand very well how to take advantage of this potential. If we examine the teaching of any subject in the curriculum, ranging from elementary mathematics to ancient history, what is striking is the great similarity between teachers and between textbooks dealing with the same subject, not the vast differences between them. It can even be argued that it is a subtle philosophical question of social policy to determine the extent to which we want to emphasize diversity in our teaching of standard subjects. Do we want a "cool" presentation of American history for some students and a fervent one for others? Do we want to emphasize geometric and perceptual aspects of mathematics more for some students, and symbolic and algebraic aspects more for others? Do we want to make learning of language more oriented toward the ear for some students and more toward the eye for those who have a poor sense of auditory discrimination? These are issues that have as yet scarcely been explored in educational philosophy or in discussions of educational policy. With the advent of the new technology they will become practical questions of considerable moment.

The third and final issue I wish to discuss is the place of individuality and human freedom in the modern technology. The crudest form of opposition to widespread use of technology in education and in other parts of our society is to claim that we face the real danger of men becoming slaves of machines. I feel strongly that the threat to human individuality and freedom in our society does not come from technology at all, but from another source that was well described by John Stuart Mill more than a hundred years ago. In discussing precisely this matter in his famous essay *On Liberty*, he said,

> . . . the greatest difficulty to be encountered does not lie in the appreciation of means towards an acknowledged end, but in the indifference of persons in general to the end itself. If it were felt that the free development of individuality is one of the leading essentials of well-being; that it is not only a co-ordinate element with all that is designated by the terms civilization, instruction, education, culture, but is itself a necessary part and condition of all those things; there would be no danger that liberty should be undervalued, and the adjustment of the boundaries between it and social control would present no extraordinary difficulty.

Just as books freed serious students from the tyranny of overly simple methods of oral recitation, so computers can free students from the drudgery of doing exactly similar tasks unadjusted and untailored to their individual needs. As in the case of other parts of our society, our new and wondrous technology is there for beneficial use. It is our problem to learn how to use it well. When a child of six begins to learn in school under the direction of a teacher, he hardly has a concept of a free intelligence able to reach objective knowledge of the world. He depends heavily upon every word and gesture of the teacher to guide his own reactions and responses. This intellectual weaning of children is a complicated process that we do not yet manage or understand very well. There are too many adults among us who are not able to express their own feelings or to reach their own judgments. I would claim that the wise use of technology and science, particularly in education, presents a major opportunity and challenge. I do not want to claim that we know very much yet about how to realize the full potential of human beings; but I do not doubt that we can use our modern instruments to reduce the personal tyranny of one individual over another, wherever that tyranny depends upon ignorance.

CHAPTER TEN

Performance Assessment

PERFORMANCE ASSESSMENT is one of the most hotly debated areas in education today. Grades are a cause of anxiety among students, parents, and teachers. The results of examinations can dictate one's future. In fact, an entire counterculture has arisen that views any evaluation of one individual by another as inherently evil. Many minority-group leaders are saying that intelligence tests and other measures used in the schools are thinly veiled instruments of discrimination that have been used to humiliate minority children and exclude them from the mainstream of American education. Groups of college students are demanding the abolition of grades and entrance examinations.

Others see performance assessment as a way of identifying and enhancing the unique talents of each individual. They envision a future in which adequate tests and other instruments will enable each student to proceed through school at his own pace, master a unit of study at his own pace, demonstrate his mastery through performance on a criterion measure, then proceed to the next unit. In such a future society, criterion measures will enable each person to determine his unique strengths and weaknesses and on this basis to plan a future in which he is most likely to find success and fulfillment.

Even the critics of testing must admit that there have been many successes in its history. For example, during World War II, the U.S. Army Air Corps developed and employed tests to screen candidates for pilot training and subsequently reduced the failure rate in flight school from 75 to 25 per cent. Perhaps it has been the successful use of a few tests that has led us to place too much faith in all tests.

Anastasi discusses how cultural differences influence test results, arguing that such variables should be taken into consideration when interpreting scores. She points out that test data provide descriptions of differences among people but do not identify the cause of the phenomena they are measuring. Ascribing too much meaning to differences in test scores is inappropriate. Dyer, too, affirms that people often assume that test scores provide more information than the authors of the tests ever claimed to provide. This has led to considerable mischief in the application of tests in the schools. He weighs the various arguments against the use of tests and concludes that the problems lie in the misuse and misinterpretation of tests rather than in the tests themselves.

Obviously, educational tests measure no more than the student's command of some area of human knowledge. Yet, frequently, the score on a test is the basis for grades, and this is controversial. Melby is one of many educators who think that the present marking system should go the way of the hickory stick and dunce cages. He claims that it produces many destructive effects and no real advantages. He finds no valid evidence that school grades serve to motivate students. As for the argument that marks are needed to communicate information to parents, other schools, and employers, he suggests other ways to achieve this end.

General background reading about measurement in school will offer a useful perspective on the various issues discussed in this chapter. For example, Thorndike and Hagen's *Measurement and Evaluation in Psychology and Education* (1969) provides a comprehensive picture of the role of measurement in education. Bauernfeind's *Building a School Testing Program* (1963) supplies an informative overview of the role of measurement in the school system. One can gain some understanding of criterion-referenced testing by reading McClelland (1973) or Ebel and Block (1971).

RECOMMENDED READING

J. H. Block. 1971. "Criterion-referenced Measurements: Potential," *School Review* 79(2), 289–97. A description of the way that tests can be used to help students formulate objectives and achieve individually determined goals.

O. K. Buros. 1965. *The Sixth Mental Measurement Yearbook* (Highland Park, N.J.: Grypon Press). The major reference book for educational and psychological tests, containing a description and critical evaluations of most of the major instruments in existence today.

R. L. Ebel. 1971. "Criterion-referenced Measurements: Limitations," *School Review*, 79(2), 282–88. Strong arguments that criterion-referenced tests do not tell us enough about educational achievement and are difficult to construct.

F. F. Elzey. 1967. A *First Reader: Statistics* (Belmont, Calif.: Wadsworth Press). A short, succinct treatment of basic statistics for the beginner.

M. G. Holmer and R. F. Docter. 1974. "Criticisms of Standardized Testing," *Today's Education* 63(1), 50–54. A fresh look at the uses and values of standardized tests, aimed at the classroom teacher.

M. L. Maehr and W. M. Stallings. 1972. "Freedom from External Evaluation," *Child Development* 43, 177–85. Discussion of the need to reduce the competitive pressures caused by the standardized measurement and evaluation of achievement.

F. T. Wilhelms. 1967. "Evaluation as Feedback," *Evaluation as Feedback and Guide* (Washington, D.C.: Association for Supervision and Curriculum Development, National Education Association). A well-balanced discussion of the values of tests and measurements to improve the retention of learning and to motivate students.

28.

ROBERT L. EBEL

WHAT DO EDUCATIONAL TESTS TEST?

The use of tests in education continues to be a focus of attention and a subject of controversy. Among the questions currently being discussed are these. Will the national assessment of educational progress now underway contribute to the improvement of education, or is it likely to do more harm than good? Should states and local school districts use tests to hold educators accountable for the results they get from the money they spend? Do the tests used in education have a middle-class bias that makes them discriminate unfairly against minority group students? Do the objective tests that are now so widely used test anything more than the student's memory for factual details? Can the essence of a good education be adequately measured by a set of paper and pencil tests, and reported in a corresponding set of numerical scores?

These are complex questions to which no simple answers are likely to be satisfactory. But our discussions of them should be more enlightened and productive if we can first get a valid answer to the more basic question, "What do educational tests test?"

Reprinted from *Educational Psychologist*, 10:2, 1973, 76–79. © Division of Educational Psychology, American Psychological Association.

A brief, direct answer to this question, applicable to most of the tests used in education, is this: *They test the student's command of some segment of human knowledge.* And because helping students attain command of knowledge is what most teachers and most schools have always spent most of their time and energy trying to do, a second, closely related answer to the question is: *They test how effectively the schools are doing their primary job.*

To understand the brief answers just given, one must know what the terms "knowledge," and "command" are intended to mean in this context. Knowledge is whatever a person has experienced, either directly or vicariously, and has remembered. Much of human knowledge is verbal knowledge: It can be expressed, communicated, anl stored in sentences. The peculiar excellence of man among other living things is his ability to produce and to use verbal knowledge. The sentences he utters can define, analyze, interpret, and record his thoughts about his experiences. Thus words are powerful aids to thinking and to learning. But they can become enemies of clear thinking and sound learning if they are accepted uncritically or repeated thoughtlessly. Words are very useful symbols, but they are only symbols. Their meaning and value rests in the last analysis on the identifiability in non-verbal experience of precisely what they symbolize.

Command of knowledge is simply the ability to use it to make decisions, to solve problems, to answer questions, or to nourish the processes of reflective thought. To command knowledge one must understand it, but understanding is nothing more than a knowledge of relationships. To achieve command of some new knowledge one must do more than ingest it. One must assimilate it into his own structure of ideas and beliefs. It must be firmly anchored to, and consistent with, his other ideas and beliefs. In the words of Scheffler, ". . . it does not follow that the student will know these new facts simply because he has been informed; . . . knowing requires that the student earn the right to his assurance of the truth of the information in question. New *information*, in short, can be intelligibly conveyed by statements, new *knowledge* cannot (Scheffler, 1965, p. 137)."

This emphasis on command of knowledge may make the task of the schools appear to be much simpler and more straightforward than it turns out to be in actual practice. But such a definition of the basic mission of the school leaves two very complex and perplexing practical problems to be solved.

1. What knowledge is likely to be useful enough to a particular child

in his future years to justify special efforts to help him get command of it?

2. How should these special efforts be managed to make them most effective in yielding command of knowledge?

Despite the perennial distractions created by revolutionary educational innovators, most good teachers spend most of their time trying to find better answers to these two questions. The problems are complex enough to keep all educators profitably employed as long as they have the will to keep working at them.

One reason some teachers have difficulty in accepting the view that the main job of the schools is cultivation of command of useful verbal knowledge, is that they do not clearly differentiate the purposes of schooling from the purposes of living. For this confusion John Dewey is at least partly to blame, with his emphasis on the half truth that education is life, and not preparation for life. The other half of the truth is that learning—learning to read, to calculate, to write, to know about the nature of the world and of man—that these are preparation for life. Of course children live while they learn. Of course adults continue to learn as they live. But this does not make learning and living identical.

Learning is only a part of living. There are also doing, and adjusting, and suffering, and loving, and enjoying. In learning, the *means* of doing and suffering and enjoying serve the *end* of knowing. In living, the *means* of learning serve the *ends* of doing and enjoying. Surely it is true that man is not all intellect. How he feels is almost always more important to him than what he knows. How he behaves is almost always more important to those about him than what he knows. But in human society learning to know is recognized as such an important part of learning to live that extensive (and expensive) efforts are made through special institutions, the schools, to promote it among all people. If those who manage the schools pay more attention to how the pupil lives than to what he learns, they give him a possibly richer present at the cost of a certainly poorer future.

Educators who conceive their ultimate purpose to be that of helping students toward the living of good lives, have a choice of two and only two ways of achieving that purpose. One is to assume control of the students' lives and to use the processes of conditioning (rewards and punishments) to build automatic, thoughtless responses into their behavior patterns. The other is to give these students the command of knowledge which will make their own free choices likely to be wise and good. The only alternative to command of knowledge as a basis for the choices free men must make are the conditioned responses of the automaton. Is there any doubt of which alternative the schools ought to choose today? Is it not the one they have chosen mainly in the past?

Let us now consider for a moment what tests do not test. They do not test, at least not directly, a person's native intelligence, i.e., the quality of his biological equipment for learning. No doubt differences exist among persons in the quality of this equipment. But the evidence purporting to show that these biological differences are important determiners of how successfully a particular person learns is far from convincing. This is not to say that all school children, or adults, are on an equal footing when trying to learn something. For all learning must build on prior learning. Deficiencies in the foundations for new knowledge, which may begin to be felt in the first years of life, tend to accumulate progressively as the years pass. The child who has suffered early educational impairment may be no better able to learn than one whose biological equipment might be deficient.

Again, the tests do not test *future* achievement. They test present ability. While present ability affects future achievement, so do a number of other factors. It is unreasonable to expect a test to predict future achievement perfectly. It is unwise to judge the quality of a test by its success in predicting future achievement *all by itself*.

Despite the extensive use made of tests in education there are many who do not like them, and who oppose their use. The most consistent and vocal opposition comes from three types of persons: the anti-intellectuals, the ultra-liberals, and the hyper-critics.

The anti-intellectuals are those who contend that what a man knows matters less than how he relates to others. They decry competition, and efforts to excel. They applaud the equality of mediocrity. They dismiss the evidences of achievement provided by tests as irrelevant to the essential purposes of the schools. But since most schools have no systematic programs of demonstrated effectiveness for cultivating non-cognitive interpersonal outcomes, the main result achieved by the anti-intellectuals is simply less concern for cognitive achievement and hence less over-all achievement. Children are short-changed on the main thing the schools were established to give them, and the only thing the schools can give them effectively, which is command of knowledge.

Anti-intellectuals find much sympathetic support among the rank and file of teachers whose excellent qualities more often include love and concern for children than outstanding intellectual ability. Anti-intellectuals are in control of teacher training in many of our colleges of education. A distressingly large proportion of young teachers believe that the schools should be more concerned with how a pupil feels than with what he knows. They are not likely to favor the use of tests in their schools. But the harm they do by opposing tests is far less than the harm they do by neglecting, or even repressing, the cultivation of intellectual excellence.

The ultra-liberals regard any differentiation among persons with respect to ability or achievement, however well justified it may be, as discriminatory, providing excuses for a denial of equal opportunity. They claim, with some justification, that most tests are biased toward middle-class culture and values. Quite irrationally they blame the tests for showing up educational deficiencies, in addition to much more rational blame of the schools and the society for having produced those deficiencies. They do not fully appreciate the value that impartial, objective measures of ability and achievement have for any who might be discriminated against on the basis of appearances alone.

The hyper-critics, for whom Hoffmann (1964) is a frequent spokesman, find in the undeniable ambiguity of some test items a general unfairness of objective tests to all of the brightest students. Their argument rests on the strange assumption that the brighter a student is the more likely he is to be puzzled by an ambiguity that was not apparent to the scholars who made the test. These hyper-critics disdain the item and test statistics that challenge their beliefs. When they cannot find in any published test an item bad enough to clinch the point they are making, they invent one. Their charges are endorsed by some who dislike tests for other reasons. The charges have had a wholesome effect in making professional test constructors more careful about the quality of the items they allow to be published. But the charges have not had, and are not likely to have, any significant influence on the extent to which educational tests are used.

One other group, while not an opponent of educational testing, has nevertheless interfered with the effective use of tests in schools. It is composed of educational mystics who will not accept anything so simple and obvious as command of knowledge as the central purpose of schooling. Instead, these mystics prefer intangible, esoteric, hard-to-measure abilities like reasoning, critical thinking, creativity, social sensitivity, aesthetic appreciation, or even learning how to learn. That these abilities are difficult even to define clearly, that they seem to be closely related to subject matter, and hence widely different in different fields of study, and that no one knows much about how to teach them; these considerations do not discourage the mystics at all. Having satisfied themselves that cultivating a few of these hypothetical qualities is the true end of education, they leave to others the task of determining what they are, how they can be attained, and how that attainment can be measured. Having rejected the obvious answer to the question, "What is the job of the schools?"

they propose alternative answers which sound impressive but which have little concrete meaning.

Even when conceived in the simplest, most obvious terms, the task of the schools is hard enough. It ought not to be complicated by vague assumptions about intangible objectives. Further, cognitive competence is important enough to the successful pursuit of happiness in living so that the schools should not be lured away from it by those whose only concern is how the child feels today. Finally, imperfect though they may be, tests are essential educational tools. Most teachers are likely to continue to use them to develop in their students the command of useful verbal knowledge.

REFERENCES

B. Hoffmann. *The Tyranny of Testing* (New York: Crowell-Collier & Macmillan, 1964).

I. Scheffler. "Philosophical Models of Teaching," *Harvard Educational Review*, 35 (1965), 131–43.

29.

ANNE ANASTASI

PSYCHOLOGICAL TESTS: USES AND ABUSES

A common misuse of psychological tests arises from the confusion of measurement with etiology. No test can eliminate causality. Nor can a test score, however derived, reveal the origin of the behavior it reflects. If certain environmental factors influence behavior, they will also influence those samples of behavior covered by tests. When we use tests to compare different groups, the only question the tests can answer directly is: "How do these groups differ under existing cultural conditions?" This limitation of tests may appear so obvious as to be trite. But it needs to be made explicit, because it is still frequently forgotten in discussing the implications of test results.

From *Teachers College Record*, 62 (1961), 389–93.

DESCRIPTION

If, then, we are to apply tests across cultural groups, what can we do to obtain a maximum of information with a minimum of misinformation? First, for purely descriptive purposes, groups should be compared in as wide a *variety* of tests as possible. This recommendation follows from the empirically established fact that groups do not occupy the same relative positions when compared in different intellectual traits. No one position or rank order, established in terms of a single test score, is any "truer" or more "basic" than any other. Just as we have been moving from the global IQ to a profile of multiple aptitude scores in the description of individuals, so we need to follow a profile approach in the description of groups.

The factorial analysis of intelligence has revealed a number of differentiable aptitudes in each of which the individual may occupy a different position. True, different factor analysts have sliced intelligence in diverse ways. The handful of primary mental abilities identified by Thurstone has been proliferating over the intervening thirty years. The hierarchical pattern favored by Vernon and other British psychologists is an alternative way of organizing the multiplicity of narrower and narrower factors that have been emerging. The large number of factors systematically mapped out by Guilford (1956, 1959) is of special interest because of their extensive coverage of creativity and reasoning.

It is apparent at this stage that we cannot prescribe a well formulated list of aptitudes to be covered for a comprehensive description of any group. Moreover, there is some evidence to suggest that the very categories in terms of which we slice intelligence may vary from one culture to another. The implication is clear, however, that no one test score, nor any small number of scores, can provide an adequate picture of the intellectual status of a group. The best we can do is to utilize as wide a variety of tests as is available to us and retain the separateness of their scores in any description of the group.

In this connection, we may also consider so-called culture-free tests. The objections that have been raised against the term "culture-free" are quite familiar, and while substitute terms have been proposed, such as "culture-fair" or "culture-common," "culture-free" seems to be easier to say and will probably survive. If we are to use this term, we must remember that the tests are not free from all cultural influences. No test can be culture-free in that sense. They are only free from the influence of those cultural factors that differentiate the groups to be compared. To put it differently, they reflect only those cultural influences *common* to the groups concerned.

A test that is culture-free in the comparison of groups A and B, therefore, may be highly culture-bound when used in comparing groups B and C. An entirely different test may be culture-free in the B-C comparison. A good example is provided by the verbal-nonverbal dichotomy into which intelligence tests are frequently classified. It has commonly been assumed that nonverbal tests are more nearly culture-free than verbal tests. Such an assumption is obviously correct in the case of persons who speak different languages. In the early testing of immigrants to this country, for example, the language barrier was paramount. It was in this connection that some of the first performance and nonlanguage tests were developed. But there are other cultural barriers besides language. There are groups speaking the same language whose cultures differ in other important respects. In the comparison of such groups, verbal tests may be less culturally loaded than tests of a predominantly spatial, numerical, or perceptual nature.

CULTURAL EFFECTS

Cultural factors may influence relative performance on verbal and nonverbal tasks in a variety of ways. Interests, value systems, work habits, problem-solving attitudes, or emotional insecurity arising from cultural conditions may in turn stimulate or retard the development of certain aptitudes. When the California Test of Mental Maturity was administered to university students in Ceylon, the Ceylonese greatly surpassed the American norms on the language part while falling far below the norms on the nonlanguage part (Straus, 1951, 1954). This difference is the reverse of what might have been expected in the case of a bilingual population such as the Ceylonese. The investigator attributed the results to the value systems of the upper-class Ceylonese culture, which included rejection of manual tasks and attachment of high prestige to verbal scholarship. The nature of the Ceylonese educational system, with its emphasis upon feats of memory and upon learning by precept and rote, was also cited as a possible contributing influence.

As a result of a somewhat different combination of cultural pressures, Jewish children tested in America usually perform much better on verbal tests than on tests involving concrete objects and spatial relations. In a study of kindergarten children in Minneapolis public schools, the Stanford-Binet was administered to groups of Jewish and Scandinavian children equated in age, sex ratio, and socioeconomic status (Brown). The Jewish children were found to be superior on tests based upon general information and verbal comprehension, while the Scandinavian children excelled on tests requiring spatial orientation and sensorimotor coordi-

school attitudes, non-academic activities, student's academic plans, peer academic plans, and parental academic plans.

One section of the PVI asks students to report their school marks in academic subjects for both the current and preceding years. These self-reported marks were used to classify students as to their levels of performance in elementary school and junior high school. There was a large attrition in the data in that only students with complete state testing records to whom the PVI was administered were included. There was no reason to expect, however, that the way in which the sample was selected biased the results.

RESULTS

Because of the oft-reported sex difference in elementary school performance, correlation matrices were calculated separately for boys and girls, utilizing the seven PVI variables, the self-reported grades, the California Mental Maturity Test scores, and the various achievement test scores. Factor analyses of the correlation matrices identified an intelligence factor that involved both achievement test scores and the mental maturity test scores, and three factors defined from the PVI scores—academic motivation, academic plans, and youth-culture involvement. The factor patterns for boys presented in Table I and for girls presented in Table II were essentially the same.

The factor analytic findings are consistent with the results of an earlier study (Finger and Schlesser, 1965) that employed a preliminary edition of the PVI and found the two factors of intelligence and academic motivation to have loadings on school marks. While the preliminary and revised edition used in the current study identified the same factors, the academic motivation factor in the revised edition is much more clearly delineated. The academic motivation factor summarized contributions from seven of the eleven PVI areas. The test items involved tended to concern themselves with ambition and work, the value that students placed on school success. The academic plans factor summarized the value the student and the significant people in his life placed on higher education. The youth-culture factor was derived from student reports of the importance they attached to pleasurable activities and thrill-seeking.

Students were classified according to marks they had received in elementary school and then cross-classified in terms of the grades they had received in junior high school. The procedure identified students who had earned junior high school marks that were "higher" than, the "same" as, "lower" than, and "much lower" than their elementary school grades. A difficulty with the classification procedure was that students who had

TABLE I

FACTOR ANALYSIS OF ACADEMIC CREDENTIALS (VARIMAX ROTATION)
BOYS—GRADE 7, N=233

	Factors			
	Intelligence	Academic Motivation	Academic Plans	Youth Culture Involvement
Personal Values Inventory Scores				
Home	—	.70	—	—
Persistence	—	.78	—	—
Self-control–deliberateness	—	.44	—	−.72
Self-views	—	.77	—	—
School defenses	.31	.64	—	—
Planning	—	.57	.32	—
School attitudes	—	.63	—	−.46
Non-academic activites	—	.37	.27	.47
Student's academic plans	.32	—	.66	—
Peer academic plans	—	—	.44	—
Parental academic plans	—	—	.75	—
California Mental Maturity				
Language	.72	—	—	—
Non-language	.77	—	—	—
California Achievement				
Reading vocabulary	.80	—	—	—
Reading comprehension	.86	—	—	—
Spelling	.71	—	—	—
Arithmetic reasoning	.56	—	—	—
Arithmetic fundamentals	.67	—	—	—
Scholastic Work Study Skills	.84	—	—	—
Marks—Junior High School	.57	.48	—	—
Elementary school	.64	.37	—	—

earned very high elementary school marks could not earn higher ones in junior high school nor could the students who had earned very low marks in elementary school go on to earn still lower ones. The students who had earned A in elementary school and continued to earn A in junior high school were classified in the gain group even though their marks remained the same. A scatter diagram was plotted at each level of elementary school performance. The percentage of students assigned to a category of junior high school marks was kept approximately equal for the various levels of elementary school marks. These procedures corrected in part for statistical regression.

Analyses of variance were calculated for all of the variables. However, only the results of four of these analyses are presented. One variable has

TABLE II

FACTOR ANALYSIS OF ACADEMIC CREDENTIALS (VARIMAX ROTATION)
GIRLS—GRADE 7, N=256

	Factors			
	Intelligence	Academic Motivation	Academic Plans	Youth Culture Involvement
Personal Values Inventory Scores				
Home	—	.71	—	—
Persistence	—	.83	—	—
Self-control–deliberateness	—	.25	—	−.82
Self-views	—	.74	—	—
School defenses	—	.65	—	−.45
Planning	—	.66	—	—
School attitudes	—	.55	—	−.63
Non-academic activities	—	—	.54	—
Student's academic plans	.40	—	.66	—
Peer academic plans	—	—	—	—
Parental academic plans	—	—	.78	—
California Mental Maturity				
Language	.72	—	—	—
Non-language	.78	—	—	—
California Achievement				
Reading vocabulary	.78	—	—	—
Reading comprehension	.85	—	—	—
Spelling	.67	—	—	—
Arithmetic reasoning	.51	—	—	—
Arithmetic fundamentals	.63	—	—	—
Scholastic-Work Study Skills	.82	—	—	—
Marks—Junior High School	.62	.52	—	—
Elementary school	.69	.33	—	—

been selected to represent each of the four factors shown in Tables I and II.

INTELLIGENCE AND THE CHANGE IN PERFORMANCE

When the California Mental Maturity–Language scores are tabulated for the various groups, there are significant differences among the categories. The differences shown in Table III were primarily related to elementary school marks rather than to change in performance at the junior high school level. Those students who earned higher marks in junior high school than elementary school had a mean mental maturity language score of 112, whereas those who earned much lower marks had a mean

TABLE III

MENTAL MATURITY LANGUAGE SCORES OF SEVENTH-GRADE STUDENTS
CROSS-CLASSIFIED BY JUNIOR HIGH SCHOOL AND
ELEMENTARY SCHOOL MARKS

Elementary Marks	Mental Maturity Language Scores				
	Junior High School Marks Compared with Elementary School Marks				
	Higher	Same	Lower	Much Lower	Total
A	126	121	119	116	120
	N = 8	N = 11	N = 15	N = 8	
A-B+	115	117	120	117	117
	N = 15	N = 27	N = 28	N = 16	
B	111	115	111	110	112
	N = 18	N = 37	N = 59	N = 22	
B-C+	111	108	104	106	107
	N = 18	N = 34	N = 42	N = 18	
C	102	101	98	101	100
	N = 16	N = 31	N = 36	N = 12	
Under C	—	—	—	—	95
TOTAL	111	111	109	110	
	$F^{20}_{468} = 6.47$		$P < .01$	$\sigma = 14.3$	

NOTE: Mean intelligence all Rhode Island sixth-grade pupils = 108.

score of 110. In contrast those students who had earned A in elementary school were 21 IQ points higher than those who had earned C. The overall trend of Table III seems to indicate that while intelligence was largely unrelated to the change in performance at the junior high school level, it was highly related to the marks earned in elementary school. Only among the students who earned the highest marks in elementary school was there any indication that intelligence was involved in this shift in marks. Those who had earned A and were classified as higher had an average intelligence score of 126 whereas those classified as much lower had an average score of 116.

ACADEMIC MOTIVATION AND THE CHANGE IN PERFORMANCE

In contrast to the results found with intelligence, academic motivation appeared to be highly related to the charge in performance at the junior high school level. The findings presented in Table IV indicate that those students who were classified as earning higher grades had a persistence score of 17.4, while those classified as earning much lower grades had an average persistence score of 12. These scores are more than seven standard errors apart. There are also differences in the persistence scores among those who received the highest marks in elementary school and those who received the lowest. While the possible cause-and-effect relationships involved will be considered later, it is of interest to note that academic motivation bears a significant relationship to school performance by the sixth grade. Furthermore, the persistence scores are very uniform in their

TABLE IV

PERSISTENCE SCORES OF SEVENTH-GRADE STUDENTS CROSS-CLASSIFIED BY JUNIOR HIGH SCHOOL AND ELEMENTARY SCHOOL MARKS

Elementary School Marks	Persistence Scores				
	Junior High School Marks Compared with Elementary School Marks				
	Higher	Same	Lower	Much Lower	Total
A	16.9	18.6	15.0	16.4	16.6
	N = 8	N = 11	N = 15	N = 8	
A-B+	17.7	15.7	15.3	11.1	15.1
	N = 15	N = 27	N = 28	N = 16	
B	19.3	15.2	15.1	11.9	15.2
	N = 18	N = 37	N = 59	N = 22	
B-C+	15.9	14.4	12.8	10.6	13.4
	N = 18	N = 34	N = 42	N = 18	
C	17.2	12.8	12.1	12.4	13.2
	N = 16	N = 31	N = 36	N = 12	
Under C	—	—	—	—	10.7
TOTAL	17.4	14.9	14.0	12.0	
	$F_{468}^{20} = 5.86$		P < .01	$\sigma = 4.5$	

downward trend with the change in performance at the junior high school level. The discrepancies in this trend, particularly apparent in those who had earned elementary school marks of A, are probably due to interactions with intelligence. (The actual influence of the persistence score can only be seen when the groups compared are equal in intelligence, for both intelligence and persistence are highly correlated with grades.)

ACADEMIC PLANS AND THE CHANGE IN PERFORMANCE

The academic plans that students have for their own future education were selected to represent the academic plan factor. The findings presented in Table V indicate that students who show a large drop in performance at the junior high school level had lower academic plans than those who went on to earn the same or higher grades. Whereas those students who earned higher grades in junior high school had a mean academic plan score of 25.3, students who experienced much lower junior high school grades had a mean score of 21.3. It is rather interesting to find academic plans to be strongly related to elementary school marks. While possible cause-and-effect relationships continue to invite speculation, it is apparent

TABLE V

ACADEMIC PLAN SCORES OF SEVENTH-GRADE STUDENTS
CROSS-CLASSIFIED BY JUNIOR HIGH SCHOOL
AND ELEMENTARY SCHOOL MARKS

Elementary School Marks	Student's Academic Plan Scores				
	Junior High School Marks Compared with Elementary School Marks				
	Higher	Same	Lower	Much Lower	Total
A	26.9	30.2	27.1	27.1	27.9
	N = 8	N = 11	N = 15	N = 8	
A-B+	31.1	28.6	26.4	24.5	27.5
	N = 15	N = 27	N = 28	N = 16	
B	25.4	25.1	23.8	20.5	23.8
	N = 18	N = 37	N = 59	N = 22	
B-C+	23.5	21.4	18.2	21.2	20.5
	N = 18	N = 34	N = 42	N = 18	
C	20.9	15.4	15.6	14.9	16.3
	N = 16	N = 31	N = 36	N = 12	
Under C	—	—	—	—	17.6
TOTAL	25.3	23.1	21.5	21.3	
	$F_{468}^{20} = 5.16$		P < .01	$\sigma = 9.7$	

that a student's educational plan bears a pronounced relationship to his performance in elementary school. As with persistence, the academic plan scores seem very uniform in their downward trend except for those students who had earned A in elementary school. It is not possible to say whether this reversal is related to the unequal intelligence of the groups or whether the performance of these students is related to different characteristics because of their higher intelligence and superior elementary school performance.

SELF-CONTROL–DELIBERATENESS AND THE CHANGE IN PERFORMANCE

The extent to which a student remains uninvolved in the youth-culture is strongly related to the fate of his grades on entering junior high school. The findings presented in Table VI indicate that while "self-control–deliberateness" bears but a weak relationship, if any, to elementary school

TABLE VI

SELF-CONTROL–DELIBERATENESS SCORES OF SEVENTH-GRADE STUDENTS
CROSS-CLASSIFIED BY JUNIOR HIGH SCHOOL AND
ELEMENTARY SCHOOL MARKS

Elementary School Marks	Self-Control–Deliberateness Scores				
	Junior High School Marks Compared with Elementary School Marks				
	Higher	Same	Lower	Much Lower	Total
A	11.6	12.5	11.4	9.4	11.3
	$N = 8$	$N = 11$	$N = 15$	$N = 8$	
A-B+	12.3	12.4	11.0	9.6	11.4
	$N = 15$	$N = 27$	$N = 28$	$N = 16$	
B	12.4	11.8	11.1	9.1	11.1
	$N = 18$	$N = 37$	$N = 59$	$N = 22$	
B-C+	· 12.4	11.3	11.2	9.6	11.1
	$N = 18$	$N = 34$	$N = 42$	$N = 18$	
C	12.0	10.7	10.0	10.6	10.6
	$N = 16$	$N = 31$	$N = 36$	$N = 12$	
Under C	—	—	—	—	10.4
TOTAL	12.2	11.6	10.9	9.6	
	$F_{468}^{20} = 2.12$		$P < .01$	$\sigma = 3.2$	

marks it is significantly related to the changes in performance at the junior high school level. Those classified as earning higher marks had "self-control–deliberateness" scores approximately five standard errors higher than those classified as earning much lower grades.

DISCUSSION

With previous research indicating that academic motivation is highly related to grades earned in college (Finger and Schlesser, 1963), prognosis for the student experiencing a decline in academic performance may be viewed as a poor one. Whatever characteristics of the student are summarized in the "academic motivation" measure, they are not only vital to his success in school as of junior high school but thereafter as well. The findings presented by Armstrong (1964) argue similarly. Students who experienced a drop in performance at the junior high school level were rarely able to improve at a later point in their educational careers. It would appear to be possible to make rather accurate predictions of eventual academic performance as early as the beginning of the seventh grade.

The question of what causes the student to drop in performance is obviously an important one. The persistence section of the PVI is largely a self-report of the students' attitudes toward studying and the effort expended in schoolwork. While this no doubt accounts for the predictive efficacy of the PVI, questions remain both as to the nature and etiology of these attitudes. One might view the decline in school performance as symptomatic of a syndrome of difficulties, as reflecting the influences of low academic plans and high involvement in youth-culture. The factor analytic data, however, suggest that these are unrelated characteristics. In an earlier report (Finger and Schlesser, 1965), it was indicated that, while the youth-culture involvement factor could not always be identified, it emerged in a sufficient number of factor analyses (Finger, 1966) to indicate that those with low academic motivation were not always youth-culture-oriented. While low academic plans may contribute to the development of low academic motivation, unsuccessful college students present obvious examples of the independence of academic plans and academic motivation. Possibly, however, the junior high school years may represent an incubation period during which low academic plans and high youth-culture involvement nurture the development of those attitudes that constitute low academic motivation.

Understanding the causes of the development of low academic motivation is an intriguing and vital issue. It would seem that at least by the sixth grade, academic motivation and academic plans bear important relationships to school marks. One might argue that the two had their origins in the early elementary school years and at some point, either in the sixth grade or earlier, helped determine the student's grades. In terms of this speculation, deficiencies in motivation and plans would cause poor school marks. It may also be conjectured, however, that poor school marks result in a diminished concern for school. This is to say that students' attitudes may be a result of a history of academic achievement rather than its cause.

While one hypothesis for the development of low academic motivation could emphasize the lack of satisfaction derived from school experience and direct attention to the influence of lack of success in creating attitudes unfavorable toward school, such a hypothesis would be inadequate to account for the drop in performance of those whose previous school performance has been high, nor would such a hypothesis account for the fact that some students who have done average or below-average work continue to strive and in many cases improve their performance.

Our assumption is that performance levels are stabilized by the development of ego defenses that enable the student to justify school performance. This repertoire of rationalizations takes many forms, such as lowering of self-expectations, changing the conceptions of what one can do ("I just can't do math"), and failing to recognize the self as responsible for low performance ("The test wasn't fair"). The rationalization system comes into being in response to school performance that is below a student's own expectations or that is below expectations of the peer group or the home. Thus, rationalizations develop as a reaction to the school performance. As they become increasingly effective in dissipating feelings of inadequacy and in fending off adult criticism, they become internalized, and stabilized, and increasingly difficult to change. Our hypothesis is that it is these ego defenses that make striving unnecessary. The data presented give evidence to support the hypothesis that these defenses have developed in some students prior to entering the seventh grade.

The question of the cause of low or lowered school performance remains. Leaving aside considerations of the function of intelligence on school performance, which has been shown to be highly related to elementary school marks, one can concentrate on the lowered performance at the junior high school level. For some students lowered performance can be attributed to the pre-existent ego defenses. The drop in performance may be wholly accounted for because in the departmentalized junior high school more demands are placed upon the student to work and strive outside of school than was the case in elementary school. However, this explanation does not account for the drop in performance of those students who had previously done well. Their lowered performance may be attributable to a wide variety of influences: the peer group norm, the learning of the rationalization system from peers and parents who developed it in response to their school experiences, the increased independence striving where school success may be interpreted as conforming to adult norms or where the self can only exert itself by standing in opposition to the imposition of parental demands.

It is apparent that many students do well in elementary school despite all of the reasons, intellectual and other, that would lead one to believe that they should not do so. These students seem to bring to school an array of abilities and capacities that satisfy demands made of them in the self-contained classroom. Their success would seem to be a function of their ability to meet demands made by the school situation. In the course of an educational career, however, demands made by the educational process and the school situation change and with these changes comes the possibility of incompatibility—the possibility of a student no longer being able to meet the demands made of him. This is to suggest that the educational process consists of a number of crisis points, points at which the compatibility of the student's abilities and the school's demands are at issue. Success or failure encountered at such crisis points would no doubt influence the student's motivation and plans for the future.

In her classic study, Ruth Benedict (1938) has described adolescence in our society as a period of developmental discontinuity. The adolescent in our culture emerges with a disquieting abruptness from the childhood period of minimal demands to the huge array of requirements thrust upon the young adult. The junior high school years would seem to be an educational period of disquieting discontinuity for many students, a period of painful crisis and important consequences. This perspective would suggest that if students are to survive these periods of crisis, the demands made of them by the school must be consistent with their abilities and capacities, both intellectual and non-intellectual.

REFERENCES

C. M. Armstrong. "Patterns of Achievement in Selected New York State Schools," Albany: New York State Education Department, 1964 (mimeographed).

R. Benedict. "Continuities and Discontinuities in Cultural Conditioning," *Psychiatry*, 1938, 1, 161–67.

J. A. Finger, Jr. "Academic Motivation and Youth-Culture Involvement: Their Relationships to School Performance and Career Success," *School Review*, 1966, 74, 177–95.

J. A. Finger, Jr., and G. E. Schlesser. "Academic Performance of Public and Private School Students," *Journal of Education Psychology*, 1963, 54, 118–22.

———. "Non-intellective Predictors of Academic Success in School and College," *School Review*, 1965, 73, 14–29.

G. E. Schlesser and J. A. Finger, Jr. *Personal Values Inventory*. Hamilton, N.Y.: Colgate University, 1962.

23.

MATINA HORNER

A BRIGHT WOMAN IS CAUGHT IN A DOUBLE BIND. IN ACHIEVEMENT-ORIENTED SITUATIONS SHE WORRIES NOT ONLY ABOUT FAILURE BUT ALSO ABOUT SUCCESS

Consider Phil, a bright young college sophomore. He has always done well in school, he is in the honors program, he has wanted to be a doctor as long as he can remember. We ask him to tell us a story based on one

Reprinted from *Psychology Today* Magazine, November, 1969. Copyright © Ziff-Davis Publishing Company.

clue: *After first-term finals, John finds himself at the top of his medical-school class.* Phil writes:

John is a conscientious young man who worked hard. He is pleased with himself. John has always wanted to go into medicine and is very dedicated. . . . John continues working hard and eventually graduates at the top of his class.

Now consider Monica, another honors student. She too has always done well and she too has visions of a flourishing career. We give her the same clue, but with "Anne" as the successful student—*after first-term finals, Anne finds herself at the top of her medical-school class.* Instead of identifying with Anne's triumph, Monica tells a bizarre tale:

Anne starts proclaiming her surprise and joy. Her fellow classmates are so disgusted with her behavior that they jump on her in a body and beat her. She is maimed for life.

Next we ask Monica and Phil to work on a series of achievement tests by themselves. Monica scores higher than Phil. Finally we get them together, competing against each other on the same kind of tests. Phil performs magnificently, but Monica dissolves into a bundle of nerves.

The glaring contrast between the two stories and the dramatic changes in performance in competitive situations illustrate important differences between men and women in reacting to achievement.

In 1953, David McClelland, John Atkinson and colleagues published the first major work on the "achievement motive." Through the use of the Thematic Apperception Test (TAT), they were able to isolate the psychological characteristic of a *need to achieve.* This seemed to be an internalized standard of excellence, motivating the individual to do well in any achievement-oriented situation involving intelligence and leadership ability. Subsequent investigators studied innumerable facets of achievement motivation: how it is instilled in children, how it is expressed, how it related to social class, even how it is connected to the rise and fall of civilizations. The result of all this research is an impressive and a theoretically consistent body of data about the achievement motive—in men.

Women, however, are conspicuously absent from almost all of the studies. In the few cases where the ladies were included, the results were contradictory or confusing. So women were eventually left out altogether. The predominantly male researchers apparently decided, as Freud had before them, that the only way to understand woman was to turn to the poets. Atkinson's 1958 book, *Motives in Fantasy, Action and Society,* is an 800-page compilation of all of the theories and facts on achievement motivation in men. Women got a footnote, reflecting the state of the science.

To help remedy this lopsided state of affairs, I undertook to explore the basis for sex differences in achievement motivation. But where to begin?

My first clue came from the one consistent finding on the women: they get higher test-anxiety scores than do the men. Eleanor Maccoby has suggested that the girl who is motivated to achieve is defying conventions of what girls "should" do. As a result, the intellectual woman pays a price in anxiety. Margaret Mead concurs, noting that intense intellectual striving can be viewed as "competitively aggressive behavior." And of course Freud thought that the whole essence of femininity lay in repressing aggressiveness (and hence intellectuality).

Thus consciously or unconsciously the girl equates intellectual achievement with loss of femininity. A bright woman is caught in a double bind. In testing and other achievement-oriented situations she worries not only about failure, but also about success. If she fails, she is not living up to her own standards of performance; if she succeeds she is not living up to societal expectations about the female role. Men in our society do not experience this kind of ambivalence, because they are not only permitted but actively encouraged to do well.

For women, then, the desire to achieve is often contaminated by what I call the *motive to avoid success*. I define it as the fear that success in competitive achievement situations will lead to negative consequences, such as unpopularity and loss of femininity. This motive, like the achievement motive itself, is a stable disposition within the person, acquired early in life along with other sex-role standards. When fear of success conflicts with a desire to be successful, the result is an inhibition of achievement motivation.

I began my study with several hypotheses about the motive to avoid success:

1. Of course, it would be far more characteristic of women than of men.

2. It would be more characteristic of women who are capable of success and who are career-oriented than of women not so motivated. Women who are not seeking success should not, after all, be threatened by it.

3. I anticipated that the anxiety over success would be greater in competitive situations (when one's intellectual performance is evaluated against someone else's) than in noncompetitive ones (when one works alone). The aggressive, masculine aspects of achievement striving are cer-

tainly more pronounced in competitive settings, particularly when the opponent is male. Women's anxiety should therefore be greatest when they compete with men.

I administered the standard TAT achievement motivation measures to a sample of 90 girls and 88 boys, all undergraduates at the University of Michigan. In addition, I asked each to tell a story based on the clue described before: *After first-term finals, John (Anne) finds himself (herself) at the top of his (her) medical-school class.* The girls wrote about Anne, the boys about John. Their stories were scored for "motive to avoid success" if they expressed any negative imagery that reflected concern about doing well. Generally, such imagery fell into three categories:

1. The most frequent Anne story reflected strong fears of social rejection as a result of success. The girls in this group showed anxiety about becoming unpopular, unmarriageable and lonely.

Anne is an acne-faced bookworm. She runs to the bulletin board and finds she's at the top. As usual she smarts off. A chorus of groans is the rest of the class's reply. . . . She studies 12 hours a day, and lives at home to save money. "Well it certainly paid off. All the Friday and Saturday nights without dates, fun—I'll be the best woman doctor alive." And yet a twinge of sadness comes thru—she wonders what she really has . . .

Although Anne is happy with her success she fears what will happen to her social life. The male med. students don't seem to think very highly of a female who has beaten them in their field . . . She will be a proud and successful but alas a very *lonely* doctor.

Anne doesn't want to be number one in her class . . . she feels she shouldn't rank so high because of social reasons. She drops down to ninth in the class and then marries the boy who graduates number one.

Anne is pretty darn proud of herself, but everyone hates and envies her.

2. Girls in the second category were less concerned with issues of social approval or disapproval; they were more worried about definitions of womanhood. Their stories expressed guilt and despair over success, and doubts about their femininity or normality.

Unfortunately Anne no longer feels so certain that she really wants to be a doctor. She is worried about herself and wonders if perhaps she isn't normal . . . Anne decides not to continue with her medical work but to take courses that have a deeper personal meaning for her.

Anne feels guilty . . . She will finally have a nervous breakdown and quit medical school and marry a successful young doctor.

Anne is pleased. She had worked extraordinarily hard and her grades showed it. "It is not enough," Anne thinks. "I am not happy." She didn't even want to be a doctor. She is not sure what she wants. Anne says to hell with the whole business and goes into social work—not hardly as glamorous, prestigious or lucrative; but she is happy.

3. The third group of stories did not even try to confront the ambivalence about doing well. Girls in this category simply denied the possibility that any mere woman could be so successful. Some of them completely changed the content of the clue, or distorted it, or refused to believe it, or absolved Anne of responsibility for her success. These stories were remarkable for their psychological igenuity:

Anne is a *code name* for a nonexistent person created by a group of med. students. They take turns writing exams for Anne . . .

Anne is really happy she's on top, though *Tom is higher than she*—though that's as it should be . . . Anne doesn't mind Tom winning.

Anne is talking to her counselor. Counselor says she will make a fine *nurse.*

It was *luck* that Anne came out on top because she didn't want to go to medical school anyway.

Fifty-nine girls—over 65 per cent—told stories that fell into one or another of the above categories. But only eight boys, fewer than 10 per cent, showed evidence of the motive to avoid success. (These differences are significant at better than the .0005 level.) In fact, sometimes I think that most of the young men in the sample were incipient Horatio Algers. They expressed unequivocal delight at John's success (clearly John had worked hard for it), and projected a grand and glorious future for him. There was none of the hostility, bitterness and ambivalence that the girls felt for Anne. In short, the differences between male and female stories based on essentially the same clue were enormous.

Two of the stories are particularly revealing examples of this male-female contrast. The girls insisted that Anne give up her career for marriage:

Anne has a boyfriend, Carl, in the same class and they are quite serious . . . She wants him to be scholastically higher than she is. Anne will deliberately lower her academic standing the next term, while she does all she subtly can to help Carl. His grades come up and Anne soon drops out of medical school. They marry and he goes on in school while she raises their family.

But of course the boys would ask John to do no such thing:

John has worked very hard and his long hours of study have paid off . . . He is thinking about his girl, Cheri, whom he will marry at the end of med. school. He realizes he can give her all the things she desires after he becomes established. He will go on in med. school and be successful in the long run.

Success inhibits social life for the girls; it enhances social life for the boys.

Earlier I suggested that the motive to avoid success is especially aroused in competitive situations. In the second part of this study I wanted to see whether the aggressive overtones of competition against men scared the girls away. Would competition raise their anxiety about success and thus lower their performance?

First I put all of the students together in a large competitive group, and gave them a series of achievement tests (verbal and arithmetic). I then assigned them randomly to one of three other experimental conditions. One-third worked on a similar set of tests, each in competition with a member of the same sex. One-third competed against a member of the opposite sex. The last third worked by themselves, a non-competitive condition.

Ability is an important factor in achievement motivation research. If you want to compare two persons on the strength of their *motivation* to succeed, how do you know that any differences in performance are not due to initial differences in *ability* to succeed? One way of avoiding this problem is to use each subject as his own control; that is, the performance of an individual working alone can be compared with his score in competition. Ability thus remains constant; any change in score must be due to motivational factors. This control over ability was, of course, possible only for the last third of my subjects: the 30 girls and 30 boys who had worked alone *and* in the large group competition. I decided to look at their scores first.

Performance changed dramatically over the two situations. A large number of the men did far better when they were in competition than when they worked alone. For the women the reverse was true. Fewer than one-third of the women, but more than two-thirds of the men, got significantly higher scores in competition.

When we looked at just the girls in terms of the motive to avoid success, the comparisons were even more striking. As predicted, the students who felt ambivalent or anxious about doing well turned in their best scores when they worked by themselves. Seventy-seven per cent of the girls who feared success did better alone than in competition. Women who were low on the motive, however, behaved more like the men: 93 per cent of them got higher scores in competition. (Results significant at the .005.)

Female Fear of Success and Performance

	Perform Better Working Alone	Perform Better in Competition
High fear of success	13	4
Low fear of success	1	12

As a final test of motivational differences, I asked the students to indicate on a scale from 1 to 100 "How important was it for you to do well in this situation?" The high-fear-of-success girls said that it was much more important for them to do well when they worked alone than when they worked in either kind of competition. For the low-fear girls, such differences were not statistically significant. Their test scores were higher in competition, as we saw, and they thought that it was important to succeed no matter what the setting. And in all experimental conditions—working alone, or in competition against males or females—high-fear women consistently lagged behind their fearless comrades on the importance of doing well.

These findings suggest that most women will fully explore their intellectual potential only when they do not need to compete—and least of all when they are competing with men. This was most true of women with a strong anxiety about success. Unfortunately, these are often the same women who could be very successful if they were free from that anxiety. The girls in my sample who feared success also tended to have high intellectual ability and histories of academic success. (It is interesting to note that all but two of these girls were majoring in the humanities and in spite of very high grade points aspired to traditional female careers: housewife, mother, nurse, schoolteacher. Girls who did not fear success, however, were aspiring to graduate degrees and careers in such scientific areas as math, physics and chemistry.)

We can see from this small study that achievement motivation in women is much more complex than the same drive in men. Most men do not find many inhibiting forces in their path if they are able and motivated to succeed. As a result, they are not threatened by competition; in fact, surpassing an opponent is a source of pride and enhanced masculinity.

If a woman sets out to do well, however, she bumps into a number of obstacles. She learns that it really isn't ladylike to be too intellectual. She is warned that men will treat her with distrustful tolerance at best, and outright prejudice at worst, if she pursues a career. She learns the truth of Samuel Johnson's comment, "A man is in general better pleased when he has a good dinner upon his table, than when his wife talks Greek." So she doesn't learn Greek, and the motive to avoid success is born.

In recent years many legal and educational barriers to female achievement have been removed; but it is clear that a psychological barrier remains. The motive to avoid success has an all-too-important influence on the intellectual and professional lives of women in our society. But perhaps there is cause for optimism. Monica may have seen Anne maimed for life, but a few of the girls forecast a happier future for our medical student. Said one:

Anne is quite a lady—not only is she tops academically, but she is liked and admired by her fellow students—quite a trick in a man-dominated field. She is brilliant—but she is also a woman. She will continue to be at or near the top. And . . . always a lady.

CHAPTER NINE

The Management of Learning

IN THE U.S. SPACE PROGRAM, THE SYSTEMS APPROACH WAS USED to mobilize vast material and human resources toward the objective of landing a man on the moon. The success of the systems approach has not been lost on educators. As a consequence, the next few years will see an increasing tendency for schools to implement systematic objectives-based management strategies both in curricula and in school organization and finance. Objectives-based systems are not gimmickry but offer a rational way of organizing the school program and making schools more accountable. In some educational circles it is now fervently believed that prospective teachers should be studying the objectives-based educational-system and computer technology with the same seriousness they devote to the methodology of their own teaching discipline.

W. James Popham's article is a sample of the way in which this space-age advance is envisioned for schools from elementary through university levels. To many teachers—beginners and veterans alike—it may seem too futuristic. Yet, computers themselves not so long ago were considered electronic gadgetry. Now they are changing our lives.

There are a number of reasons that so many educators today look with favor on objectives-based management strategies. There has always been a strong desire to find more systematic and predictable ways of teaching the basic skills in elementary schools. Also, many schools are seeking an alternative to rigid, lockstep class schedules that force learning into unreasonable time limits. Above all, teachers and administrators would like to create the conditions that will help young people to become self-directed in their learning. The educated mind is an inquiring mind. This is why many educators are so interested in trying out innovations that promise to foster self-initiated learning, freed as much as possible from bureaucratic restraints. This is not meant to imply that students should be cut loose from all supervision, as Wendel points out, but there should be greater emphasis on cooperative planning by teacher and student.

Of course, converting traditional school programs into tightly knit organizational systems is easier said than done. Any system of school organization and curriculum is an inverted pyramid perched on one key element: the teacher in the classroom. The teacher ultimately is the one who defines the learning objectives, teaches the children, and measures their performance, all according to specifications. A systems expert cannot simply pass out flow-charts and objectives-based lesson plans, plug in the necessary instructional components (teachers), and expect the mission to succeed automatically. Even if teachers were inclined to carry out such an assignment in soldierly fashion, there is still the more basic and complex problem of determining what constitutes a measurable (behavioral) objective for any given goal of instruction. Anyone who has ever undertaken the task of writing behavioral objectives will agree that the recipe for it inspires a lot more euphoria than the task itself.

A vital element of this process is the assumption that under appropriate instructional conditions virtually *all* students can and will learn most of what they are taught. Unquestionably, this "learning for mastery" strategy is a radical step in education. It has always been assumed that good instruction results in a wide distribution of achievement scores, and therefore a resultant spread of grades from "A" to "F."

Teaching for mastery means concentration on success for *everyone*— sooner or later. It also implies minimizing the harmful effects of failure. James Block's article, which received wide readership in *Today's Education*, the official publication of the National Education Association, provides a clear explanation of teaching for mastery as applied in a classroom situation. Block also discusses major research findings. He doesn't minimize the difficulties involved, and he states quite clearly that the teacher is still a vital part of the process. There is no doubt that teaching for mastery has exciting possibilities.

Another possibility for schools of the future is the application of computer technology to teaching and learning. In fact, various pilot programs already are being undertaken throughout the nation. Patrick Suppes has written and lectured extensively on this subject. Of course, like most educational innovations, computer-assisted instruction has its critics, and Suppes does an incisive job of debating their objections. In any case, because of the costs involved, the total application of computer technology to education is a long way off, but bits and pieces are already beginning to appear, such as teaching machines, dial-access systems, and computer instruction. It is not unreasonable to predict that by the end of this decade schools will begin to have a radically different learning environment.

RECOMMENDED READING

J. H. Block (ed.). 1971. *Mastery Learning: Theory and Practice* (New York: Holt, Rinehart & Winston). Applications of mastery learning techniques as well as discussion of problems of measurement; provides additional reading to Block's article in this chapter.

J. S. Bruner. 1961. "The Act of Discovery," *Harvard Educational Review* 31(1), 21–32. An analysis of creative thinking by an outstanding writer in cognitive psychology.

J. Decaroli. 1973. "What Research Says to the Classroom Teacher: Critical Thinking," *Social Education* 68, 67–69. A review of the literature pertaining to critical thinking in social studies education.

R. M. Gagne and L. J. Briggs. 1974. *Principles of Instructional Design* (New York: Holt, Rinehart & Winston). The application of the systems approach to the design of educational programs.

R. F. Mager. 1962. *Preparing Instructional Objectives* (Palo Alto, Calif.: Fearon Publishers). The steps required to convert general educational objectives into specific, behavioral outcomes.

N. M. Sanders. 1966. *Classroom Questions: What Kinds?* (New York: Harper & Row). A handbook of techniques for the conversion of subject matter to behavioral objectives, using a taxonomy of educational objectives as the structural basis.

24.

W. JAMES POPHAM

OBJECTIVES-BASED MANAGEMENT STRATEGIES FOR LARGE EDUCATIONAL SYSTEMS

There is an apparent defect in human nature which disinclines us to subject any enterprise to careful scrutiny until we sense it is in some way defective. Without debating whether this failing stems from original sin

From the *Journal of Educational Research*, 66:1 (Sept. 1972). Reprinted with permission of the author and the *Journal of Educational Research*.

or is merely an acquired shortcoming, there is little doubt that we are currently witnessing the results of this tendency in the field of education.

Americans citizens in increasing numbers have become disenchanted with the quality of our educational system, and the magnitude of this disenchantment has now passed the critical point, so that rhetoric no longer satisfies and corrective action is being demanded. The problem facing us now is easier to articulate than to answer, namely, *How should we go about promoting improvements in the educational enterprise?*

SYSTEMS-ANALYSIS STRATEGIES

Some educators are turning to systems analysis methodology as a possible source for satisfactory answers to this perplexing question. For certain of these systems analysis proponents one senses an almost religious devotion to their methodology, a devotion in which the litany of input analysis, output analysis, and servoloop feedback must be chanted daily —or at least in every published article and speech.

For me, however, systems analysis approaches derive their merits not because they border on the occult, but rather, because they reflect a rational attempt to illuminate the arenas in which we must make educational decisions. If most people are left to their own devices when they must make decisions, they will usually find that erroneous perceptions of reality and unconscious biases render those decisions less than satisfactory. Surely there are many wise human beings who will reach enlightened decisions which all of us would applaud, but there are many others who do not operate as meritoriously. If the decisions affect only the individual, we are not all that upset if the wrong choice is made; after all, an individual pretty well has the right to muck up his own life if he wishes. But in the field of education we see that imprudent decisions can penalize thousands of students, thus we cannot remain as sanguine regarding intuitively based decision-making. Therefore we find an increasing number of people, both educators and non-educators, advocating the use of more formal mechanisms for making decisions regarding large scale educational enterprises. Customarily, these mechanisms have taken a form which more or less resembles a systems analysis approach.

The distinguishing feature of a systems analysis strategy is implied by its name. Clearly, there is an attempt to analyze a system of some sort, in this instance an educational system. But equally critical is the implication that this analysis will be a *systematic* one. Indeed, many people are enamoured of systems analysis approaches for precisely that reason, i.e., they tend to reduce the capricious decision-making which is so characteristic of most human endeavors.

There is another dimension characteristically associated with systems analysis approaches which should be noticed, namely, a reliance on *evidence* of the system's effects. This orientation is in contrast to alternative approaches which, although systematic and analytic, are not essentially empirical methodologies. For instance, analytic philosophical approaches are generally not considered to be systems analysis strategies even though they may epitomize rigorous analysis.

LARGE-SCALE EDUCATIONAL SYSTEMS

This discussion will be restricted to the consideration of large scale educational enterprises such as a state school system or a large school district. For example, California legislators are currently undertaking a serious appraisal of the state's master plan for higher education. One of the considerations of the planners relates to the development of an evaluation system which will permit the state legislators and other concerned citizens within the state to judge the quality of the California higher education system. The remarks in this paper will pertain to the management of such an evaluation system.

This does not suggest that the following observations are inappropriate for small systems, such as a moderate sized school district or even a single school. Yet, in general, the focus will be on the recommendations for systems of sufficient magnitude to warrant the considerable investment in carrying out the procedures described.

OBJECTIVES-BASED SYSTEMS ANALYSIS

In most systems analysis models there are three sets of questions to be answered. These questions are associated with the three major phases of managing a system, as follows:

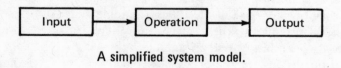

A simplified system model.

There are questions regarding which *inputs* should be made to the system, that is, the purposes for which the system exists and the types of resources which will be used to attain those purposes. A second set of questions is associated with the actual *operation* of the system, that is, how well are things working? A final group of questions stem from an appraisal of the *output* of the system, that is, was the effectiveness of the system such that it should remain essentially unmodified or do we have to make some changes in it?

Now there is nothing inherent in systems analysis models which require one to employ instructional objectives as an organizing rubric in the implementation of a model. There may be preferable classification schemes for organizing the data which must be processed in a systems analysis scheme. The present paper, however, will be addressed to a systems analysis strategy in which instructional objectives play a prominent role. The choice to employ objectives as the organizing dimension stems from a belief that statements of instructional objectives can serve as a parsimonious vehicle for communicating the information which must be considered at various points in analyzing the system. Note, for instance, that those individuals operating the National Assessment of Educational Progress, surely dealing with a large scale educational enterprise, have chosen to employ statements of instructional objectives as their organizing rubric.

For example, a learner's status in connection with an educational system may be represented by his or her performance on an examination of some sort. Rather than requiring a decision-maker to scrutinize the entire examination, we may convey an idea of what the examination entails by identifying the learner competencies it was designed to measure. Often these competencies can be described as a *desired* status for the learner, hence the equivalent of an instructional objective. In addition, many educators are quite familiar with the general concept of instructional objectives, this topic having received ample attention during the past decade.

To reiterate, it is not requisite to employ instructional objectives as the organizing theme for an educational systems analysis model. Nonetheless, the use of objectives for this purpose seems to offer some advantages and, accordingly, the remainder of this paper will describe a systems analysis model for large educational enterprises, which prominently employs instructional objectives.

MEASURABLE OBJECTIVES

It is important to note at the outset of this discussion that, unless otherwise noted, we will employ the phrase "instructional objective" to represent a *measurable* instructional objective. Because measurable objectives communicate one's instructional intentions with less ambiguity than broad, general objectives, it would seem particularly important to use such objectives in a rational decision-making scheme where any extra system noise (such as ambiguous symbology) will reduce the quality of the decisions. In recent years, of course, there have been numerous treatises written regarding technical questions of how such measurable objectives should be optimally formulated.

Returning now to the general questions which an educational systems analyst must attempt to answer, we can turn first to what is perhaps the most important question facing any systems designer. This question is, *To what ends should the system be committed?* Putting it another way, *Why should the education system be there in the first place?* For an objectives-based systems analysis approach, this essentially becomes the problem of goal determination.

GOAL DETERMINATION

In general, the proponent of systems analysis approaches subscribes to a classic means/ends paradigm. It is anticipated that if proper ends can be identified it will be worth the trouble to test the efficacy of alternative means to achieve those ends until certain means can be identified which do the job. In the field of education we are becoming increasingly more sophisticated in designing instructional sequences. It thus becomes increasingly imperative to identify the most defensible goals of our educational systems so that improved instructional means can be directed toward the proper ends.

There are at least two approaches to specifying the appropriate objectives for a large scale educational system, and these are somewhat analogous to an inductive versus a deductive approach. Characteristically, we have employed an inductive strategy over the years in education. According to this scheme the educational planner consults various groups with a series of general questions such as, *What do you want our schools to accomplish?* People typically respond to such questions with varying degrees of specificity, so it is usually up to the planner to synthesize their somewhat diffuse reactions and translate them into more or less definitive goal statements. Tyler's curriculum model which has, at least at a theoretical level, been quite influential during the past several decades represents such an approach.

An alternative attack upon the goal determination problem has become available in recent years through the establishment of large pools of measurable instructional objectives. Various clienteles can rate objectives from these pools as to the appropriateness of their inclusion in the curriculum of a given education system. In this latter approach, therefore, we do not try to derive statements of objectives from the value preferences and informal assertions of people; rather, we present people with objectives from which they choose those they consider most important.

Perhaps because the latter approach seems to offer a greater possibility of systematization through technical refinement, it has received more attention during recent months. Particularly as a consequence of the *needs assessment* operations required by federal ESEA Title III funding programs, we find more and more educators who are attempting to rigorously establish objectives for large scale educational endeavors. A number of these efforts have involved the use of deductively designated educational objectives.

The general strategy in an objectives-based goal determination operation involves presentation of alternative sets of educational objectives to groups who have a stake in deciding what the goals of the system ought to be. These groups then rate, rank, or in other ways display their preferences regarding those objectives. The expressed preferences of the various groups are then surveyed by those who must ultimately decide on the systems' goals and, hopefully, more enlightened judgments regarding what the system's goals ought to be can be made on the basis of such preference data.

The somewhat new feature of this approach to goal determination involves the use of measurable objectives. In previous efforts to employ this general strategy educators often used loose, nonmeasurable goals which almost served as Rorschach ink blots for those expressing their preferences, that is, people read into nebulous goal statements almost anything they wished. As a consequence, it was extremely difficult to make reasonable contrasts among the preferences of various groups. With the use of measurable objectives, fortunately, ambiguity is reduced, and as a consequence differences among various clienteles are more directly a function of their real differences in values rather than confusion regarding the meaning of certain goal statements.

The kinds of groups which might be involved, of course, will vary from one educational enterprise to another. For instance, in the California higher education evaluation system it would seem imperative to involve student groups from the various types of higher education institutions within the state, that is, community colleges, state colleges, and universities. It would seem equally important to involve citizen groups of various kinds, e.g., parents, businessmen, and other public spirited citizens. This would be an ideal opportunity, for example, to secure preference inputs from ethnic and other minority groups who often feel large educational systems are unresponsive to their particular curricular preferences. It might be particularly appropriate to secure the reactions of a group of specially designated *futurists* whose charge would be to consider higher education objectives in light of their suitability for the 1980's and 1990's, not merely for the next few years. The preferences of these groups can be coalesced and represented in straightforward numerical form in any one of several methods. If at any point in the goal determination operation it is discovered that important goals have been overlooked, they can be easily added to the array of objectives to be rated.

To illustrate an alternative, somewhat less quantitative method of establishing priorities among competing objectives, Prof. Robert E. Stake of the University of Illinois has recently devised an approach to priorities planning in which the decision-makers consider data such as the preferences of various clienteles. However, they also survey the system's requisite resource allocations, the payoff probabilities of various objectives, and the relevant contingency conditions, that is, special circumstances which might call for changes in instructional procedures.

Having established the preferred objectives of a system, an important second step in the goal determination is to discover the degree to which the target learners can already display the hoped-for behaviors designated by the various reference groups. This is where measurable instructional objectives offer considerable advantages, for since the objectives which have been rated by the various groups are stated in explicit and measurable terms, it is a relatively straightforward task to devise measuring devices from those objectives and, as a consequence, to measure the learner's status.

Now we would certainly employ item and person sampling techniques in this approach in order to conserve testing time and to make the task economically feasible. But by using such techniques, whereby only certain students are sampled and those sampled completed only segments of the total measuring devices, we can certainly measure student attainment of the high priority goals established via the previous rating/ranking procedure.

The next step, then, is to contrast the learners' status with the high priority goals and decide toward which of these we wish to direct our educational enterprise. Clearly, there are still a great many value judgments to be made at this point, but the hope is that by making the decisions as heavily data-based as possible, superior decisions will be made.

This system of goal determination by having different clienteles rate extant objectives has been tried out for the past two years by the Instructional Objectives Exchange (IOX) with some interesting results (Popham, 1971). Working with several school districts in Southern California,

IOX has secured a number of ratings of different objectives within the IOX collections by students, teachers, parents, and futurists. Various modifications in the directions to the rater groups have yielded some insights regarding the suitability of such matters as the inclusion of sample measurement items to further clarify the meaning of the objective, the use of rankings versus ratings, etc. Perhaps the most important conclusion drawn from these studies relates to the number of objectives to be rated. It now appears to IOX staff, in contrast to earlier expectations, that it is simply unwise to present a vast array of instructional objectives to rater groups. In other words, even though in certain of the collections of objectives currently distributed by the IOX there are upwards of one or two hundred objectives, it makes little sense to attempt to secure ratings of so many objectives. Frankly, the educational decision-maker generally is not able to process the resulting data from such rating analyses. Instead, the conclusion from the IOX work to date suggests that it would be far better to present a more moderate number of content general objectives, that is, measurable objectives which describe a class of learner behaviors rather than a single series of specific test items, and have these more general objectives rated by appropriate groups.

This is a particularly difficult procedure because one of the more persistent problems having to do with the technology of objectives concerns the level of generality of those objectives. Individuals working with instructional objectives since Tyler's early efforts have pointed out that the level of specificity question or, conversely, the level of generality issue, is one of the most important questions to be resolved in the field of instructional objectives. Yet no one seems to have come up with a very satisfactory solution. Our general estimate at this point, however, is that we must find some way to present larger "chunks" of educational objectives to various groups for ratings. Ending up with more than twenty-five or thirty objectives which must be rated presents, to most humans, an unmanageable intellectual task.

It is interesting to note that in certain relatively large school districts in California the number of reading objectives has been reduced to only three or four, thus a single objective, e.g., a student's ability to decode twenty-five words randomly drawn from a list of 500, serves to represent the bulk of that district's reading effort.

It is quite apparent that more attention must be given to the matter of how general an objective should be in order for it to prove serviceable in this type of situation. At one extreme, however, the experience at IOX to date suggests that far fewer objectives be employed than we have typically been using.

PROGRESS MONITORING

The second set of questions of concern to those involved in decisions regarding educational systems concerns the appraisal of the progress of the system toward its stipulated goals. One relatively straightforward method of discerning the degree to which the system's goals are being accomplished involves the administration of criterion-referenced tests associated with the various system goals so that indications of learner progress toward those goals can be secured. Goals which, according to measured learner progress, are not being achieved can be attacked with alternative instructional strategies, additional resources, etc. Goals which are being achieved on schedule permit the inference that the instructional program is working as well as needed. It is even conceivable, of course, that some goals will be achieved ahead of schedule, thereby permitting a shifting of resources toward less effective instructional activities.

It is particularly important in assessing progress toward system goals to gather the requisite data as economically as possible. Once more, matrix sampling (a technical term for item sampling combined with person sampling) is a valuable ally of the educational evaluator. It is even possible, when resources are short, to combine matrix sampling with goal sampling via a technique whereby progress toward only certain goals is monitored. Such an approach, of course, does not give information about all of the system's goals, hence, suffers from the defect of supplying only partial data. Nonetheless, where a system simply does not have the financial resources to investigate satisfactorily the progress toward all goals, the use of goal sampling may represent a reasonable alternative.

It is at this juncture that the evaluator should be particularly attentive to unanticipated consequences of the educational system's operation. Whereas educational designers can spell out carefully the hoped-for outcomes of an educational enterprise, it is often the case that some unintended and aversive consequences ensure which were simply unforeseen by the instructional designers. Scriven (1972), in a recent paper, argues cogently for the use of goal-free evaluation in which the educational evaluator is attentive to the consequences of an educational system, not to the rhetoric of the instructional designers. He suggests that under certain circumstances it may be more judicious to examine what happens as a consequence of the program rather than what the instructional designers say will occur via their stated objectives. Whether one uses goal-free evaluation approaches or simply employs considerable circumspection regarding what might have gone wrong, it is quite important to attend to all of the effects of a program, not only those which were intended.

OUTPUT APPRAISAL

The final set of questions regarding the management of a large scale educational system concerns the final quality of its results. Once more, since we are using objectives as an organizing rubric, it is possible to develop criterion-referenced tests which are congruent with those objectives and administer them on a matrix sampling basis to the learners served by the system. Results on such measures, combined with measures of unanticipated consequences akin to those described in the previous paragraph, will yield the kind of evidence necessary to reach a judgment regarding the quality of the educational enterprise.

A particularly thorny problem arises related to the manner in which results of such an analysis should be reported. Educational evaluators are only beginning to wrestle seriously with alternative vehicles for reporting evaluative results in such a way that decision-makers can take appropriate action based on the evaluation data. All too frequently we find evaluation endeavors resulting in encyclopedic final reports which only a person of great devotion has the patience to read completely. Brevity is a desirable criterion in reporting results of evaluation studies irrespective of the type of evaluation report involved.

Again, the organizing theme for evaluation, at least for the approach being described here, would be the use of instructional objectives. Progress toward the major instructional objectives adopted by the educational system would be reported to the appropriate decision-making groups, e.g., local school boards, state school boards, university regents, etc. In a general before-after model it is important to present the data in as succinct a fashion as possible so that those utilizing the results can make more sense out of them. Here is where the educational evaluator will have to be particularly judicious in the data he selects to report and the manner in which those data are described.

THEORY AND PRACTICE

In the foregoing paragraphs a general strategy for the management of large educational enterprises has been described. Clearly, the discussion has been at a very general, not a nuts and bolts level. Sometimes one has the feeling that in propounding a given theoretical point of view an effort to implement it in practice will result in chaos. The technical problems are seen as too serious to work out.

For example, I often hear an aptitude-by-treatment interaction specialist suggest that if we could only sort out pupils' learning styles and judiciously mesh them with relevant instructional treatments, then educational Valhalla would be upon us. At a theoretical level I can applaud such a stance, but in my pragmatic heart of hearts I really doubt that this can be pulled off, at least in my lifetime. The practical problems are too sticky.

With present propositions, however, this does not seem to be the case. Surely there will be technical, procedural questions which must be dealt with. For example, exactly which groups will be involved in rating the objectives that will result in the selection of goals for the system? How many learners should be tested in order to yield reasonable estimates regarding the progress of the system as well as its final output? What kinds of departures from anticipated progress should dictate modifications in the system? These and other problems can be faced and, I believe, resolved by individuals wishing to seriously monitor the progress of a large scale educational enterprise.

But that kind of operation takes more money than most educators have been willing to spend. Other than the recently initiated Experimental Schools Program of the U.S. Office of Education we see few large scale educational enterprises in which ample funds have been set aside for evaluation. Most state and local school systems operate under an explicit evaluation budget of less than 1 percent, if that much. The kind of evaluation endeavor we're talking about here clearly will demand resources of around 5 percent or better. The first-blush reluctance of individuals to spend that kind of money should be countered by hard-nosed estimates of the benefits, both economic and educational, which can be derived from rigorously evaluating the progress of a large scale educational undertaking. The costs of ineffectual instruction are enormous.

PERFECTION AND IMPERFECTABILITY

Some detractors will allege quite accurately that systems approaches such as those described here are laden with flaws. Surely by using objectives-based systems we will discover that certain critical features of the educational system are not appraised with sufficient sensitivity to yield the right kind of information for making proper decisions. When faced with these kinds of criticisms, however, I am reminded that decisions must currently be made regarding educational enterprises, day in and day out. And at the moment these decisions are being made with far less sophistication, far less data, and far less accuracy than might be rendered under a system such as that proposed herein. Granted that a systems analysis approach is not perfect, it nevertheless seems to offer a clear improvement over the general quality of decision-making seen so prevalently these days in educational arenas. And, perhaps more importantly, because of its systematic nature such an approach is amenable to technical self-correction and, over time, incremental improvement so that even if the management system lacks total perfection, it will be so close that the learners it serves won't know the difference.

REFERENCES

W. James Popham, "Providing Wide Ranging, Diversely Organized Pools of Instructional Objectives and Measures," final report for the U.S. Office of Education, Project No. 14–0563, Grant No. OEG–0–9–140563–4635(085), Department of Health, Education, and Welfare, 1971.

Michael Scriven, "Goal Free Evaluation," unpublished working paper for the National Institute of Education Planning Unit (available from the author), University of California, Berkeley, 1972.

Robert E. Stake, *Priorities Planning: Judging the Importance of Alternative Objectives*, Instructional Objectives Exchange, 1972.

Vimcet Associates, "Determining Defensible Goals via Educational Needs Assessment," P. O. Box 24714, Los Angeles, Calif., 1971.

25.   ROBERT WENDEL

INQUIRY TEACHING:
DISPELLING THE MYTHS

A false assumption teachers commonly make when they are introduced to inquiry as a teaching process is to interpret it as very unstructured, free-wheeling, and almost totally student centered. These opinions may seem appropriate when one compares the inquiry method with what is known as conventional content/teacher-centered education. Many times this comparison is shocking—particularly upon realizing the narrow confinement and conditioning residual in traditional education. Some people then view inquiry teaching as a radical approach to education.

Inquiry teaching may be freer than conventional approaches, but it is not unstructured. Rather, it is less rigidly structured than traditional teaching. Inquiry teaching is not completely student-centered laissez faire; moreover, it is an approach to learning that invites cooperative student-teacher

Reprinted by permission from the September, 1973, issue of *The Clearing House.*

planning. The reflective process is freer because it incorporates the principles of purposeful investigation as an aspect of the learning process. A single learner always interacting with a textbook or his own thoughts is replaced by an individual classifying and testing his insights by interacting with various resources and people in order to elaborate and verify his hunches. Learning that is dynamic, purposeful, and not just passive, is characterized by active students moving around the room, the school, the community—experiencing and interacting with various resources and each other in attempts to solve significant problems they have identified. Continuously during this inquiry, opportunities for both large group and small group instruction as well as individual reflective thinking are present.

Because students involved in inquiry-reflective learning are more purposefully interactive, both physically and psychologically, many teachers and administrators view this learning as disorderly, confused, and noisy. When all students are not quietly learning the same material, then the assumption is that the class is unstructured, unplanned, and too student centered. This is not the case at all. During the cooperative problem-raising stage of the inquiry-reflective process, several aspects of an issue are identified and adopted by individuals or small groups for continued investigation. The nature of each small group's inquiry determines largely what they will do and where they may go. Each small group experiences learning in a different manner as they interact with resources and purposely go about problem solving.

Rather than always structuring learning around a time segment, or around one activity or body of content, the reflective teacher structures learning in at least two ways. First, the teacher purposefully creates a classroom atmosphere that will maximize opportunities for students to meaningfully identify intra- and inter-personal problems and concerns and then be able to move toward their solutions. By encouraging more open discussions, questioning, and interaction within a classroom, students quickly realize that *they* are essential in giving meanings to content.

Secondly, by having created an environment responsive to student interests and concerns, the reflective teacher provides guidance in dealing with the issues raised. This guidance should lead students through the inquiry-reflective thought process. This process provides an excellent structure for both overt and cognitive activities. The stages in this process ensure some structure to thinking, yet do not restrict one to narrow thought patterns. The identification and elaboration of several hypotheses allows creative consideration of an issue within a structured process that is applicable to both thought and behavior.

Thus, reflective teaching is not unstructured: it is centered around a

nation. Similarly, in an analysis of the scores of Jewish and non-Jewish college freshmen on the ACE, the Jewish students did relatively better on the linguistic than on the quantitative parts of the test, while the reverse was true of the non-Jewish students (Held). The traditional emphasis placed in most Jewish families on formal education and abstract intelligence has often been cited as an explanation of such findings. It is also interesting to note that in a recent study of Jewish children and college students with the Wechsler scales, the difference between verbal and performance scores was not large enough to be significant at the .05 level at the time of school entrance, but reached the .001 level among school children and college students (Levinson).

Investigations of the American Negro have generally revealed poorer performance on perceptual and spatial tasks than on most types of verbal tasks. On the California Test of Mental Maturity, Negroes scored higher on the language than on the nonlanguage part (Hammer). Negro children do particularly poorly on such tests as the Minnesota Paper Form Board and the Chicago Non-Verbal Examination (Newland and Lawrence). When Negro and white boys were matched on Stanford-Binet IQ and their performance on individual items was compared, the Negroes excelled on disarranged sentences, memory for sentences, and vocabulary, but were inferior on arithmetic reasoning, repeating digits backwards, and detecting absurdities in pictures (Clarke). In several studies with the Wechsler scales, Negroes proved to be significantly poorer in Block Design, Digit Symbol, and Arithmetic than in most of the verbal tests (Davidson *et al.*; DeStephens; and Franklin). One factor that may account for some of these results is the greater emphasis put on speed in certain performance and nonlanguage tests. A second proposed explanation centers around problem-solving attitudes. Insofar as the social environment of the American Negro, especially in the South, may encourage attitudes of passive compliance rather than active exploration, it would be more conducive to rote verbal learning than to perceptual manipulation of stimuli and problem solving.

We thus find three groups—two of them bilingual and one with a relatively poor educational background—which for very different reasons perform better on verbal than on nonverbal tests. Glib generalizations can be very misleading in interpreting the test scores of different cultural groups.

ETIOLOGY

If we want to go beyond description and inquire into the *origins* of group differences, then we must look into antecedent circumstances leading up to the differences. Test scores do not provide such information. Nor are we any longer satisfied with a general answer that differences are due to "heredity" or to "environment." Heredity and environment are not entities; they refer to broad classes of factors. We need to identify the specific hereditary or environmental factors that are involved. We also need to ask the question "How?" We need to know the mechanisms whereby a given hereditary or environmental factor ultimately leads to the observed group difference in test score (Anastasi, 1958).

As an illustration, let us consider three environmental mechanisms that may produce differences in intelligence. Suppose three children obtain equally low scores on an intelligence test: one because neonatal anoxia led to brain damage; another because of inadequate schooling; and the third because he was reared in an intellectually underprivileged home where curiosity and active problem-solving attitudes were discouraged, inarticulateness was fostered, and motivation for academic achievement was low. All three deficiencies have an environmental origin, but the implications for the individual and the prognosis of progress are quite different in the three cases. We cannot simply attribute the condition to environment and apply a single solution reserved for environmentally caused conditions.

Nor can we say that it's "just an environmental difference and hence we can ignore it." Environmentally caused differences can be as pervasive, enduring, and basic in the life of the individual as those caused by heredity. To turn this around, the observation that a condition is pervasive, enduring, and basic does not in itself prove that the condition must be hereditary and cannot be used as an argument against improving the very environmental factors that brought it about. Such a circular argument represents one misuse of test findings.

PREDICTION

If we want to use test scores to *predict outcome* in some future situation, such as an applicant's performance in college, we must use tests with high predictive validity against the specific criterion. This requirement is sometimes overlooked in the development and application of culture-free tests. In the effort to include in such tests only activities and information common to many cultures, we may end up with content having little relevance to any criterion we may wish to predict (Anastasi, 1950). The fact that a test is culture-free certainly does not insure its validity for all purposes. Again it is trite to insist that in predicting a specific outcome, there is no substitute for predictive validity; but the point is sometimes forgotten in discussions of test scores.

When predicting outcomes for individuals with markedly different cultural backgrounds, a better solution is to choose test content on the basis of its predictive validity but investigate the effect of *moderator variables*. Validity coefficients, regression weights, and cutoff scores may vary as a function of certain background conditions of the subjects. For example, the same scholastic aptitude score may be predictive of college failure when obtained by an upper-middle-class student, but predictive of moderate success when obtained by a lower-class student. Follow-up studies must be conducted to establish the predictive meaning of test scores in different subgroups defined by relevant background variables. Several studies comparing the college achievement of public and private school boys in America indicate that when equated in initial IQ, public school boys obtain higher college grades than private school boys (McArthur). Similarly, recent research in Sweden suggests that children from lower social classes profit more than middle-class or upper-class children from transfer to a more favorable academic environment (Husen and Svensson).

Finally, in predicting outcome, we should also consider the possible effects of *differential treatments*. It is one of the contributions of decision theory to psychometrics that it provides ways of incorporating differential treatment into the prediction of outcomes from test scores (Cronbach). For example, given certain test scores obtained by subgroup A with a particular cultural background, what will be the predicted college achievement if we introduce remedial teaching programs, counseling designed to modify educational attitudes and motivation, or other suitable treatments? The inclusion of moderator variables and differential treatments into the prediction picture provides a more effective way of handling cultural differences than the exclusion of valid content from the tests.

In summary, I have tried to suggest a few of the procedures we can follow to improve the use of tests in intergroup comparisons—first, to describe differences as they exist in the present; second, to investigate their origins in past events; and third, to predict future outcomes.

REFERENCES

Anne Anastasi. "The Concept of Validity in the Interpretation of Test Scores." *Educational Psychology Measurement*, 1950, 10, 67–78.
———. "Heredity, Environment, and the Question 'How?'" *Psychol. Rev.*, 1958, 65, 197–208.
K. L. Bean. "Negro Responses to Verbal and Non-Verbal Test Material." *Journal of Psychology*, 1942, 13, 253–343.

F. Brown. "A Comparative Study of the Intelligence of Jewish and Scandinavian Kindergarten Children." *Journal of Genetic Psychology*, 1944, *64*, 67–92.

D. P. Clarke. "Stanford-Binet Scale L Response Patterns in Matched Racial Groups." *Journal of Negro Education*, 1941, *10*, 230–38.

L. J. Cronbach. "The Two Disciplines of Scientific Psychology." *American Psychologist*, 1957, *12*, 671–84.

K. S. Davidson, R. G. Gibby, E. B. McNeil, S. J. Segal and H. Silverman. "Form I of the Wechsler-Bellevue Scale." *Journal of Consulting Psychology*, 1950, *14*, 489–92.

W. P. DeStephens. "Are Criminals Morons?" *Journal of Social Psychology*, 1953, *38*, 187–99.

J. C. Franklin. "Discriminative Value and Patterns of the Wechsler-Bellevue Scales in the Examination of Delinquent Negro Boys." *Educational Psychology Measurement*, 1945, *5*, 71–85.

J. P. Guilford. "The Structure of Intellect." *Psychology Bulletin*, 1956, *53*, 267–93.

―――. *Personality*. New York: McGraw-Hill, 1959.

E. F. Hammer. "Comparison of the Performances of Negro Children and Adolescents on Two Tests of Intelligence, One an Emergency Scale." *Journal of Genetic Psychology*, 1954, *84*, 85–93.

O. C. Held. "A Comparative Study of the Performance of Jewish and Gentile College Students on the American Council Psychological Examination." *Journal of Social Psychology*, 1941, *13*, 407–11.

T. Husen and N. Svensson. "Pedagogic Milieu and Development of Intellectual Skills." *School Review*, 1960, *68*, 31–51.

B. M. Levinson. "Traditional Jewish Cultural Values and Performance on the Wechsler Tests." *Journal of Educational Psychology*, 1959, *50*, 177–81.

C. McArthur. "Subculture and Personality During the College Years." *Journal of Education Psychology*, 1960, *33*, 260–68.

T. E. Newland and W. C. Lawrence. "Chicago Non-Verbal Examination Results on an East Tennessee Negro Population." *Journal of Clinical Psychology*, 1953, *9*, 44–46.

M. A. Straus. "Mental Ability and Cultural Needs: A Psychocultural Interpretation of the Intelligence Test Performance of Ceylon University Entrants." *American Sociological Review*, 1951, *16*, 371–75.

―――. "Subcultural Variation in Ceylonese Mental Ability: A Study in National Character." *Journal of Social Psychology*, 1954, *39*, 129–41.

L. L. Thurstone. "Primary Mental Abilities." *Psychometric Monographs*, 1938, No. 1.

P. E. Vernon. *The Structure of Human Abilities*. London: Methuen, 1950.

30.

HENRY S. DYER

IS TESTING A
MENACE TO EDUCATION?

The title of this paper is a question: "Is Testing a Menace to Education?" Knowing who I am and what I do for a living, you would have every reason to believe that I am going to answer the question with a resounding, "No!" But you would be dead wrong, for I am going to answer the question with a tentative "Yes, but—" Yes, testing *is* a menace to education, *but* probably not for the reasons you think. It is a menace to education primarily because tests are misunderstood and test results are misused by too many educators. In his . . . book called *The Schools*, Martin Mayer speaks of testing as a "necessary evil." I disagree. It is not *necessarily* evil. Tests *could* be a blessing to education if only teachers and counselors and educational administrators would divest themselves of a number of misconceptions about what tests can and cannot do and would learn to use test results more cautiously and creatively in the educational process.

There are nine principal misconceptions that seem to stand in the way of the appropriate use of tests.

The first misconception is the notion that aptitude or intelligence tests measure something called "native ability," something fixed and immutable within the person that determines his level of expectation for all time. I am not prepared to say such an inherent entity does not exist. The chances are it does. Studies in genetics certainly support the idea, and so do many psychological studies. But intelligence or aptitude tests do not *measure* such an entity—at least not directly; and certainly not in any interpretable manner.

What intelligence tests do measure is the individual's performance on certain types of mental tasks . . . a long time after the child has first entered the world. The kinds of mental tasks that appear in any intelligence or aptitude test are clearly the kinds that a student *learns* to per-

From Henry S. Dyer, "Is Testing a Menace to Education?" *New York State Education*, XLIX (October, 1961), pp. 16–19. Reprinted with the permission of the New York State Teachers Association and the author.

form from his experiences in the world around him. The amount of learning based on such experiences may depend on many things that can vary enormously from one child to another—the number and quality of books available in his home, the kind of talk he hears, the richness and variety of his surroundings, the vividness and emotional quality of the thousands of happenings in his life from day to day. It is absurd to suppose that a child's score on an intelligence test bypasses all these factors, to suppose that such a score gets directly at the brains he was born with.

I prefer to think of an intelligence test as essentially indistinguishable from an achievement test—that is, as a measure of how well, at a given point of time, a student can perform certain well-defined tasks. The main difference between the tasks in a so-called achievement test and those in a so-called intelligence test is, generally speaking, that the tasks in an achievement test are usually learned over a relatively short time and those in an intelligence test are learned over a relatively long time.

The consequences of thinking of an aptitude test as measuring some immutable determiner of student performance can be pretty serious. First, such thinking encourages the dangerous idea that one can, from an aptitude score, decide once and for all at a fairly early age what kind and level of educational or vocational activity a student is fitted for. It nurtures that hardy perennial, for instance, that if a student has an IQ of 115 or better he ought to prepare for college, and if his IQ is below 115 he ought to make other plans—this, despite all the studies which have shown that an IQ may be highly variable for a given student, that colleges vary enormously in the quality of students they enroll, and that some low scorers succeed in college while some high scorers fail. I have often wondered how many educational crimes are annually committed on the strength of the theory that intelligence tests measure something they cannot possibly measure.

A second consequence, almost as serious, is the conception that a student with a high aptitude score and low achievement scores (or low grades in school) is an "under-achiever"—another hardly perennial. It was exploded 30 years ago, but it is back and can lead to some rather distressing treatment of individual pupils. The diagnosis goes that a student with a high aptitude score and low achievement scores is "unmotivated" or "lazy" or suffering from some sort of emotional disturbance. Granted there may be some grounds for such diagnoses, nevertheless they are scarcely inferable from the discrepancy in scores alone. And some new and possibly more useful insights about such students might be forthcoming if one frankly regarded the discrepancies simply as differences in performance on one kind of achievement test as compared to another.

Finally, the idea that aptitude tests are supposed to measure native ability leads to the persistent and embarrassing demand that they should be "culture free"; that if they are, as they must be, affected by the student's background of experience in school and at home, then *ipso facto*, they are "unfair" to the underprivileged. I wish we could get it *out* of people's heads that tests are unfair to the underprivileged and get it *into* their heads that it is the hard facts of social circumstance and inadequate education that are unfair to them. If educational opportunities are unequal, the test results will also be unequal.

A second misconception about tests is the notion that a prediction made from a test score, or from a series of test scores, or from test scores plus other quantifiable data, are, or should be, perfectly accurate, and that if they are not, the tests must be regarded as no good. This fallacy arises from a confused conception of what constitutes prediction. There are some people—maybe most people—who think of prediction as simply an all-or-none, right-or-wrong business. If a test score predicts that Johnny will get B in American History, the score is right if he actually gets a B; it is wrong if he gets a B—or a C. I suppose this is a legitimate way of thinking about prediction in certain circumstances, but it is scarcely fair to the test and it may well be unfair to Johnny. A more meaningful and useful way of thinking about a prediction is to regard it as a statement of the odds: A given test score might predict that Johnny has eight chances in ten of getting a grade of B or better in American History, and three chances in a hundred of flunking. This approach recognizes that in forecasting future events, especially human events, we never have sufficient information to be sure of being right every time, but we do have information, in the form of test scores and other data, which if appropriately organized, can help us make better decisions than would be possible without them.

The third misconception is that standardized test scores are infallible or perfectly reliable. Reliability, I remind you, has to do with the degree to which the score of an individual stands still on successive testings. It rarely occurs to the uninitiated that a test can never be more than a *sample* of a student's performance and that, in consequence, the score on any test is afflicted with sampling error. To the man-in-the-street, to many teachers, school administrators and parents, who have never reflected on the problem, a score is a score is a score, and they are shocked to find that when a student takes one test today and an alternate form of the same test tomorrow, his score can change. Anyone who deals with a test score must always be conscious that such a score, like any sort of measurement whatever, is clouded with uncertainty, that it it never more than an estimate of truth.

A fourth misconception is the assumption that an achievement test measures all there is to measure in any given subject matter area—that an achievement test in history, for example, measures everything a high school student should know about the facts of history and how to deal with them. It never seems to occur to some people that the content of a standardized achievement test in any particular subject matter area may be only partially related to what a specific course of study in that area may call for.

If people will only take the trouble to look critically at the insides of achievement tests and not just at their covers, they will almost certainly find that even the test best suited to their purposes still fails to sample *all* the types of learning that are sought in a given subject, or even all the most important types of learning. And it may also often include matters that the student is not expected to know. The consequence is, of course, that on a particular standardized achievement test a student may look considerably better or considerably worse than he really is, and decisions based on his score may miss the boat by a considerable margin.

A fifth misconception is that an achievement test can measure only a pupil's memory for facts. This used to be true. But a good modern achievement test gets at far more than a command of facts alone; it usually measures in addition the pupil's skill in reasoning with the facts he remembers and also his skill in reasoning with facts newly presented to him. It is this introduction into achievement tests of the requirement to reason, to cope with problems, to think clearly, critically and even creatively that helps to blur the distinction between aptitude and achievement tests. The modern achievement test recognizes that as students come up through the grades they are, or ought to be, learning to think as well as to know. It recognizes also that there may be many different kinds of thinking to measure, depending upon the subject matter in which the thinking is required. The result is that a well-conceived battery of achievement tests gives the same sort of information one would get from a general intelligence test plus a good deal more.

A sixth misconception has to do with profiles of achievement or aptitude scores; that a profile of scores summarizes clearly and efficiently a considerable amount of reliable information about the relative strengths and weaknesses of an individual. Test technicians have inveighed repeatedly against the use of profile charts on the grounds that they are often grossly misleading, that the differences they depict—even when they appear large —may be, and usually are, unreliable differences, that the score scales used for the several tests in the profile may not be comparable, that the several measures which show on the profile may have the appearance of being highly independent measures when, in fact, many of them may be highly correlated—in short, that the apparent clarity and efficiency of a test score profile is really an illusion covering up all sorts of traps and pitfalls in score interpretation which even the most wary can scarcely avoid. Yet the profile chart is still in much demand and in wide use, primarily, I suppose, because it is extraordinarily convenient. Mere administrative convenience is hardly sufficient justification for hiding confusion under a false coat of simplicity. Good test interpretation takes mental effort, a bit of imagination and some willingness to cope with complexity.

A seventh misconception is that interest inventories measure some kind of basic orientation of a student irrespective of the kinds of experiences to which he has been or will be exposed. Let me cite just one example. A presumably well-trained guidance counselor in a high school where the large majority of students go on to college was confronted by a girl with top-notch scholastic standing in all of the college preparatory subjects. Her parents were college-trained people, had always expected their daughter would go to a liberal arts college; the daughter had always enthusiastically entertained the same idea. The counselor, however, was apparently bewitched by one of the girl's scores on an interest inventory which indicated her major interest was in clerical work. Disregarding all the other evidence, the counselor insisted that the girl was unfitted for the work of a liberal arts college and would be happy only in a secretarial school. Tears on the part of the child, anger on the part of the parents and hell-to-pay all around. Certainly interest test scores are useful in promoting thought and self-analysis, but certainly also the tests are scarcely capable of probing deeply enough into an individual's past and future to warrant anything approaching the dogmatism which characterized this counselor.

The eighth misconception is that on a personality test an individual reveals deep and permanent temperamental characteristics of which he himself may be unaware. I suppose there is nothing about the whole testing business that frightens me more than this. Anyone close to the research in personality testing who has any critical sense at all knows that we have still barely scratched the surface of a field whose dimensions are still far from defined. To put it perhaps a little too strongly, personality tests—the inventories, the projective tests, all of them—are scarcely beyond the tea-leaf-reading stage. To be sure, there is some interesting—even exciting—research going on in the area, but none of it yet adds up to tests that can be trusted as evidence leading to important decisions about children.

There are four major weaknesses in personality tests. First, they purport to measure traits such as introversion-extroversion, neurotic tendency, gregariousness, tolerance for ambiguity, and the like—all of which are highly fuzzy concepts, to say the least, and for none of which there are any agreed-upon definitions. There is not even any general agreement on what we mean by the word "personality" itself. How can you describe or classify a person meaningfully with a test whose scores do not themselves have any clear or rigorous meaning?

Secondly, it is characteristic of current personality tests that the behavior they sample is essentially superficial nonsignificant behavior. By this I mean when a subject answers such a question as "Do you often daydream?" his response of "Yes" or "No" may well be nothing more than a purely random phenomenon quite unconnected with any of his habitual behavior tendencies. The whole essence of the measurement problem is to secure reliable samples of human behavior under standardized conditions which will have strong correlates with the universe of behavior an individual habitually exhibits in his waking life. The personality tests currently available have yet to demonstrate that they can provide such samples.

Thirdly, even if we were able to establish some meaningful personality traits, we still know little or nothing about their stability. We still don't know whether an introvert at age fifteen may not turn into an extrovert by the time he is twenty-two.

Finally, of course, practically all personality tests can be faked. I proved to my own satisfaction how fakable such tests are when I gave one to a class I was once teaching. I asked the students to take a personality inventory twice—once to prove that they were thoroughly well adjusted people and once to prove that they were ready for a mental institution. The first set of scores showed that the whole class was a bunch of apple-cheeked extroverts; the second set showed that they were all nuts.

Please do not misunderstand me. I take a very dim view of current personality tests, and I think the general public is being much too frequently taken in by the mumbo-jumbo that goes with them. On the other hand, I am very much in favor of as much solid research as we can possibly get into the fundamental dynamics of human behavior, for we shall never be in full command of the educational process until we have far more understanding than we now have of what makes children tick. There are glimmerings of hope, but we are not out of the woods yet, and who can tell when we will be? In the meantime, let's not kid ourselves by putting our trust in gimmicks.

The ninth and final misconception is this: that a battery of tests can tell all one needs to know in making a judgment about a student's competence, present and potential, and about his effectiveness as a human being. The fact is that no test or series of tests now available is capable of giving the total picture of any child. Tests can illuminate many areas of his development, suggest something about his strengths and weaknesses, show in certain respects how he stands among his peers. But there are still many important aspects of learning and human development where we must still rely upon the observation and judgment of teachers if we are to get something that approaches a complete description of the child as a functioning individual. There are subtle but supremely important human elements in the teaching-learning situation that no combination of tests yet devised is able to capture. Such elements are elusive, but if ever we lose sight of them, the educational process in all its ramifications will become something less than the exciting human enterprise it should always be.

These are the nine misconceptions which I think most frequently lead to wide misuse of tests and test results. Some of our brasher critics have argued that, since tests are so widely misused, they do constitute a menace to sound education and therefore should be abolished. This argument is specious. It is the same as saying that automobiles should be abolished because they are a menace to human life when reckless drivers are at the wheel. Or it is the same as saying that teachers should be abolished because too many of them make psychometric hash out of marks and test scores.

In any case, I think it is highly unlikely that tests will be abolished any more than that textbooks will be abolished. Too many schools have discovered that, menace or not, they cannot operate effectively without them. The problem is not one of doing away with tests and testing but of getting people to use tests intelligently. When this happens testing will cease to be a mere administrative convenience or, worse still, a burden on the souls of teachers and pupils; it will become an effective instrument for vitalizing the total educational process and for helping to insure that in these days of sky-rocketing enrollments the individual pupil will not be lost in the shuffle.

31.

ERNEST O. MELBY

IT'S TIME FOR SCHOOLS
TO ABOLISH THE MARKING SYSTEM

The marking system is damaging in its impact on the education of our children. It should go the way of the hickory stick and dunce cages. It should be abandoned at all levels of education.

Our marking system is no longer relevant to the needs and educational programs of our society. It says nothing meaningful about a pupil. It glosses over exceptional effort on the part of some pupils and lack of effort on the part of others. It says nothing about the most important outcomes of education. It leads us to measure the outcomes of our educational programs in terms of what people know, when we ought to be measuring them in terms of what people are and are in the process of becoming. It tells us a little about what the pupil has done to the subject he studies but nothing about what his study of the subject has done to him. We think we must use this worn-out system to motivate pupils, but all the studies I have seen show that marks have no motivating effect.

But the marking system is not only irrelevant and mischievous. It is destructive. It destroys the self-concepts of millions of children every year. Note the plight of the deprived child. He often enters school at six with few of the preschool experiences that the middle-class children bring to school. We ask him to learn to read. He is not ready to read. We give him a low mark—we repeat the low mark for each marking period—often for as long as the child remains in school. At the end of perhaps the ninth grade, the child drops out of school. What has he learned? He has learned he cannot learn. We have told him so several dozen times. Why should he think otherwise?

We have lied to him. He can learn. If we were worth our salt as teachers and as a school, we should have taught him he can learn. We

From *Nation's Schools*, 77 (1966), 104. Reprinted with permission of the author and publisher.

should have asked him to do things he can do, not what we know he can't do. Every day we should have sent him home with more confidence in himself, liking himself better than when he came in.

But don't tell me it's only the deprived who suffer from our marking system. All children are injured. They are injured because they are induced to seek the wrong goals—to be satisfied when their performance reaches a given level, rather than when they have done their best. They are injured because they develop a dislike for subjects in which they get a low grade, literature, for example. Often these dislikes are lifelong. Think of all the college graduates and high school graduates who dislike mathematics, for example. The low grade they received told them they were deficient in mathematical ability when most often they were merely the victims of bad teaching.

When I say these things about our obsolete marking system, someone always asks "What shall we tell the parents about the child?" "What shall we report to the university?" My answer is let us be both informative and conducive to the growth of the pupil's self-concept. Let us describe his growth in meaningful terms that are really descriptive of the pupil's effort, unique qualities, interests, attitudes, and behaviors. As for standards, we should evaluate each pupil in terms of his own capacity and growth, not in comparison with others, who are very different. A slow learner may become a better self-actualizing person than a fast learner.

We should be engaged with parents in the joint undertaking of helping the pupil to grow as a self-actualizing person. Our marking system injures the self-concepts of many children and is an obstacle to self-actualization. As for university entrance, from four years of high school experience, we should be able to decide what kind of post high school education the student should undertake. We either recommend him to a state university or junior college. On what basis?

When you go to a doctor for a history and physical check-up, the doctor writes constantly as you talk, describing your condition. He accumulates your medical history. He does not give you an A or a C. He does not use meaningless terms which blot out your individuality. He uses descriptive language which, when he reads it, causes you to come alive as a unique person—in health terms.

Why can't we in education do the same? Why do we bury the observations of a pupil's teachers over a dozen years in meaningless symbols? Why do we ignore the specific judgments of all the teachers who worked hard with the pupil and had much to pass on both to parents and the next teacher?

In American schools today perhaps a third of the children get very little in effective education. What is worse, their experience in school destroys their self-confidence. On a nationwide basis we are belatedly coming to grips with the problem. We are trying many plans. But, unless we abandon our crude and destructive marking system, nothing else we do will have much value.

CHAPTER ELEVEN

The Culturally Deprived Child

WHAT EXACTLY IS A CULTURALLY OR SOCIALLY DISADVANTAGED CHILD? Is he intellectually inferior to the mainstream of American youth, or is his handicap a product of our social and educational system? How can the U.S. public school system, with its middle-class environment, effectively cope with children from diverse cultural and socio-economic backgrounds?

We must begin with the basic assumption (which, of course, is supported by law) that all children are entitled to the benefits of a public education. This means that school authorities must no longer encourage poor, black, dissident, unlikable, or unsophisticated youth to leave school early, or, as the only other alternative, allow them to experience teacher indifference and classroom failure.

A popular liberal response to cultural deprivation was based on the assumption that the school should force-feed the deprived child until he is brought up to the standards of the dominant, middle-class society. This paternalistic strategy is being challenged by many, especially with respect to the black child. William Labov presents the position that the black child has a culture of his own, of considerable worth and complexity. The so-called deprived child is not deficient, just different. After studying the language of the black ghettoes, he concluded that the problem of ghetto children lies not in any verbal deficits but in the relationship between black children and the school system. The critical element in this relationship is the language of the ghetto. Labov discovered characteristics of black English vernacular that are far too subtle for detection in ordinary contact with the language. Black English, he maintains, is a rich, expressive language in its own right, not a substandard ver-

325

sion of English. Once the teacher understands the nature of this language, he will begin to understand the ghetto child's cognitive and perceptual world.

Recent research suggests that black children comprehend information and encode it into their memory in their most familiar dialect. The schools require these children to translate their thoughts into standard English when writing or speaking. This may account for the fact that many black children appear to learn more slowly in school surroundings than one would expect. It may also lead to lower achievement, especially on timed tests. Perhaps the schools should be more concerned about the rate of improvement in black children's performance than about their levels of achievement. Thus, not only the nature of black language, as described by Labov, but also its function in the child's world must be taken into account when evaluating the achievement and verbal skills of the culturally disadvantaged.

The analysis by Labov has important implications because it puts the black child in a new perspective, one that requires innovative teaching practices. Also, it goes far toward answering Jensen, Herrndon, Galton, Shockley, and others who believe that heredity is substantially more important than environmental forces in determining intelligence.

Because the deprived child has been made to feel so alien in the school system, he can easily develop negative feelings toward the school and toward himself. Most research studies have underscored the supposedly poor self-concepts of low socio-economic youth—especially blacks. Generally, self-concept has been shown to be related to measures of general and test anxiety, ethnicity, achievement measures, and socio-economic factors. Frerichs' well-designed study of black sixth-graders in Chicago's inner city found that low self-concept was not all-pervasive but was related to school achievement. In other words, if these disadvantaged children did well in school, they also tended to feel good about themselves, regardless of social-class handicaps or IQ level. This underscores the importance of success in school as it relates to a child's feelings about himself.

The problems involved in the education of Spanish-speaking youth appear to be even more complex. As Justin points out, discrimination against the Mexican-American child is based on a host of factors: socio-economic status, skin color, language, cultural traits and customs, and religion. Further complicating this problem is the fact that Mexican-Americans have preferred to hold to their Mexican ways and Spanish language. Justin reminds us that America never has been especially kind to ethnic groups that resisted assimilation.

Cultural deprivation as an obstacle to learning is not solely a problem of blacks or Spanish-speaking children. In fact, the majority of culturally deprived children are lower-social-class whites. But these youth present motivational problems that schools have always had, which relate to the conflict of social-class values and attitudes in the predominantly middle-class public school. The education of children from ethnic and racial minorities constitutes a far more complex challenge, for it involves cultural as well as social-class conflict.

RECOMMENDED READING

F. P. Bazeli. 1971. "Educating Teachers for the Inner City." In P. A. Dionisopoulos (ed.), *Racism in America* (DeKalb, Ill.: Northern Illinois University Press). Realistic and practical insights into the classroom environment that prospective teachers can expect to experience in inner city schools, with the focus on the learning styles of the children.

R. R. Butters. 1972. "A Linguistic View of Negro Intelligence," *The Clearing House* 46(5), 259–63. A well-documented plea for increasing the teacher's awareness of the nature of Black culture and Black English, with a rebuttal to current studies linking genetics to I.Q. scores of Black youth.

D. Drake. 1973. "Culture and Education: Mexican-American and Anglo-American," *The Elementary School Journal* 74(2), 97–105. A review of research on the personal and learning styles of Mexican children, with recommendations for ways to foster a greater sense of self-worth in children from the Spanish culture.

J. D. Finn. 1972. "Expectation and the Educational Environment," *Review of Educational Research* 42, 387–410. A summary of current studies of the "Hawthorne Effect," the extent to which teachers' perceptions of disadvantaged children influence classroom achievement.

K. R. Johnson. 1970. "The Culturally Disadvantaged—Slow Learners or Different Learners?" *Journal of Secondary Education* 45(1), 43–47. An objective argument against current efforts to teach the culturally disadvantaged student as if he or she were only a slow learner, without consideration of cultural factors.

R. S. Moore, R. D. Moon and D. R. Moore. 1972. "The California Report: Early Schooling for All?" *Phi Delta Kappan* 53(10), 615–21. A criticism of the conventional wisdom regarding the value of pre-school intervention programs for culturally deprived children; cites numerous studies that suggest that many children are not helped by early pre-schooling outside the home.

W. Raspberry. 1970. "Should Ghettoese Be Accepted?" *Today's Education* 59(4), 30–31, 61–62. A balanced, point-by-point discussion of the values of teaching standard English as a second language, *vs.* the need for ghetto and Spanish-speaking children to concentrate on acquiring the verbal skills that will help them get ahead in American society.

H. Schueler. 1965. "The Teacher of the Disadvantaged," *Journal of Teacher Education* 16(2), 174–80. An underscoring of the need for the teacher to understand the environment from which the disadvantaged child comes and to develop skill in human relations, particularly as they affect the attitudes and behaviors of his students.

32.

WILLIAM LABOV

ACADEMIC IGNORANCE AND BLACK INTELLIGENCE

In the past decade, a great deal of federally sponsored research has been devoted to the educational problems of children in ghetto schools. To account for the poor performance of children in these schools, educational psychologists have tried to discover what kind of disadvantage or defect the children are suffering from. The viewpoint which has been widely accepted and used as the basis for large-scale intervention programs is that the children show a cultural *deficit* as a result of an impoverished environment in their early years. A great deal of attention has been given to language. In this area, the deficit theory appears as the notion of "verbal deprivation": black children from the ghetto area are said to receive little verbal stimulation, to hear very little well-formed language, and as a result are impoverished in their means of verbal expression. It is said that they cannot speak complete sentences, do not know the names of common objects, cannot form concepts or convey logical thoughts.

Unfortunately, these notions are based upon the work of educational psychologists who know very little about language and even less about black children. The concept of verbal deprivation has no basis in social reality; in fact, black children in the urban ghettos receive a great deal of verbal stimulation, hear more well-formed sentences than middle-class children, and participate fully in a highly verbal culture; they have the same basic vocabulary, possess the same capacity for conceptual learning, and use the same logic as anyone else who learns to speak and understand English. The myth of verbal deprivation is particularly dangerous because it diverts the attention from real defects of our educational system to imaginary defects of the child; and as we shall see, it leads its sponsors inevitably to the hypothesis of the genetic inferiority of black children, which the verbal-deprivation theory was designed to avoid.

The deficit theory attempts to account for a number of facts that are known to all of us: that black children in the central urban ghettos do badly on all school subjects, including arithmetic and reading. In reading, they average more than two years behind the national norm. Furthermore, this lag is cumulative, so that they do worse comparatively in the fifth grade than in the first grade. The information available suggests that this bad performance is correlated most closely with socioeconomic status. Segregated ethnic groups, however, seem to do worse than others: in particular, Indian, Mexican-American, and black children.

We are obviously dealing with the effects of the caste system of American society—essentially a "color-marking" system. Everyone recognizes this. The question is, By what mechanism does the color bar prevent children from learning to read? One answer is the notion of "cultural deprivation" put forward by Martin Deutsch and others: the black children are said to lack the favorable factors in their home environment which enable middle-class children to do well in school. These factors involve the development, through verbal interaction with adults, of various cognitive skills, including the ability to reason abstractly, to speak fluently, and to focus upon long-range goals. In their publications, the psychologists Deutsch, Irwin Katz, and Arthur Jensen also recognize broader social factors. However, the deficit theory does not focus upon the interaction of the black child with white society so much as on his failure to interact with his mother at home. In the literature we find very little direct observation of verbal interaction in the black home; most typically, the investigators ask the child if he has dinner with his parents, and if he engages in dinner-table conversation with them. He is also asked whether his family takes him on trips to museums and other cultural activities. This slender thread of evidence is used to explain and interpret the large body of tests carried out in the laboratory and in the school.

The most extreme view which proceeds from this orientation—and one that is now being widely accepted—is that lower-class black children have no language at all. Some educational psychologists first draw from the writings of the British social psychologist Basil Bernstein the idea that "much of lower-class language consists of a kind of incidental 'emotional accompaniment' to action here and now." Bernstein's views are filtered through their strong bias against all forms of working-class behavior, so that Arthur Jensen, for example, sees middle-class language as superior in every respect—as "more abstract, and necessarily somewhat more flexible, detailed and subtle." One can proceed through a range of such views until one comes to the practical program of Carl Bereiter, Siegfried Engelmann, and their associates. Bereiter's program for an academically oriented preschool is based upon the premise that black children must have a language which they can learn, and their empirical findings that these children come to school without such a language. In his work with four-year-old black children from Urbana, Illinois, Bereiter reports that their communication was by gestures, "single words," and "a series of badly connected words or phrases," such as *They mine* and *Me got juice*. He reports that black children could not ask questions, that "without exaggerating . . . these four-year-olds could make no statements of any kind." Furthermore, when these children were asked, "Where is the book?" they did not know enough to look at the table where the book was lying in order to answer. Thus Bereiter concludes that the children's speech forms are nothing more than a series of emotional cries, and he decides to treat them "as if the children had no language at all." He identifies their speech with his interpretation of Bernstein's restricted code: "The language of culturally deprived children . . . is not merely an underdeveloped version of standard English, but is a basically non-logical mode of expressive behavior." The basic program of his preschool is to teach them a new language devised by Engelmann, which consists of a limited series of questions and answers such as *Where is the squirrel / The squirrel is in the tree*. The children will not be punished if they use their vernacular speech on the playground, but they will not be allowed to use it in the schoolroom. If they should answer the question "Where is the squirrel?" with the illogical vernacular form "In the tree," they will be reprehended by various means and made to say, "The squirrel is in the tree."

Linguists and psycholinguists who have worked with black children are likely to dismiss this view of their language as utter nonsense. Yet there is no reason to reject Bereiter's observations as spurious: they were certainly not made up. On the contrary, they give us a very clear view of the behavior of student and teacher which can be duplicated in any classroom. Our own research is done outside the schools, in situations where adults are not the dominant force, but on many occasions we have been asked to help analyze the results of research into verbal deprivation in such test situations.

Here, for example, is a complete interview with a black boy, one of hundreds carried out in a New York City school. The boy enters a room where there is a large, friendly white interviewer, who puts on the table in front of him a block or a fire engine, and says, "Tell me everything you can about this!" (The interviewer's further remarks are in parentheses.)

> [*12 seconds of silence*]
>
> (What would you say it looks like?)
> [*8 seconds of silence*]

A spaceship.
(Hmmmmm.)

> [*13 seconds of silence*]

Like a je-et.

> [*12 seconds of silence*]

Like a plane.

> [*20 seconds of silence*]

(What color is it?)
Orange. [*2 seconds*] An' whi-ite. [*2 seconds*] An' green.

> [*6 seconds of silence*]

(An' what could you use it for?)

> [*8 seconds of silence*]

A je-et.

> [*6 seconds of silence*]

(If you had two of them, what would you do with them?)

> [*6 seconds of silence*]

Give one to some-body.
(Hmmm. Who do you think would like to have it?)

> [*10 seconds of silence*]

Cla-rence.
(Mm. Where do you think we could get another one of these?)
At the store.
(Oh-ka-ay!)

We have here the same kind of defensive, monosyllabic behavior which is reported in Bereiter's work. What is the situation that produces it? The child is in an asymmetrical situation where anything he says can, literally, be held against him. He has learned a number of devices to *avoid* saying anything in this situation, and he works very hard to achieve this end.

If one takes this interview as a measure of the verbal capacity of the child, it must be as his capacity to defend himself in a hostile and threatening situation. But unfortunately, thousands of such interviews are used as evidence of the child's total verbal capacity, or more simply his verbality: it is argued that this lack of "verbality" *explains* his poor performance in school.

The verbal behavior which is shown by the child in the test situation quoted above is not the result of ineptness of the interviewer. It is rather the result of regular sociolinguistic factors operating upon adult and child in this asymmetrical situation. In our work in urban ghetto areas, we have often encountered such behavior. For over a year Clarence Robins had worked with the Thunderbirds, a group of boys ten to twelve years old who were the dominant preadolescent group in a low-income project in Harlem. We then decided to interview a few younger brothers of the Thunderbirds, eight to nine years old. But our old approach didn't work. Here is an extract from the interview between Clarence and eight-year-old Leon L.:

CR: What if you saw somebody kickin' somebody else on the ground, or was using a stick, what would you do if you saw that?
LEON: Mmmm.
CR: If it was supposed to be a fair fight—
LEON: I don't know.
CR: You don' know? Would you do anything? . . . huh? I can't hear you.
LEON: No.
CR: Did you ever see somebody get beat up real bad?
LEON: . . . Nope ? ? ?
CR: Well—uh—did you ever get into a fight with a guy?
LEON: Nope.
CR: That was bigger than you?
LEON: Nope.
CR: You never been in a fight?
LEON: Nope.
CR: Nobody ever pick on you?
LEON: Nope.
CR: Nobody ever hit you?
LEON: Nope.
CR: How come?
LEON: Ah 'on' know.
CR: Didn't you ever hit somebody?
LEON: Nope.
CR: [*incredulous*] You never hit nobody?
LEON: Mhm.
CR: Aww, ba-a-a-be, you ain't gonna tell me that.

This nonverbal behavior occurs in a relatively *favorable context* for adult-child interaction, since the adult is a black man raised in Harlem, who knows this particular neighborhood and these boys very well. He is a skilled interviewer who has obtained a very high level of verbal response with techniques developed for a different age level, and has an extraordinary advantage over most teachers or experimenters in these respects. But even his skills and personality are ineffective in breaking down the social constraints that prevail here.

When we reviewed the record of this interview with Leon, we decided to use it as a test of our own knowledge of the sociolinguistic factors which control speech. We made the following changes in the social situation; in the next interview with Leon, Clarence:

1. Brought along a supply of potato chips, changing the "interview" into something more in the nature of a party.
2. Brought along Leon's best friend, eight-year-old Gregory.
3. Reduced the height imbalance. When Clarence got down on the floor of Leon's room, he dropped from 6 feet, 2 inches to 3 feet, 6 inches.
4. Introduced taboo words and taboo topics, and proved to Leon's surprise that one can say anything into our microphone without any fear of retaliation. It did not hit or bite back. The result of these changes is a striking difference in the volume and style of speech.

[The tape is punctuated throughout by the sound of potato chips.]
CR: Is there anybody who says, "Your momma drink pee"?
⎰LEON: *[rapidly and breathlessly]* Yee-ah!
⎱GREG: Yup.
LEON: And your father eat doo-doo for breakfas'!
CR: Ohhh! *[laughs]*
LEON: And they say your father—your father eat doo-doo for dinner!
GREG: When they sound on me, I say "C.B.M."
CR: What that mean?
⎰LEON: Congo booger-snatch! *[laughs]*
⎱GREG: Congo booger-snatcher! *[laughs]*
GREG: And sometimes I'll curse with "B.B."
CR: What that?
GREG: Oh, that's a "M.B.B." Black boy. *[Leon crunching on potato chips]*
GREG: 'Merican Black Boy.
CR: Oh.
GREG: Anyway, 'Mericans is same like white people, right?
LEON: And they talk about Allah.
CR: Oh, yeah?
GREG: Yeah.

CR: What they say about Allah?
⎰ LEON: Allah—Allah is God.
⎱ GREG: Allah—
CR: And what else?
LEON: I don't know the res'.
GREG: Allah i—Allah is God, Allah is the only God, Allah—
LEON: Allah is the *son* of God.
GREG: But can he make magic?
LEON: Nope.
GREG: I know who can make magic?
CR: Who can?
LEON: The God, the real one.
CR: Who can make magic?
GR   The son of po'—(CR: Hm?) I'm sayin' the po'k chop God! He
        only a po'k chop God! [*Leon chuckles*]

The "nonverbal" Leon is now competing actively for the floor; Gregory and Leon talk to each other as much as they do to the interviewer. The monosyllabic speaker who had nothing to say about anything and could not remember what he did yesterday has disappeared. Instead, we have two boys who have so much to say that they keep interrupting each other, who seem to have no difficulty in using the English language to express themselves.

One can now transfer this demonstration of the sociolinguistic control of speech to other test situations, including IQ and reading tests in school. It should be immediately apparent that none of the standard tests will come anywhere near measuring Leon's verbal capacity. On these tests he will show up as very much the monosyllabic, inept, ignorant, bumbling child of our first interview. The teacher has far less ability than Clarence Robins to elicit speech from this child; Clarence knows the community, the things that Leon has been doing, and the things that Leon would like to talk about. But the power relationship in a one-to-one confrontation between adult and child are too asymmetrical. This does not mean that some black children will not talk a great deal when alone with an adult, or that an adult cannot get close to any child. It means that the social situation is the most powerful determinant of verbal behavior and that an adult must enter into the right social relation with a child if he wants to find out what a child can do. This is just what many teachers cannot do.

The view of the black speech community which we obtain from our work in the ghetto areas is precisely the opposite from that reported by Deutsch, Engelmann, and Bereiter. We see a child bathed in verbal stimulation from morning to night. We see many speech events which depend upon the competitive exhibitions of verbal skills: singing, sounding, toasts, rifting, louding—a whole range of activities in which the individual gains status through his use of language. We see the younger child trying to acquire these skills from older children—hanging around on the outskirts of the older peer groups, and imitating this behavior. We see, however, no connection between verbal skill at the speech events characteristic of the street culture and success in the schoolroom; which says something about classrooms rather than about a child's language.

There are undoubtedly many verbal skills which children from ghetto areas must learn in order to do well in school, and some of these are indeed characteristic of middle-class verbal behavior. Precision in spelling, practice in handling abstract symbols, the ability to state explicitly the meaning of words, and a richer knowledge of the Latinate vocabulary may all be useful acquisitions. But is it true that *all* of the middle-class verbal habits are functional and desirable in school? Before we impose middle-class verbal style upon children from other cultural groups, we should find out how much of it is useful for the main work of analyzing and generalizing, and how much is merely stylistic—or even dysfunctional. In high school and college, middle-class children spontaneously complicate their syntax to the point that instructors despair of getting them to make their language simpler and clearer.

Our work in the speech community makes it painfully obvious that in many ways working-class speakers are more effective narrators, reasoners, and debaters than many middle-class speakers, who temporize, qualify, and lose their argument in a mass of irrelevant detail. Many academic writers try to rid themselves of the part of middle-class style that is empty pretension, and keep the part necessary for precision. But the average middle-class speaker that we encounter makes no such effort; he is enmeshed in verbiage, the victim of sociolinguistic factors beyond his control.

I will not attempt to support this argument here with systematic quantitative evidence, although it is possible to develop measures which show how far middle-class speakers can wander from the point. I would like to contrast two speakers dealing with roughly the same topic: matters of belief. The first is Larry H., a fifteen-year-old core member of another group, the Jets. Larry is being interviewed here by John Lewis, our participant-observer among adolescents in South Central Harlem.

JL: What happens to you after you die? Do you know?
LARRY H: Yeah, I know. (What?) After they put you in the ground, your body turns into—ah—bones, an' *shit*.
JL: What happens to your spirit?

LARRY: Your spirit—soon as you die, your spirit leaves you. (And where does the spirit go?) Well, it all depends. (On what?) You know, like some people say if you're good an' shit, your spirit goin' t'heaven . . . 'n' if you bad, your spirit goin' to hell. Well, *bullshit!* Your spirit goin' to hell anyway, good or bad.

JL: Why?

LARRY: Why? I'll tell you why. 'Cause, you see, doesn' nobody really know that it's a God, y'know, 'cause, I mean I have seen black gods, pink gods, white gods, all color gods, and don't nobody know it's really a God. An' when they be sayin' if you good, you goin' t'heaven, tha's *bullshit,* 'cause you ain't goin' to no heaven, 'cause it ain't no heaven for you to go to.

Larry is a gifted speaker of the Black English vernacular (BEV) as opposed to standard English (SE). His grammar shows a high concentration of such characteristic BEV forms as negative inversion [*don't nobody know*], negative concord [*you ain't goin' to no heaven*], invariant *be* [when they be sayin'], dummy *it* for SE *there* [*it ain't no heaven*], optional copula deletion [*if you're good . . . if you bad*], and full forms of auxiliaries [*I have seen*]. The only SE influence in this passage is the one case of *doesn't* instead of the invariant *don't* of BEV. Larry also provides a paradigmatic example of the rhetorical style of BEV: he can sum up a complex argument in a few words, and the full force of his opinions comes through without qualification or reservation. He is eminently quotable, and his interviews give us a great many concise statements of the BEV point of view. One can almost say that Larry speaks the BEV culture.

It is the logical form of this passage which is of particular interest here. Larry presents a complex set of interdependent propositions which can be explicated by setting out the SE equivalents in linear order. The basic argument is to deny the twin propositions:

(A) If you are good, (B) then your spirit will go to heaven.
(not A) If you are bad. (C) then your spirit will go to hell.

Larry denies (B), and allows that if (A) or (not A) is true, (C) will follow. His argument may be outlined:

(1) Everyone has a different idea of what God is like.
(2) Therefore nobody really knows that God exists.
(3) If there is a heaven, it was made by God.
(4) If God doesn't exist, he couldn't have made heaven.
(5) Therefore heaven does not exist.

    (6) You can't go somewhere that doesn't exist.
(not B) Therefore you can't go to heaven.
    (C) Therefore you are going to hell.

This hypothetical argument is not carried on at a high level of seriousness. It is a game played with ideas and counters, in which opponents use a wide variety of verbal devices to win. There is no personal commitment to any of these propositions, and no reluctance to strengthen one's argument by bending the rules of logic as in the (2, 4) sequence. But if the opponent invokes the rules of logic, they hold. In John Lewis' interviews, he often makes this move, and the force of his argument is always acknowledged and countered within the rules of logic.

JL: Well, if there's no heaven, how could there be a hell?
LARRY: I mean—ye-eah. Well, let me tell you, it ain't no hell, 'cause this is hell right here, y'know! (This is hell?) Yeah, this is hell right here!

Larry's answer is quick, ingenious, and decisive. The application of the (3-4-5) argument to hell is denied, since hell is here, and therefore conclusion (not B) stands. These are not ready-made or preconceived opinions, but new propositions devised to win the logical argument in the game being played. The reader will note the speed and precision of Larry's mental operations. He does not wander, or insert meaningless verbiage. It is often said that the nonstandard vernacular is not suited for dealing with abstract or hypothetical questions, but in fact, speakers of the BE vernacular take great delight in exercising their wit and logic on the most improbable and problematical matters. Despite the fact that Larry H. does not believe in God, and has just denied all knowledge of him, John Lewis advances the following hypothetical question:

JL: . . . But, just say that there is a God, what color is he? White or black?
LARRY: Well, if it is a God . . . I wouldn' know what color, I couldn' say—couldn' nobody say what—
JL: But now, jus' suppose there was a God—
LARRY: Unless'n they say . . .
JL: No, I was jus' sayin' jus' suppose there is a God, would he be white or black?
LARRY: . . . He'd be white, man.
JL: Why?
LARRY: Why? I'll tell you why. 'Cause the average whitey out here

got everything, you dig? And the nigger ain't got *shit*, y'know? Y'unnerstan'? So—um—for—in order for *that* to happen, you know it ain't no black God that's doin' that *bullshit*.

No one can hear Larry's answer to this question without being convinced of being in the presence of a skilled speaker with great "verbal presence of mind," who can use the English language expertly for many purposes.

Let us now turn to the second speaker, an upper-middle-class, college-educated black man being interviewed by Clarence Robins in our survey of adults in South Central Harlem.

CR: Do you know of anything that someone can do, to have someone who has passed on visit him in a dream?

CHAS. M.:   Well, I even heard my parents say that there is such a thing as something in dreams, some things like that, and sometimes dreams do come true. I have personally never had a dream come true. I've never dreamt that somebody was dying and they actually died (Mhm), or that I was going to have ten dollars the next day and somehow I got ten dollars in my pocket. (Mhm.) I don't particularly believe in that, I don't think it's true. I do feel, though, that there is such a thing as—ah—witchcraft. I do feel that in certain cultures there is such a thing as witchcraft, or some sort of *science* of witchcraft; I don't think that it's just a matter of believing hard enough that there is such a thing as witchcraft. I do believe that there is such a thing that a person can put himself in a state of *mind* (Mhm), or that—er—something could be given them to intoxicate them in a certain—to a certain frame of mind—that—that could actually be considered witchcraft.

Charles M. is obviously a "good speaker" who strikes the listener as well-educated, intelligent, and sincere. He is a likable and attractive person—the kind of person that middle-class listeners rate very high on a scale of "job suitability" and equally high as a potential friend. His language is more moderate and tempered than Larry's; he makes every effort to qualify his opinions, and seems anxious to avoid any misstatements or overstatements. From these qualities emerges the primary characteristic of this passage—its *verbosity*. Words multiply, some modifying and qualifying, others repeating or padding the main argument. The first half of this extract is a response to the initial question on dreams, basically:

(1) Some people say that dreams sometimes come true.
(2) I have never had a dream come true.

(3) Therefore I don't believe (1).

This much of Charles M.'s response is well directed to the point of the question. He then volunteers a statement of his beliefs about witchcraft which shows the difficulty of middle-class speakers who (a) want to express a belief in something but (b) want to show themselves as judicious, rational, and free from superstitions. The basic proposition can be stated simply in five words:

> But I believe in witchcraft.

However, the idea is enlarged to exactly one hundred words, and it is difficult to see what else is being said. The vacuity of this passage becomes more evident if we remove repetitions, fashionable words, and stylistic decorations:

> But I believe in witchcraft.
> I don't think witchcraft is just a belief.
> A person can put himself or be put in a state of mind that is witchcraft.

Without the extra verbiage and the OK words like *science, culture,* and *intoxicate,* Charles M. appears as something less than a first-rate thinker. The initial impression of him as a good speaker is simply our long-conditioned reaction to middle-class verbosity: we know that people who use these stylistic devices are educated people, and we are inclined to credit them with saying something intelligent.

Let us now examine Bereiter's own data on the verbal behavior of the black children he dealt with. The expressions *They mine* and *Me got juice* are cited as examples of a language which lacks the means for expressing logical relations—in this case characterized as "a series of badly connected words." In the case of *They mine,* it is apparent that Bereiter confuses the notions of logic and explicitness. We know that there are many languages of the world which do not have a present copula, and which conjoin subject and predicate complement without a verb. Russian, Hungarian, and Arabic may be foreign, but they are not by the same token illogical. In the case of black English we are not dealing with even this superficial grammatical difference, but rather with a low-level rule which carries contraction one step further to delete single consonants representing the verbs *is, have,* or *will.* We have yet to find any children who do not sometimes use the full forms of *is* or *will,* even though they may frequently delete it.

The deletion of the *is* or *are* in black English is not the result of erratic or illogical behavior: it follows the same regular rules as standard English contraction. Wherever standard English can contract, black children use either the contracted form or (more commonly) the deleted zero form. Thus *They mine* corresponds to standard English *They're mine*, not to the full form *They are mine*. On the other hand, no such deletion is possible in positions where standard English cannot contract: just as one cannot say *That's what they're* in standard English, *That's what they* is equally impossible in the vernacular we are considering. The appropriate use of the deletion rule, like the contraction rule, requires a deep and intimate knowledge of English grammar and phonology. Such knowledge is not available for conscious inspection by native speakers: the rules we have worked out for standard contraction have never appeared in any grammar, and are certainly not a part of the conscious knowledge of any standard English speakers. Nevertheless, the adult or child who uses these rules must have formed at some level of psychological organization clear concepts of "tense marker," "verb phrase," "rule ordering," "sentence embedding," "pronoun," and many other grammatical categories which are essential parts of any logical system.

Bereiter's reaction to the sentence *Me got juice* is even more puzzling. If Bereiter believes that *Me got juice* is not a logical expression, it can only be that he interprets the use of the objective pronoun *me* as representing a difference in logical relationship to the verb; that the child is in fact saying that "the juice got him" rather than "he got the juice"! If on the other hand the child means "I got juice," then this sentence form shows only that he has not learned the formal rules for the use of the subjective form *I* and oblique form *me*.

Bereiter shows even more profound ignorance of the rules of discourse and of syntax when he rejects "In the tree" as an illogical or badly formed answer to "Where is the squirrel?" Such elliptical answers are of course used by everyone, and they show the appropriate deletion of subject and main verb, leaving the locative which is questioned by *wh + there*. The reply *In the tree* demonstrates that the listener has been attentive to and apprehended the syntax of the speaker. Whatever formal structure we wish to write for expressions such as *Yes* or *Home* or *In the tree*, it is obvious that they cannot be interpreted without knowing the structure of the question which preceded them, and that they presuppose an understanding of the syntax of the question. Thus if you ask me, "Where is the squirrel?" it is necessary for me to understand the sentence from an underlying form which would otherwise have produced *The squirrel is there*. If the child had answered *The tree*, or *Squirrel the tree*, or *The in tree*, we would then assume that he did not understand the syntax of the full form, *The squirrel is in the tree*. Given the data that Bereiter presents, we cannot conclude that the child has no grammar, but only that the investigator does not understand the rules of grammar. It does not necessarily do any harm to use the full form *The squirrel is in the tree,* if one wants to make fully explicit the rules of grammar which the child has internalized. Much of logical analysis consists of making explicit just that kind of internalized rule. But it is hard to believe that any good can come from a program which begins with so many misconceptions about the input data. Bereiter and Engelmann believe that in teaching the child to say *The squirrel is in the tree* or *This is a box* and *This is not a box,* they are teaching him an entirely new language, whereas in fact they are only teaching him to produce slightly different forms of the language he already has.

If there is a failure of logic involved here, it is surely in the approach of the verbal-deprivation theorists, rather than in the mental abilities of the children concerned. We can isolate six distinct steps in the reasoning which has led to programs such as those of Deutsch, Bereiter, and Engelmann:

1. The lower-class child's verbal response to a formal and threatening situation is used to demonstrate his lack of verbal capacity, or verbal deficit.

2. This verbal deficit is declared to be a major cause of the lower-class child's poor performance in school.

3. Since middle-class children do better in school, middle-class speech habits are said to be necessary for learning.

4. Class and ethnic differences in grammatical form are equated with differences in the capacity for logical analysis.

5. Teaching the child to mimic certain formal speech patterns used by middle-class teachers is seen as teaching him to think logically.

6. Children who learn these formal speech patterns are then said to be thinking logically, and it is predicated that they will do much better in reading and arithmetic in the years to follow.

This article has proved that numbers 1. and 2. at least are wrong. However, it is not too naïve to ask, What is wrong with being wrong? We have already conceded that black children need help in analyzing language into its surface components, and in being more explicit. But there are, in fact, serious and damaging consequences of the verbal-deprivation theory. These may be considered under two headings: (a) the theoretical bias and (b) the consequences of failure.

It is widely recognized that the teacher's attitude toward the child is an important factor in the latter's success or failure. The work of Robert Rosenthal on "self-fulfilling prophecies" shows that the progress of children in the early grades can be dramatically affected by a single random labeling of certain children as "intellectual bloomers." When the everyday language of black children is stigmatized as "not a language at all" and "not possessing the means for logical thought," the effect of such a labeling is repeated many times during each day of the school year. Every time that a child uses a form of BEV without the copula or with negative concord, he will be labeling himself for the teacher's benefit as "illogical," as a "nonconceptual thinker." This notion gives teachers a ready-made, theoretical basis for the prejudice they may already feel against the lower-class black child and his language. When they hear him say *I don't want none* or *They mine*, they will be hearing, through the bias provided by the verbal-deprivation theory, not an English dialect different from theirs, but the primitive mentality of the savage mind.

But what if the teacher succeeds in training the child to use the new language consistently? The verbal deprivation theory holds that this will lead to a whole chain of successes in school, and that the child will be drawn away from the vernacular culture into the middle-class world. Undoubtedly this will happen with a few isolated individuals, just as it happens in every school system today for a few children. But we are concerned not with the few but the many, and for the majority of black children the distance between them and the school is bound to widen under this approach.

The essential fallacy of the verbal-deprivation theory lies in tracing the educational failure of the child to his personal deficiencies. At present, these deficiencies are said to be caused by his home environment. It is traditional to explain a child's failure in school by his inadequacy; but when failure reaches such massive proportions, it seems necessary to look at the social and cultural obstacles to learning and the inability of the school to adjust to the social situation.

The second area in which the verbal-deprivation theory is doing serious harm to our educational system is in the consequences of this failure and the reaction to it. As Operation Head Start fails, the interpretations which we receive will be from the same educational psychologists who designed this program. The fault will be found, not in the data, the theory, or the methods used, but rather in the children who have failed to respond to the opportunities offered them. When black children fail to show the significant advance which the deprivation theory predicts, it will be further proof of the profound gulf which separates their mental processes from those of civilized, middle-class mankind.

A sense of the failure of Operation Head Start is already commonplace. Some prominent figures in the program have reacted to this situation by saying that intervention did not take place early enough. Bettye M. Caldwell notes that the research literature of the last decade dealing with social-class differences has made abundantly clear that all parents are not qualified to provide even the basic essentials of physical and psychological care to their children.

The deficit theory now begins to focus on the "long-standing patterns of parental deficit" which fill the literature. "There is, perhaps unfortunately," writes Caldwell, "no literacy test for motherhood." Failing such eugenic measures, she has proposed "educationally oriented day care for culturally deprived children between six months and three years of age." The children are returned home each evening to "maintain primary emotional relationships with their own families," but during the day they are removed "hopefully to prevent the deceleration in rate of development which seems to occur in many deprived children around the age of two to three years."

There are others who feel that even the best of the intervention programs, such as those of Bereiter and Engelmann, will not help the black child no matter when they are applied—that we are faced once again with the "inevitable hypothesis" of the genetic inferiority of the black people. Arthur Jensen, for example, in his *Harvard Educational Review* paper (1969), argues that the verbal-deprivation theorists with whom he has been associated—Deutsch, Whiteman, Katz, Bereiter—have been given every opportunity to prove their case and have failed. This opinion forms part of the argument leading to his overall conclusion that the "preponderance of the evidence is . . . less consistent with a strictly environmental hypothesis than with the genetic hypothesis."

Jensen argues that the middle-class white population is differentiated from the working-class white and black population in the ability for "cognitive or conceptual learning," which Jensen calls Level II intelligence as against mere "associative learning," or Level I intelligence.

Thus Jensen found that one group of middle-class children were helped by their concept-forming ability to recall twenty familiar objects that could be classified into four categories: animals, furniture, clothing, or foods. Lower-class black children did just as well as middle-class children with a miscellaneous set, but showed no improvement with objects that could be so organized.

But linguistic data strongly contradict Jensen's conclusion that these children cannot fully form concepts. In the earliest stages of language learning, children acquire "selectional restrictions" in their use of words. For example, they learn that some verbs take ANIMATE subjects, but others only INANIMATE ones: thus we say *The machine breaks* but not *John breaks; The paper tears* but not *George tears*. A speaker of English must master such subtle categories as the things which *break*, like *boards, glasses,* and *ropes*; things which *tear*, like *shirts*, *paper*, and *skin*; things which *snap*, like *buttons*, *potato chips*, and *plastic*, and other categories which *smash*, *crumple*, or *go bust*.

In studies of Samoan children, Keith Kernan has shown that similar rules are learned reliably long before the grammatical particles that mark tense, number, and so on. The experimentation on free recall that Jensen reports ignores such abilities, and defines intelligence as a particular way of answering a particular kind of question within a narrow cultural framework. Recent work of anthropologists in other cultures is beginning to make some headway in discovering how our tests bias the results so as to make normally intelligent people look stupid. Michael Cole and his associates gave the same kind of free recall tests to Kpelle speakers in Liberia. Those who had not been to school—children or adults—could only remember eight or ten out of the twenty and showed no "clustering" according to categories, no matter how long the trials went on. Yet one simple change in the test method produced a surprising change. The interviewer took each of the objects to be remembered and held it over a chair: one chair for each category, or just one chair for all categories. Suddenly the Kpelle subjects showed a dramatic improvement, remembered seventeen to eighteen objects, and matched American subjects in both recall and the amount of clustering by categories. We do not understand this effect, for we are only beginning to discover the subtle biases built in our test methods which prevent people from using the abilities that they display in their language and in everyday life.

Linguists are in an excellent position to demonstrate the fallacies of the verbal-deprivation theory. All linguists agree that nonstandard dialects are highly structured systems; they do not see these dialects as accumulations of errors caused by the failure of their speakers to master standard English. When linguists hear black children saying *He crazy* or *Her my friend* they do not hear a "primitive language." Nor do they believe that the speech of working-class people is merely a form of emotional expression, incapable of relating logical thought. Linguists therefore condemn with a single voice Bereiter's view that the vernacular can be disregarded.

There is no reason to believe that any nonstandard vernacular is in itself an obstacle to learning. The chief problem is ignorance of language on the part of all concerned. Our job as linguists is to remedy this ignorance: Bereiter and Engelmann want to reinforce it and justify it. Teachers are now being told to ignore the language of black children as unworthy of attention and useless for learning. They are being taught to hear every natural utterance of the child as evidence of his mental inferiority. As linguists we are unanimous in condemning this view as bad observation, bad theory, and bad practice.

That educational psychology should be strongly influenced by a theory so false to the facts of language is unfortunate; but that children should be the victims of this ignorance is intolerable. If linguists can contribute some of their valuable knowledge and energy toward exposing the fallacies of the verbal-deprivation theory, we will have done a great deal to justify the support that society has given to basic research in our field.

33.   ALLEN H. FRERICHS

SELF-ESTEEM OF THE DISADVANTAGED AND SCHOOL SUCCESS

Lack of success experiences in school is a central concern for the education of inner-city blacks. As one source states, "the most important factor in educational achievement is that the child must repeatedly experience success in his school endeavors" (Backman and Secord, 1968). The notion that disadvantaged youngsters have negative self-images and that others have similar attitudes toward them is frequently set forth (Tannenbaum, 1967). On the other hand, Soares found that the underprivileged living in lower social class areas have higher self-perceptions than their middle-class counterparts. This report suggests that the disadvantaged are functioning satisfactorily for the adults with whom they have contact; whereas, the middle-class youngsters are working under great pressure to do better in a very competitive framework (Soares and Soares, 1969). Interestingly, other findings indicate that when inner-city children are placed in integrated schools they develop a lower self-image (Levine, 1968). The children may find it more difficult to achieve academic and social success in the midst of the more highly competitive middle-class environment.

Furthermore, evidence shows that a positive self-image enhances the degree of school success. Bledsoe (1964) found that the self-esteem and

From *Journal of Negro Education*, 40:2 (Spring, 1971), 117–20.

academic achievement of fourth- and sixth-grade boys were shown to be positively correlated to a significant degree.

DEFINITION AND DESIGN

The study reported in this manuscript sought to find out whether level of self-esteem of black children living in a lower social class neighborhood was associated with academic success in school.* Self-esteem was defined as the degree to which a person views himself in terms of what he and other persons important to him consider socially desirable. It was decided to test sixth-grade children. They have completed the grade levels in which youngsters have clearly developed patterns of school success. The children are in a critical stage for they are now entering the adolescent world. They

TABLE I

MEAN AND RANGE SCORES OF THE THREE PUPIL CATEGORIES

	School Factors		
	IQ	GPA	Reading
Top one-third			
Mean	108	3.12	6.65
Range	97 to 142	2.67 to 3.67	6.14 to 10.89
Bottom one-third			
Mean	80	1.67	3.94
Range	61 to 86	1.40 to 2.00	3.00 to 4.41

are beginning to search for an identity in the midst of rapid physical change and their need for widening interrelationships is also a growing concern for them. The children face these changes in schools that are not equipped to meet their academic needs, and this frustrating environment is apt to lead them to give up trying to achieve.

The subjects of the study were 78 black, sixth graders living in a large midwestern inner-city area. They attended a neighborhood elementary

* For a discussion of the definition and measurement of school social status, see Robert E. Herriott and Nancy Hoyt St. John, *Social Class and the Urban School* (New York: John Wiley and Sons, Inc. 1966), pp. 13–34.

school and practically all the children were from lower social class homes. The subjects lived in a low-rent-tenement housing area with a typical family income of less than $4,000. The scale used to measure self-esteem of the children was adapted from the Self-Esteem Scale developed by Rosenberg (1965). The adaptation consisted of revising sentence structure and vocabulary based on reactions of students similar to the subjects in this study. The school-related factors tested were IQ test scores, grade point average (GPA) for the academic year, and standardized achievement reading scores.

The upper and lower one-third distributions of the population for each of the three school factors were grouped into separate categories. The mean score and range of each group is shown in Table I. The GPA was computed on a four point scale with 4.00 being the highest possible average, and the reading levels were grade equivalent scores. Twenty-six students were in each category, except 27 were in the low GPA group due to a score tie at the top end of the category.

The difference between each of the three high and low groups (see Table I) as to their mean scores on the Self-Esteem Scale was measured by a two-tailed t-test. The Scale scores could range from a high of 6 to a low of 0. Children with a positive self-esteem would score high on the scale.

FINDINGS

The findings of the differences among the three groups are listed in Table II.

TABLE II

MEAN SELF-ESTEEM SCORES OF THE THREE CATEGORIES OF PUPILS

Groups	Mean Self-Esteem Score	t-Score	P
High GPA	4.55	3.468	< 0.01
Low GPA	3.37		
High Reading	4.50	2.53	< 0.02
Low Reading	3.65		
High IQ	3.97	1.401	N.S.
Low IQ	3.81		

The results show that the youngsters who had a high degree of school success as measured by GPA and reading level scored significantly higher on the Self-Esteem Scale than did the less successful students. Interestingly, the Scale scores did not significantly differentiate between the high and low IQ groups. IQ scores measure general experiences as compared to the more specific school-oriented GPA and reading levels. Also, IQ scores are not as visible to the youngsters. On the other hand, reading plays a central role in school learning, and teacher marks are clearly evident throughout the school year.

It was decided to compare the children who were in both the high GPA and reading groups with those in both the low GPA and reading categories on the basis of Self-Esteem Scores. Again a two-tailed t-test was used to measure the difference between the two groups. Nineteen students were in each group. The difference between the two categories was statistically significant at the 0.01 level. This emphasizes to an even greater degree that good performance in school is associated with high self-esteem.

CONCLUSION

This study supports the research that shows a relationship between a positive self-esteem and school success. The need for children to have a strong self-esteem is all the more urgent when it is well-known that to change an established negative self-image is exceedingly difficult (Korman, 1967). Two very critical school factors—teacher grades and reading level—were closely associated with the level of self-esteem of the children. Both of these factors are subject to change if the schools and the public are willing to exert some effort in this direction. Instructors are reluctant to evaluate their grading procedures, but this area needs closer study. Teacher marks are constant reminders to the youngsters about their success or failure in

TABLE III

Groups	Mean Self-Esteem Score	T-Score	P
High GPA — High Reading	4.47		
		2.79	< 0.01
Low GPA — Low Reading	3.42		

school. It appears reasonable that disadvantaged children are also receiving parental pressure on grades for everyone knows the worth of A, B, C, and D on report cards. The reading problem in inner-city schools is a well-publicized scandal, and this report just adds to the depressing list of evidence that surrounds reading instruction and materials for the disadvantaged.

The findings of this report lend support to the idea that education is a means of developing pride and self-worth among disadvantaged blacks. This study shows that blacks from a homeogeneous inner-city neighborhood can achieve a high degree of self-esteem if they know they are academically successful in school. It also indicates that the academically successful disadvantaged black children perceive themselves in a positive manner, just as their white suburban middle-class counterparts do. The problem is that the black children who are not successful in school face such overwhelming odds when compared with the more affluent children. Yet, greater school success is needed for all disadvantaged if the black community of the future is to have the strong sense of worth and pride to cope with the rapidly changing American society.

REFERENCES

Carl W. Backman and Paul F. Secord. *A Social Psychological View of Education* (New York: Harcourt, Brace and World, Inc., 1968), p. 47.

J. C. Bledsoe. "Self Concepts of Children and Their Intelligence, Achievement, Interests and Anxiety," *Journal of Individual Psychology.* XX (May, 1964), 55–58.

Abraham K. Korman. "Self Esteem as a Moderator of the Relationship Between Self-Perceived Abilities and Vocational Choice," *Journal of Applied Psychology* LI, 1. (February, 1967), 65–67.

Daniel U. Levine. "The Integration-Compensatory Education Controversy," *The Educational Forum,* XXXII (March, 1968), 323–32.

Morris Rosenberg. *Society and the Adolescent Self Image* (Princeton, New Jersey: Princeton University Press, 1965), pp. 12–16.

Anthony T. Soares and Louise M. Soares. "Self-Perception of Culturally Disadvantaged Children," *American Educational Research Journal,* VI, No. 1 (January, 1969), 42.

Abraham J. Tannenbaum. "Social and Psychological Considerations in the Study of the Socially Disadvantaged." In P. A. Witty (ed.), *The Educationally Retarded and Disadvantaged,* Sixty-sixth yearbook, Part I. (Chicago, Ill.: National Society for the Study of Education, 1967), pp. 45–63.

34

NEAL JUSTIN

CULTURE CONFLICT AND
MEXICAN-AMERICAN ACHIEVEMENT

It appears that the least-educated citizens in the U.S. are the Mexican-Americans. Nearly 1,000,000 Spanish-speaking children in the Southwest never will go beyond the eighth grade (Department of Rural Education, 1966). In some areas, up to 90% of the Mexican-Americans fail to complete high school (Chilcott, 1968).

What are some of the causes of deprivation and failure among the Mexican-Americans? Four closely related areas are of concern: language, discrimination, lower socioeconomic status, and culture.

The most obvious identifying characteristic of the Mexican-Americans is their language. The Tucson Survey of the Teaching of Spanish to the Spanish-Speaking by the National Education Association placed great emphasis on the influence of the Spanish language and its use as related to academic achievement (Department of Rural Education, 1966). In fact, the language barrier currently is given more attention than any other factor affecting Mexican-American achievement.

The use of the Spanish language by the Mexican-Americans has played a definite role in the isolation and discrimination of these people by the Anglos. The preservation of the Spanish language has been interpreted by the dominant group as "a persistent symbol and instrument of isolation" (Broom and Shevsky, 1952). While the Anglo tends to consider the use of Spanish as an indication of foreignness, the Mexican-Americans consider it a symbol of their unity and loyalty to *La Raza* (Madsen, 1965).

In his discussion on barriers to Mexican integration, Officer (1951) stated that "the greatest hindrance to complete cultural assimilation of Tucson's Mexicans is the language problem." Apparently, this opinion has been shared widely by educators, if we can judge from the adjustments made for Mexican-Americans in curricula.

There is evidence that the language barrier, although important, may

Reprinted from *School & Society*, January, 1970, by permission of the author and publisher.

be overrated. Available research shows that language need not be an insurmountable barrier to the academic and intellectual achievement of youngsters who come from foreign language-speaking homes (Tyler, 1956). Henderson points out that "the current mania for structural linguistics as a panacea for educational problems of Mexican-American children is another example of a language centered curriculum emphasis" (Henderson, 1966). Moreover, he shows that the Mexican-American pupils who spoke the most Spanish also could speak the most English. Nevertheless, most educators consider the language barrier as the major obstacle to the Mexican-American's success and achievement in school.

There is substantial evidence, however, that the greater emphasis should be placed on the socio-cultural problems of the Mexican-American. The ugly factors of discrimination and prejudice have played and continue to play an important role in keeping the Mexican-Americans in a subservient position. The Mexican coming to the U.S. is confronted with a double problem of prejudice. In Mexico, class discrimination is commonplace, but discrimination against color is unusual. Here, unfortunately, discrimination and prejudice commonly are based on both class and color.

Prejudice against the Mexicans and Mexican-Americans in the Southwest generally follows this pattern: lack of job opportunities, lack of educational opportunities, segregation in housing, lack of equality before the law, and various kinds of social discrimination (Burma, 1954). Among the major reasons for this situation are a strong history of lower socioeconomic status, darker skin color, language, conflicting cultural traits and customs, and religion.

For the most part, discrimination against the Mexican-Americans is subtle in nature. While the Mexican-American enjoys all the legal rights of citizenship, he is the victim of extralegal discrimination. It is this special type of discrimination which led Tuck (1946) to call her book *Not with the Fist*. In it, she comments: "Rather than having the job of battering down a wall, the Mexican-American finds himself entangled in a spider web, whose outlines are difficult to see but whose clean, silken strands hold tight" (p. 198).

The inferior socioeconomic status of the Mexican-Americans may be greater than most Americans would like to admit. Although Mexican-Americans are found in all walks of life, an examination of the 1960 U.S. Census data shows that they occupy an overwhelmingly large position in the lower-ranking occupations. Almost 75% of the Mexican-Americans are employed as manual workers. This concentration in the unskilled occupations has had a severe effect upon their incomes. The 1960 Census data indicate that the Mexican-Americans in the Southwest earned between $1,000 and $2,000 less per year than did the Anglo unskilled workers. In all of the five Southwestern states, the average incomes of Mexican-Americans are far below that of the population in general.

The greatest barrier to the acculturation, assimilation, and achievement of the Mexican-Americans probably is culture conflict. Other immigrant groups to the U.S. have felt the blow of discrimination (Mack, 1963). The Chinese, Jews, Italians, Irish, Polish, etc., are common examples. However, the faster the immigrant group moves toward adopting the customs and language of the dominant culture, the less discrimination they seem to experience. Madsen (1965) believes that any ethnic group that fails to show a maximum faith in America, science, and progress will be subject to discrimination. It would be additionally difficult for the members of this group to assimilate if they are physically distinguishable, if they use a foreign language, and if they hold to cultural ways that are not compatible with the dominant culture (Madsen).

Unlike other immigrant groups, the Mexican-Americans have preferred to hold to their Mexican cultural ways and Spanish language. This may be attributed to their close proximity to Mexico.

The question then arises: Which of the Mexican-American cultural ways is in greatest conflict with the dominant Anglo culture? Extensive and careful review of numerous studies by Angell, Chilcott, Kluckhohn, Madsen, Simmons, Strodtbeck, Zintz, and others indicates that there are two Mexican cultural characteristics that are the mirror image of the Anglo culture. These are concerned with feelings of personal control (fatalism) and delay of gratification (future orientation). Could it be that even third- or fourth-generation Mexican-American students are actually more fatalistic and present-time oriented than their Anglo peers? What might this mean in terms of curriculums and cultural conflict?

To answer these questions, the writer set up an exploratory study at the College of Education, University of Arizona (Justin, 1969). A total of 168 male, Mexican-American seniors and 209 male, Anglo seniors were selected randomly for testing at four urban Tucson high schools. A special questionnaire, adapted from a similar instrument developed by the Institute of Behavioral Science, University of Colorado, was revised, judged for content validity, tested for reliability, and then administered to the sample population.

The statistical analysis of the data pertaining to the two cultural characteristics of delayed gratification (future orientation) and feelings of personal control (fatalism) provided a number of significant differences when the means of the two sample populations were subjected to independent tests.

The Mexican-Americans showed a mean of 6.90 on the measurement of their feelings of personal control, while their Anglo peers had a mean of 8.51. Measurement of the tendency to delay gratification provided a mean of 3.99 for the Mexican-Americans and 4.63 for the Anglos. In each case, the differences between these means were significant at the .05 level.

Marked contrast, therefore, is seen between the Mexican-Americans and the Anglos. The Mexican-Americans are significantly lacking in feelings of personal control and concern with delayed gratification when compared to their Anglo peers. These findings indicate that, whatever culture change has taken place among the second-, third-, and fourth-generation Mexican-Americans, it has not been great with reference to these two characteristics. It also should be considered that the students selected for this study were second-semester seniors and were, therefore, a select group of achievers in relation to their many peers who already have dropped out of school. One may have good cause to wonder how great these differences would have been if the study had been done with junior high students. Even with these very conservative results, the Mexican-Americans are seen to be significantly different from their Anglo peers.

Assuming that most of our school curricula are constructed by Anglos who apparently have significantly different orientations to life, then what over-all effect does this have upon the Mexican-American youngsters? What conflicts may be built into the curriculum that could permeate the whole subculture of education. Kneller provides a word to the wise when he asserts that, before we can attain our educational goals, we must be aware of the internalized antagonisms of the culture that may thwart the efforts of teachers. Could it be that our Anglo-dominated curricula inadvertently thwart the efforts of both the Mexican-American students and their teachers? There may be a good reason to consider the findings of this study. Perhaps, we should examine the appropriateness of our curricula as they apply to the Mexican-American student in particular.

REFERENCES

Leonard Broom and Eshref Shevsky, "Mexicans in the United States . . . A Problem in Social Differentiation," *Sociology and Social Research*, 36: 153, January–February, 1952.

John H. Burma, *Spanish-Speaking Groups in the United States* (Durham, N.C.: Duke University Press, 1954), p. 107.

John H. Chilcott, "Some Perspectives for Teaching First Generation Mexican-Americans," in John H. Chilcott, et al., eds., *Readings in the Socio-Cultural Foundations of Education* (Belmont, Calif.: Wadsworth, 1968), p. 359.

Department of Rural Education, National Education Association, *The Invisible Minority*, Report of the National Education Association-Tucson Survey on the Teaching of Spanish to the Spanish-Speaking (Washington: National Education Association, 1966), p. 6.

Ronald W. Henderson, *Environmental Stimulation and Intellectual Development of Mexican-American Children: An Exploratory Study* (unpublished Ph.D. dissertation, University of Arizona, 1966), pp. 142, 144.

Neal Justin, *The Relationships of Certain Socio-Cultural Factors to the Academic Achievement of Male, Mexican-American, High School Seniors* (unpublished Ed.D. dissertation, University of Arizona, 1969).

George F. Kneller, *Educational Anthropology: An Introduction* (New York: Wiley, 1965), p. 14.

Raymond W. Mack, *Race, Class and Power* (New York: American Book Co., 1963), p. 118.

William Madsen, *The Mexicans of South Texas* (New York: Holt, Rinehart, and Winston, 1965), pp. 1, 106.

James Officer, "Barriers to Mexican Integration in Tucson," *The Kiva.* 17: 7, May, 1951.

Ruth Tuck, *Not with the Fist* (New York: Harcourt, Brace, 1946), p. 198.

Leona Elizabeth Tyler, *The Psychology of Human Differences* (New York: Appleton-Century-Crofts, 1956), p. 305.

PART 4

Humanism in Education

CHAPTER TWELVE

Humanism in the Classroom

A COMMON CRITICISM OF EDUCATION is that it is too prescriptive in style and too cognitive in content. A very articulate core of critics, calling themselves "humanists," are scrutinizing current school practices with intensity. Their concern is not whether Johnny can read or write or understand set theory, but whether children are deriving *personal meaning* from schooling. Although there is a wide range of outlooks among contemporary humanists, this concern for personal meaning is a pervasive theme in their works. William Bridges, in his article, says, "What is lost is learning to do and to perceive in ways that unlock the innate human potential and provide the person with a great deal of pleasure." Bridges denies that humanists have a bias against information. He says humanistic education should not be dichotomized into personal meaning and the acquisition of information; the two domains are intermingled; one should not preclude the other. Although Bridges discusses humanism in reference to older students, the principles he advocates are applicable to children as young as first grade. In fact, some humanists insist that humanistic teaching should begin precisely at early school levels. These are the impressionable years, when self-concepts are formed. In the past few years there have been numerous books and articles showing how humanism can be applied within almost every subject area.

Humanism is not a recent invention. Many school practices of the past were intended to make school a more personal experience for the child—e.g., role-playing in speech classes—but they were described in less romantic terms than those used by humanists. Also, current organizational practices (advanced by pragmatic school administrators), such as flexible scheduling, open spaces in school buildings, and "schools without walls," are at least intended to "humanize" learning. Finally, it should be reaffirmed from time to time that good teachers have always been humanistic. They evolved toward the high art of teaching probably by sheer intuition. The creative teacher responds instinctively to a child's feelings and needs.

Humanists offer a convincing argument. After all, how could anyone argue that education should *not* involve personal meaning and involvement? Isn't direct, sensory experience the best—and *only*—teacher? Yes, perhaps, except that an imperative of modern, dynamic societies is that the child must also learn what is not immediately available to his senses, in order to prepare himself for the future. Behaviorists (and others) contend that most humanistic teaching practices will result in the child's opting only for what most interests him personally, and which he can learn on his own terms. What he *really* needs, for his own good, is systematic, positive help from a teacher.

This argument is advanced in forceful but good-humored fashion by B. F. Skinner in "The Free and Happy Student." Obviously, there is truth on both sides of the argument. Indeed, any clear distinction between humanists and behaviorists becomes blurred when one considers the requirements for developing the whole child. Each teacher must determine for himself how he can facilitate the student's acquisition of knowledge and skills while making the learning personally relevant and significant.

If one could be assured that behavioral techniques would always be used in humane ways for ethical purposes, some of the fear and criticism might be alleviated. The behaviorist has the heavy responsibility of accepting and maintaining the principle that no educational goal is worth the price if it can be achieved only by taking away the learner's freedom of action. But the humanist, too, has the responsibility of stating his goals in clear and workable terms.

It is appropriate, we believe, to end a collection of research and point-of-view articles in educational psychology with two papers on the issue of freedom versus control. Most educational innovations involve in one way or another the question of whether students will be teacher-directed or expected to direct themselves. The prospective teacher must decide for himself where he stands regarding this complex issue and how his position will help him to become a better teacher.

RECOMMENDED READING

G. I. Brown. 1971. *Human Teaching for Human Learning: An Introduction to Confluent Education* (New York: Viking Press). A general overview of humanistic psychology applied to both elementary and secondary schools, in conversational, anecdotal form.

C. Buhler. 1971. "Basic Theoretical Concepts of Humanistic Psychology," *American Psychologist* 26(4), 278–86. A comprehensive presentation of the psychological principles that support the integration of humanistic, affective objectives with the subject matter goals of the classroom.

G. Castillo. 1974. *Left-handed Teaching: Procedures in Affective Education* (New York: Praeger). Applications of humanism to classroom instruction, ranging from sensory awareness activities to affective experiences with concepts from the physical environment.

L. P. Porter. 1972. "The Movement Movement," *Today's Education* 61(5), 42–44. Humanism in the classroom through the medium of physical education.

J. G. Saylor and J. L. Smith (eds.). 1971. *Removing Barriers to Humaneness in the High School* (Washington, D.C.: Association for Supervision and Curriculum Development, National Education Association). Various applications of humanistic psychology to the teaching of high school subjects.

A. B. Smith. 1973. "Humanism and Behavior Modification: Is There a Conflict?" *The Elementary School Journal* 74(2), 59–67. A reconciliation of the advantages of directing student learning by reinforcement with the need to foster self-determination and personal growth.

B. B. Stretch. 1970. "Rise of the Free School," *Saturday Review* June, 76–79. Growth trends and an analysis of the major problems encountered by free schools.

G. Weinstein and M. D. Fantini. 1970. *Toward Humanistic Education: A Curriculum of Affect* (New York: Praeger). The report of a Ford Foundation–supported project aimed at developing methods and materials relevant to the affective needs of elementary school children, especially low-income and Black youth.

35.

WILLIAM BRIDGES

THOUGHTS ON HUMANISTIC EDUCATION, OR IS *TEACHING* A DIRTY WORD?

Ten years ago I was dismayed to hear Carl Rogers tell a Harvard audience, "Teaching is, for me, a relatively unimportant and vastly overvalued activity." At the time, I was just beginning full-time teaching and struggling to be a good teacher. Having read *On Becoming a Person*, I even

From *The Journal of Humanistic Psychology*, 13:1 (Winter, 1973).

fancied that I was something of a Rogerian in the way in which I conducted a literature class. I was pretty informal and supportive, but I was still *teaching*. Stop *teaching*? My God, better to stop breathing!

Yet, in the next several years, I slowly stopped "teaching." As a result of reading, workshops, and my own experimentation, I gradually shifted to the role of facilitator—the one who helps students learn what they want or need to learn without "teaching" it to them. At the same time, I began to acquire (as all those workshop brochures promised that I would) a sizable repertoire of techniques drawn from Gestalt therapy, encounter, psychosynthesis, sensitivity training . . . you know the list. Each semester a higher percentage of my class meetings included some unexpected "experience" for the students. Most of my classes continued to be literature classes in name, but more and more time was spent on ourselves and less and less on literature.

Having spent a lifetime being sensible, level-headed, reliable, highly organized, and uncontroversial, I was startled (and shyly pleased) to find myself coming to be known as controversial and even radical. My colleagues began to treat me with the mixture of interest and mistrust that might come the way of someone whose hair has turned white over night. Before long, I had a kind of a niche in the institution: There was the resident poet, the black militant, the ecology freak, and *me*.

I can't really say just when the whole thing began to pall, but I know that about a year ago I finally had to admit to myself that I wasn't at all clear any longer about what I was really doing in the classroom. What was my purpose? How were my classroom techniques serving that purpose? It was a very disturbing realization. Only a year earlier I was so sure of my vision of the educational promised land that I was ready to leave teaching entirely in favor of running The Center for Innovative Studies, an exciting but (fortunately) never-funded institute to set up programs to bring the *word* to the unredeemed. My *hubris* level at that time was high, and if it had all happened 2,500 years ago, the gods probably would have made me fall in love with a seal, thus making a complete fool out of me.

To reiterate, this past year has been very different indeed; it has been a whole series of grudging acknowledgments of some of the serious problems of nonteaching, as well as an awakening to some other possibilities that I had not explored. At the same time, as coordinator of the AHP Education Network, I have been talking and corresponding with many other teachers whose difficulties and desires are very like my own. It now appears crucial to take a critical look at some of the common assumptions about humanistic education, and this is precisely what I propose to do.

TRADITIONAL EDUCATION TODAY

The time is past when it is important just to turn teachers on and crack them loose from their unquestioned ways of doing things. Teachers in increasing numbers everywhere are already out of their ruts. It is astounding to find how many traditionally trained teachers—people who have used the same notes and class plans for years—are trying new and very unconventional approaches in their classrooms. From periodicals and books, from the example of free schools and free universities, from growth-center workshops and university extension courses come a flood of information on new classroom techniques. But in this welter of innovation some important questions are being bypassed.

Two of the key complaints against traditional education are (*a*) that it is prescriptively structured ("This is what you need to know, and this is how to learn it") and (*b*) that is it too exclusively cognitive in style and content ("Forget how you feel about it, just get the information accurate"). It is natural, then, that humanistic education has come to be associated with unstructured learning situations and the use of nonverbal techniques. The corollary of these characteristics of the humanistic classroom is the facilitator role for the teacher—the role of the "real" and unauthoritarian resource person who is there to help the students learn what they want to learn.

Put this way, there is hardly anything about the role that could be argued with. But, in fact, these ideas are full of various dilemmas and contradictions, some of which are elaborated upon in the following paragraphs.

1. There is an implicit conflict between the exhortation to be non-prescriptive and the desire to introduce to the class those wonderful "experiences" that one enjoys so much. For, actually, there is not much difference between saying, "Now, everyone shut your eyes and I'll take you on a fantasy trip," and the old business of "Read pages 345–378 and do the exercises on page 379." When pressed to explain the justification for the fantasy trip, I used to say that it was an interesting rewarding experience that would provide students with another dimension of knowing. This was a dishonest answer though. For some students they *weren't* interesting rewarding experiences. And the latter part of the answer is simply a more sophisticated way of saying that these experiences are good for them—which I believe to be true, but which is also just what my fourth-grade teacher used to say about drawing all those stinking little spirals in penmanship class.

2. There is also an implicit conflict between the humanistic ideal of working with students *where they are* (as the real individuals that they are right now) and the fact of laying a very heavy trip on them (a set of expectations that masquerade as total freedom). To say to a class, "What do you want to learn? This is your chance to explore something that really interests you," is also to say, "Your difficulties in this situation reflect your difficulties in dealing with freedom." Now, that's true; but how painful such freedom really is is seldom acknowledged by the classroom teacher. Instead, the impression is left that it is only hung-up people who can't deal with freedom (i.e., who have trouble with my class). If a teacher is really ready to take on the exploration of the person's resistances to full awareness and his anxieties over the implications for his life of absolute freedom, he is embarking on a long journey that quickly transforms the undertaking into something that he had better be more ready for than I was. Students are, of course, amazingly resilient as well as resourceful, so my concern is only partly for those for whom the class provides too little support in such an undertaking. My concern is also with the much greater number who size up the situation, find themselves unable or unwilling to risk so much, and then simply fake their way through the class with the same skill that they have faked their way through traditional courses for years. I have been startled to learn how many of my students have taken the latter route, saying and writing things that made me think that I was doing great things with them, when actually they were just figuring out what was appropriate to the situation and passing that off as their own experience.

3. The context in which it would be possible to freely explore this anxiety-laden experience would be a group context, and there are some classes led by some teachers that can profitably turn themselves into encounter or even therapy groups. For a while, I was willing to go this route and even encouraged it in my classes, but I do not do so now. There are many reasons for this decision. First, students enroll in classes for very different reasons (including its convenient meeting hour) from those which lead people to join groups. A person's presence in the class does not mean the same thing as his presence in a group, and there is not the same degree of commitment to the sort of honesty and openness that makes a group work. Second, my particular field of literature does not justify turning the class into an encounter group in the same way that a course in, for example, interpersonal behavior would. The students whose genuine desire to learn involves the field of literature would rightly feel upstaged when the focus of the class shifted permanently to the group itself. And third, I really don't want to lead a group; I want to teach literature, which brings us back to "teaching."

INFORMATIONAL BIAS

Is teaching really such a damaging operation as I thought when I became a facilitator? As I have puzzled over this question, I have realized that humanistic psychology really represents a blending of two traditions. One of them mistrusts teaching, emphasizing nondirective work with others. It grew out of the field of clinical psychology on a one-to-one basis. The other tradition grows out of the idea of the spiritual discipline and represents a way of working with initiates toward new kinds of insight into the nature of things. In our day of instant gurus, this latter stream often seems polluted. But it is still an important one, for there are simply some very rewarding and growthful things that a person will not discover on his own.

The question of how to help people learn is complicated by the fact that each of these two traditions within the humanistic fold is directed toward a different kind of "learning." Learning itself is a concept that covers quite different kinds of experiences. The facilitator role deals most adequately with two kinds of learning: the acquisition of information and personal learning ("I realize that I get anxious when I'm around angry people"). In each case, such learning demands assistance but not intrusion, and in neither case is it possible to impose one's own views without making the student's task more difficult. The teacher role, on the other hand, deals better with other kinds of learning, particularly those which involve training in a technique, procedure, or new kinds of discriminatory perception ("That blur on the X-ray plate is a rib, but *that* blur is a scar"). These distinctions between different kinds of learning are customarily distorted by our culture's bias toward the purely informational and the consequent tendency to convert things into informational form: "I am an obsessive person because of my early training"; "Clovis was a good king—true or false?" "To carve a leg of lamb, turn it so that . . ."

Perhaps I am the more conscious of this informational bias and the distortions of reality that it encourages because it is so strong in me that I am always running afoul of it. When I decided to learn to ski at the age of thirty, I did what only someone with a graduate-school education would do: I bought a book on skiing, read it through, buckled on my skis, and fell down. I was really offended at the thought that I needed a teacher, that I needed someone to say, "Hey, keep the weight on the downhill ski . . . tuck your tail in . . . bend your knees." I finally gave up and took classes, and I learned more than skiing in the process. I realized how different it is to do something and *at the same time* get instruction. In my literature classes, people did things outside of class and then brought them in for instruction (or rather they did until I grandly swore off instructing for a while). But productive learning just doesn't happen after the fact; you need it while you are doing the thing. You read a line of a poem and misunderstand a word, or don't hear the sound, or miss a metaphor, and if someone can say right at that moment, "Well, I thought that he was saying. . . ," then something productive happens. This, incidentally, is not the stimulus-response phenomenon that the teaching-machine people are always talking about, because it's not saying, "Wrong, try again." It is saying something more like, "Keep your weight on the downhill ski and see how much better you do when you turn." The payoff is not in getting the right piece of information, the teacher's approval, or the machine's methodical advance to the next question. It is finding that you can do something that *works*.

This informational bias of which I have been speaking has confused discussions of teaching by leaving the erroneous impression that there were basically only two kinds of learning: experiential and personal learning of the sort that goes on in therapy or in an encounter group, and the acquisition of information about the extrapersonal world. If you accept this view, it is natural to conclude that teaching gets in the way of learning because it predetermines the information and precludes intrapersonal encounter. But if you are seeking to work with the other kinds of learning that are left out of this falsely polarized picture—something beyond the facilitation of natural processes—some other sort of teaching is required. This is a crucial point because if humanistic education is falsely dichotomized into personal learning and the acquisition of information, a great deal is lost. What is lost is learning to do and to perceive in ways that unlock the innate human potential and provide the person with a great deal of pleasure.

This dichotomization of learning burdens the educational process in another way as well by suggesting that the solution must be found in the classroom rather than in the institution. If working with the student's authentic need to know is the basis of the humanistic endeavor, then the institution's task is to provide him with access to learning situations. Today's institutions don't do that. They provide him with access to "courses" —chunks of academic work that only faintly correspond to his actual situation. It would be interesting to speculate whether the heavy emphasis on warm and accepting teacher-student relations within the classroom doesn't result from the fact that so few of the students in a class have anything vital to relate to besides the teacher. This occurred to me recently when I asked for and received a lesson in tree pruning from a man who broke all the rules of humanistic education. He was judgmental, compulsive, and impersonal; he talked down to me, made light of my reactions, and taught me to prune an apple tree, which is what I wanted to learn. This apparently technical operation had deep personal significance for me, for it was part of my growing interest in a more land-related, self-sustaining, and integrated way of living. This interest is carrying me into fields of information and technique that I would have found terribly boring five years ago, fields on which books are written and in which universities offer courses. But if I were an undergraduate today, I would have to try to convert these interests into a schedule of classes that told me more than I wanted to know about subjects only vaguely related to my interests.

PROBLEMS OF HUMANISTIC TEACHING

Clearly, the problems facing the humanistic teacher come partly from his institutional situation. The student who is longing for a new mode of living naturally, and who wishes he knew how to prune an apple tree, shows up in my poetry class. I ask what he wants to learn about, and he says that he's into tree pruning. Well, I can be as unstructured as the next teacher, so he develops a project on tree pruning (in poetry, of course) and leads a class on it. But that falls flat because the class is made up of people who are into I Ching and black nationalism and creative writing and impeaching Nixon and astrology and computer programming. Of course, I can bring them together on a purely interpersonal level (except for the I Ching girl who doesn't relate well and the black nationalist who thinks that self-exploration is white, middle-class bullshit). And I can give them some growth-oriented experiences that fill up the class periods. But I can't really give them what they need, because the institution insists that we convert needs into three-unit, semester-long classes that don't conflict with one another. Until we can restructure institutions to become educational resource places, we will mistakenly, but understandably, be trying to do the impossible—make each individual classroom what the the institution ought to be.

I suspect that one reason so many out of my generation of teachers have been swayed toward this willingness to try to meet every student's needs is that we have lost our faith in the importance of what we have learned and of what we have to offer others. Traditional teachers, like my tree-pruning mentor, have a profound advantage on us in this matter. They care about and feel the importance of what they know. Often I mistrust them, feeling that the certainty is bought at the price of awareness, and sometimes I fall into the despair that William Butler Yeats must have felt when he wrote.

Things fall apart; the centre cannot hold;
Mere anarchy is loosed upon the world,
The blood-dimmed tide is loosed, and everywhere
The ceremony of innocence is drowned;
The best lack all conviction, while the worst
Are full of passionate intensity.

These lines remind me that what is needed is not faith in some subject or procedure or value system, but a centeredness, a rootedness in the place/time where we stand. They serve to make me remember that the drift I have experienced is not an uprootedness (for my old faith in what I knew was a rootless clinging) but a detachment from connections which provided safety though lacking sustenance. So I can see the drift in positive terms as the opportunity to home in on a genuine standpoint, the place from which my profession (which comes from the Latin word for confess or acknowledge) will be authentic.

As detachment from extrinsic values, this rootlessness provides the opportunity for a homecoming. Yet, it is also a state of anguish, and one that I and others have too often misrepresented and rationalized as a positive state in which we can help others without laying our trip on them. In fact, we too often lay a very heavy trip on others when we work with them in this condition. We are living vicariously through them as they search for the meaning that we have not ourselves been able to find. It is not just that we project our own confusions onto them in the name of liberating them from the false; it is that we project onto them the hope of and responsibility for finding the relation to reality that we ourselves cannot find.

The fault here does not by any means lie in the humanistic ideal of each person's discovery of his own angle of vision—an ideal that I dearly cherish. It is simply that the ideal provides an unfortunately convenient rationale for abandoning the learner to his own devices. If we are all lost, it is indeed a good idea to be lost together. But the value of the experience begins with the acknowledgment that it is in fact the case, not with misrepresenting it as a guided experiment in freedom and self-discovery.

The humanistic ideal in education is gravely endangered by this situation, but the ideal itself remains for me the only hope in a world where traditional value systems and the myths that embody them have lost their hold on our imaginations and, hence, their power to connect us to the living reality. The humanistic goal of self-knowledge and of what Emerson called "an original relation to the universe" can only be reached by providing people with several different kinds of educational opportunities. We must create institutions which are truly resource centers, networks of persons and libraries and nonwritten resources to which we can turn whenever we know what we need to learn. Profoundly alienated from ourselves, however, many of us do not yet know what we need, so we must devise ways in which to enable ourselves to recover that experiential center from which our own situations and their demands on us are revealed. To do this we must draw upon both of the great humanistic traditions mentioned earlier—the tradition that emphasizes nondirective assistance in discovering one's personal reality, and the tradition that emphasizes the masterly unfolding of new ways of doing and perceiving. Each path is perilous, the former liable to degeneration into abandonment, the latter liable to degeneration into authoritarian control. But the dangers come from misuse rather than use.

Had I been addressing this article to a traditionally oriented audience, I would have spent far more space on the dangers of the model of the teacher as master. It is all too obvious that for every teacher who errs in the direction of abandonment, ten err in the misuse of authority. Until recently it has seemed to me unnecessary to worry about a scale that was already so heavily weighted in the "wrong" direction: any change would be beneficial when things are so bad. But now I feel differently, and it is the very successes of the humanistic thrust that make me feel this way. It is time to set our own house in order, to stop measuring ourselves against an obviously decrepit status quo, and to begin to look critically at our own assumptions and accomplishments.

REFERENCE

C. Rogers. *Freedom to Learn.* Columbus, Ohio: Charles E. Merrill, 1969.

36.   B. F. SKINNER

THE FREE AND HAPPY STUDENT

His name is Emile. He was born in the middle of the eighteenth century in the first flush of the modern concern for personal freedom. His father was Jean-Jacques Rousseau, but he has had many foster parents, among them Pestalozzi, Froebel, and Montessori, down to A. S. Neill and

From *New York University Education Quarterly,* 4:2 (Winter, 1972), 2–6.

Ivan Illich. He is an ideal student. Full of goodwill toward his teachers and his peers, he needs no discipline. He studies because he is naturally curious. He learns things because they interest him.

Unfortunately, he is imaginary. He was quite explicitly so with Rousseau, who put his own children in an orphanage and preferred to say how he would teach his fictional hero; but the modern version of the free and happy student to be found in books by Paul Goodman, John Holt, Jonathan Kozol, or Charles Silberman is also imaginary. Occasionally a real example seems to turn up. There are teachers who would be successful in dealing with people anywhere—as statesmen, therapists, businessmen, or friends—and there are students who scarcely need to be taught, and together they sometimes seem to bring Emile to life. And unfortunately they do so just often enough to sustain the old dream. But Emile is a will-o'-the-wisp, who has lead many teachers into a conception of their role which could prove disastrous.

The student who has been taught *as if he were Emile* is, however, almost too painfully real. It has taken a long time for him to make his appearance. Children were first made free and happy in kindergarten, where there seemed to be no danger in freedom, and for a long time they were found nowhere else, because the rigid discipline of the grade schools blocked progress. But eventually they broke through—moving from kindergarten into grade school, taking over grade after grade, moving into secondary school and on into college and, very recently, into graduate school. Step by step they have insisted upon their rights, justifying their demands with the slogans that philosophers of education have supplied. If sitting in rows restricts personal freedom, unscrew the seats. If order can be maintained only through coercion, let chaos reign. If one cannot be really free while worrying about examinations and grades, down with examinations and grades! The whole establishment is now awash with free and happy students.

DROPPING OUT OF SCHOOL, DROPPING OUT OF LIFE

If they are what Rousseau's Emile would really have been like, we must confess to some disappointment. The Emile we know doesn't work very hard. "Curiosity" is evidently a moderate sort of thing. Hard work is frowned upon because it implies a "work ethic," which has something to do with discipline.

The Emile we know doesn't learn very much. His "interests" are evidently of limited scope. Subjects that do not appeal to him he calls irrelevant. (We should not be surprised at this since Rousseau's Emile, like the boys in Summerhill, never got past the stage of a knowledgeable

craftsman.) He may defend himself by questioning the value of knowledge. Knowledge is always in flux, so why bother to acquire any particular
stage of it? It will be enough to remain curious and interested. In any
case the life of feeling and emotion is to be preferred to the life of intellect; let us be governed by the heart rather than the head.

The Emile we know doesn't think very clearly. He has had little or
no chance to learn to think logically or scientifically and is easily taken
in by the mystical and the superstitious. Reason is irrelevant to feeling
and emotion.

And, alas, the Emile we know doesn't seem particularly happy. He
doesn't like his education any more than his predecessors liked theirs.
Indeed, he seems to like it less. He is much more inclined to play truant
(big cities have given up enforcing truancy laws), and he drops out as
soon as he legally can, or a little sooner. If he goes to college, he probably
takes a year off at some time in his four-year program. And after that his
dissatisfaction takes the form of anti-intellectualism and a refusal to support education.

Are there offsetting advantages? Is the free and happy student less aggressive, kinder, more loving? Certainly not toward the schools and teachers that have set him free, as increasing vandalism and personal attacks
on teachers seem to show. Nor is he particularly well disposed toward his
peers. He seems perfectly at home in a world of unprecedented domestic
violence.

Is he perhaps more creative? Traditional practices were said to suppress
individuality; what kind of individuality has now emerged? Free and
happy students are certainly different from the students of a generation
ago, but they are not very different from each other. Their own culture
is a severely regimented one, and their creative works—in art, music, and
literature—are confined to primitive and elemental materials. They have
very little to be creative with, for they have never taken the trouble to
explore the fields in which they are now to be front-runners.

Is the free and happy student at least more effective as a citizen? Is he
a better person? The evidence is not very reassuring. Having dropped out
of school, he is likely to drop out of life too. It would be unfair to let
the hippie culture represent young people today, but it does serve to clarify
an extreme. The members of that culture do not accept responsibility for
their own lives; they sponge on the contribution of those who have not
yet been made free and happy—who have gone to medical school and
become doctors, or who have become the farmers who raise the food or
the workers who produce the goods they consume.

These are no doubt overstatements. Things are not that bad, nor is
education to be blamed for all the trouble. Nevertheless, there is a trend

in a well-defined direction, and it is particularly clear in education. Our failure to create a truly free and happy student is symptomatic of a more general problem.

THE ILLUSION OF FREEDOM

What we may call the struggle for freedom in the Western world can be analyzed as a struggle to escape. from or avoid punitive or coercive treatment. It is characteristic of the human species to act in such a way as to reduce or terminate irritating, painful, or dangerous stimuli, and the struggle for freedom has been directed toward those who would control others with stimuli of that sort. Education has had a long and shameful part in the history of that struggle. The Egyptians, Greeks, and Romans all whipped their students. Medieval sculpture showed the carpenter with his hammer and the schoolmaster with the tool of his trade too, and it was the cane or rod. We are not yet in the clear. Corporal punishment is still used in many schools, and there are calls for its return where it has been abandoned.

A system in which students study primarily to avoid the consequences of not studying is neither humane nor very productive. Its by-products include truancy, vandalism, and apathy. Any effort to eliminate punishment in education is certainly commendable. We ourselves act to escape from aversive control, and our students should escape from it too. They should study because they want to, because they like to, because they are interested in what they are doing. The mistake—a classical mistake in the literature of freedom—is to suppose that they will do so as soon as we stop punishing them. Students are not literally free when they have been freed from their teachers. They then simply come under the control of other conditions, and we must look at those conditions and their effects if we are to improve teaching.

Those who have attacked the "servility" of students, as Montessori called it, have often put their faith in the possibility that young people will learn what they need to know from the "world of things," which includes the world of people who are not teachers. Montessori saw possibly useful behavior being suppressed by schoolroom discipline. Could it not be salvaged? And could the environment of the schoolroom not be changed so that other useful behavior would occur? Could the teacher not simply guide the student's natural development? Or could he not accelerate it by teasing out behavior which would occur naturally but not so quickly if he did not help? In other words, could we not bring the real world into the classroom, as John Dewey put it, or destroy the classroom and turn the student over to the real world, as Ivan Illich has recommended. All these possibilities can be presented in an attractive light, but they neglect two vital points:

1. No one learns very much from the real world without help. The only evidence we have of what can be learned from a nonsocial world has been supplied by those wild boys said to have been raised without contact with other members of their own species. Much more can be learned without formal instruction in a social world, but not without a good deal of teaching, even so. Formal education has made a tremendous difference in the extent of the skills and knowledge which can be acquired by a person in a single lifetime.

2. A much more important principle is that the real world teaches only what is relevant to the present; it makes no explicit preparation for the future. Those who would minimize teaching have contended that no preparation is needed, that the student will follow a natural line of development and move into the future in the normal course of events. We should be content, as Carl Rogers has put it, to trust

the insatiable curiosity which drives the adolescent boy to absorb everything he can see or hear or read about gasoline engines in order to improve the efficiency and speed of his "hot rod." I am talking about the student who says, "I am discovering, drawing in from the outside, and making that which is drawn in a real part of me." I am talking about my learning in which the experience of the learner progresses along the line: "No, no, that's not what I want"; "Wait! This is closer to what I'm interested in, what I need." "Ah, here it is! Now I'm grasping and comprehending what I need and what I want to know!"

Rogers is recommending a total commitment to the present moment, or at best to an immediate future.

FORMAL EDUCATION AS PREPARATION FOR FUTURE REWARDS

But it has always been the task of formal education to set up behavior which would prove useful or enjoyable *later* in the student's life. Punitive methods had at least the merit of providing current reasons for learning things that would be rewarding in the future. We object to the punitive reasons, but we should not forget their function in making the future important.

It is not enough to give the student advice—to explain that he will have a future, and that to enjoy himself and be more successful in it, he must acquire certain skills and knowledge now. Mere advice is ineffective because it is not supported by current rewards. The positive consequences that generate a useful behavioral repertoire need not be any more explicitly relevant to the future than were the punitive consequences of the past. The student needs current reasons, positive or negative, but only the educational policy maker who supplies them need take the future into account. It follows that many instructional arrangements seem "contrived," but there is nothing wrong with that. It is the teacher's function to contrive conditions under which students learn. Their relevance to a future usefulness need not be obvious.

It is a difficult assignment. The conditions the teacher arranges must be powerful enough to compete with those under which the student tends to behave in distracting ways. In what has come to be called "contingency management in the classroom" tokens are sometimes used as rewards or reinforcers. They become reinforcing when they are exchanged for reinforcers that are already effective. There is no "natural" relation between what is learned and what is received. The token is simply a reinforcer that can be made clearly contingent upon behavior. To straighten out a wholly disrupted classroom something as obvious as a token economy may be needed, but less conspicuous contingencies—as in a credit-point system, perhaps, or possibly in the long run merely expressions of approval on the part of teacher or peer—may take over.

The teacher can often make the change from punishment to positive reinforcement in a surprisingly simple way—by responding to the student's successes rather than his failures. Teachers have too often supposed that their role is to point out what students are doing wrong, but pointing to what they are doing *right* will often make an enormous difference in the atmosphere of a classroom and in the efficiency of instruction. Programmed materials are helpful in bringing about these changes, because they increase the frequency with which the student enjoys the satisfaction of being right, and they supply a valuable intrinsic reward in providing a clear indication of progress. A good program makes a step in the direction of competence almost as conspicuous as a token.

Programmed instruction is perhaps most successful in attacking punitive methods by allowing the student to move at his own pace. The slow student is released from the punishment which inevitably follows when he is forced to move on to material for which he is not ready, and the fast student escapes the boredom of being forced to go too slow. These principles have recently been extended to college education, with dramatic results, in the Keller system of personalized instruction (*P.S.I. Newsletter*).

THE RESPONSIBILITY OF SETTING EDUCATIONAL POLICY

There is little doubt that a student can be given non-punitive reasons for acquiring behavior that will become useful or otherwise reinforcing at some later date. He can be prepared for the future. But what *is* that future? Who is to say what the student should learn? Those who have sponsored the free and happy student have argued that it is the student himself who should say. His current interests should be the source of an effective educational policy. Certainly they will reflect his idiosyncrasies, and that is good, but how much can he know about the world in which he will eventually play a part? The things he is "naturally" curious about are of current and often temporary interest. How many things must he possess besides his "hot rod" to provide the insatiable curiosity relevant to, say, a course in physics?

It must be admitted that the teacher is not always in a better position. Again and again education has gone out of date as teachers have continued to teach subjects which were no longer relevant at any time in the student's life. Teachers often teach simply what they know. (Much of what is taught in private schools is determined by what the available teachers can teach.) Teachers tend to teach what they can teach easily. Their current interests, like those of students, may not be a reliable guide.

Nevertheless, in recognizing the mistakes that have been made in the past in specifying what students are to learn, we do not absolve ourselves from the responsibility of setting educational policy. We should say, we should be *willing* to say, what we believe students will need to know, taking the individual student into account wherever possible, but otherwise making our best prediction with respect to students in general. Value judgments of this sort are not as hard to make as if often argued. Suppose we undertake to prepare the student to produce his share of the goods he will consume and the services he will use, to get on well with his fellows, and to enjoy his life. In doing so are we imposing *our* values on someone else? No, we are merely choosing a set of specifications which, so far as we can tell, will at some time in the future prove valuable to the student and his culture. Who is any more likely to be right?

The natural, logical outcome of the struggle for personal freedom in education is that the teacher should improve his control of the student rather than abandon it. The free school is no school at all. Its philosophy signalizes the abdication of the teacher. The teacher who understands his assignment and is familiar with the behavioral processes needed to fulfill it can have students who not only feel free and happy while they are being taught but who will continue to feel free and happy when their formal education comes to an end. They will do so because they will be successful in their work (having acquired useful productive repertoires), because they will get on well with their fellows (having learned to understand themselves and others), because they will enjoy what they do (having acquired the necessary knowledge and skills), and because they will from time to time make an occasional creative contribution toward an even more effective and enjoyable way of life. Possibly the most important consequence is that the teacher will then feel free and happy too.

We must choose today between Cassandran and Utopian prognostications. Are we to work to avoid disaster or to achieve a better world? Again, it is a question of punishment or reward. Must we act because we are frightened, or are there positive reasons for changing our cultural practices? The issue goes far beyond education, but it is one with respect to which education has much to offer. To escape from or avoid disaster, people are likely to turn to the punitive measures of a police state. To work for a better world, they may turn instead to the positive methods of education. When it finds its most effective methods, education will be almost uniquely relevant to the task of setting up and maintaining a better way of life.

REFERENCES

P.S.I. Newsletter. October, 1972 (Published by Department of Psychology, Georgetown University, J. G. Sherman, ed.).
Carl R. Rogers. *Freedom to Learn*, Columbus, Ohio: Merrill, 1969.

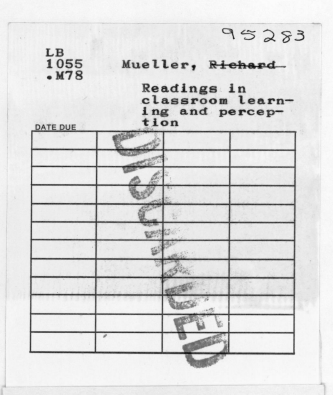